Metropolregion Nürnberg

Metropolregion Nürnberg

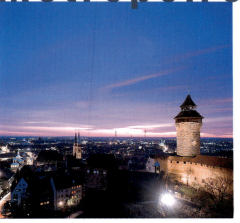

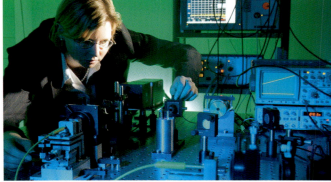

MONOGRAPHIEN
deutscher Wirtschaftsgebiete

Herausgegeben in Zusammenarbeit mit der
Industrie- und Handelskammer Nürnberg für
Mittelfranken

Redaktion:
Dr. Kurt Hesse, Industrie- und Handelskammer
Nürnberg für Mittelfranken,
Leiter des Geschäftsbereiches Kommunikation

Vierte, völlig neue Ausgabe 2006

Verlag Kommunikation & Wirtschaft GmbH,
Oldenburg (Oldb)

Bibliographische Information der Deutschen Bibliothek
Die Deutsche Bibliothek verzeichnet diese Publikation in der Deutschen Nationalbibliographie; detaillierte bibliographische Daten sind im Internet über http://dnb.ddb.de abrufbar.

Das Buch erscheint in der Edition «Städte – Kreise – Regionen»
Alle Rechte bei Kommunikation & Wirtschaft GmbH, Oldenburg (Oldb)

Printed in Germany 2006

Das Manuskript ist Eigentum des Verlages. Alle Rechte vorbehalten. Auswahl und Zusammenstellung urheberrechtlich geschützt. Dem Buch liegen neben den im Inhaltsverzeichnis genannten illustrierten Beiträgen Bilder und PR-Texte der Firmen, Verwaltungen und Verbände zugrunde, die mit ihrer finanziellen Beteiligung das Erscheinen des Bandes ermöglicht haben. Sie sind im Anhang aufgeführt. Für die Richtigkeit der auf diesen Seiten gemachten Angaben übernehmen Verlag und Redaktion keine Haftung.

Übersetzungen: Marianne Vosseler, Fachtechnische Übersetzungen – Alle Sprachen, Villingen-Schwenningen
Elektronische Bildbearbeitung:
Hoppe & Ruthe EBV GmbH, Herford
Druck: B.o.s.s Druck und Medien GmbH, Kleve

Bildquellen: Seite 274

ISBN 3-88363-258-9

Inhalt
Contents

Grußwort
Words of Welcome

Grußwort   10
Words of Welcome

Dr. Edmund Stoiber, Bayerischer Ministerpräsident

Standort in Europa
Business Location in Europe

**Die Europäische Metropolregion Nürnberg –
Regionale Governance auf gleicher Augenhöhe**   12
*The European Metropolitan Region of Nuremberg –
Regional Governance at Equal Eye Level*

Dr. Ulrich Maly, Oberbürgermeister der Stadt Nürnberg und Ratsvorsitzender der Europäischen Metropolregion Nürnberg

Wirtschaftsstandort mit DRIVE   18
A Business Location with DRIVE

Professor Dr. Klaus L. Wübbenhorst, Präsident der IHK Nürnberg für Mittelfranken

Nürnberg im Zentrum des Neuen Europa   35
Nuremberg in the Heart of the New Europe

Dr. Günther Beckstein, MdL, Bayerischer Staatsminister des Innern

**Großunternehmen und Mittelstand –
Branchenvielfalt mit geballtem Know-how**   44
*Major Concerns and Small and Medium-sized Firms –
Branch Variety with Concentrated Know-how*

Dr. Dieter Riesterer, Hauptgeschäftsführer der IHK Nürnberg für Mittelfranken

Mit Tradition in die Zukunft – innovatives Handwerk   65
With Tradition into the Future – Innovative Trades

Heinrich Mosler, Präsident der Handwerkskammer für Mittelfranken

Zukunftsperspektiven für Westmittelfranken   71
Future Perspectives for West Middle Franconia

Professor Dr. Gerhard Mammen, Präsident der Fachhochschule Ansbach

Internationaler Airport Nürnberg – tragende Säule der Infrastruktur   74
Nuremberg International Airport – Mainstay of the Infrastructure

Karl-Heinz Krüger, Geschäftsführer Flughafen Nürnberg GmbH

Güterverkehrszentrum bayernhafen Nürnberg – trimodaler Logistikprovider in einem erweiterten Europa — 78
Goods Transport Centre bayernhafen Nuremberg – Tri-mode Logistics Provider in an Extended Europe

Harald Leupold, Geschäftsführer Hafen Nürnberg-Roth GmbH

Der Verkehrsverbund Großraum Nürnberg – Vorreiter eines regionalen Bewusstseins — 82
The Public Transport Association of Nuremberg and Surroundings – Pioneer of a Regional Consciousness

Karl Inhofer, Regierungspräsident von Mittelfranken und Vorsitzender des Grundvertrags-Ausschusses des Verkehrsverbundes Großraum Nürnberg

Menschen brauchen Märkte — 87
People need Markets

Bernd A. Diederichs, Geschäftsführer NürnbergMesse GmbH

Spielend erfolgreich – die Spielwarenmesse Nürnberg — 91
Playfully Successful – the Nuremberg Toy Fair

Ernst Kick, Vorstandsvorsitzender Spielwarenmesse eG

Umbruch als Chance? Neue Gewerbe-, Wohn- und Büroflächen im Fokus — 94
Radical Change as Opportunity? Focus on New Commercial, Living and Office Premises

Gerhard Schmelzer, Immobilieninvestor und Projektentwickler

Soziales mit Rendite – familienfreundliche Personalpolitik — 99
Social Services with a Yield – Family-friendly Personnel Policy

Renate Schmidt, Bundesministerin für Familie, Senioren, Frauen und Jugend a. D.

Von Menschen für Menschen – vielfältige soziale Dienstleistungen — 104
By People for People – Manifold Social Services

Otto Kreß, Geschäftsführer Bayerisches Rotes Kreuz, Kreisverband Nürnberg-Stadt

Forschung und Technologie
Research and Technology

Zukunft des Wissens – Universitäten in der Region — 111
The Future of Knowledge – Universities in the Region

Professor Dr. Karl-Dieter Grüske, Rektor der Friedrich-Alexander-Universität Erlangen-Nürnberg

Inhalt
Contents

Die Georg-Simon-Ohm-Fachhochschule Nürnberg als Beispiel für Angewandte Wissenschaften 118
The Georg-Simon-Ohm University of Applied Sciences in Nuremberg as an Example for Applied Sciences

Professor Dr. rer. nat. Michael Braun, Rektor der Georg-Simon-Ohm-Fachhochschule Nürnberg

Zukunftsweisend – die Forschungsinstitute 124
Future-oriented – Research Institutions

Professor Dr.-Ing. Heinz Gerhäuser, Leiter Fraunhofer-Institut für Integrierte Schaltungen IIS, Erlangen

Kulturglanzlichter
Cultural Highlights

Das Nationalmuseum der deutschen Kultur steht in Nürnberg 130
The National Museum of German Culture is located in Nuremberg

Professor Dr. G. Ulrich Großmann, Generaldirektor Germanisches Nationalmuseum Nürnberg

Bayreuth – internationale Festspielstadt Richard Wagners 134
Bayreuth – Richard Wagner's International Festival City

Dr. Dieter Mronz, Oberbürgermeister der Stadt Bayreuth (von 1988 bis Mai 2006) und Geschäftsführer der Richard-Wagner-Stiftung, und
Dr. Michael Hohl, Oberbürgermeister der Stadt Bayreuth

Facetten einer Kulturregion 138
Facets of a Cultural Region

Professor Dr. Julia Lehner, Kulturreferentin der Stadt Nürnberg

Innovation – Neue Kunst und Design 144
Innovation – New Art and Design

Dr. Lucius Grisebach, Direktor Neues Museum – Staatliches Museum für Kunst und Design in Nürnberg

Bretter, die die Welt bedeuten – Oper, Schauspiel, Tanz 147
The Stage: Boards that represent the World – Opera, Theatre, Dance

Professor Dr. Wulf Konold, Staatsintendant, Staatstheater Nürnberg

Albrecht Dürer – Geniestreiche des Nürnberger Weltkünstlers 150
Albrecht Dürer – Nuremberg's Global Artist's Strokes of Genius

Eva Schickler, M.A., Kunsthistorikerin

Kompetenzfelder
Fields of Competence

Intelligenz für Verkehr und Logistik — 154
Intelligence for Transport and Logistics

Dr. Hans-Joachim Lindstadt, Leiter des Geschäftsbereichs Standortpolitik und Unternehmensförderung der IHK Nürnberg für Mittelfranken

Hightech in Information und Kommunikation — 159
High-tech in Information and Communication

Michael Nordschild, Geschäftsführer NIK Nürnberger Initiative für die Kommunikationswirtschaft e. V.

Erlangen – Hauptstadt der Medizintechnik — 167
Erlangen – Medical Technology Capital

Dr. Siegfried Balleis, Oberbürgermeister der Stadt Erlangen

Schlüssel zum Erfolg – neue Materialien — 177
The Key to Success – New Materials

Dr. Thomas Jung, Oberbürgermeister der Stadt Fürth

Metropolregion Nürnberg – Energie- und Umwelttechnologien für den Weltmarkt — 182
Metropolitan Region of Nuremberg – Energy- and Environmental Engineering for the Global Market

Dr.-Ing. Robert Schmidt, Leiter des Geschäftsbereichs Innovation | Umwelt der IHK Nürnberg für Mittelfranken

Hoch spezialisiert – Automation und Produktionstechnik — 191
Highly specialised – Automation and Production Technology

Professor Dr.-Ing. Klaus Feldmann, Lehrstuhl für Fertigungsautomatisierung und Produktionssystematik der Universität Erlangen-Nürnberg

Wachstumsmotor Innovative Dienstleistungen — 202
Innovative Services as the Drive behind Expansion

Dr. Roland Fleck, Berufsm. Stadtrat und Wirtschaftsreferent der Stadt Nürnberg

Lebensqualität pur
The Pure Quality of Life

Ein Blick zurück – die Geschichte Mittelfrankens — 222
A Look Back – the History of Middle Franconia

Professor em. Dr. Rudolf Endres, Lehrstuhl für Bayerische und Fränkische Landesgeschichte, Universität Bayreuth

Faszination und Gewalt – das Dokumentationszentrum Reichsparteitagsgelände — 228
Fascination and Power – the Reichsparteitagsgelände Documentation Centre

Dr. Franz Sonnenberger, Direktor der Museen der Stadt Nürnberg

Inhalt
Contents

Tourismus in der Metropolregion Nürnberg – vom Guten das Beste   232
Tourism in the Metropolitan Region of Nuremberg – the Best of the Best

Michael Weber, Geschäftsführer Congress- und Tourismuszentrale Nürnberg

Zur Architektur-Geschichte Frankens   239
On the Architectural History of Franconia

Dr. Oscar Schneider, Bundesbauminister a. D., Vorsitzender der Fränkischen Gesellschaft für Kultur, Politik und Zeitgeschichte e. V.

Vielfalt ist Trumpf – Hotellerie und Gastronomie   244
Variety is Trump – The Hotel and Catering Trades

Werner Behringer, Vizepräsident des Bayerischen Hotel- und Gaststättenverbandes e. V., Nürnberg

Events und Veranstaltungen mit Format   249
Events of Stature

Hartwig Reimann, Oberbürgermeister der Stadt Schwabach, Vorstandsvorsitzender Marketingverein Metropolregion Nürnberg e. V.

Naturerlebnis für Jung und Alt – der Tiergarten   254
Young and Old Experience Nature – the Zoo

Dr. Dag Encke, Leitender Direktor Tiergarten der Stadt Nürnberg

Attraktive Sportangebote für Amateure und Profis   258
Attractive Sports Arrangements for Amateurs and Professionals

Dr. Thomas Bach, Vizepräsident des Internationalen Olympischen Komitees

„Toooooooaar in Nürnberg!"   264
"Gooooooal in Nuremberg!"

Günther Koch, freier Journalist, Bayerischer Rundfunk

Kulturelle und wirtschaftliche Vielfalt in der Bierregion Bamberg   268
Cultural and Economic Variety in the Beer Region of Bamberg

Dipl.-Geogr. Rainer Keis, Wirtschaftsförderung Landkreis Bamberg

Register
Index

Metropolregion Nürnberg – Kern und Netz   272
Metropolitan Region of Nuremberg – Core and Net

Verzeichnis der PR-Bildbeiträge   274
List of Illustrated Contributions

Bildquellen   280
Picture Sources

Grußwort

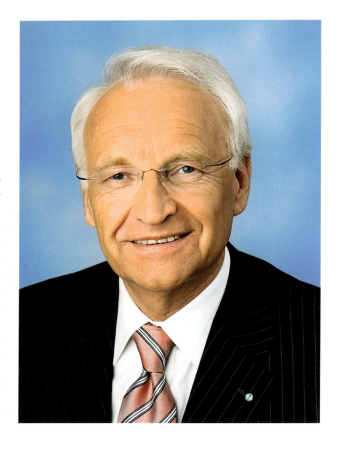

Dem Raum Nürnberg gratuliere ich zu seiner Aufnahme in den erlauchten Kreis europäischer Metropolregionen.

In dieser Auszeichnung drückt sich Anerkennung für die herausragenden Leistungen aus, die bis heute von den Menschen in der Region erbracht wurden. Das reicht weit in die Vergangenheit zurück. Die einstige Reichsstadt gehörte zu den größten und bedeutendsten wirtschaftlichen Zentren Europas. Sie nahm durch ihre Rolle als Aufbewahrungsort der Reichskleinodien und Schauplatz zahlreicher Reichstage im alten Kaiserreich politisch eine hervorgehobene Position ein. Im 19. Jahrhundert waren Nürnberg und sein Umland – noch vor der Haupt- und Residenzstadt München – Schrittmacher der Industrialisierung in Bayern. Dass zwischen Nürnberg und dem benachbarten Fürth die erste Eisenbahn Deutschlands verkehrte, kennzeichnet den weltoffenen und unternehmerischen Geist, der die Region stets prägte.

In der Region Nürnberg haben heute zahlreiche große Industrie- und Dienstleistungsbetriebe ihren Sitz oder bedeutende Niederlassungen. Eingebettet sind diese in ein dichtes Netz von Hochschulen und Forschungseinrichtungen, die sich rund um die Friedrich-Alexander-Universität Erlangen-Nürnberg und namhafte High-Tech-Unternehmen gebildet haben. Die Stärke der Region liegt nicht zuletzt in der engen Verknüpfung von Forschung und Anwendung in vielen zukunftsträchtigen Bereichen wie zum Beispiel in der Kommunikationstechnik oder in der Medizin. In solchen Clustern befruchten sich das hohe Niveau von Forschung und akademischer Bildung sowie die dynamische Entwicklung innovativer Firmen gegenseitig. Nürnberg ist zudem eine wichtige Verkehrsdrehscheibe in Zentraleuropa, die ihre traditionelle Rolle als Tor zum Osten mit der Erweiterung der Europäischen

I congratulate the Nuremberg area on its admission into the illustrious circle of European metropolitan regions.

This honour expresses recognition for the exceptional performance accomplished to date by the people of the region. This reaches well back into time. The former free imperial city was one of the largest and most important economic centres in Europe. Through its role as a place of safe-keeping for the Imperial crown jewels and as scene of numerous Imperial Diets in the old empire it was accorded a special political position. In the 19th century, Nuremberg and the surrounding areas became the pacemaker of industrialisation in Bavaria – before Munich, the capital city and residency. The fact that Germany's first railway travelled between Nuremberg and neighbouring Fürth demonstrates the cosmopolitan and entrepreneurial spirit which has always characterised the region.

Words of Welcome

Grußwort
Words of Welcome

Union zurückgewonnen hat. Nicht zuletzt als kulturelle Metropole hat Nürnberg stets große Anziehungskraft ausgeübt. Die jüngste Aufwertung des Theaters zum Staatstheater unterstreicht dies beispielhaft.

In der Erhebung zur Metropolregion sehe ich vor allem eine Ermutigung, die skizzierten Tendenzen und Entwicklungen kraftvoll und entschlossen weiterzuführen. Der engen Kooperation kommunaler Instanzen messe ich hier eine ebensolche Bedeutung bei wie Initiativen aus Wirtschaft und Gesellschaft sowie staatlichen Maßnahmen. Gemeinsame Lösungen von Aufgaben und Problemen im Innern und ein koordinierter und geschlossener Auftritt nach außen werden das Zusammengehörigkeitsgefühl und die Attraktivität der gesamten Region weiter steigern und dabei ganz Bayern wertvolle Impulse geben. Es gilt, das Netzwerk der europäischen Metropolregionen zu stärken und dabei die spezifischen Vorteile Nürnbergs zielgerichtet zu nutzen. Die Anerkennung als Metropolregion soll Ansporn sein für alle, zum Besten des fränkischen Raumes zu wirken.

Dr. Edmund Stoiber
Bayerischer Ministerpräsident
Minister-President of Bavaria

Numerous large industrial and service supply companies have their headquarters or important branches in the Nuremberg region today. They are embedded in a dense network of universities and research establishments which have been formed around the Friedrich-Alexander-University Erlangen-Nuremberg and renowned high-tech concerns. The strengths of the region lie not least in the close links between research and practice in many sectors with promising futures such as communication engineering or medicine. In such clusters the high level of research and academic education as well as the dynamic development of innovative firms has a stimulating effect on each other. Nuremberg is also an important traffic hub in central Europe having won back its traditional role as gateway to the East with the extension of the European Union. Nuremberg always held a strong attraction not least as a cultural metropolis. The recent upgrade of the theatre to state theatre is a typical example.

I see the elevation to a metropolitan region primarily as encouragement to forcefully and decisively continue with the tendencies and developments mentioned. To me, the close cooperation between communal authorities is just as important as state measures or the initiative radiating from both industry and society. The mutual solution of tasks and problems internally and a coordinated and a united appearance to the outer world will further increase the sense of togetherness and the attraction of the entire region and, while doing so, will give the whole of Bavaria valuable impulses. It is now a question of strengthening the network of European metropolitan regions and with it purposefully utilising the specific advantages offered by Nuremberg. The acknowledgement as metropolitan region should act as an incentive for all to work effectively for the benefit of the Franconian area.

Die Europäische Metropolregion Nürnberg – Regionale Governance auf gleicher Augenhöhe

Dr. Ulrich Maly

„Eine Metropolregion tritt an" – unter diesem Motto trafen sich im Juni 2004 rund 200 Akteure aus Wirtschaft, Wissenschaft, Kultur, Politik und Verwaltung zu einer Regionalkonferenz in Nürnberg. Ziel dieser Konferenz war es, den lange verwehrten Anspruch unserer Metropolregion auf förmliche Anerkennung als „Europäische Metropolregion" deutlich zu artikulieren. Gleichzeitig zeigte sich hier das neue Selbstbewusstsein, mit dem sich die Städte und Landkreise aus Franken und Teilen der Oberpfalz im neuen Europa der Regionen profilieren wollen.

Kaum ein Jahr später im April 2005 wurde dann formal von der Ministerkonferenz für Raumordnung (MKRO) bestätigt, was faktisch Realität war: Die Metropolregion Nürnberg wurde in den Kreis der europäischen Metropolregionen in Deutschland aufgenommen.

Grundlage der freiwilligen metropolitanen Zusammenarbeit ist der Aufbau einer „Regional Governance". Dies bedeutet, dass neben den politisch Verantwortlichen aus Kommunen und Landkreisen wichtige Akteure aus Wirtschaft, Wissenschaft, Sport und Verwaltung gemeinsam die Verantwortung für die Arbeit der Europäischen Metropolregion Nürnberg übernehmen.

Die Zusammenarbeit beruht auf Freiwilligkeit und Subsidiarität, das heißt, die EMN wird ausschließlich Aufgaben von metropolitaner Bedeutung wahrnehmen, die nicht bereits von anderen bestehenden Institutionen erledigt werden können.

Freiwilligkeit bedeutet zweierlei: Erstens gibt es in Bayern kein Gesetz zur Bildung von Metropolregionen, sodass wir „frei" waren und sind, unsere Instanzen selbst zu kreieren, wovon wir ausgiebig Gebrauch gemacht haben. Zweitens ist natürlich auch die Mitarbeit – weil eben nicht gesetzlich geregelt – frei-

"A Metropolitan Region makes its Entry" – under this motto some 200 players from industry, science, culture, politics and administration met for a regional conference in June 2004 in Nuremberg. The goal of this conference was to clearly articulate the long-denied claim of our metropolitan region to formal recognition as a "European Metropolitan Region". At the same time the new self-confidence with which the cities and districts of Franconia and some parts of Upper Palatinate wanted to gain a personality for themselves became obvious.

Less than one year later, in the April of 2005, the Minister Conference for Regional Development Planning (MKRO) confirmed that which had in fact become reality: The metropolitan region of Nuremberg was accepted in the circle of European metropolitan regions in Germany.

The base of the voluntary metropolitan cooperation is the construction of a "Regional Governance". This means that in addition to those politically responsible in the communities and districts, important players from industry, sport and municipal administration take over responsibility for the work of the European metropolitan region of Nuremberg.

The cooperation is of voluntary nature and on the principle of subsidiarity which means that the EMN will solely take care of tasks of metropolitan significance, tasks which cannot be fulfilled by other, existing institutions.

Being of a voluntary nature means two things: First of all there is no law in Bavaria regulating the formation of metropolitan regions so that we were and are "free" to create our authority ourselves, and we have certainly made good use of it. Secondly, and naturally, comes collaboration which – as it is not legally regulated – must be voluntary. I consider this to be an enormous

The European Metropolitan Region of Nuremberg – Regional Governance at Equal Eye Level

Standort in Europa
Business Location in Europe

Festakt zur Unterzeichnung der Charta für die Metropolregion Nürnberg in der Orangerie des Schlosses Erlangen

The ceremony of signing the Charta for the Metropolitan Region of Nuremberg in the orangery of the Erlangen castle

Das Wahrzeichen Nürnbergs: die Kaiserburg

Nuremberg's landmark: the Kaiserburg

willig. Ich sehe das als einen Riesenvorteil, denn es macht einen deutlichen Unterschied, ob sich Menschen zu einem Thema treffen, weil sie wollen oder weil sie müssen.

Obwohl der Kern der Europäischen Metropolregion Nürnberg mit zwölf Landkreisen und acht kreisfreien Städten fest definiert ist, versteht sich unsere Metropolregion als offen und dynamisch. So gibt es wichtige Verflechtungen zu Innovationszentren, Technologiestandorten oder Kultureinrichtungen im äußeren Metropolraum, die ebenfalls von internationaler Bedeutung sind. Auch die dazwischenliegenden ländlichen Räume übernehmen mit ihren naturräumlichen Qualitäten eine wichtige Rolle, vor allem als Tourismuszentren, und runden so das Spektrum ab. Dieses metropolitane Netz umfasst derzeit sieben Landkreise und drei kreisfreie Städte.

Die interne Willensbildung und die Vertretung nach außen werden legitimiert durch einen demokratischen

advantage for there is a clear difference when people meet to discuss a subject because they want to, or because they have to.

Although the core of the European metropolitan region of Nuremberg has been defined with its twelve districts and eight independent cities, our metropolitan region sees itself as open-minded and dynamic and so there are important interconnections to innovation centres, technology locations or cultural institutions in the outer areas of the metropolis which are of equal international significance. The rural areas lying in between with their natural qualities also play an important role as tourist centres, thus rounding off the spectrum. At the moment this metropolitan network covers seven districts and three independent cities (not belonging to a district).

The interior development of informed opinion and its representation to the outer world are legitimated through a democratic nucleus: the council of the metro-

Standort in Europa
Business Location in Europe

Blick auf die Markgräfliche Residenz in Ansbach

A view of the margrave's residence in Ansbach

Der Brombachsee mit dem Trimaran im Hintergrund ist ein beliebtes Ausflugsziel.

The Brombach lake with the trimaran in the background is a popular destination for a day trip.

Kern: den Rat der Metropolregion. Dieser setzt sich zusammen aus den gesetzlichen Vertretern der Gebietskörperschaften, wobei die Stimmen aller Ratsmitglieder das gleiche Gewicht haben – unabhängig von Größe und Status. Ein aus dem Rat gewählter Ratsvorsitz – bestehend aus einem Oberbürgermeister, einem Landrat und einem Bürgermeister – vertritt die Metropolregion nach außen. Dabei ist das Prinzip der gleichen Augenhöhe entscheidend für eine erfolgreiche Vertrauensbildung innerhalb der Metropolregion. Insbesondere wird damit eine mögliche dominierende Rolle der größten Stadt oder anderer Großstädte in der Region vermieden. Bei uns im Rat hat „der ländliche Raum" die Mehrheit – und zwar mit voller Absicht.

Die Bearbeitung der fachlichen metropolitanen Themen erfolgt in sechs Fachforen (Wirtschaft und Infrastruktur, Wissenschaft, Verkehr und Planung,

politan region. This is composed of the legal representatives of the corporate bodies of the areas, the voices of all committee members carrying the same weight – regardless of size and status. A chairman chosen from the council – formed by a Lord Mayor, a councillor and a mayor – represents the metropolitan region outwardly. The principle of standing at the same eye level is decisive for successful confidence-building within the metropolitan region. By using this principle the possibility of larger towns or other cities in the region playing a dominating role is avoided. On our council "the urban area" definitely carries the majority – as was fully intended.

Processing specialised metropolitan subjects is accomplished in six specialised fora (industry and infrastructure, science, transport and planning, culture and sport, culture and tourism as well as – as service supplier for these five – in the service-forum marketing). Each specialised forum has a political speaker, a speaker well-qualified in his field together with a business manager. The latter coordinates the strategic business.

In addition to building up the international trade mark of the "Metropolitan Region of Nuremberg" and the further optimisation of our inner regional cooperation we must primarily make sure that the metropolitan functions are strengthened. The most important tasks will be

– to build up a cluster policy,
– to further extend the gateway function,
– to develop a metropolitan marketing strategy,
– to push ahead international communication,
– lobbying work for the transport infrastructure impor-

Kultur und Sport, Kultur und Tourismus sowie – als Dienstleister für diese fünf – im Service-Forum Marketing). Jedes Fachforum hat einen politischen Sprecher, einen fachlichen Sprecher sowie einen Geschäftsführer. Letzterer koordiniert das operative Geschäft.

Neben dem Aufbau einer internationalen Marke „Metropolregion Nürnberg" und der weiteren Optimierung unserer innerregionalen Kooperation müssen wir uns vor allem um die Stärkung unserer metropolitanen Funktionen kümmern. Die wichtigsten Aufgaben dabei sind
- der Aufbau einer Clusterpolitik,
- der weitere Ausbau der Gateway-Funktion,
- die Entwicklung einer metropolitanen Marketingstrategie,
- das Forcieren der internationalen Kommunikation,
- die Lobbyarbeit für metropolitan bedeutsame Verkehrsinfrastruktur (Transeuropäische Netze, Bundesverkehrswegeplan) sowie für Forschungseinrichtungen und Institutionen,
- die Erstellung eines Entwicklungsleitbilds für die Metropolregion,
- die Kooperation mit Metropolregionen in Deutschland und Europa,
- die Stärkung der innerregionalen Kooperation sowie
- die Verantwortung für Stabilisierungsräume in der Metropolregion.

Ein Jahr nach der formalen Anerkennung der Metropolregion darf man feststellen, dass diese Entscheidung eine enorme Aufbruchstimmung erzeugt und die Bereitschaft zu regionaler Kooperation spürbar gestärkt hat. Die Tagung des Städtenetzwerkes METREX im Juni 2005 hat die Partner europäischer Metropolregionen bereits auf unsere junge Metropolregion aufmerksam gemacht und den vielleicht noch zweifelnden Akteuren aus unserer Region vor Augen geführt, in welchen Kategorien man sich als europäische Metropolregion bewegt und wie wichtig der Aufbau eines regionalen Netzwerkes in Europa für unsere Zukunft sein wird.

Sicherlich befinden wir uns noch am Anfang vor allem der inhaltlichen Arbeit, und wir müssen noch stärker verinnerlichen, in regionalen Kategorien zu denken und die Kirchtürme hinter uns zu lassen. Wie erfolgreich wir sind, wird sich an der Umsetzung der Arbeit in den Foren messen lassen müssen. Doch die Europäische Metropolregion Nürnberg hat sich auf den Weg gemacht, und ich bin sehr zuversichtlich, dass wir diesen Weg miteinander zum Vorteil der gesamten Region gestalten können.

tant to the metropolis (trans-European networks, Federal transport road plan) as well as for research establishments and institutions,
- *to create a development model for the metropolitan region,*
- *to cooperate with other metropolitan regions in Germany and Europe,*
- *to strengthen the inner regional cooperation as well as*
- *to take over responsibility for the stabilising areas of the metropolitan region.*

One year after the formal recognition of the metropolitan region one may ascertain that this decision created an enormous atmosphere of awakening and clearly strengthened the willingness towards regional cooperation. The conference of the city networks METREX in June 2005 made other partners of the European metropolitan regions aware of our young metropolitan region and the possible sceptics in our region were made aware in which categories one as a European metropolitan region moves and just how important the construction of a regional network in Europe will be for our future.

Of course we are still at the beginning of our work, certainly in terms of content, and we must internalise thinking even more strongly in regional categories and leave the church towers behind us. Just how successful we are will be able to be measured in the realisation of our work in the fora. However, the European metropolitan region of Nuremberg is on its way and I am quite confident that we shall be able to plan this route together to the advantage of the entire region.

Wirtschaftsstandort mit DRIVE

Professor Dr. Klaus L. Wübbenhorst

Dass die Globalisierung eine Nürnberger Erfindung ist, auf diese Idee könnte man durchaus kommen. Ist doch der Behaim-Globus die älteste erhaltene Darstellung der Erde in Kugelform. Was Martin Behaim auch immer war – Wissenschaftler, Seefahrer, Unternehmer, Entdecker oder Kosmograph – er war jedenfalls Nürnberger. Der unter seiner Anleitung 1492 geschaffene „Erdapfel" steht auch heute noch in Nürnberg, im Germanischen Nationalmuseum. Ebenfalls seit dem 15. Jahrhundert ist das Sprichwort bekannt: „Nürnberger Hand (ab dem 19. Jahrhundert: Nürnberger Tand) geht durch alle Land."

Die Linie lässt sich weiter ziehen zum Begründer der sozialen Marktwirtschaft, dem ehemaligen Wirtschaftsminister und Bundeskanzler Professor Ludwig Erhard. Er hat 1952 die Deutschen dazu aufgerufen, sich „aus protektionistischer Enge frei zu machen hin zu einer immer engeren Verbindung mit der übrigen Welt". Die Ausrichtung auf den Freihandel, so wie sie der große Franke Erhard forderte, war die wichtigste Voraussetzung dafür, dass die deutschen Unternehmen auch aktuell wieder Exportweltmeister werden konnten.

Unsere Region hat mit ihrer traditionell starken außenwirtschaftlichen Orientierung dazu beigetragen. Heute sind 2500 Unternehmen in der Außenwirtschaftsdatei des IHK-Geschäftsbereichs International erfasst. Besonders intensiv ist der Austausch innerhalb der Europäischen Union. Jeweils über 1000 Unternehmen pflegen darüber hinaus Handelskontakte zu den Staaten Mittel- und Osteuropas sowie mit Asien. Auf diese beiden Regionen wird Nürnberg als „Gateway to Eastern Europe" sowie mit Blick auf die „emerging markets" vor allem in China und Indien auch künftig seine Aktivitäten fokussieren. 750 der 2500 Außenwirtschaftsunternehmen zeichnen sich durch dauerhafte Engagements aus und unterhalten insgesamt 9000 Vertretungen, Niederlassungen, Produktionsstätten/Beteiligungen und Joint Ventures. Die Art und Intensität dieser außenwirtschaftlichen Aktivitäten hat sich in den letzten Jahren qualitativ deutlich verbessert. Vor allem in Asien ist die Zahl der

Fortsetzung Seite 22

One could almost get the idea that globalisation was a discovery made in Nuremberg. Certainly the oldest representation of the earth as a globe, the Behaim Globe, is coming from here. Whatever Martin Behaim was – scientist, sailor, entrepreneur, discoverer or cosmographist – he was in any event from Nuremberg. The "Erdapfel" created under his supervision in 1492 can still be seen today in the Germanic National Museum in Nuremberg. Also originating in the 15th century is the phrase: "The Nuremberg hand, (from the 19th century onwards: Nuremberg tand (meaning handcrafted knick-knacks)) travels around the land."

A parallel can be further drawn to the founder of social market economy and the former Minister of Economics and Chancellor Professor Ludwig Erhard. In 1952 he called on the Germans to "free themselves from protectionist confinement and have an even closer connection with the rest of the world". The orientation towards free trade which the famous Franconian Erhard demanded was the most important prerequisite for German concerns to once again being able to become export world champion.

With its traditionally strong orientation towards foreign trade, the region's contribution has been considerable. Today, some 2,500 concerns are recorded in the Chamber of Commerce's international business file. Exchange with the European Union is particularly intensive. More than 1,000 undertakings maintain trade contacts with the states of Central and Eastern Europe as well as with Asia. As the "Gateway to Eastern Europe", Nuremberg will especially focus its future activities on these two regions and with a look on the "emerging markets", primarily those of China and India. 750 of the 2,500 exporting concerns stand out for their enduring commitment and maintain a total of 9,000 branches, agencies, production facilities/partnerships and joint ventures. The type and intensity of these foreign-trade activities has shown a clear, qualitative improvement over the past few years. In Asia alone, the number of agencies and branches of our undertakings has increased by 90 percent over the last five years.

With a population of 1.7 million and a gross domes-

Continued on page 22

A Business Location with DRIVE

Standort in Europa
Business Location in Europe

Das Jahr 2005 ist das erfolgreichste Jahr in der Geschichte der GfK. Mit dem Erwerb der NOP World, Nummer 9 der Marktforschungsunternehmen weltweit, stieg die GfK in den exklusiven Club der Marktforscher auf, die mehr als eine Milliarde Euro Umsatz machen.

2005 was the most successful year in GfK's history. By acquiring NOP World, the No. 9 among the world's top market research companies, GfK entered the exclusive realms of market researchers with annual sales figures exceeding one billion euros.

GfK. Growth from Knowledge

Um ihre Position weiter zu stärken und auszubauen, definiert die GfK in ihrem neuen Strategiekonzept „5 Star Initiative" fünf Aufgabenschwerpunkte für die kommenden Jahre. Die Initiative „Fact-Based Consultancy" betrifft den konsequenten Ausbau der Dienstleistungen zu hochwertigen faktenbasierten und kontinuierlich erbrachten Beratungsleistungen für das Topmanagement in den Bereichen innovative Marktforschungsansätze und strategische Marketingentscheidungen. „TOP 3" beinhaltet die Vision der Positionierung der GfK Gruppe im Weltmarkt der Marktforschung insgesamt sowie in den wichtigsten Marktforschungsländern und in jedem ihrer fünf Geschäftsfelder. Unter dem Punkt „Globale Reichweite" definiert die GfK einen Ausbau ihres weltweiten Netzwerkes mit eigenen Unternehmen. Mit der Initiative „Full Service" verfolgt die GfK weiterhin ihr umfassendes Angebot als Full-Service-Marktforschungsunternehmen mit allen Dienstleistungen aus einer Hand. Und schließlich möchte das Unternehmen unter dem Aspekt „Hervorragende Finanzsituation" seinen jährlichen Umsatz in die Nähe der 1,5 Milliarden-Euro-Marke steigern.

GfK. Growth from Knowledge

To strengthen and expand its position, GfK defined five central tasks in its "5 Star Initiative" strategic concept for the next few years. The "Fact-Based Consultancy" initiative relates to the consistent development of services into high-value, fact-based and continuous consultancy for leaders in terms of innovative approaches to market research and strategic marketing decisions. "TOP 3" concerns the vision of the GfK Group's positioning in international market research overall, within the most important market research regions and of each of its business divisions. For GfK, "Global Reach" defines the expansion of its international network with its own companies. GfK's "Full Service" initiative is aimed at driving forward its comprehensive offering as a full service market research company, supplying all services from under one roof. Finally, the company aims to increase annual sales to around the 1.5 billion euro mark under the "Excellent Financials" initiative.

Information

Gründungsjahr: 1934

Mitarbeiter: weltweit mehr als 7500

Standorte: über 130 Tochterunternehmen in mehr als 70 Ländern der Welt

Leistungsspektrum: Informationsdienstleistungen für Kunden aus Industrie, Handel, Dienstleistung und Medien für Marketingzwecke

Geschäftsfelder:
– Custom Research
– Retail and Technology
– Consumer Tracking
– Media
– HealthCare

Year established: 1934

Employees: over 7,500 worldwide

Locations: Over 130 subsidiaries in more than 70 countries

Range of services: Information services for marketing purposes supplied to clients in industry, retail, media and the service sector

Business divisons:
– Custom Research
– Retail and Technology
– Consumer Tracking
– Media
– HealthCare

GfK Gruppe
Nürnberg

Die Erfüllung der Kundenanforderungen, hohe Qualitäts- und Sicherheitsstandards sowie die kontinuierliche Weiterentwicklung des Qualitätsmanagementsystems sind FCI ein zentrales Anliegen. Zur systematischen und nachhaltigen Sicherung der Wettbewerbsfähigkeit des Standortes gehört auch die konsequente Anwendung der Six Sigma Methodologie und eine bedarfsgerechte Qualifizierung der Mitarbeiter.

Meeting customers' needs, high standards of quality and safety as well as the continuous onward development of the quality management system are all matters of vital interest to FCI. Consistent application of the Six Sigma methodology and suitably-qualified employees are also factors in the systematic and lasting assurance of the competitiveness of the location.

Mittels vollautomatischer Fertigungslinien werden in der Montage Airbagleitungen, bestehend aus abgeschirmtem Stecker plus Kabel, in bis zu 60 Arbeitsschritten vollautomatisch produziert. Hier werden ausschließlich hoch qualifizierte Anlagenführer eingesetzt, die über eine entsprechende fachliche Qualifizierung verfügen.

Using fully automated production lines, airbag connectors consisting of isolated plug and cable are fully automatically produced in the Assembly Department in up to 60 work stages. Only highly qualified operators are employed with suitable specialised qualifications.

Standort in Europa
Business Location in Europe

FCI Automotive – und hier insbesondere der Standort Nürnberg – ist weltweit die Nummer 1 als Hersteller von Airbagsteckverbindern. Im Werk Nürnberg werden seit 1992 im Bereich Safety Restraint Systems (SRS) neben Airbagsteckverbindern auch komplette Kabelsätze für Airbag- und Gurtstrafferanwendungen und seit 2002 zusätzlich Airbagsensorgehäuse für alle namhaften Automobilhersteller und Systemlieferanten entwickelt und gefertigt.

Sensorgehäuse für Sicherheitsanwendungen werden in der Kunststoffspritzerei im Umspritzverfahren gefertigt. Aufgrund der geforderten engen Toleranzen im Bereich von bis zu 0,05 mm ist das Fertigungsverfahren komplex und bedingt den Einsatz einer vollautomatisierten Sondermaschine.

FCI Connectors Deutschland ist weltweites Kernkompetenzzentrum für das Entwickeln und Stanzen zweiteiliger Kontakte. Hier werden jährlich 2,5 Milliarden Kontaktteile hergestellt. In der Stanzerei gewährleisten direkt in die Stanzautomaten integrierte Bildverarbeitungssysteme ein effizientes Qualitätsmanagement. Der Null-Fehler-Philosophie folgend werden nur zu 100 Prozent kontrollierte und absolut einwandfreie Präzisionsstanzteile ausgeliefert oder weiterverarbeitet.

FCI Automotive – and particularly the Nuremberg location – is the world's number 1 manufacturer of airbag plug connectors. In the Nuremberg works,

complete cable sets for airbags and belt retainers have been produced since 1992 in the Safety Restraint Systems (SRS) section, in addition to airbag connectors and, since 2002, airbag sensor housings have been developed and produced for all well-known automobile manufacturers and system suppliers.

Sensor housings for safety applications are made in the synthetics moulding department in a process of extrusion. Because of the narrow tolerances demanded, in the range of up to 0.05 mm, the pro-

duction process is complex and needs the application of a special fully-automatic machine.

FCI Connectors Deutschland is a global core competence centre for the development and punching of two-part contacts. Some 2.5 billion contact parts are manufactured annually. In the press room, image processing systems integrated in the automatic presses guarantee efficient quality management. Based on the zero mistake philosophy, only those precision stampings which have been 100 percent checked and are absolutely perfect are sold or passed on for further processing.

Information

Gründungsjahr: 1957 als Daut + Rietz KG

Mitarbeiter: 590 in Nürnberg; FCI Automotive Division weltweit: über 4000 Mitarbeiter

Produktspektrum: Elektrische und elektronische Komponenten für die Automobilindustrie
- Kontaktsysteme
- Steckverbinder und Kabel für Sicherheitssysteme (Airbag und Gurtstraffer)
- Steckverbinder-Schnittstellen für elektronische Kontrolleinheiten (ABS, ESP und Motorsteuerungen)
- Umspritzte Komponenten für elektromechanische Anwendungen

Year founded: 1957 as Daut + Rietz KG

Employees: 590 in Nuremberg; FCI Automotive Division worldwide: more than 4,000 employees

Range of products: electrical and electronic components for the automobile industry
- contact systems
- plug connectors and cables for safety systems (airbags and belt retainers)
- plug connector interfaces for electronic monitoring units (ABS, ESP and motor controls)
- extrusion coated components for electromechanical applications

FCI Connectors Deutschland GmbH Nürnberg

Vertretungen und Niederlassungen unserer Unternehmen in den letzten fünf Jahren um 90 Prozent gestiegen.

Mittelfranken gehört mit 1,7 Mio. Einwohnern und einem Bruttoinlandsprodukt von über 50 Mrd. Euro zu den stärksten Wirtschaftsräumen in Deutschland. Im Kerngebiet der Metropolregion Nürnberg leben 2,5 Mio. Menschen. Das Bruttoinlandsprodukt beträgt über 70 Mrd. Euro. Das Gesamtgebiet (metropolitanes Netz) umfasst 4,3 Mio. Einwohner, die 115 Mrd. Euro erwirtschaften. Der wichtigste ökonomische Veränderungsprozess war in der jüngeren Vergangenheit die Entwicklung von der Industrie- zur Dienstleistungsgesellschaft. In Mittelfranken wurde dieser weiterhin andauernde Strukturwandel aktiv gestaltet: Seit Beginn der Zählung von sozialversicherungspflichtig Beschäftigten im Jahr 1974 sind in der Region netto über 50 000 neue Arbeitsplätze geschaffen worden. Zwar hat die Industrie in dieser Zeit fast 120 000 Beschäftigte verloren, aber im Dienstleistungssektor wurden 170 000 neue Arbeitsplätze aufgebaut. Damit ist in den vergangenen 30 Jahren der Anteil des Dienstleistungssektors von 38 auf 62 Prozent gestiegen.

Die Verschiebung der Gewichte von der Industrie zu den Dienstleistungen ist ungefähr zur Hälfte mit neuer Wertschöpfung und zur anderen Hälfte damit zu erklären, dass Aktivitäten, die vorher von Industrieunternehmen in eigener Regie erledigt wurden, in den letzten Jahren zunehmend an externe Dienstleister ausgelagert wurden (Outsourcing). Die mittelfränkische Dienstleistungswirtschaft hat die Chancen des Outsourcing genutzt und deutschlandweite Spitzenstellungen in zahlreichen innovativen Sektoren erreicht. Dazu gehören beispielsweise Informationswirtschaft und Callcenter, Marktforschung, Steuer-, Rechts- und Wirtschaftsberatung, Versicherungen, Logistikdienstleistungen, Ingenieurdienstleistungen, Gebäudemanagement und Umweltschutz.

Wir arbeiten daran, diese starke, lebens- und liebenswerte Region mit dem Erfindergeist weiterzuentwickeln, der Nürnberg schon im Mittelalter zu großer Blüte getrieben hat. Statt Erfindergeist könnte man auch DRIVE sagen. DRIVE lautet das Mission-Statement, das ich meiner Amtszeit als IHK-Präsident (2005–09) zugrunde gelegt habe. Die fünf Buchstaben stehen für Dynamisch, Regional, International/Innovativ, Vertrauenswürdig, Exzellent. Mit dieser Ausrichtung werden wir weiterhin in den internationalen Rankings Spitzenplätze belegen. Dann wird es auch in Zukunft viele Meldungen geben wie kürzlich von Spiegel Online: „Nürnberg schlägt New York."

tic product of more than 50 billion Euro, Middle Franconia is one of the strongest industrial areas in Germany. Some 2.5 million people live in the core area of the Nuremberg metropolitan region and the gross domestic product amounts to more than 70 billion Euro. The entire area (metropolitan network) has a population of 4.3 million achieving 115 billion Euro. The latest most important economic process of change has been the development from an industrial to a service supply society. In Middle Franconia this continuing structural change has been actively organised: Since beginning with the census of employees subject to social insurance in 1974 more than 50,000 new workplaces have been created in the region. It is true that industry has lost almost 120,000 employees in this period, but in the service supply sector more than 170,000 have been created. Thus the share of the service supply sector has increased from 38 to 62 percent within the last 30 years.

One half of the shift from industry to service supply is due to an increase in value and the other half due to activities which were previously carried out by industrial concerns themselves being increasingly given to external service suppliers (outsourcing). The Middle Franconian service supply industry has made best use of the changes offered by outsourcing and has achieved a top position in countless innovative sectors nationwide. Amongst them are the information industry and call centres, market research, tax, legal and economic advisors, insurance companies, logistics, engineering services, building management and environment protection.

We are working hard at developing this strong likeable region with the same inventive genius which drove Nuremberg to its heights in the Middle Ages. One could replace the words inventive genius with DRIVE. DRIVE is the mission statement that I have taken as a basis during my period of office as President of the Chamber of Commerce (2005–09). The five letters stand for dynamic, regional, international/innovative, vital, excellent. With this line of orientation we shall be able to hold our top position in the international ranks. Then there will be many more reports similar to the recent one in Spiegel Online "Nuremberg beats New York".

Standort in Europa
Business Location in Europe

Schwan-STABILO Cosmetics GmbH & Co. KG

Schwan-STABILO Cosmetics ist weltweit führender private label Hersteller hochwertiger Kosmetikstifte und somit Partner international renommierter Kosmetikunternehmen. Der Fantasie der Kunden sind mit über 10 000 Farben und 200 Texturen für alle Anwendungen keine Grenzen gesetzt. Dekorative oder Wirkstoffkosmetik: Mit avancierter Technik und intelligenten Applikationssystemen wird SCHWAN-Stabilo Cosmetics seinem Ruf als technologischer Vorreiter stets gerecht.

Schwan-STABILO Cosmetics GmbH & Co. KG

Schwan-STABILO Cosmetics is the leading private-label manufacturer of top-quality cosmetic pencils globally and thus partner to countless internationally known cosmetic firms. With more than 10,000 colours and 200 textures for all fields of application, there are no limits to customers' fantasy.
Decorative or active substance cosmetics: With advanced technology and intelligent application systems SCHWAN-Stabilo Cosmetics always matches its reputation as a technological trailblazer.

STABILO International GmbH

STABILO gilt inzwischen als „die angesagte Stiftmarke" bei jungen Leuten in ganz Europa.
Der Grund: STABILO-Produkte stehen für Design, Trends und Lifestyle. Wo früher der Schwerpunkt auf technologischen Eigenschaften lag, stehen heute vom ersten Moment an die Bedürfnisse und Wünsche derjenigen im Vordergrund, die mit einem STABILO schreiben, markieren oder zeichnen.

STABILO International GmbH

STABILO is considered in the meantime as "the brand of pencil" by young people in the whole of Europe.
The reason: STABILO products stand for design, trends and lifestyle. Where once the focal point was on technological characteristics, today the needs and desires of those people who write, mark or draw with a STABILO are in the foreground.

Information

Gründungsjahr: 1855

Mitarbeiter: rund 3000 weltweit

Leistungsspektrum: Schreib- und Zeichengeräte für die verschiedensten Anwendungen; Kosmetikstifte für die dekorative Gesichtskosmetik

Standorte: Deutschland, Tschechien, China, USA, Brasilien, Malaysia

Produkte: u. a. STABILO BOSS, STABILO point 88, STABILO's move, mechanische und flüssige Liner, holzgefasste Kosmetikstifte, Jumbos, Slims, Viscomagics

---

Year founded: 1855

Employees: some 3,000 worldwide

Range of products: writing and drawing equipment for the most various applications; cosmetic liners for decorative facial cosmetic

Locations: Germany, Czech Republic, China, USA, Brazil, Malaysia

Products: amongst others STABILO BOSS, STABILO point 88, STABILO's move, mechanical and liquid liners, wooden cosmetic liners, jumbos, slims, viscomagics

☐
Schwanhäußer
Industrie Holding
GmbH & Co. KG
Heroldsberg

Nestlé Schöller – ein Nürnberger Imageträger mit Topmarken

Das 1937 gegründete Unternehmen gehört seit 2001 zum weltweit größten Nahrungsmittelkonzern Nestlé. Seit 2002 werden die deutschlandweiten Speiseeisaktivitäten des Konzerns über die Nürnberger Zentrale von Nestlé Schöller gesteuert.
Das Unternehmen setzt im heiß umkämpften Speiseeismarkt auf innovative Eiskreationen der beiden Topmarken Mövenpick und Nestlé Schöller. Das Sortiment reicht vom Kleineis bis zur Familienpackung, von cremig bis fruchtig und von klassisch bis trendy. Das Zusammenspiel von Know-how, Kreativität und Aufgeschlossenheit für Trends sorgt für ein Produktsortiment, das höchsten Qualitätsansprüchen unterliegt. Nach der Übernahme durch Nestlé wurde die gesamte Produktpalette überarbeitet und optimiert. Gleichzeitig besetzte das Unternehmen neue Vertriebskanäle und weitete seine Aktivitäten aus. Heute ist Nestlé Schöller mit rund 25 Prozent die starke Nummer zwei auf dem deutschen Eismarkt und in der Gastronomie mit rund 50 Prozent klarer Marktführer.

Nestlé Schöller – a Nuremberg Image-carrier with top brands

*The undertaking founded in 1937 has belonged to Nestlé, the largest food concern in the world, since 2001. Since 2002 the nation-wide ice cream activities of the concern have been controlled via the Nuremberg headquarters of Nestlé Schöller.
On the hotly contested ice cream market, the undertaking relies on innovative ice cream creations from both the Mövenpick and Nestlé Schöller top brands. The assortment ranges from small ice creams to family packs, from creamy to fruity and from classic to trendy.
The interplay of know-how, creativity and open-mindedness for trends produces a product range subject to the highest quality requirements. Following the takeover by Nestlé, the entire product range was revised and optimised. Simultaneously, the concern occupied new sales channels and extended its activities. Today, Nestlé Schöller is a strong number two on the German ice cream market with approximately 25 percent and is clear market leader in catering with about 50 percent.*

Information

Gründungsjahr: 1937

Mitarbeiter: über 2000 im Dienst für über 120 000 Kunden

Standorte: Werke in Nürnberg, Uelzen und Prenzlau

Sortiment: Speiseeis für Lebensmittelhandel und Gastronomie; Tiefkühlkost und Tiefkühlbackwaren für Gastronomie

Eismarken: Mövenpick, Frubetto, Nestlé Schöller

Eissortiment für Endverbraucher: 31 Kleineis (Impulseis), 22 Haushaltspackungen, 6 Multipackungen

---

Year founded: 1937

Employees: over 2,000 working for more than 120,000 customers

Locations: works in Nuremberg, Uelzen and Prenzlau

Assortment: ice cream for the food trade and catering; frozen foods and frozen baked products for the catering industry

Ice cream brands: Mövenpick, Frubetto, Nestlé Schöller

Ice cream range for the consumer: 31 small ice creams (impulse purchases), 22 domestic packs, 6 multi-packs

☐
Nestlé Schöller GmbH & Co. KG, Nürnberg

Standort in Europa
Business Location in Europe

Faurecia, Europas zweitgrößter Automobilzulieferer ist in 28 Ländern an 160 Standorten mit 60 000 Mitarbeitern vertreten und damit einer der weltweit führenden Anbieter für sechs bedeutende Fahrzeugmodule – Sitz, Cockpit, Tür, Akustikpackage, Frontend und Abgasanlage – mit einem Konzernumsatz von 11 Mrd. Euro 2005.

Faurecia is a world leading automotive supplier of six major vehicle modules: seats, cockpits, door modules, acoustic modules, front ends and exhausts. In 2005 the Group posted sales of 11 billion Euro. It operates in 28 countries and employs 60,000 people at 160 sites.

Information

Gründungsjahr: 1960

Mitarbeiter:
ca. 2000 in Exhaust Systems Product Group in der Nord-Europa Division, am Standort Fürth ca. 300

Standorte:
Deutschland
Tschechien
Slowakei
Schweden

Produkte:
– komplette Abgasanlagen
– Dieselpartikelfilter
– Katalysatoren
– Krümmer
– Schalldämpfer

Year founded: 1960

Employees:
round about 2,000 within the Northern Europe Division of our Exhaust Systems Product Group; at Fürth Site nearly 300

Locations:
Germany
Czech Republic
Slovakia
Sweden

Products:
– complete exhaust lines
– diesel particle filters
– catalytic converters
– manifolds
– mufflers

Faurecia Exhaust Systems, Fürth

Die Hermann Gutmann Werke AG ist seit über sechs Jahrzehnten als Spezialist in der Aluminiumbranche bekannt. Durch die aktive Erschließung immer neuer Märkte konnte die Marktposition in den letzten Jahren konsequent ausgebaut werden.
Höchste Präzision und ausgereifte Produktionstechniken bei der Herstellung, Bearbeitung und Oberflächenveredelung von Aluminium-Strangpressprodukten und Aluminium-Drähten stehen an erster Stelle. Aufgrund der zahlreichen Weiterbearbeitungsmöglichkeiten (mechanische Bearbeitung bis hin zur Fertigung komplett einbaufähiger Teile) kann Gutmann seinen Kunden ein umfangreiches Leistungsspektrum aus einer Hand anbieten.
In der Summe ergibt sich ein Kompetenzspektrum, mit dem sich die Unternehmensgruppe einen Namen als zuverlässiger Partner gemacht hat. Geprüfte Qualität, fundierte Beratung und kundennaher Service sind – neben den Systemlösungen – die stabile Basis für innovative Produktentwicklungen.

*For more than six decades the Hermann Gutmann Werke AG has been known as a specialist in the aluminium branch. They have been able to consequently extend and strengthen their market position by developing ever more markets.
The highest amount of precision and matured production engineering in the manufacture, processing and surface finishing of extruded aluminium products and aluminium wires is of paramount importance. Because of the large number of possibilities of onward-processing (mechanical processing through to the production of complete ready-for-installation parts) Gutmann is able to offer its customers a wide-reaching range of services all from the same source.
In summation, a range of competences is offered with which the undertaking group has made itself a name as a reliable partner. Verified quality, well-founded advice and customer-close services are – alongside the system solutions – a steady base for innovative product development.*

Information

Gründungsjahr: 1937

Mitarbeiter: 1000

Produkt- und Leistungsspektrum:
- Bausysteme für Fenster, Fassaden und Wintergärten in Aluminium und in Kombination Holz-Aluminium
- Aluminium-Verbundplatten
- Aluminium-Spezialdrähte
- Aluminium-Industrieprofile

Year founded: 1937

Employees: 1,000

Range of products and services:
- building systems for windows, facades and winter gardens in aluminium and in wood- aluminium combination
- aluminium-composite boards
- special aluminium wires
- aluminium-industrial structural materials

Hermann Gutmann Werke AG
Weißenburg

Standort in Europa
Business Location in Europe

Aus dem Konkurs der Firma Schmotzer entsteht 1980 die Gießerei Heunisch in Bad Windsheim. Vier Jahre später wird die Gießerei Hofmann übernommen. 2003 werden beide Betriebe zu einem Gesamtunternehmen verschmolzen.

Außerdem unterhält die Gießerei Heunisch zwei weitere Unternehmen in Tschechien (Slévárna Heunisch As) und in Thüringen (Gießerei Heunisch Steinach).

Heute beschäftigt Heunisch Guss über 1000 Mitarbeiter und erwirtschaftet einen jährlichen Umsatz von rund 100 Mio. Euro. Monatlich produziert die Firmengruppe ca. 160 000 Gussteile mit einem Gesamtgewicht von rund 6000 Tonnen. Und auch im Umweltschutz setzt Heunisch Guss Maßstäbe. Die hochmodernen Filteranlagen reinigen etwa 1 Mio. m³ Luft in der Stunde. Der Kupolofen hat von allen bayerischen Gießereien die besten Abgaswerte – weit unter den gesetzlich geforderten Werten. Rund 95 Prozent aller Produkte und Einsatzmaterialien sind recycelbar. Allein seit 1997 hat Heunisch mehr als 6 Mio. Euro in den Umweltschutz investiert.

In 1980 the Heunisch foundry in Bad Windsheim was created from the bankruptcy of Messrs. Schmotzer. Four years later the Hofmann foundry was taken over. In 2003 both companies were melted together into one whole enterprise.

The Heunisch foundry also maintains two further concerns in the Czech Republic (Slévárna Heunisch As) and in Thuringia (Steinach Heunisch foundry).

Today, Heunisch Guss employs more than 1,000 people and achieves an annual turnover of about 100 million Euro. Monthly, the group produces about 160,000 castings with a total weight of about 6,000 tons. The Heunisch Guss also sets standards in questions of environment conservation. Their highly-modern filter plants clean some 1 million m³ air per hour. The cupola melting furnace has the best exhaust values of all Bavarian foundries – well under the legal requirements. Some 95 percent of all their products and materials utilised are recyclable. Since 1997 alone, Heunisch has invested more than 6 million Euro in environmental protection.

Information

Gründungsjahr: 1980

Mitarbeiter: rund 1000

Leistungsspektrum:
Produktion von
- 85 000 t Grau- und Sphäroguss sowie 2500 t Aluminium-Kokillenguss jährlich durch Verarbeitung
- von 7600 t Stahlschrott und Roheisen, 2500 t Quarzsand, 1700 t sonstigen Einsatzstoffen

Year founded: 1980

Employees: some 1,000

Range of services:
production of
- 85,000 t grey castings and spheroidal castings as well as 2,500 t aluminium-permanent mould castings annually by processing of
- 7,600 t steel waste and raw iron, 2,500 t silica, 1,700 t other materials

☐
Gießerei Heunisch GmbH
Bad Windsheim

Die ECKART GmbH & Co. KG, seit 1. Oktober 2005 ein Unternehmen der ALTANA Chemie, blickt auf eine 130-jährige Firmengeschichte zurück. Den Grundstein des heute von Fürth aus weltweit agierenden Unternehmens legte Carl Eckart 1876, als er dort eine Goldschlägerei zur Herstellung von Blattgold gründete.
Nicht um Gold, sondern um Bronzepulver drehte sich alles in der 1920 gegründeten Produktionsstätte in Güntersthal. Der älteste, heute noch genutzte Standort der ECKART Gruppe ist inzwischen auf 600 000 Quadratmeter gewachsen. ECKART verfügt über insgesamt acht Produktionsstätten in fünf Ländern in Europa, den USA und Asien. Die ECKART Gruppe versorgt damit über 70 Länder mit Effektpigmenten.
Diese geben Lacken, Druckfarben oder Kosmetikartikeln ihren besonderen Glanz. Zum Produktspektrum gehören Aluminium-, Perlglanz- und PVD-Pigmente, Metallpigmentfarben, Goldbronze- und Zinkpigmente sowie fertige Metallic-Druckfarben für die Graphische Industrie. Pigmente von ECKART werden beispielsweise in der Automobilindustrie aber auch bei anderen Beschichtungen und Lackierungen eingesetzt. Die Kunststoffindustrie verwendet sie u. a. zur Einfärbung. Bei der Herstellung von Porenbeton dienen die Aluminiumpigmente als Treibmittel.

ECKART GmbH & Co. KG a member of ALTANA Chemie since October 1st, 2005 can look back on 130 years of company history.
The cornerstone of this globally operating company, today headquartered in Fuerth, was laid by Carl Eckart in 1876 when he founded a goldbeating shop for the manufacture of leaf gold.
But instead of gold it's bronze powder that glitters in the production plants in Guentersthal that were founded in 1920. The oldest location of the ECKART group still in use today has grown over the years to cover.
ECKART has altogether eight production facilities in five countries in Europe, the US and Asia. Altogether the ECKART Group supplies over 70 countries with effect pigments. These products lend special high gloss and brilliance to paints, printing inks or cosmetics. The product range includes aluminium, pearlescent and PVD pigments, metallic pigment coatings, goldbronze and zinc pigments and even press-ready metallic printing inks for the Graphic Arts industry. ECKART pigments are widely used, for example, in the automobile industry and also for other types of paint and coatings. The plastics industry uses them, among others, as dye pigments. In the manufacture of lightweight concrete aluminium pigments serve as a propellant.

Information

Gründungsjahr: 1876

Mitarbeiter: weltweit ca. 1850

Standorte:
Fürth
Güntersthal
Wackersdorf
Uden (Niederlande)
Louisville (USA)
Painesville (USA)
Hong Kong (China)
Saint Ouen (Frankreich)
Rivanazzano (Italien)
Porto Marghera (Italien)
Pori (Finnland)
Ampthill (Großbritannien)
Vétroz (Schweiz)

Year founded: 1876

Employees: worldwide approx. 1,850

Locations:
Fuerth
Guentersthal
Wackersdorf
Uden (The Netherlands)
Louisville (USA)
Painesville (USA)
Hong Kong (China)
Saint Ouen (France)
Rivanazzano (Italy)
Porto Marghera (Italy)
Pori (Finland)
Ampthill (Great Britain)
Vétroz (Switzerland)

☐
ECKART
GmbH & Co. KG
Velden

Standort in Europa
Business Location in Europe

FAUN GmbH ist die deutsche Tochtergesellschaft der TADANO Ltd. (Japan), einem der größten Hersteller und Lieferanten von Kranen und speziellen Hebezeugen.
Am deutschen Standort in Lauf werden All Terrain Krane mit einer Kapazität von 35 bis 220 t, Aufbaukrane, Bergefahrzeuge und Kranfahrgestelle hergestellt.
Die FAUN GmbH kann auf eine über 160-jährige Firmengeschichte vor Ort zurückblicken.
Der Vertrieb und Service in Europa ist über die ebenfalls in Lauf ansässige TADANO FAUN GmbH organisiert, international über das umfassende Netzwerk der TADANO Gruppe.

FAUN GmbH is the German subsidiary of TADANO Ltd. (Japan), being known as one of the world's leading manufacturer and supplier of cranes and special lifting equipment.

*At the German location in Lauf, All Terrain Cranes in the range from 35 to 220 t, Truck-Mounted Cranes, Recovery Vehicles as well as Crane Chassis are manufactured.
FAUN GmbH is looking back on a more than 160 years company history.
The sales and service in Europe is supported through the TADANO FAUN GmbH being also based at the Lauf location, whilst International through the wide spread network of the TADANO Group.*

Werksansicht der FAUN in Lauf in der Nähe von Nürnberg
The FAUN factory located in Lauf close to Nuremberg

All Terrain Kran ATF 220G-5 – das neue 220 t-Flaggschiff „Made in Germany" für den „G"lobalen Markt
All Terrain Crane ATF 220G-5 – the new 220 t flagship "Made in Germany" for the "G"lobal market

Information

Gründungsjahr: 1845
Mitarbeiter: am Standort Lauf 630; weltweit 2331 (TADANO Gruppe)
Produkte:
– All Terrain und Aufbaukrane
– Bergefahrzeuge
– Kranfahrgestelle
Leistungsspektrum: Herstellung der o. g. Produkte sowie Vertrieb inklusive von TADANO Geländekranen; 24-Stunden-Service
Standorte: Lauf a. d. Pegnitz bei Nürnberg; Muttergesellschaft in Japan mit 392 Vertriebs- und Serviceniederlassungen weltweit
Umsatz: TADANO FAUN GmbH ca. 210 Mio. Euro; TADANO Gruppe ca. 952 Mio. Dollar

Year founded: 1845
Employees: at the Lauf location 630; worldwide 2,331 (TADANO Group)
Products:
– All Terrain and Truck-Mounted Cranes
– Recovery Vehicles
– Crane Chassis
Range of Services: Manufacturing of the above products a.w.a. Sales inclusive of TADANO Rough Terrain Cranes; 24 h Product Support
Locations: Lauf a. d. Pegnitz (Germany), close to Nuremberg; Mother Company in Japan with 392 Sales and Service locations worldwide
Turnover: TADANO FAUN GmbH approx. 210 million Euro; TADANO Group approx. 952 million Dollar

TADANO FAUN GmbH
Lauf a. d. Pegnitz

Joh. Barth & Sohn ist einer der weltweit bedeutendsten Hopfenhändler.

Joh. Barth & Sohn is one of the world's most important hop traders.

Bild links/picture left: Regine Barth, Managing Partner und Peter Hintermeier, Executive Vice President Procurement

Bild unten/picture below: Adolfo Schott Steinberg, Sales Manager

Seit über 200 Jahren ein Näschen für erstklassigen Hopfen: das Familienunternehmen Joh. Barth & Sohn

A nose for first class hops for more than 200 years: Joh. Barth & Sohn, the family enterprise

Der Name Joh. Barth & Sohn ist seit über 200 Jahren untrennbar mit dem weltweiten Hopfenhandel verbunden und – ab Mitte der sechziger Jahre des vorigen Jahrhunderts – ebenso klangvoll mit dem Bereich der Hopfenverarbeitung verknüpft. Inzwischen wird das 1794 gegründete Unternehmen bereits in der achten Familiengeneration von den derzeitigen Geschäftsführern Stephan J. Barth, Alexander W. Barth, Regine Barth und Thomas C. Raiser geführt.
Gemeinsam mit den Unternehmen der Barth-Haas Gruppe ist Joh. Barth & Sohn mit einem Marktanteil von etwa 35 Prozent heute der weltweit größte Anbieter im Bereich Hopfenhandel und Hopfenverarbeitung. Zur Barth-Haas Gruppe gehören Unternehmen in den Vereinigten Staaten, Großbritannien, Australien und Deutschland.
Deutschland ist nach wie vor der größte Hopfenproduzent der Welt – vor den USA und China – mit einem Ernteanteil von 33 200 Tonnen (gesamt: 92 300 Tonnen).
Eine immer größere Rolle außerhalb der Brauwirtschaft spielen inzwischen die Einsatzmöglichkeiten

Standort in Europa
Business Location in Europe

von Hopfen in anderen Industrien wie etwa bei der Herstellung von Nahrungsmitteln oder Medizinprodukten. Joh. Barth & Sohn finanziert zahlreiche Forschungsprojekte auf diesem Feld.

Dazu gehören auch Untersuchungen beim Deutschen Krebsforschungszentrum in Heidelberg, wo bereits seit einigen Jahren Untersuchungen laufen, den Hopfenbestandteil Xanthohumol in der Krebsprävention wirksam einzusetzen.

For more than 200 years the name of Joh. Barth & Sohn has been inseparably linked with global hop trading. Since the mid-sixties of the last century it has been equally linked with the sector of hop processing. The enterprise which was founded in 1794 is run by the Barth family (Managing Directors Stephan J. Barth, Alexander W. Barth, Regine Barth and Thomas C. Raiser) already in the eighth generation.

Together with the affiliated companies of the Barth-Haas group Joh. Barth & Sohn has a market share of almost 35 percent being today the world's largest supplier in the sector of hop trading an hop processing. Affiliates in the United States, Great Britain, Australia and Germany belong to the Barth-Haas group.

With a harvest share of 33,200 tons (world total: 92,300 tons) Germany is still the world's largest hop producer – ahead of the USA and China.

In the meantime utilising hops is playing an ever-increasing role in non-brewing industries such as food and pharmaceuticals. Joh. Barth & Sohn have financed numerous research projects in this field. Some of them are carried out in the German Cancer Research Centre in Heidelberg where the effective use of Xanthohumol – one of the compounds of hops – in cancer has been examined for many years.

Information

Gründungsjahr: 1794

Mitarbeiter:
rund 500 weltweit, davon 236 in Deutschland

Leistungsspektrum:
– Hopfenhandel
– Hopfenverarbeitung

Standorte:
Deutschland, USA, China, Großbritannien, Australien

Umsatz:
rund 74 Mio. Euro (2004)

Year founded: 1794

Employees:
some 500 worldwide, of which 236 in Germany

Range of services:
– hop trading
– hop processing

Locations:
Germany, USA, China, Great Britain, Australia

Turnover:
about 74 million Euro (2004)

☐
Joh. Barth & Sohn
GmbH & Co. KG
Nürnberg

Information
Gründungsjahr: 1941
Mitarbeiter: 72
Produktspektrum:
– Transportlösungen aus Leichtmetall
– Behälter und Wagen in vielen Varianten
– umfangreiche Sonderfertigung
Schwerpunktbranchen:
– Katalogversandhandel
– Camping und Freizeit
– Chemie- und Pharmaindustrie
– Entsorgungsbranche
– Krankenhäuser
– Wäschereien
– Textilindustrie
Kompetenzen:
– Blech- und Profilbearbeitung
– Lasertechnologie
– verschiedene Schweiß- und Fügetechniken
– anwenderoptimierte Logistiklösungen

GMÖHLING fertigt seit mehr als 55 Jahren Transportbehälter und -geräte aus Leichtmetall. Die anerkannte Kompetenz der Firma GMÖHLING liegt in der Verarbeitung von Blechen und Profilen. In ihrem Marktsegment gehört sie zu den führenden Unternehmen der Branche.
GMÖHLING Transportbehälter und -geräte erfüllen höchste Ansprüche an Qualität und Innovation und bewähren sich in vielen Branchen für Verpackung, Lagerung und Transport.
Kundenorientierung wird dabei in zweifacher Weise verwirklicht:
1. Ein breites Angebot an Standardlösungen.
2. Aus speziellen Kundenwünschen werden individuelle Logistiklösungen.

*For more than 55 years GMÖHLING has manufactured transport containers and equipment made of light metal. The recognised competence of Messrs GMÖHLING lies in the processing of sheet metals and profiles. In their market segment they belong to the leading undertakings of the branch.
GMÖHLING transport containers and equipment meet the highest demands on quality and innovation and have proved themselves in many branches for packing, storage and transport.
At the same time customer-orientation is realised in two ways:
1. A wide selection of standard solutions.
2. Individual logistic solutions for special customer needs.*

Year founded: 1941
Employees: 72
Range of products:
– transport solutions made of light metal
– containers and carts in many variations
– encompassing special manufacture
Main branches:
– mail-order business
– camping and leisure
– chemical and pharmaceutical industry
– waste disposal branch
– hospitals
– laundries
– textile industry
Competence areas:
– sheet metal and profile processing
– laser technology
– various welding and jointing techniques
– user-optimised logistics solutions

GMÖHLING
Transportgeräte GmbH
Fürth

Standort in Europa
Business Location in Europe

Sasse Elektronik – Produkte zum Bedienen und Beobachten

Die Sasse Elektronik GmbH in Schwabach bietet ein umfangreiches Edelstahl-Tastaturprogramm für unterschiedlichste Anwendungsfelder. Schwerpunkte bilden Design, Entwicklung und Produktion von mechatronischen Lösungen für das industrielle Umfeld und die Medizintechnik.
Das Produktspektrum reicht von robusten Industrietastaturen bis zu integrierten Tastatur-Lösungen in Steuergehäusen und -schränken, mobilen Bedieneinheiten und kundenspezifischen Entwicklungen für die Automatisierung. Die Schnittstelle Mensch-Maschine/-Prozess steht im Fokus.

Sasse Elektronik – Products for Operating and Observing (Monitoring)

Sasse Elektronik GmbH in Schwabach offers a wide programme of stainless steel keyboards for various fields of use. The focus is on design, development and production of mechatronic solutions for the industrial sphere and medicine technology. The range of products reaches from sturdy industrial keyboards through to integrated keyboard solutions in control housings and cabinets, mobile operating units and customer-specific developments for automation. The focus is always on the man-machine/-process interface.

Information

Gründungsjahr: 1946

Mitarbeiter: 57

Leistungsspektrum: Entwicklung und Fertigung von Tastaturen, mobilen Bedieneinheiten und kundenspezifischen Sonderlösungen für den industriellen Einsatz

Umsatz: 8,5 Mio. Euro

Year founded: 1946

Employees: 57

Range of services: development and manufacture of keyboards, mobile operating units and special customer-specific solutions for industrial use

Turnover: 8.5 million Euro

☐ Sasse Elektronik GmbH – Member of the EBE Group Schwabach

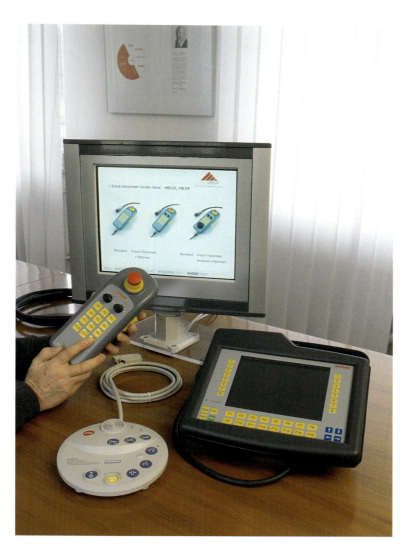

Eingabelösungen für die Automation und Medizintechnik; Bedienen und Beobachten

Input solutions for automation and medical technology; serve and observe

Design und Robustheit: Eingabekomponenten aus Edelstahl

Design and sturdiness: input components of stainless steel

Information

Gründungsjahr: 1933

Mitarbeiter: 2500

Standorte:
39 Modehäuser in Bayern, Baden-Württemberg, Berlin, Sachsen und Sachsen-Anhalt

Angebotsspektrum:
WÖHRL ist eines der größten Fachgeschäfte für Mode und Sport in ganz Europa mit den fünf Modewelten
– Damenmode
– Herrenmode
– Young Fashion
– Sportmode
– Kindermode

Year founded: 1933

Employees: 2,500

Locations:
39 fashion shops in Bavaria, Baden-Württemberg, Berlin, Saxony and Saxony-Anhalt

Range on offer:
WÖHRL is one of the largest speciality shops for fashion and sports equipment in the whole of Europe with the five fashion worlds
– ladies' fashion
– gents' fashion
– young fashion
– fashion for sports
– children's fashion

WÖHRL ist eines der führenden Unternehmen des Mode- und Sporteinzelhandels in Deutschland und verfügt über ein Filialnetz mit 39 Modehäusern in Bayern, Baden-Württemberg, Berlin, Sachsen und Sachsen-Anhalt.
Der Name WÖHRL steht für starke Marken, modische Kompetenz, exzellenten und kundenfreundlichen Service sowie ein hervorragendes Preis-Leistungs-Verhältnis.
Die WÖHRL-City Nürnberg am Weißen Turm repräsentiert dabei die ganze Leistungskraft und Kompetenz von WÖHRL als eine der ersten Adressen für Markenmode und Sport in Deutschland. Außerdem ist das WÖHRL-Stammhaus eines der größten Fachgeschäfte Europas für Mode und Sport – und ein faszinierendes Einkaufserlebnis für die ganze Familie.
WÖHRL. Willkommen in der Welt der Markenmode und des Sports.

*WÖHRL is one of the leading fashion and sports equipment retailers in Germany and maintains a network of branches consisting of 39 fashion shops in Bavaria, Baden-Württemberg, Berlin, Saxony and Saxony-Anhalt.
The name of WÖHRL stands for strong brands, fashion competence, excellent and customer-friendly service together with a first-rate price-performance relationship.
The WÖHRL-City Nuremberg at the Weißer Turm is representative of all the capabilities and competence of WÖHRL as one of the finest addresses for brand name fashion and sports equipment in Germany. In addition, the WÖHRL-parent company is one of the largest specialist retailers in Europe for fashion and sports equipment – a fascinating shopping experience for the whole family.
WÖHRL. Welcome to the world of brand name fashion and sports equipment.*

WÖHRL AG
Nürnberg

Standort in Europa
Business Location in Europe

Nürnberg im Zentrum des Neuen Europa

Dr. Günther Beckstein

Mit der größten Erweiterung in der Geschichte der Europäischen Union am 1. Mai 2004 kehrt Nürnberg wieder ins Zentrum Europas zurück. Der Beitritt der zehn neuen Mitgliedstaaten stößt für die Region Nürnberg das Tor zu einem Handels- und Wirtschaftsraum ungeahnten Ausmaßes auf. Gleichzeitig nimmt aber auch der harte Konkurrenzkampf auf dem nationalen und internationalen Markt zu. Vor diesem Hintergrund gewinnt die europäische Region mehr und mehr an Bedeutung. Innerhalb einer Region können Strukturprobleme besser erfasst und gelöst werden. Umso erfreulicher ist es, dass die Region Nürnberg am 28. April 2005 in den Kreis der europäischen Metropolregionen aufgenommen wurde.

In Nürnberg hat man sich offensiv dem Strukturwandel gestellt. Die Frankenmetropole entwickelt sich immer mehr vom traditionellen Produktionsstandort hin zu einem modernen Industrie- und Dienstleistungszentrum mit zukunftsträchtigen Clustern wie zum Beispiel in der Medizintechnik, der Informations- und Kommunikationstechnik oder der Marktforschung. Die unterschiedlichen Forschungseinrichtungen der Universität Erlangen-Nürnberg und die Institute der Max-Planck-Gesellschaft sowie die Institute der Fraunhofer-Gesellschaft arbeiten Hand in Hand mit den Unternehmen vor Ort. Das Know-how der beteiligten Firmen und Einrichtungen wird gebündelt und schnell und effektiv in innovative Produkte und Verfahren umgesetzt. Damit entstehen neue zukunftsträchtige Arbeitsplätze. Das macht Nürnberg attraktiv für Investoren.

Nürnberg präsentiert sich heute als ein besonders wirtschaftsstarker Raum in Deutschland und Europa, an dem sich drei wichtige europäische Fernstraßen treffen. Die Stadt ist auch Drehkreuz des nationalen und internationalen Flug- und Bahnverkehrs. Eine gute Verkehrsanbindung und ein gezielter Ausbau der Infrastruktur sind wichtige Weichenstellungen. Hier sind besonders
– der Ausbau der A 6 nach Osten bis Prag und die Ertüchtigung auf sechs Fahrstreifen nach Westen bis zur Landesgrenze mit Baden-Württemberg,

Fortsetzung Seite 38

With the largest expansion in the history of the European Union, Nuremberg returned once again to the centre of Europe on 1st May 2004. The entrance of the ten new member states pushed open the door to a trading and economic area in undreamed of dimensions for the region of Nuremberg. Simultaneously however, the hard competitive battle on the national and international market is on the increase. With this backdrop, the European region gains more and more in significance. Within one region, structural problems can be better understood and solved. So it was all the more pleasant that the region of Nuremberg was accepted into the circle of European metropolitan regions on 28th April 2005.

In Nuremberg structural changes have been met offensively. The Franconian metropolis is developing more and more from a traditional production location to a modern industry and services centre with forward-looking clusters, for instance such as in medical technology, information and communication technologies and market research. The various research institutions of the Erlangen-Nuremberg University and the institutes of the Max-Planck-Gesellschaft as well as the institutes of the Fraunhofer-Gesellschaft work hand in hand with local concerns. The know-how of the firms and institutions involved is bundled and quickly and effectively put into practice in innovative products and processes. Thus new workplaces with promising futures are created, making Nuremberg very attractive for investors.

Today Nuremberg presents itself as a particularly strong economic area in Germany and Europe, a location at which three significant European motorways meet. The city is also the hub of national and international flight and rail transport. Good transport connections and purposeful expansion of the infrastructure are important course settings. Here particular mention should be made of
– the expansion of the A 6 motorway in an easterly direction to Prague and the strengthening to six lanes in a westerly direction through to the county boundary with Baden-Württemberg,

Continued on page 38

Nuremberg in the Heart of the New Europe

Nordbayern ist mit über 53 000 Beschäftigten der größte Standort der Siemens AG weltweit. Sieben Bereichszentralen und 17 Werke sind hier an elf verschiedenen Standorten ansässig. Dabei war Nürnberg von Anfang an das Tor für den Vertrieb in Nordbayern, denn in der mittelfränkischen Stadt schlug bereits im 19. Jahrhundert das industrielle Herz Bayerns.

Heute nehmen die vier Niederlassungen Bayreuth, Nürnberg, Regensburg und Würzburg die Vertriebs- und Serviceaktivitäten für die rund 20 000 Kunden in den drei fränkischen Bezirken und der Oberpfalz wahr. Das Spektrum reicht von international tätigen Großkonzernen über öffentliche Auftraggeber und Einrichtungen des Gesundheitswesens bis zu kleinen und mittelständischen Betrieben aller Branchen.

Als größter Arbeitgeber mit rund 34 000 Mitarbeitern in Vertrieb, Fertigung und Entwicklung nimmt der Global Player Siemens eine herausragende Rolle im Großraum Erlangen-Nürnberg-Fürth-Forchheim ein. In Erlangen zum Beispiel ist der Name Siemens untrennbar mit der Entwicklung der Stadt nach 1945 verbunden. Heute beschäftigt das Unternehmen hier etwa 21 000 Mitarbeiter und erwirtschaftet im Großraum rund 50 Prozent seines weltweiten Jahresumsatzes.

Die Präsenz und viele innovative Projekte belegen, welche Bedeutung Siemens dem Wirtschaftsraum beimisst. Hier haben nicht nur die erfolgreichsten Unternehmensbereiche ihren Hauptsitz, hier hat Siemens seine Wurzeln.

Mit seinen Aktivitäten, der engen Kooperation mit der Region, den Universitäten und den mittelständischen Firmen sowie mit aktuellen Bauvorhaben zeigt der Global Player ganz klar: Siemens und die Metropolregion Nürnberg – zwei Namen, die auch künftig zusammengehören.

Das Siemens-Verwaltungsgebäude in Erlangen wird im Volksmund auch „Himbeerpalast" genannt.

The Siemens administration building in Erlangen is known locally as the "raspberry palace".

Von der Niederlassung Nürnberg aus steuert Siemens seine Vertriebs- und Serviceaktivitäten in der Region Nordbayern.

Siemens controls its sales and service activities in the Northern Bavarian region from the Nuremberg branch.

Standort in Europa
Business Location in Europe

Mit attraktiven und modernen Ausbildungs- und Studiengängen macht Siemens junge Leute fit für das Berufsleben.

With attractive and modern training and study courses Siemens helps young people to become fit for professional life.

With more than 53,000 employees, Northern Bavaria is the largest Siemens AG location worldwide.
Seven department head offices and 17 works are located here on eleven different sites. From the very beginning, Nuremberg was the portal for sales in Northern Bavaria as the Middle-Franconian city was the industrial heart of Bavaria as early as the 19th century.
Today, the four branches in Bayreuth, Nuremberg, Regensburg and Würzburg take care of the sales and service activities for approximately 20,000 customers in the three Franconian districts and the Upper Palatinate. The selection ranges from internationally operating major concerns via public contractors and health institutions through to small and medium-sized firms belonging to all possible branches.
As the largest employer having some 34,000 employees in sales, production and development, Siemens, the global player, takes over an outstanding role in the wide area covering Erlangen-Nuremberg-Fürth-Forchheim. In Erlangen for example the name of Siemens is inseparably associated with the town's development from 1945 onwards. Today the concern employs some 21,000 people there and achieves some 50 percent

of its global turnover in the area.
Its very presence together with the many innovative projects proves the significance Siemens has for the economic area. Not only do the most successful concern sectors have their headquarters here, this is also where Siemens has its roots.
With its activities, the close cooperation with the region, the universities and the small and medium-sized firms as well as current building plans, this global player demonstrates quite clearly: Siemens and the metropolitan region of Nuremberg are two names which will also belong together in the future.

In der Region entwickeln die Siemens-Experten innovative Produkte und Lösungen für die Welt von heute und morgen: hier der Computertomograph Somatom Definition, der klinische Aufnahmen mit nicht gekannter zeitlicher Auflösung möglich macht.

Siemens experts in the region develop innovative products and solutions for today's and tomorrow's world: here we have a computer tomograph Somatom Definition which makes clinical images with unknown temporal resolution possible.

Information

Mitarbeiter: rund 53 000 sowie etwa 1500 Auszubildende in ganz Nordbayern

Struktur:
- 7 Bereichszentralen
- 17 Werke
- 11 Standorte

Unternehmensbereiche:
- Automation & Drives (A&D)
- Industrial Solution and Services (I&S)
- Medical Solutions (Med)
- Power Generation (PG)
- Power Transmission and Distribution (PTD)
- Transportation Systems (TS)
- Siemens VDO Automotive (SV)

Employees: some 53,000 as well as approximately 1,500 trainees in the whole of Northern Bavaria

Structure:
- 7 department head offices
- 17 works
- 11 locations

Concern sectors:
- Automation & Drives (A&D)
- Industrial Solution and Services (I&S)
- Medical Solutions (Med)
- Power Generation (PG)
- Power Transmission and Distribution (PTD)
- Transportation Systems (TS)
- Siemens VDO Automotive (SV)

Siemens Aktiengesellschaft Niederlassung Nürnberg

Das Autobahnkreuz Nürnberg-Süd an der A 6 wurde um eine Direktrampe (Overfly) erweitert und Ende 2005 für den Verkehr freigegeben.

The motorway intersection Nuremberg-South on the A 6 was expanded with an overfly and was released for traffic at the end of 2005.

– der Ausbau des transeuropäischen Eisenbahnnetzes unter besonderer Berücksichtigung der neuen ICE-Trasse nach Erfurt/Berlin,
– der wichtige Europakanal, der – in Verbindung mit dem weiteren Ausbau der Donau – eine Funktion bis zum Schwarzen Meer erfüllen muss, und
– das Güterverkehrszentrum am Hafen
zu nennen.

Darüber hinaus unterstützt der Messestandort Nürnberg als Austauschplattform von Produkten und Wissen die Internationalität der Region.

Außerdem setzt Nürnberg ganz gezielt auf die Qualitäten der Region: Brauchtum, Tradition und regionale

Fortsetzung Seite 43

– *the extension of the trans-European railway network paying particular attention to the new ICE-railway line to Erfurt/Berlin,*
– *the vital European canal which – in connection with the further extension of the Danube – has to fulfil its function through to the Black Sea, and*
– *the goods transport centre at the harbour.*

Beyond this, the trade fair location Nuremberg supports the internationality of the region as an exchange platform of products and knowledge.

Furthermore, Nuremberg depends specifically on the qualities of the region: Customs, tradition and regional identity are particular strong points of Franconia. When considering the increasing intensification of international competition and the far-reaching structural changes, then the so-called soft business location factors become increasingly important. As a consequence, the provision of education, culture, leisure and recuperation, not to mention individual characteristics and local sights, carry far more weight. Frequent-

Continued on page 43

Standort in Europa
Business Location in Europe

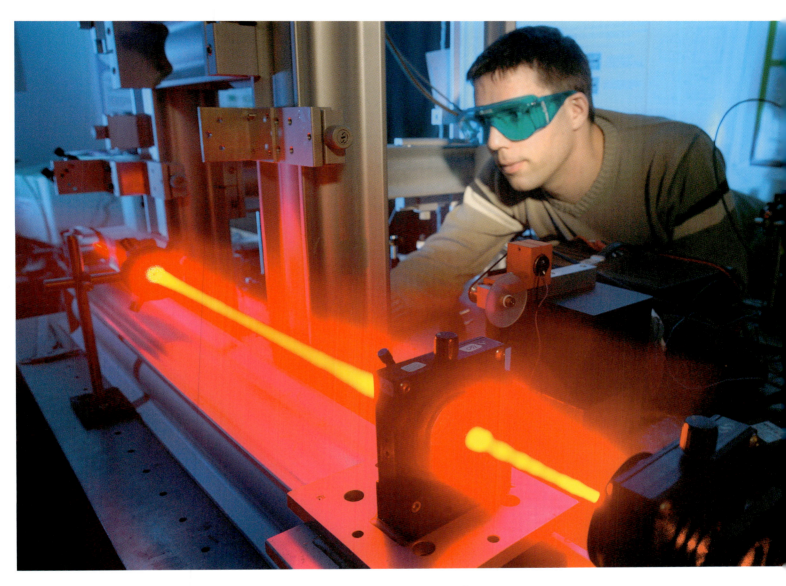

Messlabor zur Untersuchung der optimalen Strukturtiefe in der optischen Datenspeicherung der Max-Planck-Forschungsgruppe für Optik, Information und Photonik

A measuring laboratory for examining the optimal structural depth of optical data saving at the Max-Planck-Research Group for Optic, Information and Photonic

Rödl & Partner ist eine der führenden Wirtschaftsprüfungs-, Steuerberatungs- und Rechtsanwaltskanzleien. Gegründet 1977, betreut Rödl & Partner Unternehmen weltweit bei ihren Geschäftsaktivitäten. Die Kanzlei ist in allen wesentlichen Industrienationen der Welt vertreten und hat insbesondere in Mittel- und Osteuropa, Westeuropa, Asien und den USA starke Marktpositionen aufgebaut. Der im Herbst 2005 eröffnete Erweiterungsbau und die damit verbundene Schaffung des „Rödl Campus" im Herzen Nürnbergs ist Ausdruck starken Wachstums und gleichzeitig klares Bekenntnis zur Region. In der Architektur spiegelt sich die Unternehmensphilosophie: Wichtige Eckpunkte sind Offenheit und Transparenz, in der Beratung von Mandanten ebenso wie in der nationalen und internationalen Zusammenarbeit der Fachteams. Ausdruck finden diese Komponenten in der Architektur durch eine offene, kommunikative Gebäudegestaltung mit viel Raum zum persönlichen Austausch.

Von der Unternehmenszentrale in Nürnberg aus koordiniert Rödl & Partner heute 71 Niederlassungen im In- und Ausland. Zahlreiche Kerngebiete, die Rödl & Partner an sämtlichen deutschen Standorten anbietet, etwa Transaktionsberatung und internationales Steuerrecht, werden von Nürnberg aus gesteuert.

Rödl & Partner versteht sich als Professional Service Firm, die auf der Grundlage ausgeprägter Kompetenz und Erfahrung seiner Mitarbeiter und der engen, vertrauensvollen Zusammenarbeit mit Mandanten fach- und länderübergreifend individuell zugeschnittene Lösungen erarbeitet.

Standort in Europa
Business Location in Europe

Rödl & Partner is one of the leading professional service firms providing auditing, tax and legal services. Founded in 1977, Rödl & Partner look after the business activities of companies all over the world. The office is represented in all the important industrial nations of the world and has strong market positions in Central and Eastern Europe, West Europe, Asia and the USA. The extension to the office opened in Autumn 2005 and the "Rödl Campus" thereby created in the heart of Nuremberg gives expression to the strong growth and simultaneously is a clear declaration of commitment to the region. The architecture reflects company philosophy: The most important cornerstones are openness and transparency when counselling clients just as much as in the national and international cooperation of teams of specialists. These components are mirrored in the architecture of the open, communicative building design with lots of room for personal discussions.

Based in the company headquarters in Nuremberg, Rödl & Partner today coordinates 70 branches in Germany and overseas. Numerous core areas are provided for by Rödl & Partner on all their German locations, for instance transaction advice and international tax laws all of them controlled from Nuremberg.

Rödl & Partner sees itself as a professional services firm which works out interdisciplinary and international individually tailored solutions on the basis of exceptional competence and the experience of its employees together with the close, confidential cooperation with its clients.

Information

Gründungjahr: 1977
Mitarbeiter:
2430 weltweit;
1500 in Deutschland
Niederlassungen:
weltweit 71 Standorte in 31 Ländern;
22 Standorte in Deutschland
Rödl & Partner ist vertreten in:
Deutschland, Belgien, Brasilien, China, Estland, Finnland, Frankreich, Indien, Indonesien, Italien, Kroatien, Lettland, Litauen, Malaysia, Österreich, Polen, Rumänien, Russische Föderation, Schweden, Singapur, Slowakische Republik, Slowenien, Spanien, Südkorea, Thailand, Tschechische Republik, Türkei, Ukraine, Ungarn, USA, Vereinigte Arabische Emirate

---

Year founded: 1977
Employees:
2,430 worldwide;
1,500 in Germany
Branches:
worldwide 71 locations in 31 countries;
22 locations in Germany
Rödl & Partner is represented in:
Germany, Austria, Belgium, Brazil, China, Croatia, Czech Republic, Estonia, Finland, France, Hungary, India, Indonesia, Italy, Latvia, Lithuania, Malaysia, Poland, Rumania, Russian Federation, Singapore, Slovak Republic, Slovenia, South Korea, Spain, Sweden, Thailand, Turkey, Ukraine, United Arab Emirates, USA

☐
**Rödl & Partner GbR
Nürnberg**

STAEDTLER zählt weltweit zu den führenden Herstellern von Schreib- und Zeichengeräten und bürgt für höchste Markenqualität. Produkte der Marke STAEDTLER stehen für präzise Schreibergebnisse, hohe Zuverlässigkeit und exzellenten Schreibkomfort.
Das Unternehmen ist stolz auf seine lange Produktionstradition in Deutschland und auf die Erfahrung in der Entwicklung und Herstellung von professionellen Schreib- und Zeicheninstrumenten. MADE IN GERMANY gilt weltweit als Gütesiegel für höchste Qualität. Mehr als zwei Drittel aller STAEDTLER-Produkte werden am Standort Deutschland hergestellt. STAEDTLER präsentiert sich heute mit einem vielfältigen Sortiment an hochwertigen Produkten, von Blei- und Farbstiften über Tuschezeichner, Kugelschreiber, Faserschreiber, Folienstiften und Markern bis hin zu Druckbleistiften, Radierern, Zirkel und Tinten.

STAEDTLER counts as one of the world's leading manufacturers of writing and drawing equipment and guarantees top quality. Products with the STAEDTLER trademark stands for perfect writing comfort, highest reliability and superb writing comfort.
The undertaking is proud of its long tradition of production in Germany and of the experience gained in the development and manufacture of professional writing and drawing instruments. MADE IN GERMANY is known all over the world as a kite-mark for highest quality.
More than two thirds of all

Mit STAEDTLER schreibt die Welt.

The world writes with STAEDTLER.

Eine Marke gewachsen aus Tradition und Qualität.

A trademark grown from tradition and quality.

STAEDTLER products are manufactured in Germany. STAEDTLER presents itself today with a manifold assortment of high-grade products, from lead and coloured pencils via equipment for pen-and-ink drawings, ball pens, fibre tips, overhead markers and markers through to propelling pencils, erasers, pairs of compasses and ink.

Modernste Technologie ist für STAEDTLER in der Produktion genauso selbstverständlich wie in den Produkten.

For STAEDTLER cutting-edge technology in production is just as natural as in the products.

Information

Gründungsjahr: 1835

Mitarbeiter:
weltweit rund 3000

Leistungsspektrum:
– Schreib- und Zeichengeräte
– größter Hersteller in Europa für Bleistifte, Farbstifte, Folienstifte, Radierer

Standorte:
Stammsitz der Unternehmensgruppe in Nürnberg;
25 Vertriebsniederlassungen weltweit

Year founded: 1835

Employees:
some 3,000 globally

Range of services:
– writing and drawing equipment
– Europe's largest manufacturer of lead pencils, coloured pencils, overhead markers, erasers

Locations:
headquarters of the group of companies in Nuremberg;
25 sales subsidiaries all over the world

☐
STAEDTLER Mars GmbH & Co. KG
Schreib- und Zeichengeräte-Fabriken
Nürnberg

Standort in Europa
Business Location in Europe

Identität sind besondere Stärken des Frankenlandes. Gerade im Hinblick auf die weitere Verschärfung des internationalen Wettbewerbs und den tief greifenden Strukturwandel werden die so genannten weichen Standortfaktoren immer wichtiger. Somit fallen das Bildungs-, Kultur-, Freizeit- und Erholungsangebot sowie die charakteristischen Eigenarten und Sehenswürdigkeiten vor Ort stark ins Gewicht. Oftmals geben sie sogar den letzten Ausschlag bei Standortentscheidungen.

Nürnberg hat sehr schnell erkannt, auf die eigenen Potenziale zu setzen. Erklärtes Ziel ist es, Lebensqualität, Leistungsfähigkeit und Attraktivität der Region zu bewahren und weiter zu stärken. Allein das vielfältige und attraktive Kulturangebot der Metropolregion Nürnberg spricht für sich. Es reicht vom Staatstheater über das Germanische Nationalmuseum und das Staatliche Museum für Kunst und Design bis hin zum Dokumentationszentrum Reichsparteitagsgelände. Und wer kennt nicht den Nürnberger Christkindlesmarkt, der ein Magnet für Besucher aus aller Welt ist. Auch die Fußball-Weltmeisterschaft 2006 mit dem Austragungsort Frankenstadion wertet die Region zusätzlich auf. Will man „die Seele mal baumeln lassen" und herrliche Natur genießen, ist man in der Fränkischen und Hersbrucker Schweiz, im Fränkischen Seenland oder im Altmühltal bestens aufgehoben.

Mit einem Wort: Die Metropolregion Nürnberg ist im internationalen Vergleich gut aufgestellt. Sie präsentiert sich als attraktiver, internationaler Wirtschaftsstandort und behauptet ihre Stellung in der „Champions League" auf dem Weltmarkt. Sie hat sich nicht nur als Impulsgeber und Entwicklungspol für den gesamten nordbayerischen Raum entwickelt, sondern dient auch als „Gateway" für die neuen EU-Staaten. In dieser Funktion trägt sie nicht nur zum regen wirtschaftlichen Austausch, sondern auch zum menschlichen Zusammenwachsen der immer größer werdenden Europäischen Union bei.

ly, they are even the deciding factor in decisions regarding business location.

Nuremberg very quickly realised that it must depend on its own potential. It has become the declared goal to maintain and further increase the quality of life, productivity and the region's attractiveness. The metropolitan region of Nuremberg's manifold and attractive cultural range alone speaks for itself. It reaches from the state theatre via the Germanic National Museum and the state-owned Museum for Art and Design through to the documentation centre Reichsparteitagsgelände. And who has never heard of the Nuremberg Christkindlesmarkt, a magnet for guests from all over the world. The football world championships 2006 with the Frankenstadion as venue add value to the region. Whoever wishes to "let it all hang out" and enjoy splendid nature, then he is in good keeping in Franconia's natural parks "Franconian Switzerland" and "Hersbruck Switzerland", in the Franconian lake district or in the Altmühltal.

In other words: The metropolitan region of Nuremberg is well set up by international comparison. It presents itself as an attractive, international business location and can maintain its position in the "Champions League" on the world market. Not only has it developed itself as an pulse generator and development pole for the entire North Bavarian area but also serves as a "gateway" for the new EU states. In these functions, it contributes not only to lively industrial exchange but also to the growing together of peoples in the ever widening European Union.

Großunternehmen und Mittelstand – Branchenvielfalt mit geballtem Know-how

Dr. Dieter Riesterer

Die Ministerkonferenz für Raumordnung hat am 28. April 2005 beschlossen, die Region Nürnberg in den Kreis der europäischen Metropolregionen in Deutschland aufzunehmen. Dieser Entscheidung kommt herausragende Bedeutung zu, weil sie der Region hervorragende Zukunftsperspektiven eröffnet. Eine wichtige wirtschaftliche Grundlage für die Aufwertung zur Metropolregion war neben der hoch entwickelten Infrastruktur sowie den umfassenden Kompetenzen in Forschung und Technologie das starke Potenzial, das aus der Leistungsfähigkeit der über 100 000 Unternehmen resultiert.

Die Metropolregion kann auf einen gesunden Größen- und Branchenmix der Unternehmen aufbauen. Mit einem Anteil von über 80 Prozent an den Betrieben prägen mittelständische Familienunternehmen die Wirtschaftsstruktur. Die enge Verflechtung von Familie, Kapital und Unternehmensführung begünstigt eine langfristige Ausrichtung der Unternehmensziele – auch auf den internationalen Markt. Eine ebenso unverzichtbare Rolle für Wirtschaftskraft, Außenhandel und Arbeitsplätze spielen Großunternehmen: Unter den beschäftigungsstärksten Unternehmen, die zusammen weit über 100 000 Arbeitsplätze in der Region anbieten, befinden sich internationale Größen wie Siemens, Quelle, die Nürnberger Versicherungsgruppe, adidas, die GfK-Gruppe, Rehau, Rosenthal, Loewe, Grammer oder Pfleiderer, mit DATEV eine von Steuerberatern aus ganz Deutschland getragene Genossenschaft, und Familienunternehmen mit weltweit bekannten Markennamen wie INA Schaeffler, Diehl, Schwan-Stabilo, Geobra Brandstätter („Playmobil"), Cherry, Bögl oder Brose.

Schon an diesen Beispielen zeigt sich das breite Spektrum der vertretenen Branchen aus Industrie,

Fortsetzung Seite 51

On 28th April 2005 the ministers' conference for regional development planning decided to accept the region of Nuremberg in the circle of European metropolitan regions in Germany. This decision is of exceptional significance in that it opens excellent future prospects for the region. One of the important economic bases for the enhancement to a metropolitan region was, alongside the highly developed infrastructure and the extensive competence in research and technology, the strong potential resulting from the productivity of more than 100,000 undertakings.

The metropolitan region has a healthy mixture in concern sizes and concern branches on which to build. The share of medium-sized family-owned undertakings amounts to more than 80 percent and they leave a definite mark on the economic structure. The close meshing of family, capital and company management benefits long-term orientation of company targets – also on the international market while major companies play an equally indispensable role in economic power, foreign trade and workplaces. International concerns such as Siemens, Quelle, the Nürnberger Versicherungsgruppe, adidas, the GfK-Group, Rehau, Rosenthal, Loewe, Grammer are to be found amongst the companies employing the most people, together they provide far more than 100,000 workplaces in the region. Pfleiderer too, thanks to DATEV, a cooperation carried by tax consultants from all over Germany, and family undertakings with globally known trademarks such as INA Schaeffler, Diehl, Schwan-Stabilo, Geobra Brandstätter ("Playmobil"), Cherry, Bögl and Brose should be mentioned here.

These examples alone demonstrate the wide range of branches representing industry, trade and services. The services offered by medium-sized undertakings

Continued on page 51

Major Concerns and Small and Medium-sized Firms – Branch Variety with Concentrated Know-how

Standort in Europa
Business Location in Europe

**Ziele setzen.
Gemeinsam steuern.**

Durch die Vernetzung von Spezialisten aus verschiedenen Fachbereichen bietet MUNKERT · KUGLER + PARTNER seinen Kunden eine ganzheitliche Beratung und Betreuung. Von der Steuer- und Rechtsberatung bis zur Wirtschaftsprüfung und zur betriebswirtschaftlichen Beratung. Mit einem persönlichen Ansprechpartner, der alles im Sinne der Kunden steuert.

**Regional verbunden.
International vernetzt.**

In Deutschland bieten mehr als 400 Mitarbeiter an 40 Standorten eine umfangreiche persönliche Betreuung vor Ort. Als Mitglied der Geneva Group International (GGI) ist MUNKERT · KUGLER + PARTNER in mehr als 70 Ländern mit 11 400 Mitarbeitern für seine international tätigen Kunden aktiv. Flexible und effiziente Einheiten, die auf die individuellen Bedürfnisse der Kunden eingehen, sind das Versprechen von MUNKERT · KUGLER + PARTNER.

Competence meets experience.

Interdisciplinary specialist networking enables MUNKERT · KUGLER + PARTNER to give its clients comprehensive advice and support, ranging from tax and legal advice to accounting, commercial and investment advice. You will have just one point of contact who will provide you with all the advice you require.

*Strong regional links.
Strong international network.*

In Germany 400 employees at 40 locations provide clients with personalised full service. As a member of Geneva Group International (GGI) MUNKERT · KUGLER + PARTNER is actively supporting its clients in more than 70 countries with 11,400 employees. Flexible and efficient units that will respond to your individual needs are a promise made by MUNKERT · KUGLER + PARTNER.

**Visionen teilen.
Ideen voranbringen.**

Durch aktive Umsetzung der fachlichen und terminlichen Anforderungen, Kreativität, Querdenken und frühzeitigem Erkennen von Fehlentwicklungen ermöglicht MUNKERT · KUGLER + PARTNER seinen Kunden, sich auf das Wesentliche zu konzentrieren – ihr Geschäft. Flexibilität und Interdisziplinarität sind dabei Leitmotiv für MUNKERT · KUGLER + PARTNER.

*Sharing visions.
Promoting ideas.*

With active implementation of professional requirement and meeting deadlines, creativity, thinking out of the box and recognition of developments in the wrong direction MUNKERT · KUGLER + PARTNER enables its clients to focus on their projects. Flexibility and interdisciplinarity is the philosophy of MUNKERT · KUGLER + PARTNER.

Information

Gründungsjahr: 1969
Mitarbeiter: ca. 400 in Deutschland; weltweit ca. 11 400 (GGI Netzwerk)
Standorte: 40 in Deutschland; weltweit 300 (GGI Netzwerk)
Kunden:
- Familienunternehmen
- Internationale Konzerne
- Öffentliche Unternehmen
- Freiberufler
- Privatpersonen
- Stiftungen

Leistungen:
- Wirtschaftsprüfung
- Steuerberatung
- Rechtsberatung
- Unternehmensberatung
- Corporate Finance
- Vermögensberatung

Year founded: 1969
Employees: approx. 400 in Germany; worldwide approx. 11,400 (GGI network)
Locations: 40 in Germany; worldwide 300 (GGI network)
Clients:
- Family run businesses
- International groups
- Public companies
- Freelancers
- Private Individuals
- Foundations

Services:
- Auditing
- Tax Advice
- Legal Advice
- Management consultancy
- Corporate Finance
- Investment advice

☐
MUNKERT · KUGLER + PARTNER, Nürnberg

Information

Gründungsjahr: 1946
Mitarbeiter:
58 000 weltweit;
28 000 in Deutschland;
7500 im Stammhaus Herzogenaurach
Produktspektrum:
– Motorenelemente
– Kupplungs- und Getriebesysteme
– Sensor-Radlager
– Wälzlager
– Linearsysteme
– Direktantriebstechnik
Etwa 4000 hoch qualifizierte Ingenieure entwickeln weltweit neue zukunftsgerichtete Lösungen.
Standorte:
Stammhaus Herzogenaurach sowie weitere Werke und Niederlassungen in Deutschland; weltweit etwa 180 Standorte in mehr als 50 Ländern
Umsatz: 7,2 Mrd. Euro (Stand 2004)

Year founded: 1946
Employees:
58,000 worldwide;
28,000 in Germany;
7,500 in the parent company in Herzogenaurach
Range of products:
– motor elements
– clutch and gear systems
– sensor wheel bearings
– roller bearings
– linear systems
– direct drive technology
Some 4,000 highly qualified engineers develop worldwide new forward-looking solutions.
Locations:
the parent house in Herzogenaurach as well as other works and branches in Germany; some 180 locations in more than 50 countries all over the world
Turnover: 7.2 billion Euro (as at 2004)

□

Schaeffler Gruppe Herzogenaurach

„Gemeinsam bewegen wir die Welt." Die Schaeffler Gruppe, eines der größten deutschen Industrieunternehmen in Familienbesitz, ist ein weltweit führender Anbieter von Wälzlagern und Linearprodukten und ein renommierter Zulieferer der Automobilindustrie. Gesellschafter sind Maria-Elisabeth Schaeffler und ihr Sohn Lic. oec. HSG Georg F. W. Schaeffler JD/LLM. Der Erfolg basiert auf ausgeprägter Innovationskraft, globaler Kundennähe und höchster Qualität. Mit der Organisation nach den Sparten Automotive, Industrie und Aerospace hat sich die Schaeffler Gruppe kundennah ausgerichtet. Produkte der drei starken Marken INA, LuK und FAG werden von den Sparten vertrieben. Zu den Kunden der Sparte Automotive zählen alle namhaften Automobilhersteller. Die beiden Marken INA und FAG sind gemeinsam die weltweite Nummer 2 in der Wälzlager-Industrie und bieten mit mehr als 40 000 Katalogprodukten und einem Gesamtsortiment von mehr als 150 000 Artikeln eines der breitesten Produktprogramme in dieser Branche.

"Together we move the world." The Schaeffler Gruppe, one of the largest German industrial undertakings in family ownership, is a worldwide leading supplier of roller bearings and linear products and a well-known supplier for the automobile industry. Shareholders are Maria-Elisabeth Schaeffler and her son Lic. oec. HSG Georg F. W. Schaeffler JD/LLM. Their success is based on exceptional innovative power, global customer-closeness and the utmost in quality. With the organisation divided into the sections of automotive, industry and aerospace, the Schaeffler Gruppe has geared itself for customer closeness. The various sections sell products of the three strong INA, LuK and FAG brands and all the famous car manufacturers are customers of the automotive sector. Together, the INA and FAG brands are the world's number 2 in the roller bearing industry and, with more than 40,000 products in their catalogue and a range of more than 150,000 articles, offer one of the widest product programs in this branch.

Das Stammhaus Herzogenaurach ist größter F&E-Standort und koordiniert auch alle Forschungs- und Entwicklungsaktivitäten weltweit.

The parent company in Herzogenaurach is the largest R&D location where all the global research and development activities are also coordinated.

Standort in Europa
Business Location in Europe

INA steht seit mehr als 50 Jahren für Präzisionsteile im Industrie- und Automotivebereich. Der Firmengründer Dr. Ing. E.h. Georg Schaeffler verhalf mit seiner Erfindung des käfiggeführten Nadellagers dem Unternehmen 1949 zum Durchbruch. Hochwertige INA-Nadellager kommen in mehr als 60 Industriebranchen zum Einsatz. Mit INA-Motorenelementen lassen sich Verbrauch und Emissionen in Kraftfahrzeugen deutlich senken.

For more than 50 years, INA has stood for precision parts in industry and the automotive sector. The company founder Dr. Ing. E.h. Georg Schaeffler's invention of the needle bearing with cage helped the concern to its breakthrough in 1949. High quality INA-needle roller bearings are used in more than 60 branches of industry. Using INA motor elements consumption and emission in motor vehicles can be reduced considerably.

FAG-Großlager kommen zum Beispiel in Windkraftanlagen, Stahlwerken und Erzmühlen zum Einsatz. Sie können einen Durchmesser von mehreren Metern haben. FAG liefert auch Präzisionslager für die Luft- und Raumtechnik sowie Sonderanwendungen für die Medizintechnik. Die Sparte Aerospace hat jüngst mit FAG als Alleinlieferant für alle Hauptlagerungen der Triebwerke des neuen Airbus A 380 ein Stück Luftfahrtgeschichte mitgeschrieben.

FAG bearing housings for heavy industry are used for instance in wind-driven power stations, steelworks and ore mills. They can have diameters of several metres. FAG also delivers precision bearings for aerospace technologies as well as special applications for medicine technology. The aerospace division recently helped to write history with FAG as sole supplier for all main bearings of the engines of the new Airbus A 380.

LuK-Innovationen setzen seit 1965 Maßstäbe im Kupplungsbau. Heute rollt weltweit fast jedes vierte Auto mit einer LuK-Kupplung vom Band. Die neue LuK-Doppelkupplung ermöglicht zugfreies und damit komfortables Schalten. Darüber hinaus liefert LuK Komponenten für Automatikgetriebe sowie Ersatzteile für Werkstatt und Handel.

LuK innovations have set standards since 1965 in the construction of clutches. Today, almost every fourth car rolls off conveyor belts all over the world with a LuK clutch. The new LuK double clutch enables drag-free and thereby comfortable gear changes. LuK also supplies components for automatic gearboxes as well as spares for workshops and the trade.

Der Stammsitz von uvex in Fürth: Trotz der großen Internationalisierung des Unternehmens bleibt uvex dem Standort Fürth und Deutschland treu, da das Unternehmen hier neben einer wirtschaftsfreundlichen Politik und guter Infrastruktur auch über ein großes Potenzial an qualifizierten Arbeitskräften verfügt.

The headquarters of uvex in Fürth: In spite of massive internationalisation within the undertaking, uvex remains faithful to its locations in Fürth and Germany. Here, the undertaking can avail itself of a huge potential of qualified employees in addition to a business-friendly policy and an excellent infrastructure.

Ausrüster internationaler Spitzensportler:
Die Fürther Unternehmensgruppe, die vor allem durch die Ausrüstung zahlreicher Spitzensportler im Winter-, Rad-, Automobil- und Motorradsport bekannt ist, gilt heute als unbestrittener Weltmarktführer in den Bereichen Skibrille und Skihelm. Vor allem im Wintersport gibt es daher wenige sportliche Top-Ereignisse, bei denen uvex nicht mit auf dem Siegerpodest steht.

Equipper of top international sportspeople: The Fürth group of undertakings, primarily known for equipping countless top sportspeople in winter, cycling, and automobile and motor bike sports is considered today to be the undisputed global leader in the sectors of skiing goggles and helmets. Especially in winter sports, there are few sporting events where uvex doesn't appear on the winner's podium.

Standort in Europa
Business Location in Europe

Arbeitsschutz von Kopf bis Fuß: Die UVEX ARBEITSSCHUTZ GMBH gehört als innovativer Markensystemanbieter mit Herstellerkompetenz zu den weltweit größten Herstellern von Arbeitsschutzprodukten und ist mit 18 Tochtergesellschaften und Beteiligungen in mehr als 50 Ländern aktiv.

Personal protection equipment from head to toe: The UVEX ARBEITSSCHUTZ GMBH is one of the innovative brand name system suppliers with manufacturer's competence and belongs to the world's largest manufacturers of articles for health and safety protection at the workplace and with 18 subsidiaries and holding companies in more than 50 countries is active all over the world.

Weltmarktführer im industriellen Augenschutz: uvex hat seine Brillenproduktion nicht nur in Deutschland belassen, sondern auch in allen Bereichen umfassend ausgebaut. Der Weltmarktführer hat mit den Kompetenzbereichen Bügelbrille, Vollsichtbrille, Korrektionsschutzbrille, Laserschutzbrille, eigener Beschichtungstechnologie für Brillen und Visiere sowie der uvex academy einen hochmodernen Standort geschaffen, der in seiner Ausprägung weltweit einzigartig ist und das Unternehmen zur wichtigsten Innovationsschmiede im internationalen Augenschutzmarkt macht.

Global leader in industrial safety eyewear: uvex not only left its eyewear production in Germany but has also comprehensively extended it in many sectors. The global leader has created a highly modern location in the competence sectors of safety spectacles, safety goggles, prescription safety eyewear, laser protection goggles, their own coating technology for eyewear and visors as well as the uvex academy whose very distinctiveness makes it unique, making the undertaking the most important innovation forge for the international protective eyewear market.

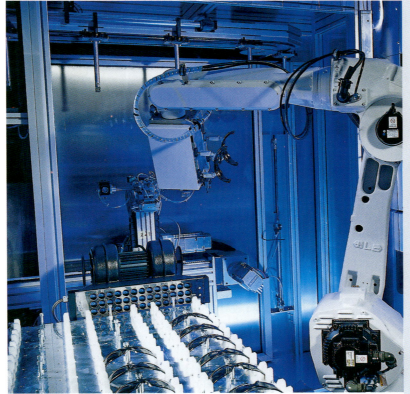

Information

Gründungsjahr: 1926
Mitarbeiter: weltweit 1738, davon 625 in Fürth
Produktspektrum:
UVEX Arbeitsschutz:
– Schutzbrillen
– Gehörschutz
– Kopfschutz
– Sicherheitsschuhe
– Schutzhandschuhe
– Schutz- und Berufsbekleidung
UVEX Sports:
– Skibrillen und -helme
– Sport- und Sonnenbrillen
– Radbrillen und -helme
– Motorrad- und Motorsporthelme
Umsatz:
262 Mio. Euro im Geschäftsjahr 2004/05

Year founded: 1926
Employees: worldwide 1738, of which 625 in Fürth
Range of products:
UVEX work protection:
– safety eyewear
– hearing protection
– head protection
– safety footwear
– safety gloves
– safety workwear
UVEX sports:
– skiing goggles and helmets
– sports and sunglasses
– cycling goggles and helmets
– motorbike and motor sport helmets
Turnover:
262 million Euro in the fiscal year 2004/05

UVEX WINTER HOLDING GmbH & Co. KG, Fürth

Das Unternehmen Eschenbach Optik ist seit über 15 Jahren Marktführer für Brillenfassungen in Deutschland und einer der führenden Anbieter in Europa.
Im Bereich optische Sehhilfen zählt das traditionsreiche Unternehmen aus Nürnberg sogar zu den Weltmarktführern. Weitere Maßstäbe in seiner Branche setzt Eschenbach Optik in den Geschäftsfeldern Fernoptische Produkte beim Augenoptiker sowie im Vertrieb von Wettergeräten beim Augenoptiker. Heute vertreibt das Unternehmen seine Produkte in über 80 Länder der Welt an mehr als 27 000 Augenoptiker. Jüngste Beispiele für die Innovationskraft von Eschenbach Optik sind die neuen TITAN*flex* Modelle, die erstmals dreidimensional bearbeitet werden können. Daraus ergeben sich eine völlig neue Technologie und eine größere Vielfalt an Designkreationen.
Außerdem entwickelte Eschenbach Optik im Bereich Sehhilfen das Modell MaxTV, mit dem selbst bei kleinen Fernsehbildschirmen – etwa beim Zweitfernseher – das Bild doppelt so groß gesehen werden kann.

The Eschenbach Optik undertaking has been market leader for spectacle frames in Germany for more than 15 years and has become one of the leading suppliers in Europe.
In the sector of optical visual aids the traditional Nuremberg concern can even be counted as a global leader. In its branch, Eschenbach Optik sets additional standards in the business sectors of tele-optical products sold by opticians as well as in the sales of weather stations sold by opticians. Today, the undertaking sells its products in more than 80 countries all over the world and to more than 27,000 opticians.
The latest examples of Eschenbach Optik's innovative power are the new TITANflex models, which, for the first time, can be three-dimensionally processed resulting in a totally new technology and a larger variety in design creations.
In the sector of visual aids, Eschenbach Optik also developed the model MaxTV, with which even with the smallest television screen – for instance a portable TV – a picture double its original size can be produced.

Information

Gründungsjahr: 1913

Mitarbeiter:
490, davon etwa 320 in Deutschland

Produktspektrum:
Bereich Eyewear:
Fassungen, Sonnenbrillen
Instrumentenoptik:
Lupen, Ferngläser, Lesehilfen, optische Spezialsysteme
Technische Optik:
Prismen, Asphären, Mikrostrukturen, Diffraktive Optiken, Linsenarrays, Reflektoren, optische Baugruppen

---

Year founded: 1913

Employees:
490 of which some 320 in Germany

Range of products:
in the sector of eyewear:
frames, sunglasses
instrument optics:
magnifying glasses, binoculars, reading aids, special optical systems
technical optics:
prisms, asphericals, microstructures, diffractive optics, lens arrays, reflectors, optical construction groups

Eschenbach Optik GmbH + Co.
Nürnberg

Standort in Europa
Business Location in Europe

Handel und Dienstleistung. Die angebotenen Leistungen der mittelständischen Unternehmen weisen eine noch weit größere Vielfalt auf. Plakativ ausgedrückt: „Intelligente Lösungen für jede Aufgabe!" Einen Eindruck davon geben wiederum einige Beispiele aus dem Angebot von Weltmarktführern – vielfach „Hidden Champions" – aus dem Mittelstand in der Metropolregion Nürnberg: Euro-Banknoten erhalten ihre Sicherheitsmerkmale, nämlich Hologramme und Silberfäden, von der Fürther Firma Leonhard Kurz, Sicherheit für Ski-, Motorrad- und Fahrradrennfahrer auf den Rennstrecken der Welt bieten die Helme von UVEX WINTER, Sicherheit für die Internet-Verbindungen von Abgeordneten verspricht die Nürnberger NCPe Network Communications Products engineering. Die besten Künstlerpinsel der Welt erhält man bei Defet in Nürnberg, internationale Stars aus dem Musikgeschäft statten sich bei Roland Meinl in Neustadt a. d. Aisch aus. Ihre Musik hört man heute weltweit im MP3-Format, das am Fraunhofer-Institut IIS in Erlangen entwickelt wurde. Dort bringt man heute gerade den elektronischen Schiedsrichter, der bei künftigen „Wembley-Toren" die richtige Entscheidung signalisiert, zu weltmeisterlicher Marktreife. In WM-Stadien sind Sitze von Stechert Stahlrohrmöbel aus Wilhermsdorf montiert, während die mobilen Tribünen vor Großleinwänden oder bei Massenveranstaltungen mit hoher Wahrscheinlichkeit von Nüssli aus Roth stammen. Auch die vielleicht auffälligste neue Sportstätte in Deutschland verlässt sich auf Ingenieur-Know-how aus Franken: Eine Tochtergesellschaft des Nürnberger Engineering-Dienstleisters is Industrial Services ist als Betreiber für die Gebäudetechnik der Münchener Allianz-Arena verantwortlich. Und sobald die Planungen von Ebert Ingenieure für den „Federation Tower" in Moskau umgesetzt werden, wird auch das höchste Gebäude Europas auf dem Expertenwissen aus Nürnberg beruhen.

Die Aufzählung lässt sich nahezu beliebig fortsetzen. Um auch künftig zu den führenden Wirtschaftsstandorten in Deutschland und Europa zu zählen, verfolgt die Region Nürnberg schon seit 1998 ein strategisches Entwicklungskonzept. Es definiert die Kernkompetenzen, in denen die Region ihre besonderen Stärken besitzt und die als globale Wachstumsfelder einzustufen sind. Dazu wurde unter Federführung der IHK im breiten Konsens von Wirtschaft, Politik, Verwaltung, Gewerkschaften und Hochschulen ein Entwicklungsleitbild erarbeitet und verabschiedet.

In diesem Entwicklungsleitbild wurden mit Verkehr

Fortsetzung Seite 56

show an even wider variety. Putting it bluntly: "Intelligent solutions for every task!" An impression of this on the other hand can be gained by some examples of offers by global leaders – in many cases "Hidden Champions" – from the small and medium-sized concerns in the metropolitan region of Nuremberg: Euro-banknotes receive their safety features, hologram and silver strip, from the Fuerth company Leonhard Kurz, safety for skiers, motor bikers and cyclists on the race courses of the world is assured by helmets from UVEX WINTER, security for the internet communication of Members of Parliament is promised by Nuremberg NCPe Network Communications Products engineering. The best artists' paintbrushes in the world can be bought at Defet in Nuremberg, international stars of the music business equip themselves at Roland Meinl's in Neustadt a. d. Aisch. Their music can be heard all over the world in MP3-format, developed at the Fraunhofer-Institute IIS in Erlangen. At the moment they are busy making an electronic referee to signalise the right decisions in future "Wembley-goals" ready for the world champions' market. Seats by Stechert Stahlrohrmöbel from Wilhermsdorf are installed in WM stadiums, whilst the mobile tribunes in front of mega-screens or during mass events very probably originated in Nüssli from Roth. The probably most conspicuous new sports arena in Germany relies on engineering know-how from Franconia: A subsidiary of the Nuremberg engineering-service supplier is Industrial Services is responsible as operator for the building technology of the Munich Allianz-Arena. And as soon as the plans drawn up by Ebert engineers for the "Federation Tower" in Moscow have been put into practice, then the highest building in Europe will be founded on the knowledge of experts from Nuremberg.

The list could be continued almost at will. In order to count among the leading economic business locations in Germany and Europe, the region of Nuremberg has followed a strategic development concept since 1998. It defines those core competences in which the region is particularly strong and which are to be classified as global fields of growth. Under the overall control of the Chamber of Commerce and with the widest approval of industry, politics, municipal administration, trade unions and colleges a development model was worked out and adopted.

In this development model six technological fields of competence in the economic region of Nuremberg were emphasized: transport and logistics, information and communication, medicine and health, energy and

Continued on page 56

NORMA – das Filialnetz: modernes Einkaufen in einer neuen NORMA-Filiale im Raum Nürnberg

NORMA – the branch network: modern shopping in a new NORMA branch in the Nuremberg area

Der Lebensmittelfilialbetrieb NORMA zählt mit über 1300 Filialen zu den bedeutendsten und erfolgreichsten Handelsunternehmen im Discountbereich. Allein im Raum Nürnberg-Fürth-Erlangen gibt es mehr als 150 NORMA-Outlets.

Hervorgegangen aus dem im Jahr 1921 gegründeten Filialunternehmen Georg Roth in Fürth, wurden schon vor über vier Jahrzehnten die ersten NORMA-Filialen eröffnet. NORMA stellt mit Konzept, Auftritt, Sortiment, Preis, Qualitätsanspruch und Organisationsstruktur einen der großen deutschen Lebensmitteldiscounter dar. NORMA definiert sich als Harddiscounter mit Schwerpunkten Frische, gekühlte und tiefgekühlte Waren sowie einem wechselnden Food- und Non-Food-

Standort in Europa
Business Location in Europe

Angebot zu Dauerniedrigpreisen bei bester Qualität. In einem ständig wachsenden Filialnetz, das sich raumgreifend über Deutschland, Österreich, Frankreich und Tschechien erstreckt, setzt NORMA kontinuierliches Wachstum erfolgreich mit einem neuen, aktualisierten Konzept fort. Neue, moderne Verkaufsräume bieten die Möglichkeit, Einkäufe schnell und bequem abzuwickeln. Unter dem Slogan „NORMA – mehr fürs Geld" setzt NORMA mit Frische, Dauerniedrigpreisen, Kreativität, Flexibilität und Reaktionsschnelligkeit neue Standards im Wettbewerb.

With more than 1,300 branches the grocery chain NORMA counts as one of the most important and successful business enterprises in the discount sector. There are more than 150 NORMA outlets in the Nuremberg-Fürth-Erlangen area alone. Arising from the company of Georg Roth founded in Fürth in 1921, the first NORMA branches were opened as long as four decades ago. In concept, appearance, assortment, price, standard of quality and organisational structure, NORMA is one of the largest German food discounters. NORMA defines itself as a hard discounter focussed on freshness, cooled and deep-frozen goods as well as changing food and non-food articles at permanently low prices with top quality.

With a constantly growing branch network stretching over Germany, Austria, France and the Czech Republic, NORMA is successfully carrying on its steady growth by applying a new, updated concept. New, modern sales rooms provide the opportunity of shopping quickly and comfortably. Under the slogan "NORMA – more for your money" NORMA is setting new standards for competitors with its freshness, constant low prices, creativity, flexibility and the speed of their reactions.

NORMA – das Filialnetz: ein 360° Rund-um-Blick über das reichhaltige NORMA-Sortiment

NORMA – the branch network: a 360° all-round view of the rich NORMA assortment

Information

Unternehmen:
Lebensmitteldiscount mit über 1300 Filialen in Deutschland, Österreich, Frankreich und Tschechien

Historie:
Hervorgegangen aus dem schon im Jahr 1921 gegründetem Filialunternehmen Georg Roth in Fürth

Konzept:
Rationelles, einfaches, klares und effizientes Verkaufskonzept: Hohe Qualität zum Niedrigpreis!

The company:
Grocery discounter with more than 1,300 branches in Germany, Austria, France and the Czech Republic

History:
Arose from the branch company Georg Roth in Fürth founded in the year 1921

Concept:
Rational, simple, clear and efficient sales concept: Top quality at a low price!

☐
NORMA
Lebensmittelfilialbetrieb GmbH & Co. KG
Nürnberg

Tabak ist die Basis. Moderne Strukturen sichern den Erfolg.

Tobacco is the basis. Modern structures assure success.

tabacon is one of the largest distributors of tobacco products in Germany. The company, which was founded by Fridolin Spengler in 1922, looks back on a successful past full of changes. Over the decades it developed into a logistics company and combined its original wholesaling business with major innovations in the use of vending machines. In 1981, tabacon expanded its tradional focus on northern Bavaria to the south. In 1990, the company ventured into the markets of former Eastern Germany. tabacon provides its customers, which include pubs and restaurants, smaller distributors using cigarette vending machines, and retailers, with tobacco products, convenience and prepaid products. As a distributor of these products to more than 45,000 outlets, tabacon both reports trends to customers and makes trends for its suppliers' latest product innovations. tabacon is synonymous with innovation, sustainable growth, and profitability. Besides, tabacon is well aware of its responsibility towards its employees and customers. Based on these values, tabacon has become one of the most modern and technically advanced distributors of tobacco products in the world.

tabacon ist einer der größten Tabakwarengroßhändler Deutschlands. Das im Jahr 1922 von Fridolin Spengler in Nürnberg gegründete Unternehmen kann auf eine wechselvolle und erfolgreiche Vergangenheit zurückblicken. Seit Jahrzehnten vereint es sein traditionelles Großhandelsgeschäft mit bedeutenden Innovationen auf dem Gebiet der Automatenaufstellung. In den letzten Jahren entwickelte sich tabacon verstärkt zum Logistikdienstleister.
Im Jahr 1981 begann die Expansion der tabacon-Gruppe, ausgehend von der Region Nordbayern, nach Südbayern. Mitte 1990, noch vor der offiziellen Wiedervereinigung Deutschlands, eröffnete tabacon den Geschäftsbetrieb in den neuen Bundesländern. tabacon versorgt seine Kunden, zu denen Gastronomen, andere Zigarettenauto-

matenaufsteller sowie Einzelhändler gehören, mit Tabakwaren, Convenience- und Prepaid-Artikeln. Als Verteiler dieser Produkte an mehr als 45 000 Vertriebsstellen übermittelt tabacon neueste Trends an Kunden und setzt zudem Trends für aktuelle Produktentwicklungen seiner Lieferanten. tabacon steht für Innovation, nachhaltiges Wachstum und Wirtschaftlichkeit. Darüber hinaus ist sich tabacon seiner Verantwortung gegenüber den Mitarbeitern und Kunden bewusst. Mit diesen Werten wurde tabacon zu einem der modernsten Tabakwarengroßhändler der Welt.

Standort in Europa
Business Location in Europe

Information

Gründungsjahr: 1922

Mitarbeiter:
mehr als 400

Umsatz der tabacon-Gruppe:
850 Mio. Euro

Standorte:
Berlin, München, Nürnberg, Ronneburg

Leistungsspektrum:
– Großhandel mit Tabakwaren, Prepaid- und Convenience-produkten
– Betreiben von über 40 000 Zigaretten- und Verkaufsautomaten für Prepaid-produkte

---

Year founded: 1922

Employees:
more than 400

Turnover of the tabacon-group:
850 million Euro

Locations:
Berlin, Munich, Nuremberg, Ronneburg

Range of services:
– wholesalers of tobacco products, prepaid and convenience products
– running more than 40,000 vending machines for cigarettes and prepaid products

tabacon Tabakwaren GmbH & Co. Holdinggesellschaft KG
Nürnberg

und Logistik, Information und Kommunikation, Medizin und Gesundheit, Energie und Umwelt, Neue Materialien sowie Automation und Produktionstechnik sechs technologische Kompetenzfelder der Wirtschaftsregion Nürnberg hervorgehoben. Nach dem Motto „Die Stärken stärken" soll das Fundament der regionalen Wirtschaft auch künftig in einer international ausgerichteten Industrie mit dem Anspruch auf die weltweite technologische Führungsrolle liegen. Die Vernetzung der sechs Kompetenzfelder untereinander sowie die Entwicklung und Verknüpfung mit wichtigen Querschnittstechnologien bietet darüber hinaus vielfältige Ansatzpunkte für eine zusätzliche Wertschöpfung und damit auch für neue wettbewerbsfähige Arbeitsplätze in zahlreichen Branchen und in allen Teilräumen der Metropolregion Nürnberg.

Ebenso wie die Aufnahme in den Kreis der Metropolregionen eröffnet das Entwicklungsleitbild neue Chancen für Wirtschaftsdynamik und internationale Profilbildung. Mit dem Ausbau von Infrastruktur und Forschungseinrichtungen, Standortmarketing, der Erschließung neuer Märkte und einem unternehmensfreundlichen Klima wird die Metropolregion Nürnberg auch weiterhin vordere Plätze in nationalen und internationalen Rankings zur technologischen und wirtschaftlichen Leistungsfähigkeit belegen. Damit bleibt sie ein hoch attraktiver Standort für ein breites Spektrum an Unternehmen aus allen Branchen mit geballtem Know-how.

environment, new materials as well as automation and production engineering. Following the motto "strengthen the strengths" the foundation of regional industry is also to lay claim to a global technologically leading role in an internationally-oriented economy. The linking of the six fields of competence among themselves as well as the development and linking with important cross-sections of technology will offer manifold starting points for an additional increase in value and thereby also new competitive workplaces in countless branches and in all areas of the metropolitan region of Nuremberg.

Just as the acceptance into the circle of metropolitan regions does, the development model opens new chances for economic dynamics and international image forming. With the extension of infrastructure and research institutions, business location marketing, the development of new markets and an entrepreneur-friendly climate the metropolitan region of Nuremberg will carry on occupying front seats in national and international quality assessments on technological and industrial productivity. With its concentrated know-how it will thereby remain a highly attractive business location for a wide range of concerns from all branches.

Standort in Europa
Business Location in Europe

Information

Gründungsjahr: 1897 (2002)

Mitarbeiter:
gesamte Gruppe 34 000, davon am Standort Nürnberg 3600

Produktspektrum:
- Schnelllaufende Diesel- und Gasmotoren
- Leistungsbereich 47 kW/64 PS – 1140 kW/1550 PS

Year founded: 1897 (2002)

Employees:
the entire group 34,000 of which 3,600 at the Nuremberg location

Range of products:
- fast diesel and gas-driven engines
- power range 47 kW/64 PS – 1,140 kW/1,550 PS

In der Geschäftseinheit Motoren in Nürnberg ist die Kernkompetenz der MAN Nutzfahrzeuge Gruppe in Forschung, Entwicklung, Produktion und Lieferung von Diesel- und Gasmotoren konzentriert.
Die Tradition der am 1. Januar 2002 gegründeten Geschäftseinheit Motoren reicht bis auf Rudolf Diesel zurück, der zwischen 1893 und 1897 den ersten voll betriebsfähigen Dieselmotor der Welt bei MAN entwickelte und baute.
Die von MAN in Nürnberg gefertigten Motoren werden zum großen Teil (85 Prozent) in Nutzfahrzeuge von MAN eingebaut. Darüber hinaus ist die MAN Geschäftseinheit Motoren in weiteren Marktsegmenten erfolgreich und liefert Diesel- und Gasmotoren zum Antrieb von Schienenfahrzeugen, Ackerschleppern, landwirtschaftlichen Maschinen, stationären Energieanlagen und schnellen Schiffen, insbesondere Motoryachten.
Insgesamt stellte MAN 2005 in Nürnberg 89 700 Motoren her, was einem Umsatz von ca. 1,2 Mrd. Euro entspricht.
Mit zurzeit 3600 Mitarbeitern ist die MAN Nutzfahrzeuge AG, Geschäftseinheit Motoren, der größte Industrieeinzelbetrieb in Nürnberg.

In the Business Unit "Engines" in Nuremberg the core competence of the MAN utility vehicles group is concentrated on research, development, production and supply of diesel and gas-driven engines.
The tradition of the Business Unit "Engines" which was founded on 1. January 2002 reaches back to Rudolf Diesel who, between 1893 and 1897, developed and built the world's first fully operable diesel engine in the MAN works.
The majority (85 percent) of the engines produced by MAN in Nuremberg are built into MAN utility vehicles. The MAN Business Unit "Engines" is also successful in other market segments and supplies diesel and gas engines for driving rail vehicles, farming tractors, agricultural machines, stationary energy plants and fast ships, particularly motor yachts. MAN in Nuremberg produced a total of 89,700 engines in 2005 corresponding with a turnover of about 1.2 billion Euro. With its present 3,600 employees, the Business Unit "Engines" of the MAN Nutzfahrzeuge AG, is the largest individual industrial operation in Nuremberg.

MAN Nutzfahrzeuge Gruppe Geschäftseinheit Motoren, Nürnberg

SUSPA ist ein weltweit führender Anbieter von maßgeschneiderten Systemlösungen und Produkten in den Bereichen Automobil und Industrie, gerade wenn es darum geht, Ergonomie, Komfort und Sicherheit von Kundenprodukten zu verbessern. Die SUSPA-Gruppe mit Hauptsitz in Altdorf bei Nürnberg (Deutschland) ist ein spezialisierter und innovationsstarker Hersteller von Gasfedern, Hydraulikdämpfern, Schwingungsdämpfern, Crash- und Sicherheitssystemen und automatischen Verstellsystemen.

Durch seine engagierten und intelligenten Mitarbeiter hat sich das Unternehmen zum Entwicklungs- und Systempartner bedeutender Produzenten aus der Automobil-, Büromöbel-, Gebrauchsgüter- und Waschmaschinenindustrie entwickelt. Das weltweite Vertriebsnetz sichert die nahe Betreuung der Kunden an fast allen Plätzen der Welt. Seit vielen Jahren verfügt SUSPA über Produktionsstätten in USA, China und Indien. SUSPA bietet seinen Kunden individuelle Lösungen, Produkte und Services aus einer Hand: von der Konzeption, Planung und Entwicklung, dem Prototypenbau, dem Testen in eigenen Laboren, der Einzelfertigung bis hin zur Massenserienproduktion. Der Einsatz umweltbewusster Materialien, modernster Fertigungstechniken sowie kurze Liefer- und Servicezeiten runden das Portfolio der SUSPA-Gruppe ab.

So stellt das Unternehmen eines sicher: SUSPA gehört mit seinen Lösungen und Produkten zum Heben, Senken, Neigen und Dämpfen zu den führenden Anbietern – zum Nutzen und zum Vorteil der Kunden rund um den Globus.

SUSPA is a global leading supplier of tailor-made system solutions and products in the sectors of automobile and industry in places where it is a matter of improving the ergonomics, comfort and security of customer products.
The SUSPA-Group with headquarters in Altdorf near Nuremberg (Germany) is a specialised and innovative manufacturer of pneumatic springs, hydraulic absorbers, vibration absorbers, crash and safety systems and automatic adjustment systems. Thanks to its committed and intelligent employees, the undertaking has developed itself into a development and system partner for important producers in the automobile, office furniture, consumer goods, and washing machine industries. The worldwide sales network provides close customer service in almost all places in the world. SUSPA has maintained production facilities in the USA, China and India for many years. SUSPA offers its customers individual solutions, products and services from the one source: from conception, planning and development, building the prototype, testing in their own laboratories, individual manufacture through to series production.
The use of environment-friendly materials, state-of-the-art technologies as well as short delivery and service terms round off the portfolio of the SUSPA-Group.
Thus the undertaking guarantees one thing: With its solutions and products for lifting, sinking, inclining and absorbing, SUSPA belongs to the leading suppliers – to the benefit and advantage of customers all round the world.

Information

Gründungsjahr: 1951

Mitarbeiter: 954

Produktspektrum:
Gasfedern und Gasfedersäulen für die weltweite Büromöbelindustrie

---

Year founded: 1951

Employees: 954

Range of products:
pneumatic springs and pneumatic spring columns for the global office furniture industry

SUSPA Holding GmbH
Altdorf

Standort in Europa
Business Location in Europe

Erfolgreich bauen, renovieren und modernisieren heißt heute: wertbeständig und kostensparend bauen. Die BAUSTOFF UNION als Baustoff-Fachhändler unterstützt sowohl den Profi als auch den Privatkunden mit qualifizierten Produkt- und Problemlösungen. In ihrer Funktion als Fachvertriebspartner der Baustoffindustrie ist das Unternehmen frühzeitig über aktuelle Produkte und neue Verarbeitungstechniken informiert. Im umfassenden Sortiment mit über 20 000 Artikeln finden sich modernste, leistungsfähige Baustoffe und Baustoffsysteme für die unterschiedlichsten Einsatzbereiche.
Die BU Holding mit über 1000 Mitarbeitern besteht aus den Firmen BAUSTOFF UNION, OBI Baumarkt Franken und OBI Regnitztal, die zusammen einen Umsatz von über 230 Mio. Euro erwirtschaften.

To build, renovate and modernise successfully today means: building so that it is stable in value and cost-saving.
As a building material specialist supplier, the BAUSTOFF UNION supports the professional as much as the private customer with well-qualified products and problem solutions. In their function as specialist sales partner to the building material industry, the undertaking is informed well in time of current products and new processing technologies. Cutting-edge, extremely efficient building materials and material systems for varied areas of utilisation can be found in their all-encompassing assortment of more than 20,000 articles.
The BU Holding with more than 1,000 employees consists of the firms BAUSTOFF UNION, OBI Baumarkt Franken and OBI Regnitztal, who together make a turnover of more than 230 million Euro.

Information

Gründungsjahr: 1969
Mitarbeiter: ca. 1000, davon rund 150 in der BAUSTOFF UNION
Verkaufsbereiche:
– Hochbau/Estriche
– Tief-, Straßen-, Garten- und Landschaftsbau
– Stuck, Putz, Trockenbau, Bauelemente
– Dach, Dämmstoffe, Fassade
– Baugeräte und Werkzeuge
Dienstleistungen:
– Logistik – „just-in-time"
– Beratung vor Ort
– Mietservice
– kundenfreundliche Öffnungszeiten
– ständige Baubetreuung
Niederlassungen: Nürnberg, Forchheim, Langenzenn, Weißenburg

Year founded: 1969
Employees: about 1,000, of which some 150 are in the BAUSTOFF UNION
Sale sectors:
– building construction/composition floors
– civil engineering, road building, horticulture and landscaping
– stucco, plastering, dry mortarless construction, building elements
– roofs, insulating materials, facades
– building equipment and tools
Services:
– logistics – "just-in-time"
– advisory service on site
– rental service
– customer-friendly opening hours
– constant building supervision
Branches: Nuremberg, Forchheim, Langenzenn, Weißenburg

☐
BAUSTOFF UNION GmbH & Co. KG
Nürnberg

Die Leitidee der qualitativen Marktforschung verdeutlicht die Aussage des Nobelpreisträgers Sir Norman Angell: „Nicht Tatsachen bestimmen das menschliche Handeln, sondern die Meinung der Menschen über Tatsachen."

Die Kernkompetenz der Psyma liegt in der Motivforschung von Verbrauchern und Entscheidungsträgern in jenem Sinne. In Ergänzung zu multinationalen Marktforschungsfirmen, die sich zu Informationsfabriken mit Standardlösungen weiterentwickelt haben, setzt Psyma auf individuell angewandtes Expertenwissen in Methoden, transkulturelles Know-how bei multinationalen Studien sowie auf fundierte marktspezifische Erfahrung. Unter dem Dach der PSYMA GROUP AG explorieren heute über ein Dutzend hoch spezialisierter Psyma-Firmen weltweit Verbraucherverhalten, Marktchancen und Eintrittsbarrieren. Das über Jahrzehnte akkumulierte Fachwissen bleibt zum Nutzen der Kunden abrufbar: Die Psyma ist rein eigentümergeführt, was eine hohe Konstanz des multikulturellen Führungs- und Fachpersonals gewährleistet. Die PSYMA GROUP AG setzt ihr fachspezifisches und internationales organisches Wachstum stetig fort und zählt in einigen Fachgebieten zur Weltspitze.

The fundamental idea behind qualitative market research becomes clear in the statement by the Nobel prize winner Sir Norman Angell: "It is not the facts which guide the conduct of men, but their opinions about facts."

The core competence of Psyma lies in researching consumers' and decision-makers' motivation in every sense of the word. Supplementary to multinational market research firms, which have developed onwards into information factories with standard solutions, Psyma relies on individually applied expert knowledge of methods, trans-cultural know-how gained in multinational studies as well as on well-founded market-specific experience. Under the umbrella of the PSYMA GROUP AG more than a dozen highly-specialised Psyma-firms are today exploring consumer behaviour, market opportunities and entrance barriers all over the world. The specialised knowledge acquired over decades remains retrievable for the customer's use: That Psyma is purely owner-managed, guarantees high consistency in the multicultural management and specialised personnel. The PSYMA GROUP AG steadily continues its subject-specific and international organic growth and, in some subject sectors, counts as one of the world's best.

Information

Gründungsjahr: 1957

Mitarbeiter: insgesamt rund 200

Leistungsspektrum:
Markt- und Marketingforschung für die Branchen
- Pharma und Medizintechnik
- Konsumgüter
- Medien
- Finanzdienstleistungen
- Automobil und Transport
- Investitionsgüter
- Online

Standorte:
Deutschland, USA, Mexiko, China, Spanien, Frankreich, Tschechien, Polen, Ungarn, Slowakei

---

Year founded: 1957

Employees: around 200 in total

Range of services:
market and marketing research for the branches of
- pharmaceuticals and medicine technology
- consumer goods
- media
- financial services
- automobile and transport
- capital equipment
- online

Locations:
Germany, USA, Mexico, China, Spain, France, Czech Republic, Poland, Hungary, Slovakia

☐
PSYMA GROUP AG
Rückersdorf

Standort in Europa
Business Location in Europe

Information

Gründungsjahr: 1931

Mitarbeiter: 80

Leistungsspektrum:
- Spezialmotoren für Schiffsausrüstungen
- Motoren für den Offshorebetrieb, wie zum Beispiel Plattformhebeanlagen auf Bohrinseln
- Motoren für Ventilatorantriebe
- Motoren für die Lebensmittelindustrie
- Motoren für Verkehrstechnik, Kranbau und Schwerindustrie
- Elektromotoren als Sondermaschinen

Year founded: 1931

Employees: 80

Range of services:
- special motors for ship's equipment
- motors for offshore use as i.e. for jacking-systems on rigs
- motors for fans/blowers
- motors for food-industry
- motors for traffic technology, cranes and heavy industry
- electrical motors for special machines

Die BEN Buchele Elektromotorenwerke GmbH kann auf über sieben Jahrzehnte erfolgreiche Firmengeschichte zurückblicken und ist bis heute zu einem modernen, mittelständischen Industriebetrieb gewachsen.
Zum Leistungsspektrum gehören vorwiegend Sondermotoren für höchste Qualitätsansprüche aus Grauguss und Stahl, die nach unterschiedlichsten Kundenanforderungen in kleinen bis mittleren Stückzahlen hergestellt werden. Das Programm umfasst dabei Drehstrommotoren mit Käfigläufern und Schleifringläufern für Leistungen bis zu 1200 kW je nach Schutzart, Betriebsart und Drehzahl.
Für die Projektierung maritimer Elektroausrüstungen aus Motoren, Schalt- und Bediengeräten steht auch die Firma BEN Marine Equipment Service GmbH in Schenefeld bei Hamburg zur Verfügung.

The BEN Buchele Elektromotorenwerke GmbH can look back over seven decades of successful company history and has grown into what is today a modern, medium-sized industrial company. Primary amongst its range of services are special engines to meet the highest demands, made of grey cast iron and steel and produced in small to medium-sized groups to fulfill the varying needs of customers. The programme also includes three-phase motors with squirrel-cage rotors and slip ring rotors for capacities of up to 1,200 kW depending on the protective system, duty cycle and speed.
Messrs BEN Marine Equipment Service GmbH in Schenefeld near Hamburg is also available for drawing up plans for maritime electrical equipment consisting of engines, switch and operating units.

□
BEN Buchele Elektromotorenwerke GmbH, Nürnberg

Information

Gründungsjahr: 1879

Mitarbeiter: 65

Produkte:
Speziallacke für die graphische Industrie sowie für die Bleistift- und Kosmetikindustrie

Leistungsspektrum:
hohe Produktqualität, technischer Service, umfangreiches Produktprogramm, Innovationen, Problemlösungen, Umweltprogramm, zertifiziert nach DIN ISO 9001

Year founded: 1879

Employees: 65

Products:
special varnishes for the graphics industry and for the pencil and cosmetics industry

Range of services:
high product quality, technical service, extensive product programme, innovative products, contribution to the environment, certified in accordance with DIN ISO 9001

☐ WEILBURGER Graphics GmbH
Gerhardshofen

WEILBURGER Graphics GmbH ist einer der weltweit führenden Hersteller von Speziallacken für die Druck- und Veredelungsindustrie. Unter dem Markennamen SENOLITH® werden wässrige Dispersionslacke und strahlenhärtende UV-Lacksysteme vertrieben. Sie verleihen den Druckerzeugnissen zusätzliche Attraktivität und Funktionalität. Der Markenname SENOCELL® steht für innovative Beschichtungen für die Holz- und Bleistiftindustrie. Die WEILBURGER Graphics GmbH gehört mit elf Schwesterfirmen zur international tätigen GREBE Gruppe, einem der führenden mittelständischen Hersteller von Industrielacken.

WEILBURGER Graphics GmbH is one of the world's leading manufacturers of special coatings for the graphics and print finishing industry. SENOLITH® stands for water-based dispersion coatings and UV lacquers, which provide the printed product with added value and functionality. SENOCELL® stands for innovative coatings for the wood and pencil industry. WEILBURGER Graphics GmbH is one of eleven sister companies of the GREBE Group, one of the leading manufacturers of industrial coatings.

Standort in Europa
Business Location in Europe

Die Firma Telle ist einer der anerkannten Lieferanten von Schläuchen, Armaturen, Dichtungen und anderen Produkten rund um die Materialien Gummi, Metall und Kunststoff.

Das breite Sortiment umfasst ausschließlich hochwertige Produkte namhafter Hersteller. Derzeit sind mehr als 20 000 verschiedene Artikel ab Lager vorrätig. Eine flexible Logistik gewährleistet die schnelle und zuverlässige Lieferung an jeden Bestimmungsort. Und erfüllt ein Produkt „von der Stange" einmal nicht die gewünschten Anforderungen, so finden die Fachleute von Telle in der eigenen Fertigung garantiert die individuelle und maßgeschneiderte Lösung.

Messrs Telle is a recognised supplier of tubing, fittings, seals and other products surrounding the materials of rubber, metal and plastics.
Their wide range is composed solely of high-grade products from renowned manufacturers. At the moment there are more than 20,000 various articles in stock. Flexible logistics guarantee the speedy and reliable delivery at any destination. And should, very rarely, an "off the peg" article not fulfil the customer's needs then the specialists from Telle will find an individual and tailor-made solution from their own production.

Information

Gründungsjahr: 1970

Mitarbeiter: 57

Leistungsspektrum:
– technische Elastomer- und Kunststoffprodukte
– individuelle Kleinserienfertigung
– Entwicklung und Herstellung kundenspezifischer Produkte

Produktspektrum:
Schlauchleitungen, Armaturen, Dichtungen, Halbzeuge aus Kunststoffen, Elastomerprofile

Standorte:
Nürnberg, Sulzbach-Rosenberg, Bayreuth

Year founded: 1970

Employees: 57

Range of services:
– technical elastomer and plastics products
– individual small production series
– development and manufacture of customer-specific products

Range of products:
flexible hose lines,
fittings,
seals,
semi-finished products made of plastics,
elastomer profiles

Locations:
Nuremberg, Sulzbach-Rosenberg, Bayreuth

☐
Erwin Telle GmbH
Nürnberg

Elektrische Stellantriebe in ihrem „natürlichen Lebensraum". Sie werden zum Fernbetätigen von Armaturen aller Art u. a. in Kraftwerken, Wasserwerken und Kläranlagen eingesetzt.

Electric actuators in their "natural environment". They are used to remote control all kind of valves, mainly in power plants, water and waste water stations.

Die SIPOS Aktorik GmbH entstand 1999 durch die Ausgliederung des Geschäftszweigs Elektrische Stellantriebe aus der Siemens AG. Innerhalb der AUMA-Gruppe ist SIPOS Aktorik ein selbstständiges Unternehmen.
Wie kaum ein anderes Unternehmen seiner Branche kennt SIPOS Aktorik die Anforderungen und Wünsche seiner Kunden auf dem Gebiet elektrischer Stellantriebe und ist so in der Lage, bei Neuanlagen ebenso wie bei Nachrüstungen optimale Lösungen anzubieten.

SIPOS Aktorik GmbH was founded in 1999 by separating the subdivision "Electric Actuators" from Siemens AG. It is now an independent company within the AUMA group. Like hardly any other in this field, SIPOS is familiar with the requirements and wishes of its customers and thus is in the position to offer optimum solutions in the case of both retrofits and new plants.

Information

Gründungsjahr: 1999

Mitarbeiter: etwa 60

Leistungsspektrum:
– Entwicklung, Montage und Vertrieb von elektrischen Stellantrieben
– Entwicklung und Vertrieb von Antriebssteuerungen
– Servicedienstleistungen

Umsatz:
rund 20 Mio. Euro
(in 2005)

Year of foundation: 1999

Employees: about 60

Business activities:
– development, assembly and sales of electric actuators
– development and sales of electric actuator controls
– provision of actuator services

Turnover:
approx. 20 million Euro
(in 2005)

Montage und Prüfung der Antriebe – Kernkompetenzen des Unternehmens

Assembly and test of the actuators – core competences of the company

☐ SIPOS Aktorik GmbH
Nürnberg

Mit Tradition in die Zukunft – innovatives Handwerk

Heinrich Mosler

„Der meist Theil sich mit Handwerk nährt – Allerlei Handwerk ungenannt – Was je erfunden Menschenhand", preist 1510 Hans Sachs seine Heimatstadt Nürnberg. Der „Nürnberger Witz" – will heißen Erfindergeist – ist sprichwörtlich. Nürnberg gilt nicht nur als „des Deutschen Reiches Schatzkästlein", Nürnberger Handwerke erwarben sich frühzeitig hervorragende Bedeutung und einen weltweiten Ruf: Peter Henlein, der Erfinder der Taschenuhr, Wenzel Jamnitzer, der Gold- und Silberschmied, der erste Weltglobus von Martin Behaim, eine Gemeinschaftsarbeit vieler Gewerke, der Romweg von Erhard Etzlaub, die erste Straßenkarte Europas und viele andere. Sie sind noch heute unvergessen.

Erfindergeist und Qualitätsbewusstsein ziehen sich wie ein roter Faden durch die Geschichte der Stadt: Der Flaschnermeister Ernst Plank erregt auf der Bayerischen Landes-Gewerbe-Industrieausstellung im Jahr 1882 mit der Vorstellung der ersten elektrischen Eisenbahn großes Aufsehen. Der Feinmechaniker Sigmund Schuckert erlangt in den 70er und 80er Jahren des 19. Jahrhunderts mit seinen dynamo-elektrischen Maschinen Weltruhm und wird zum Begründer der Siemens-Schuckert-Werke. Die Kreativität und Erfindungsgabe Nürnberger Handwerker, ihre Innovationen schreiben Technikgeschichte. Das moderne Weltbild wird von der Nürnberger Handwerkerschaft entscheidend mitgeprägt.

Das Handwerk in Nürnberg hat auch schlechte Zeitläufe letztlich erfolgreich hinter sich gelassen. Das Festhalten an überkommenen Gewerbestrukturen erweist sich an der Schwelle zum Industriezeitalter als kaum zu überwindendes Hindernis und verhindert moderne Produktionsformen. Wer Neues wagt, wird abgestraft. Die Wettbewerbsfähigkeit des Handwerks geht vorübergehend verloren. Doch es verharrt zu jener Zeit nicht in Depression, sondern ergreift nach einem sehr schmerzlichen Umdenkungsprozess die Initiative. Das Handwerk schöpft seinen Fortschritt aus der Tradition.

"Der meist Theil sich mit Handwerk nährt – Allerlei Handwerk ungenannt – Was je erfunden Menschenhand" ("Most people feed themselves with trade – all sorts of trades are not even mentioned – those which the human hand ever discovered"), was how Hans Sachs praised his home town of Nuremberg in 1510. The "Nuremberg Wit" – should be read as "spirit of invention" – is proverbial. Nuremberg is not only considered to be "the treasure chest of the German Empire", Nuremberg traders had achieved outstanding significance and a global reputation for themselves at a very early stage: Peter Henlein, the inventor of the pocket watch, Wenzel Jamnitzer, the gold and silversmith, the first globe of the world from Martin Behaim, mutual work of many crafts, the Romweg by Erhard Etzlaub, the first European map and many others. Even today, they have not been forgotten.

Inventive genius and quality consciousness are the central themes running through the history of the city: The master plumber Ernst Plank caused a sensation on the Bavarian Trade-Industrial Exhibition in 1882 with the introduction of the first electric train. Sigmund Schuckert, precision engineer, became world-famous in the 70's and 80's of the 19th century with his dynamo-electrical machines and became the founder of the Siemens-Schuckert-Works. The creativity and inventive talents of Nuremberg's tradesmen, in other words their innovations write engineering history. Nuremberg's tradesmen leave their marks quite distinctly on today's conception of the world.

The trades in Nuremberg have also managed in the long run to successfully survive bad periods. Stubbornly clinging to traditional commercial structures proved, on the treshold of the industrial era, to be an almost insurmountable obstacle and prevented modern forms of production. But he who risks anything new is punished. The competitiveness of the trades gets temporarily lost. But instead of sinking into depression, the trades, after a very painful change of mind, grasp the initiative. From tradition, they have moulded progress for themselves.

With Tradition into the Future – Innovative Trades

Die Handwerkskammer für Mittelfranken (HWK) ist insbesondere im Bereich Umweltschutz Vorreiter in ganz Deutschland. Beispiele hierfür sind der „Qualitätsverbund umweltbewusster Handwerksbetriebe" (QuH), der inzwischen seinen Siegeszug durch Bayern angetreten hat und auf dem Sprung in weitere Bundesländer ist, sowie das 2004 eingeführte Umwelt- und Qualitätsmanagement, welche die Handwerkskammer für Mittelfranken zum Kompetenzzentrum Umwelt nicht nur in Bayern, sondern in ganz Deutschland machen. Darüber hinaus bietet die HWK in den neuen Technologien und Materialien – EDV, CNC, CAM, CAD und Laser sind nur einige Beispiele – qualifizierte Schulungen in einem der vier Berufsbildungs- und Technologiezentren der Handwerkskammer. Außerdem engagiert sich die HWK für Handwerkerfrauen und verhilft ihnen über Weiterbildungsangebote und andere Maßnahmen zu einer angemessenen Plattform im Kammerbezirk. Zu einem öffentlichkeitswirksamen „Renner" entwickelte sich die Kür der „Meisterfrau des Jahres" der Handwerkskammer für Mittelfranken – auf Kammerebene einmalig in Deutschland. Gewürdigt wird damit der Einsatz im Betrieb ebenso wie die Bereitschaft zur Weiterbildung oder das außerbetriebliche soziale oder politische Engagement.

The Chamber of Handicrafts for Middle Franconia (HWK) leads the whole of Germany particularly in the sector of environmental protection. One example of this is the "Qualitätsverbund umweltbewusster Handwerksbetriebe" QuH (quality association of environmental-conscious handicraft firms) which has, in the meantime, carried its triumphal march into Bavaria and is now ready to move into other Federal counties. Another one is the environmental and quality management introduced in 2004, which is making the Chamber of Handicrafts for Middle Franconia into an environmental competence centre not only for Bavaria, but for the whole of Germany. In addition, the HWK offers qualified training courses in new technologies and materials – EDP, CNC, CAM, CAD and laser being just a few examples – in one of the four professional training and technology centres of the Chamber of Handicrafts. The HWK has also committed itself to women in handicrafts, helping them to get a suitable basis in the Chamber's area by means of, amongst other measures, providing further education and training. The Chamber of Handicrafts for Middle Franconia's title of "Mistress of the Year" has developed into an effective publicity feature – at Chamber level something quite unique in Germany. In this way appreciation is shown of her commitment to her firm as well as the willingness to undertake additional training or even out-of-house social or political commitment.

Information

Kompetenzspektrum:
- Beratung in betriebswirtschaftlicher, rechtlicher und technischer Hinsicht und in den Bereichen Umweltschutz, Tarifrecht und Sozialversicherung
- Nachwuchswerbung und Berufsorientierung
- Regelungen der beruflichen Bildung und der überbetrieblichen Ausbildung
- Fortbildungen
- Meisterprüfungen

Spectrum of competence:
- counselling in economic, legal and technical questions and in the sectors of environmental protection, collective bargaining law and social insurance
- recruitment of trainees and professional orientation
- regulating professional training and interworks training
- advanced vocational training
- master craftsman's qualifying examinations

Handwerkskammer für Mittelfranken Nürnberg

Standort in Europa
Business Location in Europe

Dachdecker beim Montieren einer Solaranlage

A roofer installing solar equipment

Zum Handwerk in Mittelfranken mit seinen heute über 20 000 mittelständischen Betrieben gehören die in einer langen Tradition stehenden Gewerbe wie die Bürsten- und Pinselmacher im westlichen Mittelfranken, die Gold-, Silber- und Aluminiumschläger im Raum Schwabach und die Streich- und Zupfinstrumentenbauer im Umkreis von Erlangen. Alle diese Unternehmen sind in hohem Maße exportorientiert. Weltweit operieren auch Handwerksbetriebe in der Medizintechnik, Kommunikationstechnik und im Bereich der elektrostatischen Oberflächenbeschichtung. Das Handwerk in der Metropolregion prägen aber ebenso die Werkzeug- und Formenbauer, Elektromaschinenbauer und Maschinenbaumechaniker, die der Industrie zuliefern.

Zunehmende Bedeutung gewinnt insbesondere der Dienstleistungssektor, dessen Berufsspektrum breit gefächert ist. Es reicht vom Anlagenbauer oder Augenoptiker über Bäcker oder Brauer und Mälzer bis zum Chirurgiemechaniker. Der Dachdecker gehört ebenso dazu wie der Fotograf oder Friseur, Glaser, Konditor, Stuckateur oder Zimmerer. Und die Liste erhebt keinen Anspruch auf Vollständigkeit.

Der Handwerker der Zukunft ist jedoch nicht nur am Wohnort oder in der Region tätig, sondern muss auch die Wünsche überregionaler Kunden wie beispielsweise einer Bank oder einer gemeinnützigen Einrichtung erfüllen können. Dazu bedarf es neuer Allianzen und Kommunikationsstrukturen im Handwerk. Und auch politisch haben Großeinheiten naturgemäß ein stärkeres Gewicht. Einigkeit macht stark. Dieses Motto aus der Gewerkschaftsbewegung

Fortsetzung Seite 70

Trades with long-standing traditions such as the brush manufacturers in Western Middle Franconia, gold-leaf, silver-leaf and aluminium-leaf makers in the Schwabach area and the string and plucked string instrument manufacturers near Erlangen also belong to the trades in Middle Franconia which can currently count more than 20,000 medium-sized concerns. All these undertakings are, to a large extent, export-oriented. Handicraft firms operate globally in medicine technology, communication technology and in the sector of electrostatic surface coating. As suppliers to industry, tool-makers, mould-constructors, electro machine constructors and mechanical engineers also leave their mark on trades in general.

Of increasing importance is the service sector, which today encompasses a widely spread spectrum of professions. This stretches from plant constructor or optician via baker or beer brewer and maltster through

Continued on page 70

Die WEILER Werkzeugmaschinen GmbH kann auf eine fast 70-jährige Tradition als zuverlässiger und kompetenter Hersteller von Drehmaschinen zurückblicken und befindet sich seit 1995 im Besitz der Familie Eisler. Die Firma wird von dem Geschäftsführenden Gesellschafter, Herrn Dkfm. Friedrich K. Eisler, geleitet. Eingesetzt werden WEILER Präzisions-Drehmaschinen weltweit in den unterschiedlichsten Branchen wie zum Beispiel Drehereien, Ausbildungsstätten, Forschung und Entwicklung, Werkzeug- und Formenbau, in der Erdölindustrie, im Flugzeugbau, in der Medizintechnik, in der Stahlindustrie, in Wasserkraftwerken, usw. Wesentliche Merkmale aller WEILER-Produkte und zentrales Thema jeder Innovation sind der hohe Bedienkomfort, höchste Präzision und Kundenzufriedenheit. Um diese auch in Zukunft zu gewährleisten, legt das Unternehmen größten Wert auf die ständige Aus- und Weiterbildung seiner Mitarbeiter sowie auf einen konzentrierten Dialog mit seinen weltweiten Kunden, zum Beispiel auch auf nationalen und internationalen Messen.

WEILER Werkzeugmaschinen GmbH looks back on almost 70 years of tradition as a reliable and competent lathe manufacturer. Since 1995 it has been owned by the Eisler family and is headed by the managing shareholder, Friedrich K. Eisler, a master in business Administration. WEILER precision lathes are in use all over the world in a wide variety of fields such as turneries, training centres, research and development, tool and mould makers, in the petroleum industry, in aircraft construction, in medicine technology, in the steel industry and in hydroelectric power stations, etc. The important characteristics of all WEILER products and main focus of each innovation are user-friendly operation, absolute precision and total customer satisfaction. To guarantee that this remains so in the future, management places the utmost importance on continuous further education and training of employees as well as on the concentrated dialogue with global customers taking place, for instance, at national and international trade fairs.

Information

Gründungsjahr: 1938

Mitarbeiter: 500

Leistungsspektrum: Entwicklung und Herstellung von Präzisions-Drehmaschinen

Year founded: 1938

Employees: 500

Range of services: development and manufacture of precision turning lathes

☐
WEILER Werkzeugmaschinen GmbH
Emskirchen

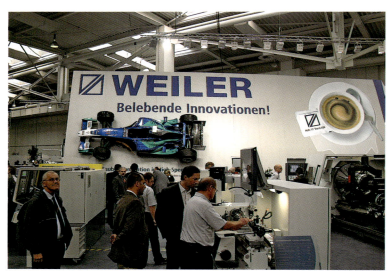

Standort in Europa
Business Location in Europe

Die Firma ESAB ARCOS Georg Hartner GmbH, kurz EAGH, kann auf eine lange Tradition verweisen. Bereits 1934 begann der Vertrieb von ARCOS-Schweißelektroden durch den Firmengründer Georg Hartner in Unterfranken. 1985 wurden die Vertriebsaktivitäten der Firmen ESAB, ARCOS und Georg Hartner in dem neu gegründeten Unternehmen EAGH zusammengeschlossen.

Das große Engagement und die kompetente fachliche Beratung überzeugen die stetig wachsende Kundschaft bereits seit Jahrzehnten. Diese konsequente Kundenorientierung zusammen mit der permanenten Erweiterung des Sortiments machen die EAGH zu einem der renommiertesten Schweißfachhändler in Deutschland.

Messrs ESAB ARCOS Georg Hartner GmbH, in short EAGH, can refer to a long tradition. Georg Hartner, the company founder, began selling ARCOS welding electrodes in Lower Franconia as early as 1934. In 1985 the sales activities of the firms ESAB, ARCOS and Georg Hartner were amalgamated in the newly founded concern EAGH. Their enormous commitment and competent specialised counselling has convinced their steadily growing circle of customers for decades. This consequent customer orientation together with the permanent extension of the product range make the EAGH one of the best known welding specialist suppliers in Germany.

Information

Gründungsjahr: 1985 (G. Hartner seit 1934)

Mitarbeiter: insgesamt 16, davon 2 in der Außenstelle Regensburg und 1 in der Außenstelle Würzburg

Produkte:
– Schweißen
– Schneiden
– Arbeitsschutz
mechanisiertes Schweißen:
– Vorrichtungen
– Roboter

Year founded: 1985 (G. Hartner since 1934)

Employees: altogether 16, of which 2 are in the branch office in Regensburg and 1 in the branch office in Würzburg

Products:
– welding
– cutting
– work protection
mechanised welding:
– equipment
– robots

☐
ESAB ARCOS
Georg Hartner GmbH
Nürnberg

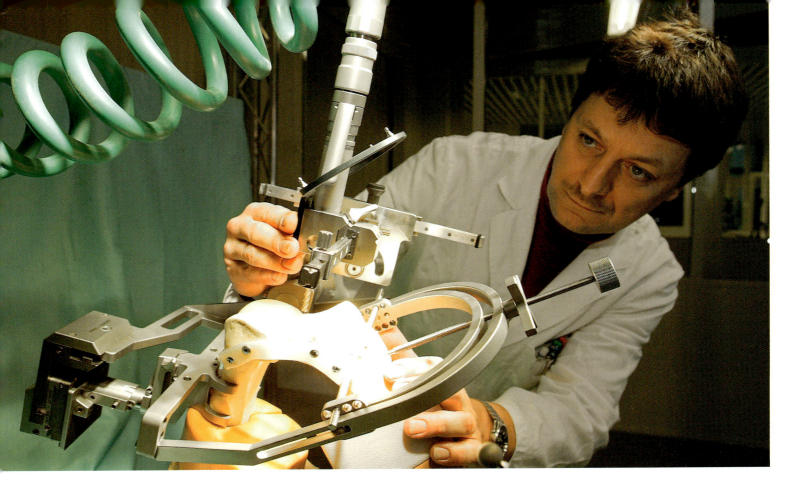

High-Tech-Handwerk aus der Metropolregion: Justieren eines künstlichen Kniegelenks aus biokompatiblen Titan-Implantaten

High-tech handicraft from the metropolitan region: adjusting an artificial knee joint made of biocompatible titan implants

gewinnt im Handwerk beträchtlich an Bedeutung. Deshalb denkt das Handwerk in den Dimensionen der Metropolregion, die auch Landkreise und Städte wie Bayreuth, Amberg oder Neumarkt mit einschließt.

Das Handwerk schöpft seine innovative Kraft auch aus dem Bewusstsein, dass es seine Kunden vor Ort, in der Region hat. Dort gilt es, die Lebensqualität der Menschen zu erhalten und zu steigern. Denn eine der Stärken des Handwerks liegt in seinem direkten menschlichen Kontakt zum Kunden. Nicht zuletzt daraus gewinnt es seine innovative Kraft. ☐

to surgery mechanic. The roofer belongs just as much to them as do the photographer or hairdresser, glazer, confectioner, plasterer and carpenter. And the list is by no means complete.

The craftsman of the future is, however, not only busy in his home town or in the region, but must be prepared to fulfil the demands made by supra-regional customers, for instance one of the banks or a charitable institution. To do this will require new alliances and communication structures within the trades. In the natural course of things, large units carry more weight and this also applies to politics. Unity strengthens. This motto from the union movement is gaining considerable meaning within the trades. Which explains why they are thinking in the dimensions of the metropolitan region which encloses districts and cities such as Bayreuth, Amberg or Neumarkt.

Trade also draws innovative strength from the awareness that it has customers on location, in the region. It is a case of maintaining and increasing the quality of life for people there, as one of their strengths lies in the direct human contact to the customer. Not least from here, does it gain its innovative strength. ☐

Standort in Europa
Business Location in Europe

Zukunftsperspektiven für Westmittelfranken

Professor Dr. Gerhard Mammen

„Herzlich willkommen in Westmittelfranken!" Hinweistafeln dieser Art sucht man vergebens an den Verwaltungsgrenzen der Landkreise Ansbach, Neustadt/Aisch-Bad Windsheim und Weißenburg-Gunzenhausen. Sie umschließen die Region Westmittelfranken – und mittendrin das Oberzentrum: die Stadt Ansbach. Auch auf Landkarten ist Westmittelfranken nicht zu finden. Und doch ist es ein Markenzeichen für Raumordnung und Landesplanung, für Zuversicht, Fleiß und Kreativität seiner Bevölkerung und für den entschlossenen politischen Willen, die Lebensverhältnisse in dieser von den negativen Folgen des Strukturwandels in der Landwirtschaft besonders stark betroffenen Region anzuheben und ihr Entwicklungspotenzial nachhaltig zu aktivieren.

Das ist eindrucksvoll gelungen. Die Autobahnen A 6 und A 7 haben Westmittelfranken angebunden, näher an überregionale Absatzmärkte herangeführt und neue Produktivkräfte in der Region freigesetzt. Heute ist Westmittelfranken ein begehrter Lebensraum für Fach- und Führungskräfte aus dem nahe gelegenen Ballungsraum Nürnberg. Ebenso haben zahlreiche innovative Unternehmen Westmittelfranken als attraktiven Wirtschaftsstandort entdeckt – mit preis- und verkehrsgünstigen Gewerbeflächen, qualifizierten Arbeitskräften und einem Umfeld, das die Vereinbarkeit von Produktion und Umweltschutz leichter als in Ballungsräumen ermöglicht. Die Neuansiedlungen und die erfolgreiche Entwicklung heimischer Unternehmen haben eine leistungsstarke mittelständische Wirtschaft herangebildet, die in den letzten drei Jahrzehnten eine Vielzahl von Arbeitsplätzen außerhalb der Landwirtschaft geschaffen hat.

Branchenschwerpunkte bilden die Kunststoffverarbeitung, Elektrotechnik und Lebensmittelherstellung. Viele der Firmen sind als System- und Komponentenhersteller hochgradig technologisch orientiert, geschäftlich eng mit „Global Playern" verbunden und ebenso wie diese auf den Weltmärkten zu

"A hearty welcome to West Middle Franconia!" It is futile to look for information boards of this type on the administrative borders of the districts of Ansbach, Neustadt/Aisch-Bad Windsheim and Weißenburg-Gunzenhausen. They encompass the region of West Middle Franconia – with the upper centre in the middle: the city of Ansbach. Nor can West Middle Franconia be found on any map although it is a trademark for regional development planning and county planning, for the confidence, diligence and creativity of its population. It also stands for the resolute political intentions to improve the living conditions in this region, which were strongly affected by the negative results of structural changes in agriculture, and to activate and sustain their development potential.

This has been impressively successful. The A 6 and A 7 motorways have linked up West Middle Franconia, brought them nearer to supra-regional sales markets and released new productive power in the region. Today West Middle Franconia is a desirable habitat for specialists and management working in the neighbouring heavily populated centre of Nuremberg. Equally, numerous innovative concerns have discovered West Middle Franconia as an attractive business location – with reasonably priced commercial land conveniently situated for public transport, with a well-qualified workforce and an environment which enables the compatibility of production and environmental protection easier than in densely populated centres. The new settlements and the successful development of local companies have developed and trained an efficient medium-sized economy, which, in the last three decades, has created a number of workplaces outside the agricultural sector.

Branch focal points are synthetic processing, electrical engineering and foodstuff manufacture. Many companies are, as system and component manufacturers, highly technologically oriented, closely linked in business with "global players" and, as they, at home on

Future Perspectives for West Middle Franconia

Angewandte Forschung und Entwicklung: Quelle von Innovation und Fortschritt

Applied research and development: source of innovation and progress

Hause. Selbst traditionelle Wirtschaftszweige wie die Bürsten- und Pinselhersteller gehören inzwischen weltweit zur technologischen Avantgarde. Neue unternehmerische Aktivitäten entstehen im Bereich innovativer Energie- und Umweltsysteme.

Wichtige wirtschaftliche Impulse gehen auch vom Tourismus aus. Rothenburg ob der Tauber genießt weltweites touristisches Interesse. Als Ausflugs- und Urlaubsgebiet gewinnt das Fränkische Seenland an Bedeutung, das als eines der größten wasserwirtschaftlichen Bauprojekte in Bayern entstanden ist. Und mit drei ortsgebundenen Heilmitteln verfügt Bad Windsheim über ein Alleinstellungsmerkmal als Standort für Gesundheits- und Wellnesstourismus.

Die Stadt Ansbach ist das Oberzentrum Westmittelfrankens. Als Einzelhandelsstandort besitzt Ansbach ein weit in das Umland hineinragendes Einzugsgebiet. Trotz hoher Investitionen – etwa in den Aufbau der Fachhochschule und des Technologiezentrums – kommt die Stadt seit Jahren ohne Neuverschuldung aus.

Bildung, Wissenschaft, angewandte Forschung

world markets. Even traditional branches of industry such as brush manufacturers belong in the meantime to the technical avantgarde all over the world. New entre-preneurial activities are being created in the sector of innovative energy and environmental systems.

Meaningful economic impulses are also being sent out from the tourism sector. Rothenburg ob der Tauber enjoys the interests of tourists from all over the world. As a destination for tours and holidays the Franconian lake district is gaining in importance, one of the largest water management construction projects in Bavaria. And with three residential medicinal remedies, Bad Windsheim has a unique standing in the health and well-being tourism branch.

Standort in Europa
Business Location in Europe

Schaltstelle für Information, Kommunikation und Innovation – die Fachhochschule Ansbach

Control centre for information, communication and innovation – the university of applied sciences in Ansbach

The city of Ansbach is the upper centre of West Middle Franconia. As retail location Ansbach's catchment area reaches far into the surrounding countryside. In spite of high investments – for instance in the set-up of the university of applied sciences and the technology centre – the city has managed for years without making new debts.

Education, science, applied research and development as well as an intensive technology transfer between universities and regional businesses are gaining in importance for the future strengthening of the region. The universities of applied sciences in Ansbach and Triesdorf have key functions, they are the switchboard for information, communication and innovation, essential for a forward-looking infrastructure.

With unmistakable profile and independent indentity as a highly efficient rural area, West Middle Franconia will find its own position in the developing metropolitan region of Nuremberg. The requirements have been met. In this spirit: A hearty welcome to West Middle Franconia!

Anziehungspunkt für Touristen aus der ganzen Welt: Rothenburg ob der Tauber

An attraction for tourists from all over the world: Rothenburg ob der Tauber

und Entwicklung sowie ein intensiver Technologietransfer von Hochschulen und regionaler Wirtschaft gewinnen für die zukünftige Stärkung der Region zunehmend an Bedeutung. Den Fachhochschulen in Ansbach und Triesdorf kommen dabei Schlüsselfunktionen zu, sie sind Schaltstellen von Information, Kommunikation und Innovation, die für eine zukunftsweisende Infrastruktur unentbehrlich sind.

Mit unverwechselbarem Profil und eigenständiger Identität als leistungsstarker ländlicher Wirtschaftsraum wird sich Westmittelfranken in der entstehenden Metropolregion Nürnberg positionieren. Die Voraussetzungen dafür sind gegeben. In diesem Sinne: Herzlich willkommen in Westmittelfranken!

Internationaler Airport Nürnberg – tragende Säule der Infrastruktur

Karl-Heinz Krüger

Der Nürnberger Flughafen ist ein Garant für Mobilität, Verlässlichkeit und Dynamik. Als leistungsstarke Luftverkehrsdrehscheibe ist der Airport Nürnberg damit ein wichtiges Standbein der Infrastruktur für die Metropolregion Nürnberg und macht den Wirtschaftsstandort zum Global Player.

Mehrfach gekürt wegen seiner guten Serviceleistungen, zeichnet sich der Airport Nürnberg durch seine reibungslosen Abläufe bei der Abfertigung aus: Vom Check-in bis zur Gepäckrückgabe geht es dank kurzer Wege und hoher Übersichtlichkeit jeweils nur um wenige Meter und Minuten. Um die kurzen Aufenthaltszeiten so angenehm wie möglich zu gestalten, stehen dem Fluggast diverse Einkaufs-, Verpflegungs- und Informationsmöglichkeiten zur Verfügung. Der Airport verfügt zudem über komfortable Lounges.

Der Airport Nürnberg liegt zentral und gewährt eine erstklassige Anbindung in die Innenstadt und das Messezentrum NürnbergMesse: Mit der direkten U-Bahnverbindung beträgt die Fahrzeit zum Hauptbahnhof nur 12 und zum Messegelände 20 Minuten. Alternativ stehen zu Messezeiten Sonderbusse, ein großer Taxi-Pool sowie ein Limousinen-Service zur Verfügung. Das Mietwagen ServiceCenter liegt unmittelbar gegenüber der Ankunftshalle.

„Vielfalt, Qualität und Beständigkeit" sind laut Geschäftsführer Karl-Heinz Krüger die drei Grundpfeiler des Erfolgs: Mit einem zweistelligen Passagierplus auf rund 3,8 Millionen Fluggäste und einem positiven Jahresergebnis schloss der Airport Nürnberg das Jahr 2005 ab. Vor allem die Ausweitung der Euro-Shuttle-Strecken der Air Berlin mit günstigen Low-Fare-Tarifen ab 29 Euro (oneway inklusive Steuern und Gebühren) hat den stabilen Aufschwung der letzten Jahre unterstützt. Belebt wurde der Trend zudem durch vielversprechende Markteintritte wie beispielsweise von der dba (auf den Strecken Düsseldorf, Hamburg und Berlin), der polnischen Low-Cost-Airline Centralwings und der dänischen SAS. Für die weitere

The airport in Nuremberg is a guarantee for mobility, reliability and dynamic. As an efficient hub for air traffic the airport in Nuremberg is therefore an important support for the infrastructure of the Nuremberg metropolitan region allowing the business location to be a global player.

Having been praised many times for its excellent service, the Nuremberg airport is especially notable for its smooth service: Thanks to very short routes and overall openness, the routes from the check-in desk through to baggage return are short in both time and distance. To make the short stays as comfortable as possible for the passenger, there are various opportunities for shopping, catering and collecting information. Needless to say, the airport also maintains comfortable lounges.

The airport in Nuremberg is located centrally and provides first class connections to the inner city and to the NürnbergMesse, the trade fair centre in Nuremberg: The underground has a direct link and the journey to the main railway station takes 12 minutes and 20 minutes to the trade fair grounds. Alternatively, there are special busses available for trade fair visitors, a large taxi pool as well as a limousine service. The car rental service centre is located directly opposite the arrival hall.

"Diversity, quality and dependability" are, according to the business manager Karl-Heinz Krüger, the three cornerstones for success: the Nuremberg airport completed the year 2005 with a two-digit passenger growth to some 3.8 million flight passengers and a positive annual result. Most of all, the extension of Air Berlin's Euro Shuttle routes with their economic low fare prices starting at 29 Euro (one way including taxes and charges) has supported the stable upswing of the last few years. The trend was also animated through promising market introductions such as dba (on the Dusseldorf, Hamburg and Berlin routes), the Polish low cost airline Centralwings and the Danish SAS. To cater

Nuremberg International Airport – Mainstay of the Infrastructure

Entwicklung wird der Airport Nürnberg qualitativ hochwertigen Low-Fare-Angeboten und dem weiteren Ausbau des Liniennetzes einen größeren Umfang einräumen. Eine solide Basis für diesen Fortschritt ist, dass nahezu alle etablierten europäischen Carrier Nürnberg ansteuern, darunter klassische Airlines wie Lufthansa und Swiss, Air France, KLM, Austrian Airlines und Turkish Airlines.

Auch im Cargogeschäft ist der Airport Nürnberg ein stabiles Standbein für die Wirtschaft in der Metropolregion: Mit einem jährlichen Frachtaufkommen von über 80 000 Tonnen steht Nürnberg auf Platz sechs im Ranking der deutschen Verkehrsflughäfen. Rund 30 Spediteure und Dienstleister rund um das Produkt Fracht sowie bis zu 50 verschiedene nationale und internationale Airlines sind im Cargobereich am Airport Nürnberg aktiv. Am Airport Nürnberg können

Vom Airport Nürnberg aus sind die wichtigsten europäischen Flughäfen nonstop zu erreichen.

The most important European airports can be reached non-stop from the airport in Nuremberg.

for further development, the Nuremberg airport will grant the expansion of qualitatively high-value lowfare offers as well as the route network on a larger scale. A solid base for such progress is, of course, that almost all established European carriers head for Nuremberg, amongst them the classic airlines such as Lufthansa and Swiss, Air France, KLM, Austrian Airlines and Turkish Airlines.

Im Herbst 1986 begann das Unternehmen K&M Transporte eine Marktlücke im Nürnberger Speditionswesen zu schließen. Mit zunächst nur einem Lkw wurden die Spediteure am Nürnberger Flughafen unterstützt. Heute ist K&M Transporte einer der Hauptanbieter von Fuhrleistungen für Speditionen und Airlines am Flughafen Nürnberg im Bereich Luftfracht. Das umfassende Angebot reicht von Teil- und Komplettsendungen an den Flughäfen Nürnberg, München und Frankfurt (Main) im Import und Export, inklusive SITA und DGR Check. Sechs Linien zu europäischen Flughäfen bedient K&M Transporte täglich im Nachtsprung mit mehreren Fahrzeugen. Mit über 40 firmeneigenen Fahrzeugen kann der Logistikdienstleister äußerst flexibel auf die Wünsche seiner Kunden reagieren. K&M Transporte befördert ausschließlich Luftfracht und weiß daher um die Sensibilität aller Sendungen und der damit gebotenen Sorgfalt im Umgang mit diesen.

In the autumn of 1986 the undertaking K&M Transporte began to close a market gap in the Nuremberg transport sector. At the beginning, they supported the forwarding agents at the Nuremberg airport using just one motor lorry.
Today K&M Transporte is one of the main providers of carrier services for forwarding agencies and airlines in the air cargo sector at the Nuremberg airport. Their wide range reaches from partial and complete consignments at airports in Nuremberg, Munich and Frankfurt (Main) in import and export, including SITA and DGR checks. K&M Transporte serves six routes to European airports daily in night jumps using several vehicles. The logistics suppliers have more than 40 self-owned vehicles at their disposal enabling them to react extremely flexibly to customer requirements. K&M Transporte hauls exclusively air cargo and is therefore aware of the sensitivity of all consignments and the proficiency in the care needed with them.

Information

Gründungsjahr: 1986

Mitarbeiter: 65

Leistungsspektrum:
– tägliche Abholungen und Zustellungen im gesamten nordbayerischen Raum
– Linienverkehre im Nachtsprung zu den Flughäfen Düsseldorf, Frankfurt, Köln, München, Amsterdam, Luxemburg
– Kurier- und Sonderfahrten (In- und Ausland)
– Handling (Dokumentenhandling, Zollabfertigung von Exportsendungen, Lagerlogistik)

Zertifizierung:
DIN EN ISO 9001:2000

Year founded: 1986

Employees: 65

Range of services:
– daily collection and delivery in the entire North Bavarian area
– regular overnight services in night jumps to the airports in Dusseldorf, Frankfurt, Cologne, Munich, Amsterdam and Luxemburg
– courier- and special tours (inland and overseas)
– handling (dealing with documents, customs clearance for export consignments, storage logistics)

Certification:
DIN EN ISO 9001:2000

☐
K&M Transporte
Nürnberg

Standort in Europa
Business Location in Europe

Durch den konsequenten Ausbau der Euro Shuttle-Strecken zu günstigen Tarifen werden im Jahr 2006 rund vier Millionen Fluggäste am Airport Nürnberg erwartet.

By the consistent expansion of the Euro shuttle routes at economic prices, some four million passengers are expected at the Nuremberg airport in 2006.

Information

Der Airport Nürnberg bietet Nonstopverbindungen zu den wichtigsten europäischen Wirtschaftszentren sowie den großen Hub-Flughäfen. Verlässliche Direktanbindungen nach Frankfurt, München, Zürich, Wien, Amsterdam, Paris, London, Kopenhagen und Istanbul gewährleisten Anschlussflüge an weltweit über 300 Ziele. Neue Destinationen in Osteuropa wie Budapest sowie ein wachsender Anteil an Low-Fare-Flügen geben der Erreichbarkeit durch die Luft zudem ständig neue Impulse.

rund um die Uhr Frachtflugzeuge abgefertigt werden. Im Gegensatz zu manch größerem Flughafen bietet der Airport Nürnberg zudem übersichtlichere Strukturen und dadurch eine höhere Flexibilität, um auf individuelle Kundenwünsche eingehen zu können. Firmen von Weltrang wie etwa Siemens, Bosch, MAN, Audi und BMW, Leistriz und INA Schaeffler Wälzlager nutzen die Möglichkeiten, die sich ihnen am Airport Nürnberg bieten. Das Spektrum der Luftfracht reicht von Textilien über hoch technisierte Industriegüter und komplette Schalt- und Röntgenanlagen sowie andere besonders sensible Waren.

Für die weitere Entwicklung des Airport Nürnberg setzt die Geschäftsführung auf eine anhaltende Stabilisierung der Linie und Erweiterungen im Touristikverkehr.

In the cargo business too, the Nuremberg airport is a stable support for the economy in the metropolitan region: With annual freight amounting to more than 80,000 tons Nuremberg stands in sixth place in the ranks of the German commercial airports. Some 30 haulage contractors and service suppliers surrounding the product of freight as well as up to 50 different national and international airlines are active in the cargo sector at Nuremberg airport. Freight planes can be processed round the clock in Nuremberg's airport. And in contrast to many another decent-sized airport, the Nuremberg airport offers clear structures and a high

Information

The Nuremberg airport offers non-stop connections to the most important European industrial centres as well as large airports with lifting capacities. Reliable direct connections to Frankfurt, Munich, Zurich, Vienna, Amsterdam, Paris, London, Copenhagen and Istanbul guarantee connecting flights to more than 300 destinations all over the world. New destinations in Eastern Europe such as Budapest together with a growing share of low fare flights give constant new impulses to accessibility by air.

amount of flexibility in order to meet the demands of individual customers. Firms of global reputation such as Siemens, Bosch, MAN, Audi and BMW, Leistriz and INA Schaeffler Wälzlager make use of the possibilities offered them by the Nuremberg airport. The range of air cargo reaches from textiles via highly technical industrial goods and complete switchgears and x-ray equipment through to other particularly sensitive goods.

For the further development of the Nuremberg Airport the management is relying on continuing course stabilisation and the extensions in tourist traffic.

Güterverkehrszentrum bayernhafen Nürnberg – trimodaler Logistikprovider in einem erweiterten Europa

Harald Leupold

Mit einer jährlichen Umschlagleistung von über 10 Millionen Tonnen ist das GVZ bayernhafen Nürnberg das größte und bedeutendste multifunktionale Logistikzentrum in Süddeutschland. Auf einer Fläche von 337 Hektar sind im bayernhafen Nürnberg 260 Unternehmen aus den Bereichen Spedition, Transport, Umschlag, Lagerung, Verpackung, Recycling, Industrie, Handel und logistische Dienstleistungen angesiedelt, die über 5300 Menschen Arbeit bieten. Im bayernhafen Roth mit seinen 5,8 Hektar Fläche sind spezialisierte Unternehmen aus den Bereichen Recycling und Baustoffhandel tätig.

Die Region Nürnberg wird von der EU als Gateway-Region definiert, die als grundlegend für den Ausbau der Wirtschaftsbeziehungen zu Ost- und Südosteuropa angesehen wird. Als zentraler Distributionsstandort in Süddeutschland und Gateway für Südosteuropa erreicht der Standort ca. 27 Millionen Einwohner im Umkreis von 200 Kilometern.

Das GVZ bayernhafen Nürnberg ist einer der führenden trimodalen Logistikstandorte in Europa und somit ein idealer Wirtschaftsstandort mit Zukunft in geozentraler Lage. Zugleich ist es an die Transeuropäischen Netze (TEN) der Verkehrsträger Straße, Schiene und Wasser angebunden und verknüpft diese Infrastrukturen in idealer Weise für multimodale Transportketten.

Durch zukunftsweisende Investitionen in Infrastruktur- und Erschließungsmaßnahmen und mit nachhaltigem Verkehrsausbau wird die kundenorientierte Systemvernetzung der Verkehrsträger Schiff, Bahn und Lkw des Standorts konsequent vorangetrieben. Ziel ist es, die Wachstumspotenziale im weltweit boomenden Containerverkehr und die Verlagerungs-

Goods Transport Centre bayernhafen Nuremberg – Tri-mode Logistics Provider in an Extended Europe

Standort in Europa
Business Location in Europe

Das GVZ bayernhafen Nürnberg ist eines der führenden trimodalen Logistikzentren Europas.

The GVZ bayernhafen Nuremberg is one of the leading tri-modal logistics centres in Europe.

With an annual transhipment tonnage of more than 10 million tons the GVZ bayernhafen Nuremberg is the largest and most significant multi-functional logistics centre in Southern Germany. 260 firms from the branches of haulage, transport, transhipment, storage, packaging, recycling, industry, trade and logistics services are located on an area of 337 hectares in the bayernhafen Nuremberg where more than 5,300 people have found work. In the bayernhafen Roth, with its 5.8 hectare area, undertakings specialising in the sectors of recycling and building materials are active.

The Nuremberg region has been defined by the EU as a gateway-region and is considered to be fundamental for the extension of economic relations to East and Southeast Europe. As a central distribution location in Southern Germany and gateway for Southeast Europe the location reaches about 27 million inhabitants in an orbit of 200 kilometres.

The GVZ bayernhafen Nuremberg is one of the leading tri-mode logistics locations in Europe and thus an ideal industrial location of the future in a geographically central position. At the same time, it is linked with the trans-European networks (TEN) of the transport carriers road, rail and water and combines these infrastructures in an ideal way for multimode transport chains.

Customer-oriented systematic linkage of the location's ship, railway and HGV transport carriers is being consequently driven ahead by making forward-looking investments in infrastructure and development and by sustaining development in transport. The target is to open up and develop both growth potential in the globally-booming container transport and the potential in moving from the road to the environmental-friendly

Rund 155 000 Ladungseinheiten werden pro Jahr im GVZ umgeschlagen.

Some 155,000 loads are transferred per year in the GVZ.

potenziale von der Straße auf die umweltfreundlichen Verkehrsträger Schiene und Wasser zu erschließen. Die bedeutendste Infrastrukturmaßnahme ist die Realisierung einer leistungsstarken und trimodalen Umschlaganlage im kombinierten Ladungsverkehr (KV) mit einem Investitionsvolumen von 31 Mio. Euro. Mit einer jährlichen Umschlagkapazität von ca. 155 000 Ladungseinheiten (Container, Lkw-Aufbauten) und dem Teilausbau eines dritten Hafenbeckens werden die drei Verkehrsträger noch effizienter zusammengeführt.

In einem weiteren Ausbauschritt ist geplant, den derzeitig innerstädtischen Umschlagbahnhof der DB in das GVZ bayernhafen Nürnberg zu verlagern. Die Realisierung dieses zweiten Moduls erfolgt voraussichtlich bis Ende 2008.

Ergänzend zum Infrastrukturausbau wird die Standortqualität durch die Vernetzung mit bedeutenden Logistikzentren forciert. Die Vernetzungsstrategie beruht auf folgenden wesentlichen Entwicklungen:
– Ausbau von Seehafen-Hinterlandverkehren (Container) mit allen bedeutenden Nord-, West- und Südhäfen in Europa
– Integration des Standortes in das nationale und europäische Netz für den unbegleiteten Kombinierten Verkehr (KV) für Lkw-Wechselbrücken und Sattelauflieger
– Ganzzugsysteme mit wichtigen europäischen GVZ
– Binnenschiff-/Bahn-Verkehrsketten mit dem Donauraum

Die Hafen Nürnberg-Roth GmbH, Betreibergesellschaft der bayernhäfen Nürnberg und Roth, ist ein marktaktives und kundenorientiertes Infrastruktur- und Dienstleistungsunternehmen. Neben der aktiven Vermarktung und dem Management von Grundstücken, Hafenumschlag sowie dem Betrieb der Hafenbahn werden den im GVZ ansässigen Unternehmen umfangreiche Services und Dienstleistungen in Form von Facility-Management-Angeboten offeriert. ☐

transport carriers of rail and water. The most important infrastructural measure is the realisation of a powerful and tri-mode transhipment plant in combined carrier traffic (KV) with an investment volume of 31 million Euro. With an annual transhipment capacity of about 155,000 loading units (container, HGV body erections) and the partial extension of a third harbour basin, the three transport carriers will be brought together even more efficiently.

In a further extension stage it is planned to move the present inner city transhipment railway head belonging to the DB (German Federal Railway) into the GVZ bayernhafen Nuremberg. The realisation of this second module will probably be at the end of 2008.

Supplementary to the extension of the infrastructure, the business location quality is being pushed along by linking with important logistic centres. This strategy of linking rests on the following essential developments:
– *the extension of the seaport's ninterland traffic (container) with all the significant northerly, westerly and southerly ports in Europe*
– *the integration of the location into the national and European network for unaccompanied combined traffic (KV) for HGV interchangeable bodies and semi-trailers*
– *entire towing systems with important European GVZ*
– *inland waterway transport/rail transport links with the Danube area*

The Hafen Nürnberg-Roth GmbH, operating company of the bayernhäfen Nuremberg and Roth, is a market-active and customer-oriented infrastructure and service supply concern. In addition to actively marketing and managing property, harbour transhipping and operating the harbour train, the firms residing in the GVZ are provided with a wide range of services in the form of facility management. ☐

Standort in Europa
Business Location in Europe

Die Vernetzung von Binnenschiff- und Bahn-Verkehrsketten mit dem Donauraum ist eines der Ziele des GVZ.

The linking of inland shipping and rail traffic chains with the Danube area is one of the GVZ's targets.

Der Verkehrsverbund Großraum Nürnberg – Vorreiter eines regionalen Bewusstseins

Karl Inhofer

Mit hohen Erwartungen startete am 27. September 1987 der Verkehrsverbund Großraum Nürnberg (VGN). Gleichzeitig nahm die Deutsche Bundesbahn als erste S-Bahn-Strecke im Großraum die Strecke Nürnberg Hauptbahnhof–Lauf (links d. Pegnitz) in Betrieb. Ein gemeinsames Fahrplanbuch und ein einheitlicher Tarif sowie nur eine Fahrkarte für alle beteiligten Verkehrsunternehmen waren ein erster großer Schritt hin zu mehr Kundenfreundlichkeit. Denn bis dahin waren die Fahrgäste gezwungen, für jedes Umsteigen neue Fahrausweise zu lösen. Der Nahverkehr war mit einem Schlag übersichtlicher und damit auch attraktiver geworden. Bereits Mitte der neunziger Jahre schwärmte der damalige Regierungspräsident von Mittelfranken, Heinrich von Mosch: „Wenn es den Verkehrsverbund nicht schon gäbe, müsste er schleunigst erfunden werden." Obwohl dies für niemanden wirklich vorhersehbar war, war mit dem Verkehrsverbund ein wichtiger Baustein für eine künftige Metropolregion entstanden.

Erwartungen übertroffen

Im Lauf der zurückliegenden Jahre hat sich der Verkehrsverbund zu einem unverzichtbaren Bestandteil der Mobilität in Franken entwickelt. Er ist mit einer Fläche von 11 500 Quadratkilometern der drittgrößte Verkehrsverbund in Deutschland. Im Verbundgebiet, das sind sechs kreisfreie Städte und elf Landkreise in Mittel- und Oberfranken sowie in der Oberpfalz, leben rund 2,2 Millionen Menschen. In diesem Gebiet betreiben 90 Verkehrsunternehmen rund 540 Linien. Neben den 20 Regional- und drei S-Bahn-Linien gibt es zwei U-Bahn-Linien, sechs Straßenbahn- und etwa 500 Buslinien.

Fortsetzung Seite 86

The VGN Verkehrsverbund Großraum Nürnberg (Public Transport Association) started on 27th September 1987 with high expectations. At the same time, the German railway began operating the Nuremberg main railway station–Lauf (left of the Pegnitz) line as the first suburban train in the area. A mutual book of time-tables and a common tariff as well as only one ticket for all the transport undertakings involved were the first large steps towards more customer friendliness. Until then all passengers had to buy a new ticket for each transfer. With one stroke, local transport had become clearly structured and considerably more attractive. As early as the middle of the nineties, Heinrich von Mosch, the then president of the regional council of Middle Franconia, said: "If we hadn't already got the transport combine then it would need to be invented as soon as possible." Although it wasn't really foreseeable for anyone, in the public transport association an important element for the future metropolitan region had been created.

Expectations surpassed

In the course of the past few years the public transport association has developed into an essential component of mobility in Franconia. With an area of 11,500 square kilometres it is the third largest transport association in Germany. Some 2.2 million people live in the association's area which covers six independent cities and eleven districts in Middle and Upper Franconia as well as in the Upper Palatinate. 90 different transport undertakings operate approximately 540 routes in the area. There are two underground lines, six trams and about 500 bus routes in addition to the 20 regional and three suburban train lines.

Continued on page 86

The Public Transport Association of Nuremberg and Surroundings – Pioneer of a Regional Consciousness

Standort in Europa
Business Location in Europe

Mit dem Verkehrsverbund Großraum Nürnberg (VGN) durch die Metropolregion: Moderne Züge werten auch die Regionalstrecken auf.
With the Verkehrsverbund Großraum Nürnberg (VGN) through the metropolitan region: Modern trains also increase the value of regional lines.

Unten: Die VAG überwacht in ihrer neuen Leitstelle den Bus-, Straßenbahn- und U-Bahnverkehr im Großraum Nürnberg mit digitaler Funktechnik.
Below: From its new headquarters the VAG uses digital radio technology to monitor bus, tram and underground traffic in Nuremberg and surroundings.

83

Der flächenmäßig drittgrößte Verkehrsverbund in Deutschland baut seine Verkehrsleistung und Tarifangebote stetig aus. Auch bei der Fahrgastinformation setzt man auf Innovation. Traditionelle Informationsmedien wie Fahrplanbuch und Servicetelefon werden durch Internet, WAP und Auskunft per SMS ergänzt. In Vorbereitung sind die dynamische Fahrgastinformation an Haltestellen und in den Neuen Medien sowie eine Echtzeitauskunft, die auch Verkehrsbehinderungen, Betriebsstörungen und Verspätungen aktuell verarbeitet.

The third most widespread transport association in Germany is continuously extending its efficiency and tariffs. Innovation is also prevalent in passenger information. Traditional information methods such as timetable and service telephone are supplemented by the internet, WAP and information via SMS. Dynamic passenger information boards at bus stops and in the new media together with realtime information giving traffic obstructions, service interruptions and delays updates are at the moment in the preparation process.

Information

Gründungsjahr: 1987

Verbundgebiet:
– 6 kreisfreie Städte
– 11 Landkreise

Fläche: 11 541 km²

Einwohner: 2,2 Mio.

Beförderte Personen:
190 Mio. pro Jahr

Verkehrsunternehmen: 90

Linien insgesamt:
rund 540
S-Bahn: 3
Regionalbahn: 20
U-Bahn: 3
Straßenbahn: 6
Bus: über 500

Year founded: 1987

Area covered by the association:
– 6 towns not belonging to an administrative district
– 11 administrative districts

Area: 11,541 km²

Citizens: 2.2 million

Persons carried:
190 million per annum

Traffic concerns: 90

Total services:
approx. 540
Suburban trains: 3
Regional trains: 20
Undergrounds: 3
Trams: 6
Buses: more than 500

☐
Verkehrsverbund
Großraum Nürnberg
GmbH (VGN)

Standort in Europa
Business Location in Europe

Der OVF als größte bayerische Regionalbusgesellschaft bietet auf fast einem Drittel der Fläche Bayerns ÖPNV-Leistungen an. Die Grundlage hierfür bildet eine enge Zusammenarbeit einerseits mit Landkreisen und Kommunen, andererseits mit mittelständischen Busunternehmern, die vielfach Hand in Hand mit dem OVF Verkehrsleistungen durchführen. Tag für Tag befördert der OVF etwa 150 000 Personen im ländlichen Raum Frankens sowie im Umland der großen Städte. Die drei Niederlassungen und sieben Verkaufsbüros sorgen für den reibungslosen Betriebsablauf und den Kontakt zu den Kunden vor Ort.
Als qualitätsbewusstes und ökologisches Unternehmen ist der OVF in den Bereichen Qualität, Arbeitsschutz und Umwelt zertifiziert und Mitglied im Umweltpakt Bayern. Sein Engagement zeigt sich u. a. in der Flottenpolitik: Inzwischen besteht der Fuhrpark zu mehr als der Hälfte aus innovativen und umweltfreundlichen Erdgasbussen.

*The OVF, as the largest Bavarian regional bus company, supplies rural public transport services covering almost one third of the area of Bavaria. The basis for this is, on the one hand, formed by close cooperation with country districts and communes and on the other hand with medium-sized bus undertakings that frequently run traffic services hand in hand with the OVF.
Day after day, the OVF carries some 150,000 persons in the rural area of Franconia as well as in the areas surrounding the large cities. The three branches and seven sales offices provide smooth operation and on-the-spot-contact with customers. The OVF, as a quality conscious and ecological undertaking, is certified in the areas of quality, industrial safety and environment and is a member in the Bavarian environmental pact. Its commitment can be seen, amongst others, in the fleet policy: In the meantime more than half of their fleet of vehicles consists of innovative and environment-friendly natural gas buses.*

Information

Gründungsjahr: 1988

Mitarbeiter: rund 700

Standorte:
Niederlassungen in Nürnberg, Coburg und Gemünden (Main); Verkaufsbüros in Nürnberg, Erlangen, Würzburg, Gemünden, Bad Neustadt (Saale), Coburg und Bayreuth

Fuhrpark:
286 Busse (davon 144 Erdgasbusse), ca. 1100 Subunternehmerfahrzeuge

Linien:
305 (Gesamtlänge: 17 300 km)

Umsatz:
87 Mio. Euro (2004)

Year founded: 1988

Employees: some 700

Locations:
branches in Nuremberg, Coburg and Gemünden (Main); sales offices in Nuremberg, Erlangen, Würzburg, Gemünden, Bad Neustadt (Saale), Coburg and Bayreuth

Fleet of vehicles:
286 buses (144 of which are run on natural gas), about 1,100 subcontractor vehicles

Routes: 305 (total length: 17,300 km)

Turnover: 87 million Euro (2004)

Omnibusverkehr Franken GmbH (OVF) Nürnberg

Gerade das Anwachsen der Zahl der Omnibuslinien von ursprünglich 118 auf 500 macht das Anliegen des Verkehrsverbundes deutlich, den öffentlichen Personennahverkehr zum Vorteil der Fahrgäste auch in der Region zu stärken. Und diese Anstrengungen werden von der Bevölkerung honoriert, so ist zum Beispiel die Zahl der beförderten Fahrgäste von 109 auf 190 Millionen gestiegen. Mit diesen Fahrgastzahlen gehört der VGN zu den Top Ten der deutschen Verbünde.

Dieses gute Ergebnis basiert auf ständigen Verbesserungen im Leistungs- und Tarifangebot. S- und U-Bahn-Netz wurden und werden ausgebaut, die Regionalbahnstrecken weitgehend vertaktet. Durch die Einführung des „Bayerntaktes" wurde das Verkehrsangebot auf den Schienenstrecken der DB AG besonders an den Wochenenden stark verbessert. Günstige und auf bestimmte Zielgruppen zugeschnittene Tarifangebote des Verkehrsverbunds erleichtern zusätzlich das Umsteigen auf Busse und Bahnen. Für Fahrgäste, die täglich mit öffentlichen Verkehrsmitteln unterwegs sind, sind MobiCard oder Jahres-Abo unentbehrliche Begleiter geworden. Für Ausflüge hat sich speziell das VGN-Angebot „TagesTicket Plus" bewährt.

Zufriedene Kunden

Ein hervorragender Beweis, dass der öffentliche Personennahverkehr im Großraum Nürnberg auf dem richtigen Weg ist, belegen die Angaben im jährlich vom Institut TNS Emnid durchgeführten ÖPNV-Barometer. Von allen getesteten Verkehrsverbünden schneidet der VGN in der Regel am besten ab.

Visionen

Der Ballungsraum Nürnberg und mit ihm die gesamte Metropolregion ist ohne flächendeckenden öffentlichen Personennahverkehr nicht denkbar. Ein stetig anwachsender motorisierter Individualverkehr würde die Lebensqualität unserer Bevölkerung immer stärker beeinträchtigen. Unumgänglich ist deshalb eine Vervollständigung des S-Bahn-Netzes. Neue S-Bahn-Strecken nach Ansbach, Neumarkt (OPf) und nach Forchheim, mit Anschluss nach Bamberg, sowie die Verlängerung der S1 bis Hartmannshof, aber auch Verbesserungen in den Korridoren nach Neustadt a. d. Aisch und nach Hersbruck (rechts d. Pegnitz) sind für den ÖPNV unbedingt notwendig. Diese Strecken erschließen den Kern der Metropolregion. Sie sind deshalb unverzichtbar für die Entwicklung unseres Wirtschaftsraumes. Der Verkehrsverbund Großraum Nürnberg hat im wahrsten Sinne des Wortes die Weichen gestellt für die Europäische Metropolregion Nürnberg.

It is the increase in the number of omnibus routes from the original 118 to 500 which makes clear the transport association's request also to strengthen local public transport in the region to the advantage of passengers. That these efforts are appreciated by the population becomes obvious by reading that the number of passengers carried have increased from 109 to 190 million. With these passenger figures, the VGN belongs to the top ten of the German associations.

This excellent result is based on the constant improvements made in performance and tariffs. Suburban and underground networks have been and are being extended and, to a large extent, regional trains run at fixed intervals. By the introduction of the "Bayerntakt" (Bavarian interval), transport on the DB AG's railway routes has been considerably improved, particularly at the weekend. Low-cost tariffs targeting certain groups which are offered by the public transport association additionally simplify switching between buses and trains. For passengers who use public transport daily the MobiCard or an annual season ticket have become indispensable companions. For day-trippers the special VGN-offer "TagesTicket Plus" (Day-Ticket-Plus) has proved to be very popular.

Satisfied Customers

First-rate proof that local public transport in the Nuremberg area is on the right path can be read from the ÖPNV-barometer, carried out each year by the TNS Emnid institute. Of all the public transport associations tested, the VGN as a rule came off best.

Visions

The conurbation area of Nuremberg, and indeed the entire metropolitan region, would be unimaginable without a blanketing local public transport system. Constant growth in individual motorised transport would influence the living quality of the population increasingly strongly. It is therefore essential that the suburban train network be completed. New suburban train routes to Ansbach, Neumarkt (Upper Palatinate) and to Forchheim with connections to Bamberg, as well as the extension of the S1 to Hartmannshof, are absolutely imperative for the ÖPNV (Public passenger traffic) as are the improvements to the corridors to Neustadt a. d. Aisch and Hersbruck (on the right bank of the Pegnitz). These stretches open up the core of the metropolitan region and are therefore indispensable for the development of our economic area. The Verkehrsverbund Großraum Nürnberg has, in the true sense of the word, set the points for the European metropolitan region of Nuremberg.

Standort in Europa
Business Location in Europe

Menschen brauchen Märkte

Bernd A. Diederichs

Das Messewesen in Deutschland ist mit dem legendären VW Käfer zu vergleichen: Es lief und lief und lief. Wie beim Käfer gilt jedoch auch hier: Eine lange Tradition sichert noch lange nicht die Zukunft. Und die Frage nach der Existenzberechtigung von Messen wird gerade in dieser Zeit immer lauter. Wenn sich heute fast alles im Wirtschaftsleben wandelt, kann das Messewesen nicht bleiben wie es ist. Der Messe- und Kongressplatz Nürnberg hat in den vergangenen Jahren deutlich von diesem Wandel profitiert und sich erfolgreich als Gastgeber hoch spezialisierter internationaler Fachmessen und Kongresse etabliert. Inzwischen kommt jeder dritte Aussteller und jeder fünfte Fachbesucher bei unseren Messen aus dem Ausland. Für eine Exportnation wie Deutschland ein überlebenswichtiger Faktor.

Heute sind die Messen in Nürnberg für zahlreiche globale Branchen wichtige Drehscheiben: Der Spiel-

The exhibition and trade fair sector in Germany can be compared with the legendary VW Beetle: It just kept on running. But the same applies here as with the Beetle: A long tradition by no means secures the future. And the question of exhibitions and trade fairs' rights to exist is at the moment getting increasingly loud. Today, when almost everything in business is undergoing change, then the exhibition and trade fair sector cannot remain as it is. Over the past few years Nuremberg, as an exhibition and congress centre, has clearly profited from this change, successfully establishing itself as host to highly specialised international trade fairs and congresses. In the meantime every third exhibitor and every fifth trade visitor to our trade fairs come from abroad. A vital factor for an exporting nation such as Germany.

Today, trade fairs and exhibitions in Nuremberg are an important turntable for countless global branches:

Das Asien-Pazifik-Forum Bayern im Messezentrum Nürnberg ist eine der hochkarätigsten Kontaktbörsen internationaler Wirtschaftsexperten.

The Asian-Pacific-Forum Bavaria in the Trade Fair Centre in Nuremberg is one of the best-rated contact exchanges for international economic experts.

People need Markets

Die Messebau Wörnlein GmbH ist eines der modernsten und größten Messebauunternehmen in Deutschland. Eng verknüpft mit dem stetigen Wachstum des Messestandortes Nürnberg, entwickelte sich Messebau Wörnlein zu einem kompetenten Partner, der von der Messestandsplanung bis zur Durchführung einer ganzen Veranstaltung das komplette Leistungsspektrum anbietet.

The Messebau Wörnlein GmbH is one of the most modern and largest exhibition stand construction firms in Germany. Closely linked with the steady growth of the Nuremberg trade fair location, Messebau Wörnlein has developed into a competent partner offering the entire range of services from planning the exhibition stands through to the execution of an event.

Information

Gründungsjahr: 1907
Mitarbeiter: 65
Leistungsspektrum:
– Entwurf und Planung
– System Standbau
– individueller Standbau
– Mietmöbel
– Digitaldruck und Schriften

Year founded: 1907
Employees: 65
Range of services:
– design and planning
– system stand construction
– individual stand construction
– furniture to rent
– digital printing and inscribing

☐
Messebau Wörnlein GmbH, Nürnberg

---

warenhersteller aus China blickt ebenso nach Nürnberg wie der Kaffeeproduzent aus Brasilien, der damit rechnen kann, auf der BioFach seine gesamte Jahresernte zu verkaufen. Der Hersteller von italienischen Natursteinbearbeitungsmaschinen reist alle zwei Jahre über den Brenner nach Nürnberg, um seine Produkte vorzustellen.

Insgesamt werden in Nürnberg inzwischen über 50 Messen und Kongresse, letztere häufig mit begleitender Ausstellung, durchgeführt. Zwei Drittel tragen das Prädikat „Internationale Fachmesse", darunter befinden sich sieben Weltleitmessen.

Dazu zwei Beispiele: Die Jagd- und Sportwaffen-Fachmesse IWA & OutdoorClassics ist selbstverständlich international aufgestellt. Immerhin exportieren die deutschen Hersteller von Jagd- und Sportwaffen über 90 Prozent ihrer Produkte. Gleichzeitig macht es genauso viel Sinn, die Verpackungs-Fachmesse FachPack überwiegend auf den deutschen Verpackungsmarkt auszurichten, den größten in Europa und den drittgrößten der Welt.

Wir sind auf dem Weg zur Informations- und Wissensgesellschaft. Es ist der Weg von der Hardware zur Software. Das heißt: Die Produkte werden immer

The toy manufacturer from China keeps one eye on Nuremberg as does the coffee producer from Brazil who can count on selling his entire annual harvest at the BioFach. The manufacturer of Italian natural stone processing machines travels over the Brenner to Nuremberg every second year to introduce his products.

In the meantime, a total of more than 50 trade fairs and congresses are held in Nuremberg, the latter frequently with accompanying exhibitions. Two thirds are rated as "International Trade Fairs"; amongst them are seven leading world fairs.

Here are just two examples: The Hunting and Sports Weapon Trade Fair IWA & OutdoorClassics are of course drawn up on an international basis. After all, German manufacturers of hunting and sports weapons export more than 90 percent of their products. At the same time it is just as sensible to direct the packing trade fair FachPack mainly towards the German packing market, the largest in Europe and the third largest in the world.

We are well on the way to becoming an information and scientific society. It is the route from hardware to software. Which means: Products will need more ex-

Standort in Europa
Business Location in Europe

Blick auf das Areal der NürnbergMesse

A glimpse of the grounds of the NürnbergMesse

erklärungsbedürftiger, komplexer und weniger anschaulich. Dieser Entwicklung tragen auch die Messen Rechnung, indem ergänzende Kongresse immer stärker das Zeigen und Vorführen übernehmen. Natürlich gibt es immer noch genügend Hardware zu erklären. Natürlich gibt es immer noch Weine, die man verkosten und Stoffe, die man fühlen muss. Aber auch Blue Tooth, SAP R3 und E-Procurement müssen dargestellt werden. Deswegen entstehen immer raffiniertere Mischungen von Messen, Kongressen, Workshops und Events.

Messen und Kongresse haben viel gemeinsam: Sie laden zum Wissensaustausch, zur Kommunikation und zur direkten persönlichen Begegnung ein. Nirgends sonst besteht die Möglichkeit, in kurzer Zeit eine derartige Konzentration an Fachleuten und Ideen zu nutzen. Beide profitieren von einem wohl überlegt eingeladenen Publikum, und beide besitzen eine Magnetfunktion für die umliegende Region. Nicht überraschend also, dass Messen und Kongresse immer mehr zusammenwachsen. Eine internationale Fachmesse im Technologiesektor ohne begleitenden Kongress? Heute kaum noch vorstellbar. Kongresse bieten Fachmessen einen deutlichen Mehrwert, indem

planation, they will become more and more complex and less clear. This development is also borne in mind by trade fairs in that their supplementary congresses are increasingly taking in presentations and demonstrations. Of course there is still more than enough hardware to be explained. Of course there are still wines to be tasted and materials to be felt. But a Blue Tooth, SAP R3 and e-procurement also need to be demonstrated. Which is why ingenious combinations of trade fairs, congresses, workshops and events are on the increase.

Fairs and congresses have much in common: They invite one to exchange knowledge, to communicate and to have direct personal encounters. Nowhere else can one find a similar opportunity of making use of such a concentration of specialists and ideas in such a short time. Both profit from a well-considered invited public, and both possess a magnet function for the surrounding region. It is therefore not surprising that fairs

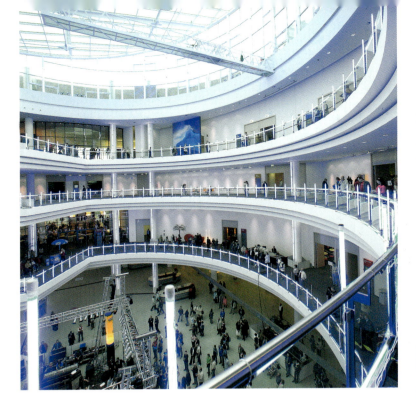

Das 2005 eröffnete CCN Ost in Nürnberg ist eines der modernsten Kongresszentren Europas.

The CCN Ost in Nuremberg opened in 2005 is one of Europe's most modern congress centres.

sie der Absatzplattform, dem gelenkten Zusammentreffen von Angebot und Nachfrage, eine wissenschaftliche Komponente beimischen. Spezialisten aus Forschung und Industrie begegnen sich – mit außerordentlich fruchtbaren Ergebnissen für beide Seiten.

Im Kongressmarkt liegt ein großes Wachstumspotenzial, das nach der Eröffnung des CCN Ost (CongressCenter Nürnberg) in der Metropolregion Nürnberg nun noch besser ausgeschöpft wird. Das derzeit modernste Kongresszentrum Europas bietet eine Kapazität von 3200 Sitzplätzen. Insgesamt stehen damit im Messezentrum Nürnberg über 11 000 Plätze für Kongresse zur Verfügung. Kongresse sind jedoch national wie international heiß umkämpfte Veranstaltungen. CCN, Congress- und Tourismuszentrale, Meistersingerhalle, Airport Nürnberg, die Kongresshotels sowie die Verkehrsbetriebe (VAG) haben sich unter der Führung des Wirtschaftsreferates der Stadt Nürnberg zu einer strategischen Allianz zusammengeschlossen, um eine einheitliche Positionierung des Messe- und Kongressstandorts Nürnberg zu dokumentieren. Dieses Ziel verfolgt in Nürnberg die übergreifende Kongressinitiative. Bislang überaus erfolgreich: Nürnberg ist auf dem Sprung, eine europäische Kongressmetropole zu werden.

Information

Mehr zu Messen und Kongressen in Nürnberg unter www.nuernbergmesse.de und www.congressing.de. Die NürnbergMesse ist Mitglied der Gemeinschaft Deutscher Großmessen (GDG e. V.). In der Rangliste der deutschen Messemacher liegt die NürnbergMesse heute auf Platz 7. Gemessen an Ausstellern, Besuchern und verfügbarer Fläche zählt die NürnbergMesse weltweit zu den 20 führenden Messeplätzen.

Information

More information on trade fairs and congresses in Nuremberg under www.nuernbergmesse.de and www.congressing.de. The NürnbergMesse is member of the Gemeinschaft Deutscher Großmessen (GDG e. V.). In the German trade fair makers' rankings, the NürnbergMesse is today at 7th place. Measured by exhibitors, visitors and available space, the NürnbergMesse is amongst the top 20 leading trade fair locations in the world.

and congresses are growing closer. An international trade fair in the technology sector without an accompanying congress? Almost inconceivable nowadays. Congresses offer trade fairs a clear added value in that they add a scientific component to the sales platform, that managed encounter of offer and demand. Specialists from research and industry meet – with exceptionally fertile results for both parties.

In the congress market lies an enormous growth potential which, following the opening of the CCN East (CongressCenter Nürnberg) in the metropolitan region of Nuremberg, can now be made full use of. At present Europe's most modern congress centre, it has a seating capacity of 3,200. There are therefore altogether more than 11,000 seats available for congresses in the Trade Fair Centre in Nuremberg. Congresses however, are hotly contested events both nationally and internationally. CCN, Congress- and Tourism centre, the Meistersinger Hall, the Nuremberg airport, the congress hotels as well as the transport services (VAG) have joined forces under the management of the Economic Section of the city of Nuremberg to form a strategic alliance to document the uniform positioning of Nuremberg's trade fair and congress location. This is the target set in Nuremberg by the overlapping congress initiative. To date, very successfully: Nuremberg is on the way to becoming a European congress metropolis.

Standort in Europa
Business Location in Europe

Spielend erfolgreich – die Spielwarenmesse Nürnberg

Ernst Kick

Spielen hat Tradition und Zukunft in der Metropolregion Nürnberg. Zahlreiche Spielwarenhersteller, Spielwarenhändler und die größte Spielwarenmesse weltweit machen Produktion von und Handel mit Spielwaren zu einem bedeutsamen Wirtschaftsfaktor für die Region. Zur „Spielwarenmesse International Toy Fair Nürnberg" treffen sich jährlich rund 2700 Aussteller aus 65 Ländern und über 75 000 Spielwarenfachbesucher in der Spielzeugstadt der Metropolregion. Keine andere Messe für Spielwaren bildet das internationale Angebot annähernd so kontinentsübergreifend und komplett ab wie die Fachmesse für Spielwaren, Hobby und Freizeitgestaltung in Franken.

1950 fand die erste Spielwarenmesse in Nürnberg statt. Schon zur Veranstaltung 1958 mischten sich unter die 830 Aussteller erstmals 60 internationale Unternehmen. Das beständige Wachstum der Spiel-

Games have a long tradition in the metropolitan region of Nuremberg. Countless toy manufacturers, toy dealers and the largest toy fair in the world make the production and trade with toys a significant economic factor for the region. Some 2,700 exhibitors from 65 countries and more than 75,000 visitors meet annually at the "Spielwarenmesse International Toy Fair Nürnberg" in the region's toy town. No other fair for toys forms an international assortment nearly so trans-continental and complete as the trade fair for toys, hobby and leisure in Franconia.

The first toy fair took place in Nuremberg in 1950, and already at the event in 1958 there were 60 international firms mingling amongst the 830 exhibitors. The steady growth of the toy fair led to the construction of the Nuremberg Messezentrum, where the toy fair first took place in 1973 with 1,560 exhibitors and

Die Spielwarenmesse International Toy Fair Nürnberg ist die größte Fachmesse für Spielwarenhersteller und -händler weltweit.

The International Toy Fair Nuremberg is the largest specialised fair for toy manufacturers and dealers in the world.

Playfully Successful – the Nuremberg Toy Fair

Mehr als 2700 Fachhändler aus 65 Ländern treffen sich jährlich auf der Spielwarenmesse in Nürnberg und zeigen die neuesten Trends.

More than 2,700 specialists from 65 countries meet annually on the Toy Fair in Nuremberg to show the latest trends.

warenmesse führte zum Bau des Nürnberger Messezentrums, auf dem 1973 erstmals die Spielwarenmesse mit 1560 Ausstellern und 25 480 Fachbesuchern stattfand. Der Ausbau des Geländes wird parallel zur Weiterentwicklung der Spielwarenmesse fortgesetzt und mit dem Bau der Halle 4A im Jahr 2007 vorläufig abgeschlossen. Damit sind die Weichen für eine Bestandssicherung des Messeprojektes gestellt.

Das vielseitige Sortiment der Spielwarenmesse bietet alles, was Spielwarenhändler brauchen, um die Wünsche ihrer Kunden erfüllen zu können: Modellbau, Modelleisenbahnen, Mechanisches und elektronisches Spielzeug, Puppen, Plüsch, Spiele, Bücher, Lernen und Experimentieren, Multimedia, Karneval, Fest- und Scherzartikel, Feuerwerk, Holzspielwaren und Kunsthandwerk, Basteln, Malen, Kreatives Gestalten, Outdoor und Freizeit. Die Fachhandelsmesse schafft Transparenz im weltweiten Spielwarenangebot und ist das optimale Forum für nationale und internationale Hersteller sowie für weltweite Fachhändler und Einkäufer.

Als Genossenschaft gegründet, übernimmt das Unternehmen Spielwarenmesse eG bis heute die Organisation der „Spielwarenmesse International Toy Fair Nürnberg". Die Geschäftsaktivitäten des Unternehmens, das Eigentum der Spielwarenhersteller ist, konzentrieren sich auf Messeveranstaltungen und Marketingdienstleistungen für die Spielwarenindustrie weltweit. Mit der Shanghai Toy Expo erschließt die Spielwarenmesse eG in Kooperation mit der China Toy

25,480 trade visitors. Extension of the grounds is being carried out parallel with the onward development of the toy fair and the construction of hall 4A in 2007 will, for the time being, bring it to conclusion. Thus the points have been set for the continuation of the Trade Fair project.

The wide assortment at the toy fair offers everything needed by toy dealers to be able to fulfil their customers' needs: model construction, model railways, mechanical and electronic toys, dolls, soft toys, games, books, learning and experimenting, multimedia, carnival, gags and tricks, fireworks, wooden toys and handicrafts, practising handicraft, painting, creative design, outdoor and leisure. The specialised trade fair creates transparency in the global toy assortment and is the optimal forum for national and international manufacturers as well as for traders and buyers from all over the world.

Founded as a cooperative, the undertaking Spielwarenmesse eG takes over the organisation of the "Spielwarenmesse International Toy Fair Nürnberg". The business activities of the undertaking, owned by the toy manufacturers, is concentrated on trade fair events and marketing services for the toy industry all over the world. With the Shanghai Toy Expo the Spielwarenmesse eG in cooperation with the China Toy Association has, since 2002, developed the increasingly important Chinese toy and toy fair market. On the domestic market too, the Spielwarenmesse eG probes for new sales opportunities for toy manufacturers. The

Standort in Europa
Business Location in Europe

Association seit 2002 den bedeutsam werdenden chinesischen Spielwaren- und Messemarkt. Auch im Inland sondiert die Spielwarenmesse eG neue Absatzmöglichkeiten für Spielwarenhersteller. Der Gemeinschaftsstand Spiele und Spielen auf der Frankfurter Buchmesse 2005 zum Beispiel bot Spielwarenherstellern den direkten Geschäftskontakt zu Buchhändlern und Grossisten, deren Interesse an Non-Book-Artikeln wächst.

Für die Metropolregion Nürnberg ist die Spielwarenmesse das Highlight der Unternehmensaktivitäten der Nürnberger Genossenschaft. Der Handel mit Holzspielwaren machte Nürnberg im 16. Jahrhundert bereits als Spielzeugstadt bekannt. Die Erfindung des Zinnsoldaten im 17. Jahrhundert und die Blechspielzeugproduktion ab 1850 schlugen international Wellen. Heute löst die Spielwarenmesse jährlich eine Woge der Medienberichterstattung aus und zieht Menschen aus über 100 Ländern in die Region. Die Messegäste sorgen für einen Umsatzzuwachs bei Hotellerie, Gastronomie, Handel, Standbau, Service-Dienstleistern, NürnbergMesse, Regionalverkehr und Taxiunternehmen. Die Weiterentwicklung der Spielwarenmesse, entsprechend den Bedürfnissen der Händler und Einkäufer, wird auch in Zukunft Spielwarenprofis aus aller Welt jährlich in die Metropolregion Nürnberg führen. Mit dieser wirtschaftlichen Dynamik zählt die Spielwarenmesse zu einem der wichtigen Wirtschaftsfaktoren der Metropolregion.

Auch Hersteller aus der Region sind auf der Spielwarenmesse vertreten.

Manufacturers from the region are also represented on the Toy Fair.

common stand Spiele und Spielen at the Frankfurter Buchmesse 2005 for example offered toy manufacturers a direct business contact to book dealers and wholesalers whose interest in non-book articles is on the increase.

For the metropolitan region of Nuremberg the toy fair is the highlight of the activities of the Nuremberg cooperative. The trade in wooden toys established Nuremberg's reputation as toy city as early as the 16th century. The invention of the tin soldier in the 17th century and the production of tin toys from 1850 onwards created an international stir. Nowadays the toy fair releases a surge of media reports every year, drawing people from more than 100 countries into the region. The trade fair visitors also provide growth in turnover in the hotel sector, catering, trade, stand construction, service suppliers, NürnbergMesse, regional transport and taxi companies. The further development of the toy fair, according to dealers' and buyers' demands, will continue to draw toy professionals every year into the metropolitan region of Nuremberg from all over the world. With such a dynamic economic force, the toy fair counts as one of the most significant economic factors of the metropolitan region.

Umbruch als Chance? Neue Gewerbe-, Wohn- und Büroflächen im Fokus

Gerhard Schmelzer

Ab der Mitte des 19. Jahrhunderts entwickelte sich die Region um Nürnberg zum industriellen Zentrum Bayerns. Die vorherrschenden Branchen damals waren Metallverarbeitung, Maschinenbau und später die Elektrotechnik. Mit dem wirtschaftlichen Aufschwung ging ein starkes Bevölkerungswachstum einher. Bis zu Beginn der siebziger Jahre des 20. Jahrhunderts dominierte Nürnberg als zweitgrößte Stadt Bayerns vor München die industrielle Produktion des Freistaats.

Der Umbruch von der Industriegesellschaft zur Dienstleistungs- und Informationsgesellschaft traf Nürnberg verstärkt ab Mitte der achtziger Jahre – später als viele andere traditionelle deutsche Industrieregionen. Die jahrzehntelange Prägung Nürnbergs durch den sekundären Sektor verlor nun rapide und schmerzhaft an Bedeutung, verbunden mit dem Niedergang einst großer Namen der Region wie Triumph-Adler, GRUNDIG, Philips PKI oder jüngst AEG Hausgeräte.

Doch mit dem Strukturwandel wurden plötzlich große Entwicklungsflächen einer neuen Art freigesetzt: zentral gelegen, erschlossen und bebaut mit Zeugnissen der Industriearchitektur („Revitalisierungsflächen"). Ab 1990 wurden diese Flächenpotenziale durch freiwerdende militärische Nutzflächen („Konversionsflächen") insbesondere in Fürth, aber auch Erlangen und Nürnberg, noch erweitert.

Wo liegen nun die Chancen dieses Strukturwandels für die Bereitstellung neuer Gewerbe- und Büroflächen?

Zum einen geht mit steigender Bedeutung des tertiären Sektors ein allgemeiner Paradigmenwechsel mit neuen Nutzeranforderungen einher, von dem auch Nürnberg und seine Region profitieren können. Arbeitsraum wird heute zunehmend als Lebensraum gesehen. Individualität, Flexibilität und die architektonische Verbindung von Tradition und Modernität

The region around Nuremberg developed into Bavaria's industrial centre from the middle of the 19th century onwards. The predominant branches at that time were metal processing, mechanical engineering and, somewhat later, electrical engineering. The economic growth was accompanied by a strong population explosion. Up to the beginning of the seventies of the 20th century Nuremberg, as the second largest city in Bavaria and before Munich, controlled the Free State's industrial production.

The change from industrial society to service and information society affected Nuremberg more strongly from the middle of the eighties – much later than many other traditional German industrial regions. The decade-long impression on Nuremberg left by the secondary sector began rapidly and painfully to lose meaning, doubtlessly linked to the decline of once important names in the region such as Triumph-Adler, GRUNDIG, Philips PKI or later AEG domestic appliances.

However, the structural change abruptly caused the release of massive development areas of a new type: centrally situated, fully developed and already built upon with witnesses of industrial architecture ("revitalised areas"). From 1990 onwards, this potential was added to by utilisable military space becoming free ("conversion areas") in Erlangen and Nuremberg and especially in Fürth.

But exactly where are the opportunities which have been provided by the structural change and how can they be utilized for providing new commercial and office premises?

On the one hand with the tertiary sector increasing in importance there is a general change in the paradigms accompanying new consumer requirements, from which Nuremberg and its region could profit. Today, working space is increasingly considered as living space. Individuality, flexibility and the architec-

Radical Change as Opportunity? Focus on New Commercial, Living and Office Premises

Standort in Europa
Business Location in Europe

Das Auto- und Motorradmuseum „Dauphin Speed Event" in Hersbruck hat eine ehemalige Industriehalle in einen exklusiven Veranstaltungsort verwandelt.

The car and motorbike museum "Dauphin Speed Event" in Hersbruck has transformed a former industrial hall into an exclusive event location.

Für Liebhaber ein Augenschmaus: Die Oldtimer-Ausstellung der Familie Dauphin

A feast for the eyes: the old-timer exhibition of the Dauphin family

Wohnen, Leben, Arbeiten und Zukunft sind die Schlüsselwörter der täglichen Arbeit der alpha Gruppe. Mit innovativen Immobilienkonzepten schafft und organisiert das Unternehmen seit 1979 individuelle Lebensräume. Neben der Projektierung und Umsetzung hat für die alpha Gruppe vor allem die Erhaltung und Weiterentwicklung einmal entstandener Strukturen eine große Bedeutung. Zu den beispielhaften Objekten gehören u. a. das Mittelstandszentrum TA – ein Revitalisierungsprojekt auf dem ehemaligen Triumph-Adler-Gelände – wo bis heute rund 80 000 Quadratmeter moderne Büro- und Dienstleistungsflächen entstanden sind, sowie das Projekt Sebalder Höfe. Auf dem ehemaligen Druckereigelände im Herzen Nürnbergs entsteht ein attraktiver Standort zum Wohnen und Arbeiten in der Altstadt. Das städtebauliche Konzept sieht vor, das Viertel mit Gespür für die Altstadt und für die Bedürfnisse der heutigen Zeit zu gestalten.

Wohnen und Arbeiten in den Sebalder Höfen

Living and working in the Sebalder Höfe

Mittelstandszentrum TA

Mittelstandszentrum TA

Living, working and future are the key words frequently found in the daily work of the alpha Gruppe. Since 1979 the undertaking has managed and organised individual living space using innovative property concepts.
For the alpha Gruppe, the maintenance and further development of already existing structures is of utmost importance, in addition to drawing up plans and their implementation. Amongst the exemplary objects are the Mittelstandszentrum TA – a revitalising project on the former Triumph-Adler grounds – where some 80,000 square metres of modern offices and services area have been created to date, as well as the Sebalder Höfe project. An attractive location for living and working is in process of being built in the old town on the site of the former printery in the centre of Nuremberg. According to the urban development concept, the district is to be laid out with a feeling for the old town taking into consideration the needs of present-day life.

Information

Gründungsjahr: 1979

Mitarbeiter: ca. 40

Leistungsspektrum:
- Entwicklung für Wohn- und Gewerbeimmobilien
- Immobilienverkauf und -vermietung
- Property Management
- Hausverwaltung nach WEG
- Facility Management
- Consulting

Year founded: 1979

Employees: about 40

Range of services:
- development of residential and commercial properties
- property sales and rental
- property management
- management of residential blocks in accordance with WEG (tenant owner regulations)
- facility management
- consulting

☐
alpha Gruppe
Nürnberg

gewinnen bei den Ansprüchen der Gewerbeflächen Suchenden spürbar an Bedeutung. Dieser Trend begünstigt die Durchmischung von Wohn- und Büroflächen, was an zahlreichen neueren Immobilienentwicklungsvorhaben unter dem Schlagwort „Wohnen und Arbeiten" sichtbar wird.

Zum anderen begünstigen objektive wirtschaftliche Grundlagen das „Redevelopment" von Brachflächen. Die vergleichsweise niedrigen Bodenpreise in Nürnberg spiegeln die niedrigen erzielbaren Neubaumieten wider, deren Abstand zu den Bestandsmieten nur gering ist.

Der gefühlvoll revitalisierte Altbau hat demnach sogar die Chance, eine höhere Rendite zu erzielen als ein Neubau. Zumal die architektonische Großzügigkeit und Extravaganz (Stichwort „Loftbüros") in der Bestandssanierung quasi ohne Mehrpreis darstellbar ist und eine zusätzliche Attraktivität am Markt schafft.

Viele Revitalisierungsprojekte dieser neuen Art wie zum Beispiel das Mittelstandszentrum TA (vormals Triumph-Adler), das Deutschherrnkarrée (vormals Sandoz), das Nürbanum (ehemals PKI/TeKaDe) oder die in der Entwicklung befindliche Uferstadt in Fürth (ehemals GRUNDIG) bilden heute gewerbliche Nutzeranforderungen zeitgemäß ab und behaupten sich erfolgreich am Markt. Sogar erste themenbezogene Revitalisierungen als Beispiel extremer Nutzerdifferenzierung werden in Nürnberg sichtbar, wie das Ofenwerk – ehemals Riedhammer Ofenbau – als „Zentrum für mobile Klassik" (für historische Automobile) zeigt.

Die Flächenressourcen der Region werden weiterhin auf Jahre von einem vielfältigen Potenzial innerstädtischer „Redevelopments" geprägt sein, wie die zum Teil bereits laufenden Entwicklungen der Brachen Cebal, Hercules, GRUNDIG-Langwasser oder des Milchhofs in Nürnberg zeigen. Ein Beispiel für die kommenden Herausforderungen ist das Projekt Sebalder Höfe am östlichen Stadteingang der Nürnberger Altstadt. Diesem liegt das Konzept einer zeitgemäßen Verbindung von Wohnen und Gewerbe und der architektonischen Verschmelzung von Tradition und Moderne zugrunde. Der Weg in die Zukunft moderner Gewerbeimmobilien weist in diese Richtung.

tonic combination of tradition and modernity are noticeably gaining importance in the requirements of commercial premises seekers. This trend favours the mixing of living and office space and becomes obvious when one reads the catchphrase "living and working" applied to countless newer property development plans.

On the other hand, objects of a commercial basis benefit from the "redevelopment" of fallow land. The relatively low price of ground in Nuremberg reflects the low achievable rents for new buildings, the difference to existing rents being very small.

The sensitively revitalised old building therefore has a chance of achieving an even higher return than a new one. Particularly as, in the reorganisation of stocks, the architectural generosity and extravagance (slogan "loft offices") can almost be portrayed without having to increase the price which, and in turn, adds to the attraction for the market.

Many revitalisation projects of this new type such as the medium-sized centre TA (formerly Triumph-Adler), the Deutschherrnkarrée (formerly Sandoz), the Nürbanum (formerly PKI/TeKaDe) or the river bank area in Fürth which is currently undergoing development (formerly GRUNDIG) today depict commercial user demands in modern design and assert themselves very successfully on the market. Even the first "theme" revitalisations, as examples of extreme differences in consumer demands, are visible in Nuremberg, as for example the furnace works – formerly Riedhammer Ofenbau – as the "Centre of mobile classic (old-timers)" (for historical cars) demonstrates.

The land resources of the region will continue for many years to be characterised by a manifold potential of inner-city "redevelopments" such as the partially running developments of the fallows Cebal, Hercules, GRUNDIG-Langwasser or the Milchhof in Nuremberg. One example of challenges to be awaited is the Sebalder Höfe project at the easterly entrance to the old Nuremberg city. This has taken the concept of a contemporary combination of residence and commerce and the architectural melting of tradition and modernity as a basis. The route into the future of modern commercial property points in this direction.

Der SÜD-WEST-PARK Nürnberg ist ein moderner Businesspark in Nürnberg-Gebersdorf – ein paar Autominuten vom Messegelände entfernt –, der 190 000 Quadratmeter an modernen Büro- und Serviceflächen bereitstellt.

Bei variierenden Gebäudetiefen können sowohl Einzelbüros als auch moderne Team-Varianten oder Call-Center effizient zugeschnitten werden. Empfangs-, Ausstellungs-, Verkaufs- und Dispositionszonen lassen sich nahtlos mit Verwaltungsflächen kombinieren. Bei der Ausstattung reicht der Spielraum vom „veredelten Rohbau" über robuste Flächen (Rampen, Deckenlast, Aufzüge etc.) bis hin zum schlüsselfertigen Headquarter. Diese Flexibilität und dichte Glasfasernetze haben den SÜD-WEST-PARK zu einem Zentrum der Informations- und Kommunikationstechnik in Bayern gemacht. Dazu zählen etwa die Bereiche Fortbildung/Tagung oder der MediPark, ein medizinisches Netzwerk mit abgestimmten Fachrichtungen und einer ambulanten OP-Klinik, das derzeit integriert wird.

The SÜD-WEST-PARK Nuremberg is a modern business park in Nuremberg-Gebersdorf – just a few minutes by car from the exhibition grounds – providing 190,000 square metres of modern office and services areas. With varying building depths, the needs of single offices as well as modern team variations or call centres can be efficiently dealt with. Zones for reception, exhibition, sales and planning can be seamlessly combined with administrative areas. The range of fittings reaches from "refined raw building" via rugged areas (ramps, floor loading, lifts, etc.) through to turn-key headquarters. This flexibility and the dense glass fibre networks have turned the SÜD-WEST-PARK into a centre of information and communication technology for Bavaria. The sectors of training/conferences and the MediPark, a medical network with balanced subject areas and a day OP clinic which is being integrated at the moment, can also be added to these features.

Information

Grundsteinlegung: 1990

Mieter: ca. 230 Unternehmen

Mitarbeiter: ca. 6000

Angebotsspektrum:
- flexible Mieteinheiten ab 100 m²
- individuelle Ausbauberatung
- gute Verkehrsanbindung und 4000 Parkplätze
- aktives Management und Serviceteams vor Ort
- integrierte Aus- und Fortbildungsinstitute
- Hotel, Tagungscenter, Forum, Gastronomie-Angebote
- Einkaufs- und Fitness-Möglichkeiten
- angenehmes Umfeld mit viel Grün

Laying of the foundation-stone: 1990

Tenants: about 230 firms

Employees: about 6,000

Range supplied:
- flexible rental units from 100 m²
- individual counselling regarding fittings
- good traffic links and 4,000 parking spaces
- active management and service teams on location
- integrated education and advanced training institutes
- hotel, conference centre, forum, catering
- shopping and fitness training possibilities
- pleasant environment with plenty of greenery

SÜD-WEST-PARK Management GmbH Nürnberg

Soziales mit Rendite – familienfreundliche Personalpolitik

Renate Schmidt

Bereits Mitte der achtziger Jahre sollte ich bei einem Seminar über Frauenförderung im Betrieb reden, und zwar vor Führungskräften der deutschen Wirtschaft. Fünfunddreißig von ihnen saßen da in Hufeisenform, alphabetisch sortiert.

Ich wollte das Ganze ein bisschen lockerer angehen, bin außerdem der Meinung, dass Frauen jetzt genug gefördert sind, genügend qualifiziert und genügend berufsorientiert. Die beste Frauenförderung ist die Emanzipation des Mannes, sein Vatersein wirklich anzunehmen. Das wollte ich mit einem fiktiven Einstellungsgespräch des Jahres 2000 darstellen und begann:

„Stellen Sie sich vor: Ein Großunternehmen, die Personalchefin, nennen wir sie der Einfachheit halber Schmidt, sitzt dem Bewerber für eine gehobene Führungsposition, nennen wir ihn Herrn Dr. Zeitz, verheiratet, drei Kinder, 37 Jahre alt, gegenüber.

Frau Schmidt blättert in den Unterlagen und sagt: ‚Also, Herr Dr. Zeitz, Sie haben ja ganz ausgezeichnete Qualifikationen. Nur eines finde ich nicht, Sie sind doch verheiratet und haben drei Kinder?'

Dr. Zeitz: ‚Ja.'

Frau Schmidt: ‚Dann habe ich es wahrscheinlich überblättert. Sagen Sie, wann haben Sie Ihre Erwerbstätigkeit wegen der Kinder unterbrochen, waren teilzeitbeschäftigt oder haben Elternzeit in Anspruch genommen?'

Herr Dr. Zeitz merkt, worauf das hinausläuft, wird trotz seines Selbstbewusstseins verlegen, kommt sogar ein bisschen ins Stottern und sagt: ‚Meine Frau, also ich und meine Frau haben beschlossen, dass diese Aufgabe meine Frau übernimmt.'

Daraufhin klappt die Personalchefin Schmidt bedauernd die Bewerbungsunterlagen zu und sagt: ‚Dann kommen Sie für eine Führungsposition in unserem Hause leider nicht infrage. Wir legen Wert darauf, dass unsere Führungskräfte, soweit sie Kinder haben, die Kompetenzen, die man in der Familien-

As early as the middle of the eighties I was asked to speak at a seminar on women's promotion at work, namely to an audience composed of leaders of German industry. Thirty-five of them sat there in horseshoe form, in alphabetical order.

I wanted to approach the whole thing in a more relaxed manner and besides it is my opinion that women receive enough support, are sufficiently qualified and professionally well oriented. The best support for women is the emancipation of the man so that he really takes on his role as father. This is what I wanted to portray with a fictitious interview from the year 2000 and so I began:

"Just imagine: A big concern, the personnel manageress, for the sake of simplicity we shall call her Schmidt, sits opposite an applicant for a senior management position, let's call him Dr Zeitz, married, three children, 37 years old.

Mrs Schmidt leafs through the documents and says: 'Well, Dr Zeitz, you have excellent qualifications. There is only one thing I can't find. You are married and have three children?'

Dr Zeitz: 'Yes.'

Mrs Schmidt: 'Then I have probably missed it. Tell me, when did you interrupt your career because of the children, were you employed part time or when did you take parents' leave because you had become a father?'

Dr Zeitz notices in which direction the discussion was heading and, in spite of his self-confidence, becomes embarrassed. He even starts to stutter a little and says: 'My wife, well, I and my wife decided that she should take over the job.'

Mrs Schmidt, the personnel manageress, then regretfully closes the application file and says: 'I am afraid then that there is no question of your being offered a position in our management. We consider it important that our managers, inasmuch as they have children, themselves actually gain the competence which can only be gained in family work.'"

Social Services with a Yield – Family-friendly Personnel Policy

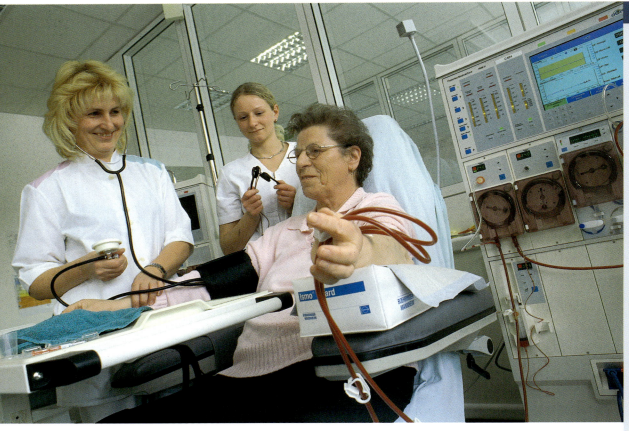

Die DTZ Dialyse Trainings-Zentren ist eine gemeinnützige Gesellschaft zur Förderung des Gesundheitswesens und der Altenhilfe durch den Betrieb von Dialyseeinrichtungen, insbesondere von ambulanten Dialysezentren. Derzeit bietet die DTZ in Deutschland und Österreich rund 30 Einrichtungen zum Einsatz von Nierenersatztherapien.
Ziel der Gesellschaft ist es, den Patienten unter ärztlicher Aufsicht auf die Selbstdialyse (Heim- und Limited-Care-Dialyse) vorzubereiten bzw. die notwendigen Dialyseverfahren sicherzustellen. Dabei setzt die DTZ auf eine enge Zusammenarbeit mit Universitätskliniken, allgemeinen Krankenhäusern und niedergelassenen Ärzten sowie einer Kooperation mit den Krankenkassen und anderen Kostenträgern.

The DTZ Dialyse Training-Centres is a charitable institution for the promotion of the health sector and geriatric welfare by operating dialysis installations, especially out-patient dialysis centres.

At the moment the DTZ maintains some 30 institutions in Germany and Austria set up for kidney replacement therapies. It is the target of the institution to prepare patients, under medical supervision, for self-dialysis (home and limited-care-dialysis) and/or to guarantee the necessary dialysis processes. The DTZ relies on close cooperation with university clinics, general hospitals and general practitioners to complete their tasks as well as cooperating with medical insurance companies and other cost bearers.

Information

Gründungsjahr: 1971; seit 1990 Firmierung als gGmbH

Leistungsspektrum:
- je nach Indikation: Zentrums-Dialyse, Limited-Care-Dialyse (LC), Heim-Dialyse, Trainings-Dialyse, Peritonial-Dialyse, Aphereseverfahren
- Bereitstellung von Räumlichkeiten und notwendigen Ausstattungen
- Wartung und Reparatur aller Anlagen
- Betreuung durch ausgebildetes Pflegepersonal
- Organisation und Überwachung des pflegerischen und technischen Bereitschaftsdienstes
- Abrechnung der erbrachten Leistungen

Year founded: 1971; since 1990 trading under the name of gGmbH

Range of services:
- according to symptoms: centre-dialysis, limited-care-dialysis (LC), home-dialysis, training-dialysis, peritoneal-dialysis, aphaeresis process
- preparation of rooms and their fitting-out
- maintenance and repair of all plant
- care by well-trained nursing personnel
- organisation and supervision of care and technical emergency services
- calculation and invoicing of the services rendered

☐
DTZ Dialyse Trainings-Zentren gGmbH
Nürnberg

arbeit erwerben kann, auch tatsächlich selbst erwerben.'"

Anhand dieser kleinen Anekdote wird deutlich, was heute leider noch immer nach Zukunftsmusik klingt. Personalchefs müssen nach und nach erkennen, dass die Motivation der Mitarbeiter und Mitarbeiterinnen und das Leistungsvermögen für den Betrieb eng mit ihrem Familienleben im Zusammenhang steht. Mitarbeiter und Mitarbeiterinnen mit Familien stehen vor doppelten Herausforderungen: Das berufliche Leben mit dem der Familien zu vereinbaren ist eine existenzielle Aufgabe.

Information

Franconian International School, Herzogenaurach

Fakten
- Im Schuljahr 2005/06 ca. 220 Kinder vom Kindergarten bis zur 9. Klasse
- Sukzessiver Ausbau der High School mit Jahrgangsstufe 12, 2008/09 abgeschlossen; Internationale Baccalaureate als Abschluss; Zugangsberechtigung für Universitäten weltweit (inkl. Deutschland)
- Schüler aus ca. 20 Nationen; in erster Linie Kinder von Expats, die für international tätige Firmen in die Region kommen. Auch deutsche Kinder, deren Eltern an einer Alternative zum öffentlichen Schulsystem interessiert sind, werden aufgenommen.
- Internationaler Lehrplan, der auf die Bedürfnisse „global" aufwachsender Kinder abgestimmt ist
- Unterrichtssprache Englisch
- Fokus auf Lerntechniken, Lernen im Team, Präsentationsfähigkeiten, Projektarbeit
- Baubeginn eines eigenen Schulgebäudes für 500 bis 600 Schüler im Röthelheimpark in Erlangen im Jan./Feb. 2007; Fertigstellung 2008

http://fis.ecis.org

Vätern und Müttern muss die notwendige Zeit für ihre Kinder eingeräumt werden. Zum Abholen vom Kindergarten, für den Arztbesuch oder auch dadurch, was viele Firmen in der Region bereits praktizieren: durch eine Kinderkrippe, für die sich auch mehrere Firmen zusammenschließen können. Ein Unternehmen, das einen Personalchef hat, der sich dieses Spannungsfeldes bewusst ist, kann sich so klare betriebswirtschaftliche Vorteile schaffen.

Mitarbeiter, die sich nicht darum kümmern müssen, was abends für Familie und Kinder gekocht wer-

This small anecdote clearly demonstrates that which is unfortunately still a long way off. Personnel managers must come to realise that employees' motivation and capability concerning work are closely related to their family life. Employees with families are faced with double challenges: Making professional life compatible with the family is an existential task.

Fathers and mothers must be given the time necessary for their children. For picking them up from nursery school, for a visit to the doctor or even, as is already practiced by many firms in the region: by a day-nursery for which even several firms may combine to maintain. Any undertaking having a personnel manager who is aware of this area of tension can create clear economic advantages for itself.

Employees who do not need to worry about what should be cooked for the family in the evening because they can take food for the family from the canteen will be able to concentrate more on their work, bringing better results at their workplace.

It is difficult to specifically express the advantages which a family-friendly personnel policy brings. A feasibility study by Prognos AG carried out on behalf of the Bundesfamilienministerium (Federal Ministry for Families) examined the concrete saving potential in various concerns spread over the entire federal territory with quite different numbers of employees (between 150 and 13,000 employees) – with amazing results: The study "The Economic Effects of Family-friendly Measures" revealed that even in medium-sized undertakings the saving potential achieved by introducing family-friendly measures was in the magnitude of several hundred thousand Euro.

The first example for savings in costs is the fluctuation cost. When one parent – unfortunately this is still usually the mother – takes time off because they are a new parent, this means for the concern, that they have to either look for a temporary replacement for the duration of the "maternity leave", bringing acquisition and qualification costs for the new employee with it, or the position is held vacant – when other colleagues must take over their tasks placing an enormous extra burden on them as well as overtime. Using soft transitional arrangements, part-time work and flexible care services the fluctuation costs can be clearly minimised.

The second example is the cost of re-entry. Parents who return to work after their parent leave must once again become accustomed to the changes within the firm. A renewed training period will be necessary. Estimates say that returning to work after the three-year

den soll, weil man aus der Betriebskantine das Abendessen für die Familie mitnehmen kann, werden sich ihrer Arbeit konzentrierter widmen können und an ihren Arbeitsplätzen bessere Leistungen bringen.

Die Vorteile, die eine familienfreundliche Personalpolitik mit sich bringt, sind nur schwer konkret auszudrücken. Eine Studie der Prognos AG im Auftrag des Bundesfamilienministeriums hat bei verschiedenen Unternehmen im gesamten Bundesgebiet mit ganz unterschiedlichen Mitarbeiterzahlen (zwischen 150 und 13 000 Beschäftigte) die konkreten Einsparpotenziale untersucht – mit erstaunlichen Ergebnissen: Die Studie „Betriebswirtschaftliche Effekte familienfreundlicher Maßnahmen" ergab selbst bei mittelständischen Unternehmen Einsparpotenziale bei der Einführung familienfreundlicher Maßnahmen in einer Größenordnung von mehreren hunderttausend Euro.

Als erstes Beispiel für Kostenersparnis lassen sich die Fluktuationskosten nennen. Wenn ein Elternteil – es ist ja leider meist immer noch die Mutter – in die Elternzeit geht, bedeutet dies für den Betrieb, dass er entweder für die Dauer der Elternzeit einen befristeten Ersatz suchen muss, was Akquise- und Qualifizierungskosten für neue Mitarbeiter mit sich bringt, oder die Stelle vakant lässt – hier müssen dann andere Mitarbeiter die Aufgaben wahrnehmen und haben damit enorme Mehrbelastungen und Überstunden. Durch weiche Übergangsregelungen, Teilzeitarbeit und flexible Betreuungsangebote lassen sich die Fluktuationskosten deutlich minimieren.

Als zweites Beispiel sind die Wiedereinstiegskosten zu nennen. Eltern, die nach der Elternzeit in den Betrieb zurückkehren, müssen sich erst wieder an die Veränderungen innerhalb des Betriebes gewöhnen. Eine neuerliche Einarbeitungsphase wird nötig. Schätzungen gehen davon aus, dass ein Wiedereinstieg nach der dreijährigen Elternzeit immerhin 75 Prozent der Kosten einer Neueinstellung verursacht. Bei einem Wiedereinstieg nach nur einem halben Jahr fallen lediglich 15 Prozent der Kosten an. Ein triftiges Argument also, die Rahmenbedingungen für ein Miteinander von Familie und Beruf zu verbessern.

Zum Dritten sind noch die Kosten für Fehlzeiten zu nennen. Bei der Krankheit eines Kindes, das sonst in einer Tagesbetreuungseinrichtung untergebracht ist, muss der Vater oder die Mutter zu Hause bleiben, um das kranke Kind zu betreuen. Bei flexiblen Arbeitszeitmodellen oder bei Teleheimarbeitsplätzen fallen diese Fehlzeiten erst gar nicht an.

All diese Kosten sind zwar schwer zu beziffern, las-

Information

Franconian International School, Herzogenaurach

Facts
- in the school year 2005/06 about 220 children from nursery school up to the 9th year
- successive extension of the High School finishing with 12th year 2008/09; International Baccalaureate as finals; qualifies for entrance in worldwide universities (incl. Germany)
- students from about 20 nations, primarily children of expats, who are employed in the region by international firms. Also German children whose parents are interested in alternatives to the public school system are accepted.
- international curriculum tailored to meet the needs of children growing up "globally"
- lessons are taught in English
- focus on learning techniques, learning in a team, presentation ability, project work
- start of construction on their own school building for 500 to 600 schoolchildren in the Röthelheimpark in Erlangen in Jan./Feb. 2007; completion 2008

http://fis.ecis.org

parent leave creates costs amounting to almost 75 percent of the costs of a new employee. By returning to work after only half a year, only 15 percent of the costs are incurred. A convincing argument for improving frame conditions for combining career and family.

As a third example, the cost of absences should be given. When a child, who is usually in a day-care institution, becomes sick, then the father or the mother must stay at home to look after the child. With flexible working hour models or when work can be done at home these absence costs no longer arise.

All these costs are difficult to estimate, but they are easy to avoid by using family-friendly personnel policies at the same time increasing employee satisfaction with their employer.

Concrete family-policy measures are many and varied. Many concerns in the metropolitan region of Nuremberg also have committed themselves to a family-friendly personnel policy. The measures which can be taken are widespread: From company-owned childcare via financial support for the costs of childcare or concrete assistance in the mediation of childminders – these are all assistance measures supporting mothers

Standort in Europa
Business Location in Europe

Die Franconian International School in Herzogenaurach besuchen derzeit rund 220 Schülerinnen und Schüler aus mehr als 20 Nationen.

Some 220 students from more than 20 nations are currently attending the Franconian International School in Herzogenaurach.

sen sich aber durch familienfreundliche Personalpolitik leicht vermeiden und steigern damit gleichzeitig die Zufriedenheit der Mitarbeiter mit ihrem Betrieb.

Konkrete familienpolitische Maßnahmen sind vielfältig. Auch in der Metropolregion Nürnberg haben sich zahlreiche Unternehmen einer familienfreundlichen Personalpolitik verpflichtet. Die Maßnahmen sind breit gefächert: Von betriebseigener Kinderbetreuung über finanzielle Förderung der Kinderbetreuungskosten oder der konkreten Hilfe bei der Vermittlung von Tagesmüttern – dies sind alles Hilfestellungen, die Mütter und Väter dabei unterstützen, Familie und Beruf besser zu vereinbaren.

Eine familienfreundliche Personalpolitik spart nicht nur Kosten und verbessert die Wettbewerbssituation des Unternehmens, sie sorgt auch für zufriedenere Mitarbeiterinnen und Mitarbeiter – also eine echte Win-Win-Situation.

and fathers in their efforts to better coordinate family and job.

A family-friendly personnel policy not only saves costs and improves the company's competitiveness, it also results in more satisfied employees – a truly win-win situation.

Von Menschen für Menschen – vielfältige soziale Dienstleistungen

Otto Kreß

In allen Bereichen des Lebens bietet die Metropolregion Nürnberg ihren Bürgerinnen und Bürgern ein dichtes Netz an sozialen Dienstleistungen. Diese unterstützen und sichern das gesellschaftliche Zusammenleben und wirtschaftliche Handeln. Obwohl die sozialen Dienste so wichtig sind, werden sie in der Öffentlichkeit kaum wahrgenommen, da diese Leistungen in der Regel unauffällig erbracht werden. Dabei zählen zum Beispiel die Wohlfahrtsverbände zu den größten Arbeitgebern in der Bundesrepublik und ebenso in der Metropolregion Nürnberg.

Die Geschichte „sozialer Dienstleistungen" beginnt bereits im frühen Mittelalter mit privaten Stiftungen wohlbetuchter Bürger. Als Beispiele können hier das Heilig-Geist-Spital im 14. Jahrhundert in Nürnberg, die Caritas-Pirckheimer-Stiftung und die Gustav-Schickedanz-Stiftung im 20. Jahrhundert oder aktuell die Dr. Hans und Elisabeth Birkner-Stiftung genannt werden. Neben diesen Privatpersonen gab und gibt es Bürger, deren Wirken zur Gründung von Wohlfahrtsorganisationen führte. In dieser Tradition stehen Wilhelm Löhe mit der Diakonie Neuendettelsau, die Rummelsberger Anstalten, die Stadtmission und andere Einrichtungen. Hinzu kommen die jeweiligen Kreisverbände überregionaler Organisationen wie das Rote Kreuz, das 1886 in Nürnberg eine eigenständige Organisation mit heute über 900 ehrenamtlichen und 450 hauptamtlichen Mitarbeitern aufbaute. Außerdem sind die Arbeiterwohlfahrt (AWO), die Caritas, die Diakonie (DW) und der Paritätische Wohlfahrtsverband (DPWV) zu nennen.

Alle diese Einrichtungen bieten vielfältige Dienstleistungen im sozialen Bereich an. Das Spektrum umfasst nahezu alle Lebensbereiche und reicht von der Geburtsvorbereitung bis zur Sterbebegleitung. Dabei wurden und werden stets die Herausforderungen der jeweiligen Zeit aufgegriffen und hierfür Lösungen angeboten. Aktuell ist hier das Entstehen von Kinderkrippen in der Region zu nennen, um Beruf und Familie in Einklang bringen zu können. Unterstützt

The metropolitan region of Nuremberg offers its citizens a dense network of social services covering all areas of life. These services support and safeguard them in social cohabitation as well as in business matters. Although the social services are very important, they are usually so unobtrusively supplied that they are hardly perceived by the public even though some charitable institutions for instance count amongst the largest employers in the Federal Republic and also in the metropolitan region of Nuremberg.

The history of "social services" began already in the early middle ages with private foundations set up by wealthy citizens. As examples we could mention the Holy Ghost Hospital in the 14th century in Nuremberg, the Caritas-Pirckheimer-Foundation and the Gustav-Schickedanz-Foundation in the 20th century and the current Dr. Hans and Elisabeth Birkner-Foundation. Alongside these private persons, there were, and still are, citizens whose works led to the foundation of charitable institutions. Following this tradition is Wilhelm Löhe with the Diakonie (social welfare organisation) in Neuendettelsau, the Rummelsberg Institutes, the city mission and other organisations. To them can be added the various district branches of national organisations such as the Red Cross, which built up an independent organisation in 1886 in Nuremberg and which today has more than 900 voluntary and 450 full-time employees. In addition, the Arbeiterwohlfahrt (AWO), the Caritas, the Diakonie (DW) and the Paritätische Wohlfahrtsverband (DPWV) should be mentioned.

All these organisations provide manifold services in the social sector. The range covers almost all areas of life and reaches from ante-natal preparation through to care for the terminally ill. In fulfilling these tasks, the challenges of the prevailing times are taken up, and, as was always the case, suitable solutions are offered. At the moment, the creation of day-nurseries in the region is very topical, necessary to be able to harmonise jobs and families. These efforts are supported, amongst

By People for People – Manifold Social Services

Die Pflege von alten und hilfsbedürftigen Menschen hat in der Region eine lange Tradition.

The care of old people and those needing assistance has a long tradition in the region.

werden diese Bemühungen u. a. durch das „Bündnis für Familie" der Stadt Nürnberg. Hier helfen zahlreiche gesellschaftliche Gruppen mit, familienfreundliche Strukturen zu schaffen. Ein weiteres Beispiel ist die Integration von Ausländern in die Gesellschaft. Dies gelingt in der Metropolregion unter Einbeziehung aller gesellschaftlichen Kräfte inklusive der Verbände und dem in Nürnberg ansässigen Bundesamt für Migration und Flüchtlinge (BAMF). So wird die „Zentrale Rückkehrberatung für Flüchtlinge in Nordbayern" (ZRB) von Wohlfahrtsverbänden in Kooperation mit der Landesaufnahmestelle für Flüchtlinge gemeinsam getragen. An der „Zentralen Anlaufstelle für Migration" (ZAM) sind die Wohlfahrtsverbände und das Bildungszentrum der Stadt Nürnberg beteiligt.

Im Bereich der Pflege sind neben den Wohlfahrtsverbänden auch private Anbieter, städtische Einrichtungen, Krankenkassen, Kliniken und der Bezirk Mittelfranken in eine gemeinsame Beratungsstelle „Zentrale Anlaufstelle Pflege" (ZAPF) eingebunden. Dies trägt zu einer optimalen Versorgung im Bereich der ambulanten und stationären Pflege bei. Aufgrund der demographischen Entwicklung der Bevölkerung werden Angebote für Senioren zunehmend wichtig, denn bereits heute ist jeder vierte Einwohner über 60 Jahre alt. Die Metropolregion bietet Versorgungsdienste wie den Hausnotruf und Essen

Fortsetzung Seite 110

others, by the "Bündnis für Familie" (Alliance for Family) organised by the city of Nuremberg. Numerous social groups assist in the creation of family-friendly structures. Another example is the integration of aliens into society. This has become successful in the metropolitan region by including all the social forces as well as the associations and BAMF, the Bundesamt für Migration und Flüchtlinge (Federal Office for Migration and Refugees) located in Nuremberg. Thus the charitable associations and the Landesaufnahmestelle für Flüchtlinge (Admission Office of the Land for Refugees) are the mutually responsible body for the "Zentrale Rückkehrberatung für Flüchtlinge in Nordbayern" (ZRB) (Central Advisory Office in North Bavaria for the return of refugees). The charitable organisations and the city of Nuremberg's education centre participate in ZAM, the "Zentrale Anlaufstelle für Migration" (Central Contact Office for Migration).

On the care sector, alongside the charitable institutions, private suppliers, municipal institutions, medical insurance offices, clinics and the district of Middle Franconia are also linked in a communal advisory office "Zentrale Anlaufstelle Pflege" (ZAPF) (Central Advisory Office for Nursing). This makes a considerable contribution towards optimal care in the sector of out-patient and in-patient care. Because of the demographic development in the population and because every fourth

Continued on page 110

Das Kompetenzzentrum Demenz im Nürnberger Stadtteil Tillypark setzt neue Maßstäbe in der Beratung und Betreuung von Menschen mit Demenz.

The dementia competence centre in the Nuremberg district of Tillypark sets new standards in the counselling of and caring for people with dementia.

Im Namen Jesu Christi Leben zu gestalten, ist bis heute das zentrale Anliegen der Diakonie Neuendettelsau, die 1854 von Pfarrer Wilhelm Löhe gegründet wurde.
Heute sind in der Diakonie Neuendettelsau fast 6000 Mitarbeiterinnen und Mitarbeiter an Standorten in Bayern, Baden-Württemberg und im europäischen Ausland tätig.

Die Diakonie Neuendettelsau führt u. a. Senioreneinrichtungen, Einrichtungen für Menschen mit Behinderung, Krankenhäuser sowie Schulen und Ausbildungsstätten.
Wie jedes Unternehmen hat die Diakonie Neuendettelsau Ziele, die die Grundlage des Handelns bilden:
– professionelles Arbeiten,
– verantwortliches Wirtschaften und
– christliches Leben.

Die Qualität der Arbeit wird durch eine gezielte Aus-, Fort- und Weiterbildung, eine moderne Personalentwicklung und ein gezieltes Qualitätsmanagement gesichert (Integriertes Managementsystem).
Die Summe aus Tradition und Innovation auf der Grundlage des christlichen Glaubens: Das ist die Diakonie Neuendettelsau.

Direkt an der Pegnitz mitten in Nürnberg liegt das Wohnstift Hallerwiese, eine der modernsten Senioreneinrichtungen für Service-Wohnen im Stadtgebiet.

The Wohnstift Hallerwiese, one of the most modern senior installations for serviced residences in the city area, is situated direct on the river Pegnitz in the middle of Nuremberg.

Standort in Europa
Business Location in Europe

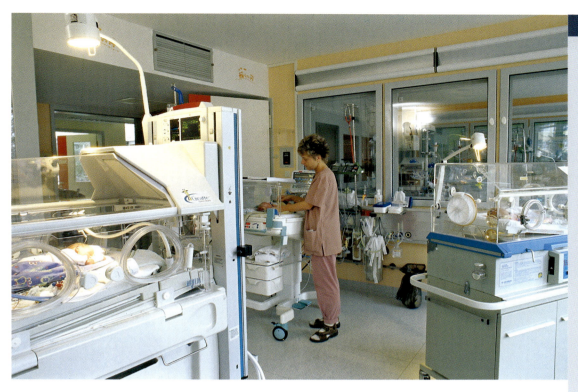

Enabling life to be lived in the name of Jesus Christ remains the central theme of the Diakonie (ecclestical social welfare) Neuendettelsau, founded in 1854 by the pastor Wilhelm Löhe.
Today there are almost 6,000 people employed in the Diakonie Neuendettelsau active in locations in Bavaria, Baden-Württemberg and other European countries.
The Diakonie Neuendettelsau runs, amongst other things, senior residences, installations for people with handicaps, hospitals as well as schools and training centres.

As in every concern, the Diakonie Neuendettelsau has targets which form the basis of their works:
– functioning professionally,
– responsible management and
– a Christian life.
The quality of work is secured through purposeful further education and training, an up-to-date personnel development and well-directed quality management (integrated management system).
The sum of tradition and innovation on the basis of Christian faith: This is the Diakonie Neuendettelsau.

Blick in die neonatologische Intensivstation der Cnopf'schen Kinderklinik.

A glimpse of the neonatal intensive-care ward at the Cnopf'sche Children's Clinic.

Information

Gründungsjahr: 1854
Mitarbeitende: 6000
Angebotsspektrum:
- Senioreneinrichtungen (u. a. Kompetenzzentrum Demenz, Wohnstift Hallerwiese, Seniorenwohnpark Neulichtenhof, Service-Wohnen Sonnen-Seite in Nürnberg)
- Behindertenhilfe
- Schule & Ausbildung (u. a. Berufsfachschulen für Krankenpflege und Kinderkrankenpflege in Nürnberg)
- Krankenhäuser (u. a. Klinikum Hallerwiese mit Cnopf'scher Kinderklinik und Klinik Hallerwiese in Nürnberg)
- DiaLog Conference Center (mit DiaLog-Hotel und Internationaler Akademie DiaLog)

Year founded: 1854
Employees: 6,000
Range on offer:
- installations for seniors (amongst others dementia competence centre, Wohnstift Hallerwiese, Neulichtenhof senior residential estate, SonnenSeite serviced residences in Nuremberg)
- assistance for handicapped people
- schools and training (amongst others training colleges for nursing and paediatric nursing in Nuremberg)
- hospitals (amongst others the Hallerwiese clinic with Cnopf'sche Children's Clinic and the Hallerwiese Clinic in Nuremberg)
- DiaLog Conference Centre (with DiaLog-Hotel and international academy DiaLog)

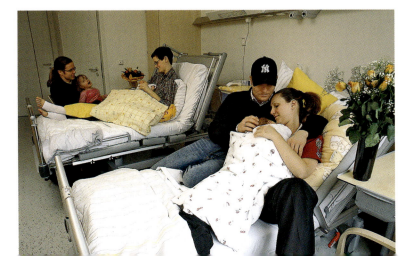

Die Zimmer in der Klinik Hallerwiese – wie hier auf der Wochenstation – haben Hotelstandard.

The rooms in the Hallerwiese clinic – this one is of the lying-in ward – are up to the standard of hotels.

Diakonie Neuendettelsau

Die uniVersa Versicherungen sind eine Unternehmensgruppe mit einer langjährigen Tradition und großer Erfahrung. Der Ursprung geht auf das Jahr 1843 zurück, als mit der Gründung eines Krankenunterstützungsvereins durch Tabakfabrikarbeiter die erste private Krankenversicherung Deutschlands entstand. Als moderner Finanzdienstleister ist die uniVersa heute auf die Rundum-Lösung von Versorgungsproblemen vornehmlich der privaten Haushalte sowie kleinerer und mittlerer Betriebe spezialisiert. Ein flächendeckendes Netz von Geschäftsstellen garantiert Kunden- und Beraternähe. Ihr Hauptsitz ist Nürnberg.

uniVersa Insurance is a group of companies with a long-standing tradition and wide-ranging experience.
Its origins go back to 1843, when tobacco factory workers founded a mutual benefit association for invalids that became Germany's first private health insurance company. As a modern financial service provider, uniVersa now specializes in comprehensive solutions for health and well-being, primarily for private households, as well as for small to medium-sized companies. A wide network of branch offices guarantees optimum proximity between customers and insurance agents. uniVersa is headquarted in Nuremberg.

Information

Gründungsjahr:
1843 uniVersa Krankenversicherung a.G.
1857 uniVersa Lebensversicherung a.G.
1951 uniVersa Allgemeine Versicherung AG

Mitarbeiter: mehr als 6000 Mitarbeiter und Vertriebspartner

Leistungsspektrum:
– Versicherungsschutz für alle Lebenslagen, umfassend, modern, anerkannt preiswert und auf hohem Leistungsniveau
– Baufinanzierung
– Bausparen
– Vermögensanlagen

Kapitalanlagen:
rund 2,6 Mrd. Euro; Eigenkapitalausstattung rund 91 Mio. Euro

---

Year of founding:
uniVersa Krankenversicherung (health insurance) a.G. in 1843;
uniVersa Lebensversicherung (life insurance) a.G. in 1857;
uniVersa Allgemeine Versicherung (general insurance) AG in 1951

Workforce: more than 6,000 employees and sales partners

Range of services:
– insurance coverage for all ages and situations: comprehensive, modern, known for its value and high level of performance
– construction financing
– home loan banking
– investment services

Assets:
approx. 2.6 billion Euro; equity capital approx. 91 million Euro

☐
uniVersa Versicherungen Nürnberg

Standort in Europa
Business Location in Europe

Der Versicherungsdienst BEV GmbH entstand vor über 40 Jahren aus einer Ein-Mann-Agentur. Mittlerweile ist das Unternehmen zu einem der größten Versicherungsdienste gewachsen, der ausschließlich Produkte der Versicherungskammer Bayern anbietet.
Koordiniert von der Zentrale Nürnberg, befinden sich derzeit 13 weitere Filialen im Geschäftsgebiet, um kurze Wege für den Kunden zu gewährleisten. Von A wie Autoversicherung bis Z wie Zahnersatzabsicherung ist der Versicherungsdienst der Bayerischen Beamtenkrankenkasse ein kompetenter Partner in allen Kranken-, Sach- und Lebensversicherungsfragen.

The Versicherungsdienst BEV GmbH arose more than 40 years ago from a one-man agency. In the meantime, the undertaking has grown into one of the largest insurance service suppliers solely offering products of the Bavarian Versicherungskammer (insurance chamber). Coordinated from the headquarters in Nuremberg, there are at the moment a further 13 branches in their business area set up to guarantee customer proximity.
From A as in automobile insurance to Z as in Zahnersatzabsicherung (denture protection) the insurance service of the Bayerische Beamtenkrankenkasse is a competent partner in all questions of sickness, property and life insurance.

Information

Gründungsjahr: 1963

Mitarbeiter: 90 (Innen- und Außendienst sowie Auszubildende)

Leistungsspektrum:
Vermittlung von Personen-, Sach- und Lebensversicherungen für Privatpersonen, Firmen und Verbände

Tätigkeitsgebiete:
13 Standorte in Mittelfranken, Oberfranken und der Oberpfalz

Kunden: ca. 100 000

Year founded: 1963

Employees:
90 (in-office and outside workers together with trainees)

Range of services:
mediating personal, property and life insurance for private persons, firms and associations

Activity sectors:
13 locations in Middle Franconia, Upper Franconia and the Upper Palatinate

Customers:
about 100,000

☐
Bayerische Beamtenkrankenkasse Versicherungsdienste BEV GmbH
Nürnberg

auf Rädern sowie Betreutes Wohnen und ambulante Pflegedienste, die ein möglichst langes Verbleiben in den eigenen vier Wänden ermöglichen. Aber auch im stationären und teilstationären Bereich ist die Versorgung der Bevölkerung gesichert. Neben traditionellen Pflegeheimen gibt es Angebote mit neuen zukunftsweisenden Konzepten wie zum Beispiel selbstbestimmte Wohnformen bei Pflegebedarf oder beschützende Stationen für Menschen mit Demenzerkrankungen. Begleitet wird dieses Aufgabenfeld durch entsprechende Lehrstühle an den Fachhochschulen und Hochschulen der Region, zum Beispiel für Gerontopsychiatrie. Themenbezogene Veranstaltungen und Messen, etwa die jährlich stattfindende „ConSozial" oder die Seniorenmesse, sorgen für entsprechende Resonanz über die Grenzen der Metropolregion hinaus.

Die gute Zusammenarbeit verschiedener Organisationen in der Region zeigt sich auch bei den Hilfsorganisationen wie Arbeiter-Samariter-Bund (ASB), Bayerisches Rotes Kreuz (BRK), Johanniter Unfallhilfe (JUH) und Malteser Hilfsdienst (MHD). Neben der gemeinsamen Durchführung des Rettungsdienstes erfolgt hier eine Kooperation im Sanitätsdienst, insbesondere bei Großveranstaltungen wie „Rock im Park" oder Norisring-Rennen sowie im Katastrophenschutz. Die gute Zusammenarbeit mit Polizei, Feuerwehr und Technischem Hilfswerk bewährt sich gerade bei der Vorbereitung und Durchführung der Fußball-Weltmeisterschaft 2006. Besonders hervorzuheben ist, dass hierbei ein hohes Maß an ehrenamtlicher Leistung einfließt.

Bürgerschaftliches Engagement findet sich sowohl bei den traditionsreichen Verbänden wie der Bergwacht, der Wasserwacht oder dem Jugendrotkreuz als auch in neuen Formen freiwilliger Arbeit wie zum Beispiel der „Tafel", die günstig Lebensmittel an Bedürftige in verschiedenen Orten ausgibt oder dem Verein „Klabautermann", der chronisch kranke Kinder in Nürnberg unterstützt.

Alle diese sozialen Dienste – verbunden mit vielfältigem bürgerschaftlichem Engagement – tragen dazu bei, dass sich jede Bürgerin und jeder Bürger in der Metropolregion gut aufgehoben und wohl fühlen kann.

citizen is already older than 60, the care of seniors is becoming increasingly important. The metropolitan region provides care services such as house emergency calls and meals on wheels as well as senior living facilities and out-patient care services enabling seniors to remain as long as possible within their own four walls. But also in the in-patient and day-care sectors the care of the population is guaranteed. In addition to traditional nursing homes for the elderly, there are many with forward-looking concepts such as self-determined forms of living for those in need of care or sheltered wards for people with dementia illnesses. These task areas are accompanied by suitable professorial chairs at the universities of applied sciences and universities of the region, for instance for geronto-psychiatry. Specific thematic events and trade fairs, for example the "ConSozial" held every year, or the Senior Trade Fair, provide an appropriate response far beyond the boundaries of the metropolitan region.

The excellent cooperation between various organisations in the region can also be seen with aid organisations such as the Arbeiter-Samariter-Bund (ASB) (Workers' Samaritan Association), Bavarian Red Cross (BRK), St. John's Brigade (JUH) and Malteser Hilfsdienst (MHD) (Maltese Emergency Service). In addition to carrying out mutual rescue services, there is a large amount of cooperation within the medical services, especially during big events such as "Rock in the Park" or the Noris Ring Races as well as disaster control. Excellent cooperation with the police, fire brigades and Technischem Hilfswerk (Technical Emergency Service) has proved itself in the preparation and execution of the World Football Championship 2006. It should be specially mentioned at this point that a large amount of the work is done by volunteers.

Citizens' commitment can also be found in traditional organisations such as the Bergwacht (Mountain Rescue Service), the Wasserwacht (Water Rescue Service) or Jugendrotkreuz (Youths' Red Cross) and the new form of voluntary work such as the "Tafel" which distributes low-cost food to the needy in various towns or the association "Klabautermann" which supports sick children in Nuremberg.

All these social services – combined with the manifold citizens' commitments – make their contribution towards each individual citizen in the metropolitan region feeling that he is well taken care of.

Forschung und Technologie
Research and Technology

Zukunft des Wissens – Universitäten in der Region

Professor Dr. Karl-Dieter Grüske

Zukunft ist für Menschen des 21. Jahrhunderts kein unabänderliches Schicksal, nichts, was uns prinzipiell verborgen bleibt und ergeben abzuwarten ist. Wir sind uns bewusst, dass wir der Welt von morgen durch alles, was wir heute tun, Form verleihen. Das macht das Entscheiden nicht leichter: Der Versuch, alle Konsequenzen einer Handlung im Voraus abzuschätzen, kann in Verwirrung enden, statt Klarheit zu schaffen. Die beste Basis für sinnvolle Entscheidungen ist gesichertes Wissen, wie es auf vielen Gebieten eben nur durch methodisches Beobachten, Erproben und Durchdenken erreichbar ist.

For people of the 21st century the future is not an irreversible fate, it is not a thing which remains fundamentally hidden and to be awaited with humility. We are conscious that we shape tomorrow's world by that which we do today. Which does not make decision-making any easier: The attempt to assess all the consequences of something in advance can, instead of bringing clarity, end in confusion. The best basis for making sensible decisions is solid knowledge and this can only be achieved in many fields by means of methodical observation, trial and by thorough consideration.

Wissbegierig: Studierende im Hörsaal der Wirtschafts- und Sozialwissenschaftlichen Fakultät (WISO)

Eager to learn: students in the lecture hall of the Economics and Social Sciences Faculty (WISO)

Wenn der Blick allerdings auf die Forschung alleine begrenzt ist, bleibt ihr Beitrag zur gesellschaftlichen Entwicklung beschränkt. Die Wissenschaftlerinnen und Wissenschaftler der Universität Erlangen-Nürnberg halten trotz der notwendigen Konzentration auf

However, when observation is restricted purely to research, then its contribution to social development is also restricted. In spite of the necessary concentration on details, the scientists of the Erlangen-Nuremberg university keep their eyes open for the "look over the

The Future of Knowledge – Universities in the Region

Details die Augen offen für den „Blick über den Zaun". Seit dem Gründungsjahr 1743 ist an der Friedrich-Alexander-Universität reichlich Nahrung für den menschlichen Wissensdurst gesammelt worden, der auf willkürlich gesetzte Stoppsignale nicht achtet, Denkmodelle überprüft, verwirft oder präzisiert, Querverbindungen aufdeckt und so im Rückgriff auf überliefertes Wissen unablässig Neues schafft.

Nahezu 6000 junge Frauen und Männer haben im November 2005 ein Studium an der mittelfränkischen Zwei-Städte-Universität aufgenommen und sich damit deren Tradition der Erneuerung angeschlossen. Mit 25 800 Studierenden wurde im Wintersemester 2005/06 ein neuer Höchststand erreicht. Diese Studenten und Studentinnen bringen wie keine andere Personengruppe Leben in die Metropolregion Nürnberg, auf kulturellem, sozialem und wirtschaftlichem Gebiet. Sie nehmen Sachverstand und wissenschaftliche Kenntnisse auf, die an den elf Fakultäten mit insgesamt 550 Professorenstellen bewahrt und laufend neu erarbeitet werden, und tragen sie weiter: in die

Information

Friedrich-Alexander-Universität Erlangen-Nürnberg
Zahlen und Fakten:
11 Fakultäten
89 Institute
23 Kliniken
260 Lehrstühle
550 Professoren
12 000 Mitarbeiter
25 800 Studierende
17 Interdisziplinäre Zentren
10 Sonderforschungs- und Transferbereiche
5 DFG-Forschergruppen
8 Graduiertenkollegs

Universitäten:
Friedrich-Alexander-Universität Erlangen-Nürnberg
www.uni-erlangen.de
Otto-Friedrich-Universität Bamberg
www.uni-bamberg.de
Universität Bayreuth
www.uni-bayreuth.de
Bayerische Julius-Maximilians-Universität Würzburg
www.uni-wuerzburg.de
Augustana-Hochschule, Neuendettelsau
www.augustana.de
(Kirchliche Hochschule der Evangelisch-Lutherischen Kirche in Bayern, den Universitäten gleichgestellt)

Information

Friedrich-Alexander-University Erlangen-Nuremberg
Figures and facts:
11 faculties
89 institutes
23 clinics
260 professorial chairs
550 professors
12,000 employees
25,800 students
17 interdisciplinary centres
10 special research and transfer sectors
5 DFG (German Research Association) research groups
8 graduated colleges

Universities:
Friedrich-Alexander-University Erlangen-Nuremberg
www.uni-erlangen.de
Otto-Friedrich-University Bamberg
www.uni-bamberg.de
University of Bayreuth
www.uni-bayreuth.de
Bavarian Julius-Maximilians-University Würzburg
www.uni-wuerzburg.de
Augustana-High School, Neuendettelsau
www.augustana.de
(Ecclesiastical College of the Protestant-Lutheran Church in Bavaria, at the same level as the Universities)

fence". Since its foundation in 1743, at the Friedrich-Alexander-University a plentiful supply of nutrition has been collected to satisfy human hunger for knowledge, hunger that does not react to arbitrarily set stop signals, but which examines, rejects or states hypotheses more precisely, discovers links and so, while making recourse to knowledge handed down, continuously creates something new.

Almost 6,000 young women and men took up studies in November 2005 at the Middle Franconian twin-city university, thus joining this tradition of rejuvenation. In the winter semester 2005/06 a new record level of 25,800 students was reached. As no other group of people, these students bring life into the metropolitan region of Nuremberg on a cultural, social and economic level. They absorb the expertise and scientific knowledge which is maintained and continually newly processed on the eleven faculties with a total of 550 professors, and carry it forward into schools, industrial companies, into start-up concerns, into the health sector and into administrative and com-

Antikensammlung (Gipsabdruck-Galerie) des Instituts für klassische Archäologie der Universität Erlangen-Nürnberg

The antique collection (plaster-cast gallery) of the Institute for Classical Archaeology at the Erlangen-Nuremberg University

Schulen, die Industriebetriebe, in Start-up-Unternehmen, ins Gesundheitswesen, in Verwaltungs- und Kommunikationsbereiche. Das Reservoir von gut ausgebildeten und hoch motivierten Arbeitskräften direkt vor der Haustür versorgt die Region mit dem „Rohstoff", auf dem Deutschlands Wirtschaftskraft beruht.

Als zweitgrößter Arbeitgeber in der Metropolregion beschäftigt die Universität selbst über 12 000 Mitarbeiterinnen und Mitarbeiter. Das stabilisiert die Wirtschaftsstruktur in Mittelfranken ebenso wie die zahlreichen Kooperationsprojekte zwischen Industrie und Hochschule und den Transfer von praxisrelevanten Forschungsergebnissen, speziell auch in mittelständische Betriebe. Neuheiten in den Bereichen, die zu den international ausgewiesenen Stärken der Universität zählen, finden dadurch zügig den Weg in die Anwendung. Dies betrifft an erster Stelle Fortschritte in der Molekularen Biomedizin und der Medizintechnik, die Entwicklung von maßgeschneiderten Materialien und effizienten Fertigungsprozessen, die Grundlagen

munication sectors. This reservoir of well-educated and highly motivated workforce on the doorstep provides the region with the "raw material" on which Germany's economic power rests.

As the second largest employer in the metropolitan region, the university itself employs more than 12,000 people. This stabilises the economic structure in Middle Franconia as do the numerous cooperation projects between industry and colleges and the transfer of practicable research results, especially in medium-sized companies. Anything new in those sectors, which are classed as internationally acknowledged

Information

Die **Otto-Friedrich-Universität Bamberg** ist die jüngste und zugleich eine der ältesten Universitäten Bayerns. Ihre Wurzeln reichen zurück bis in das Jahr 1647. Nach einer wechselvollen Geschichte wird die Universität 1972 als Gesamthochschule wieder gegründet und trägt seit 1979 offiziell die Bezeichnung Universität. Charakteristisch für die Otto-Friedrich-Universität ist ihr geistes- und kulturwissenschaftliches Profil, das durch vier der sechs Fakultäten besonders geprägt wird. Der andere große Studien- und Forschungsschwerpunkt sind die Sozial- und Wirtschaftswissenschaften.

Die **Universität Bayreuth** – gegründet 1975 – ist eine der jüngsten Universitäten in Deutschland. Individuelle Betreuung, hohe Leistungsstandards und eine entschiedene Ausrichtung an beruflichen Chancen und Perspektiven bestimmen das Studienangebot. Es reicht von den Natur- und Ingenieurwissenschaften über die Rechts- und Wirtschaftswissenschaften bis hin zu den Sprach-, Literatur- und Kulturwissenschaften. In regionaler wie überregionaler Hinsicht versteht sich die Universität Bayreuth als wichtige Transferstelle für Wissenschaft, Kultur und Technologie.

Im Jahr 1582 wurde die heutige **Bayerische Julius-Maximilians-Universität Würzburg** gegründet und nahm mit einer Theologischen und Philosophischen Fakultät ihren Betrieb auf. Bald darauf kamen eine Juristische und eine Medizinische Fakultät hinzu, von denen letztgenannte noch heute mit rund 3000 Studierenden die größte Einzelfakultät bildet. Die Universität Würzburg verfügt mit einem auf 12 Fakultäten verteilten Fächerspektrum über nahezu alle traditionellen Gebiete einer gewachsenen Universität und gehört mit insgesamt über 20 000 Studierenden zu den vier großen Universitäten Bayerns.

der Wachstumsbranchen Elektronik und Informationstechnik sowie Optik und optische Technologien.

Beispielhaft für Letzteres stehen die Max-Planck-Forschungsgruppe für Optik, Information und Photonik in Erlangen und die im November 2005 beschlossene International Max Planck Research School „Optics and Imaging", für welche das Fraunhofer-Institut für Integrierte Schaltungen und Siemens Medical Solutions als Partner gewonnen werden konnten. Beleg für den hohen Forschungsstand sind im biomedizinischen wie im technisch-naturwissenschaftlichen Bereich die gegenwärtig zehn DFG-Sonderforschungsbereiche der Universität.

strengths of the university, finds its way quickly into practice. This is particularly true of progress in molecular bio-medicine and medicine technology, the development of made-to-measure materials and efficient manufacturing processes, the basis of the growing branches of electronics and information engineering as well as in optics and optic technologies.

Exemplary for the latter is the Max-Planck-Research-Group for Optics, Information and Photonic in Erlangen and the International Max Planck Research School "Optics and Imaging", agreed upon in November 2005 for which the Fraunhofer-Institut für Integrierte Schaltungen (Institute for Integrated Circuits) and Siemens Medical Solutions were able to be won as partners. Proof of the high research status is, in the biomedical as in the technical natural science sectors, the current ten DFG-Sonderforschungsbereiche (special research sectors) of the university.

Information

The **Otto-Friedrich-University Bamberg** is the youngest and at the same time one of the oldest universities in Bavaria. Its roots reach back into the year 1647. After a varied history, the university was refounded in 1972 as a comprehensive university (polytechnic) and since 1979 has had the official title of university. Charactaric of the Otto-Friedrich-University is its humanities and cultural sciences profile, particularly pronounced in four out of six faculties. The other study and research focal points are the social and economic sciences.

The University of Bayreuth – founded in 1975 – is one of the youngest universities in Germany. Individual counselling, high standards of performance and a purposeful orientation towards professional opportunities and perspectives determine the study selection. It reaches from the natural and engineering sciences via law and economics through to language, literature and cultural sciences. From a regional point of view, and indeed beyond, the Bayreuth university sees itself as an important transfer point for science, culture and technology.

In 1582 today's **Bavarian Julius-Maximilians-University Würzburg** was founded and began its work with a theological and philosophical faculty. Shortly afterwards, a law and medical faculty was added, the latter today forming the largest individual faculty with some 3,000 students. The university of Würzburg has almost all the traditional sectors of a grown university, divided over 12 faculties and today, with more than 20,000 students, is one of the four largest universities in Bavaria.

Forschung und Technologie
Research and Technology

Berührungsloses Messen von Wasserströmungen mittels Laser im Wasserkanal am Lehrstuhl für Strömungstechnik der Technischen Fakultät der Universität Erlangen-Nürnberg

Contactless measuring of water currents by laser in the water channel at the Institute for Current Technology of the Technical Faculty of the Erlangen-Nuremberg University

Studenten der Wirtschafts- und Sozialwissenschaftlichen Fakultät in der Langen Gasse in Nürnberg

Students of the Economics and Social Sciences Faculty in the Langen Gasse in Nuremberg

Rechts: Blick auf das Erlanger Schloss, den Sitz der Universitätsverwaltung

Right: A view of the Erlangen castle, seen the residence of the University administration

Die wachsende Überzeugung, dass gemeinsames Vorgehen jedem Einzelnen ebenso wie der Gesamtheit nützt, war Anlass einer Erklärung aller Hochschulen im Raum Nürnberg zur Bekräftigung ihrer Absicht, die Kernkompetenzen der mittelfränkischen Region zu stärken. Die Universität Erlangen-Nürnberg, seit jeher eng in ihrem regionalen Umfeld verankert, ist sich ihrer regionalen Verantwortung bewusst. Die Zusammenarbeit mit der Fachhochschule Nürnberg, etwa bei Praktika der Studierenden oder beim Höchstleistungsrechnen, hat ohnehin in jüngster Zeit deutliche Fortschritte gemacht.

Bei der Weltoffenheit, die Mittelfranken in vieler Hinsicht auszeichnet, ist eine Konzentration auf die eigenen Stärken kein Widerspruch zur Aufgeschlossenheit gegenüber fernen und fremden Kulturen, ohne die auch eine Metropolregion nicht denkbar ist. Über ihre weit gespannten Auslandskontakte stößt die Friedrich-Alexander-Universität die Tore zu Welten auf, die nach wie vor wenig vertraut sind.

Zwei Beispiele sollen dies illustrieren. Nach dem Vorbild der Goethe-Institute richtet China weltweit Konfuzius-Institute ein, um die chinesische Sprache und Kultur zu verbreiten. Für Deutschland sind zwei solcher Institute vorgesehen: eines in Berlin, das andere, in Kooperation mit der Universität Erlangen-Nürnberg, in der Nürnberger Region. Ähnlich steht es mit der Errichtung eines Koreanisch-Europäischen Internationalen Kooperationszentrums in Erlangen, das die wirtschaftlichen und wissenschaftlichen Beziehungen zwischen Südkorea und der Europäischen

The growing conviction that mutual action benefits each individually as much as the whole was the reason for a declaration of all the colleges in the Nuremberg area to confirm their intention of strengthening the core competences of the Middle Franconian region. The Erlangen-Nuremberg university, which has always been closely anchored to its regional surroundings, is conscious of its regional responsibility. The cooperation with the university of applied sciences in Nuremberg, be it regarding students' practical periods or high-performance computers, has made clear progress recently.

In the liberal-mindedness for which Middle Franconia is in many respects well known, a concentration on their own strengths does not contradict the open-mindedness for far-removed and foreign cultures, without which no metropolitan region could be imagined. It is widely spread overseas contacts by which the Friedrich-Alexander-University pushes wide open the doors to worlds which are still, now as before, unfamiliar.

Two examples will illustrate this. Following the ideals of the Goethe-Institute, China organised Confucius-Institutes to promote the spread of the Chinese language and culture. Two such institutes are planned for Germany: one in Berlin and the other, in cooperation with the university, in the Nuremberg region. It is a similar story with the foundation of a Korean-European International Cooperation Centre in Erlangen which is to care for and coordinate scientific and economic relations between South Korea and the

Forschung und Technologie
Research and Technology

Union pflegen und koordinieren soll. Auf jedem Kontinent gibt es eine derartige Einrichtung nur ein einziges Mal.

Die Zukunft des Wissens liegt in erheblichem Maße im Wissensaustausch – interkulturell ebenso wie zwischen den Disziplinen. Das Konzept einer Leonardo-Akademie, wie sie an der Friedrich-Alexander-Universität geplant ist, reicht über eine Vermittlerposition zwischen Natur- und Geisteswissenschaften hinaus. Hier sollen Forschungsziele von Anfang an gemeinsam beschrieben und angegangen werden: damit Wissen in Zukunft weder bruchstückhaft bleibt noch weltabgewandt agiert, sondern in einer äußerst komplexen Umwelt geisteswissenschaftlich reflektiert wird. ☐

European Union. There is only one such organisation on each continent.

The future of knowledge lies to a large extent in the exchange of knowledge – inter-culturally as well as between the various disciplines. The concept of a Leonardo Academy as is planned for the Friedrich-Alexander-University stretches beyond taking over a mediator position between nature and the humanities. This is where research goals will be mutually described and approached: so that knowledge in the future remains neither fragmentary nor will it turn away from the world but rather will be reflected in a humanistic way in an extremely complex environment. ☐

Die Georg-Simon-Ohm-Fachhochschule Nürnberg als Beispiel für Angewandte Wissenschaften

Professor Dr. Michael Braun

International, kompetent, innovativ: 1823 als städtisches Polytechnikum gegründet, vereint die Georg-Simon-Ohm-Fachhochschule große Tradition und Moderne. Heute sind rund 8500 Studierende in zwölf Fachbereichen eingeschrieben, womit die Fachhochschule zu den größten in ganz Deutschland zählt. 250 Professoren lehren und forschen mitten im Herzen Nürnbergs und machen den Campus zwischen Wörder See und Prinzregentenufer zu einem der wissenschaftlichen Zentren der Metropolregion. Unterstützt werden sie von zahlreichen Lehrbeauftragten aus Wirtschaft und Industrie, die die praxisnahe Ausbildung garantieren. Der weltbekannte Physiker Georg-Simon Ohm ist übrigens nicht nur Namensgeber: Er lehrte in Nürnberg als Professor und war von 1839 bis 1849 Rektor der Hochschule.

Den größten Fachbereich stellen die Wirtschaftswissenschaften, die zusammen mit dem Sozialwesen an der Bahnhofstraße residieren. Am Keßlerplatz und in der Wassertorstraße sitzen die Gestaltung und die Fachrichtungen der Ingenieurwissenschaft. Von Architektur und Angewandter Chemie über Werkstofftechnik, Maschinenbau, Elektro-, Feinwerk- und Informationstechnik, Verfahrenstechnik und Informatik bis hin zu Bauingenieurwesen reicht die Palette quer durch alle Disziplinen. Über 30 Studiengänge bieten dabei 64 individuelle Vertiefungs- und Spezialisierungsmöglichkeiten.

Durch ihren großen Praxisbezug ist die Georg-Simon-Ohm-Fachhochschule für Wirtschaft und Industrie stets ein gefragter Partner. High-Tech-Keramiken und -Gläser, Mechatronik, Automatisierungstechnologien oder das europäische Anwendungszentrum für polymere optische Fasern (POFAC) stehen stellvertretend für die vielen Kompetenzfelder

International, competent, innovative: Founded in 1823 as the municipal polytechnic, the Georg-Simon-Ohm University of applied sciences combines tradition with modernity. Today, some 8,500 students are registered in twelve faculties making the university of applied sciences one of the largest in all Germany. 250 professors teach and carry out research in the heart of Nuremberg and make the campus between Lake Wörder and Prinzregentenufer into one of the scientific centres of the metropolitan region. They are supported by countless temporary lecturers from commerce and industry who guarantee close-to-practice training. The well-known physicist Georg-Simon Ohm, by the way, not only gave his name: He taught in Nuremberg as a professor and was from 1839 to 1849 vice-chancellor of the university of applied sciences.

The largest faculty is formed by economics, which, together with social welfare, is resident in the Bahnhofstraße. Design and the faculties of engineering are to be found on Keßlerplatz and in the Wassertorstraße. The range stretches across all the disciplines from architecture and applied chemistry via material technology, mechanical engineering, electro-, precision mechanics and information technology, process technology and informatics through to civil engineering. More than 30 study courses provide 64 possibilities of individual consolidation and specialisation.

Because of its practical orientation the Georg-Simon-Ohm-University of applied sciences is a much sought-after partner for trade and industry. High-tech ceramics and glass, mechatronic, automation engineering or the Europäische Anwendungszentrum für polymere optische Fasern (POFAC) (European application centre for polymere optical fibres) represent just some of the many fields of the institute's competence

The Georg-Simon-Ohm University of Applied Sciences in Nuremberg as an Example for Applied Sciences

Forschung und Technologie
Research and Technology

Die Georg-Simon-Ohm-Fachhochschule zählt zu den größten in Deutschland.

The Georg-Simon-Ohm-Fachhochschule (university of applied sciences) counts as one of the largest in Germany.

der forschungsintensivsten aller 17 bayerischen Fachhochschulen. Im Bereich der Drittmittel – der Einnahmen aus externen Forschungsaufträgen und eigener unternehmerischer Tätigkeit als Hochschule – liegt die FH Nürnberg ebenfalls vorne. Möglich wird dies nicht zuletzt durch die umfangreichen Laborausstattungen, zu denen u. a. ein Hochspannungslabor bis 1200 Kilovolt, ein Wasserbaulabor, ein Reinraum für Mikrotechnologien sowie ein Video- und Fotostudio für die Designer gehören.

Die Lehre profitiert stark vom stets aktuellen Stand der technischen Ausstattung: Studierende aus rund 90 Nationen erwerben an der Georg-Simon-Ohm-Fachhochschule ihre beruflichen Qualifikationen. Partnerschaften zu mehr als 100 Hochschulen in 30 Ländern weltweit machen das Haus zu einem Global Player. Im Zuge des Bologna-Prozesses stellt die Georg-Simon-Ohm-Fachhochschule alle ihre Studiengänge sukzessive auf die neuen gestuften Abschlüsse Bachelor und Master um, die das klassische Diplom in Deutschland ablösen. Dabei übernahm das „Ohm" früh eine Pionierrolle, schon Ende der neunziger Jahre wurden die ersten Bachelor-Studiengänge eingeführt, bis zum Wintersemester 2007/08 werden alle Erstsemester ihre Ausbildung in den neuen Studiengängen beginnen. Die akkreditierten Master-Programme eröffnen den beruflichen Zugang zum höheren Dienst.

In der Zeit nach dem Studium sollte eine Ausbildung nicht enden. Im „Ohm-Netzwerk für lebenslanges Lernen" bietet die Hochschule ein hochkarätiges und sehr praxisorientiertes Weiterbildungspaket unterschiedlicher Richtungen, das im Jahr 2004 vom Stifterverband für die Deutsche Wissenschaft als eines der drei besten in der Bundesrepublik ausgezeichnet wurde. MBA-Programme oder spezielle Weiterbildungen für Ingenieure und vieles mehr stehen exemplarisch für das umfassende Angebot.

Information

Fachhochschulen/Universities of applied sciences:

Georg-Simon-Ohm-Fachhochschule Nürnberg
www.fh-nuernberg.de

Fachhochschule Ansbach
www.fh-ansbach.de

Evangelische Fachhochschule Nürnberg
(staatlich anerkannte nichtstaatliche Hochschule)
www.evfh-nuernberg.de

Fachhochschule Weihenstephan, Abteilung Triesdorf, Freising
www.fh-weihenstephan.de/triesdorf

Fachhochschule Amberg-Weiden, Amberg
www.fh-amberg-weiden.de

Fachhochschule Coburg
www.fh-coburg.de

Fachhochschule Hof
www.fh-hof.de

Fachhochschule Würzburg-Schweinfurt, Würzburg
www.fh-wuerzburg.de

Fachhochschule für öffentliche Verwaltung und Rechtspflege in Bayern
Fachbereich Allgemeine Innere Verwaltung, Hof
www.fhvr-aiv.de

Fachbereich Polizei, Sulzbach-Rosenberg
www.fhvr-polizei.bayern.de

which has the most intensive research programme of all 17 Bavarian universities of applied sciences. In the sector of third party (financial) resources – income from external research assignments and their own entrepreneurial activities as a university of applied sciences – the FH Nuremberg is also in the front line. This has been made possible not least by the extensive laboratory equipment, amongst which, for instance, is a high-voltage laboratory with up to 1200 kilovolt, a river engineering laboratory, and a clean room for micro technology as well as a video and photo studio for designers.

Education profits strongly from the constant up-to-date status of the technical equipment: Students from about 90 nations obtain their professional qualifications at the Georg-Simon-Ohm University of applied sciences, and partnerships with more than 100 universities and colleges in 30 countries all around the world make the institution a global player. In the course of the Bologna Process, the Georg-Simon-Ohm University of applied sciences has gradually changed all its study courses to the newly classified final exams of Bachelor and Master which, in Germany, take over from the classical diploma. The "Ohm" has always had a pioneering role, the first Bachelor study courses were introduced as early as the end of the nineties and by the winter semester 2007/08 all the first semester (students) will begin their education in the new study courses. The accredited Master programmes open up professional admission into the upper (civil) services.

Education should not finish once one has finished studying. In the "Ohm network for life-long learning" the university of applied sciences offers a top-notch and extremely practice-oriented further education parcel in different directions and which in 2004 was honoured by the Stifterverband für die Deutsche Wissenschaft as one of the three best in the Federal Republic. MBA pro-

Forschung und Technologie
Research and Technology

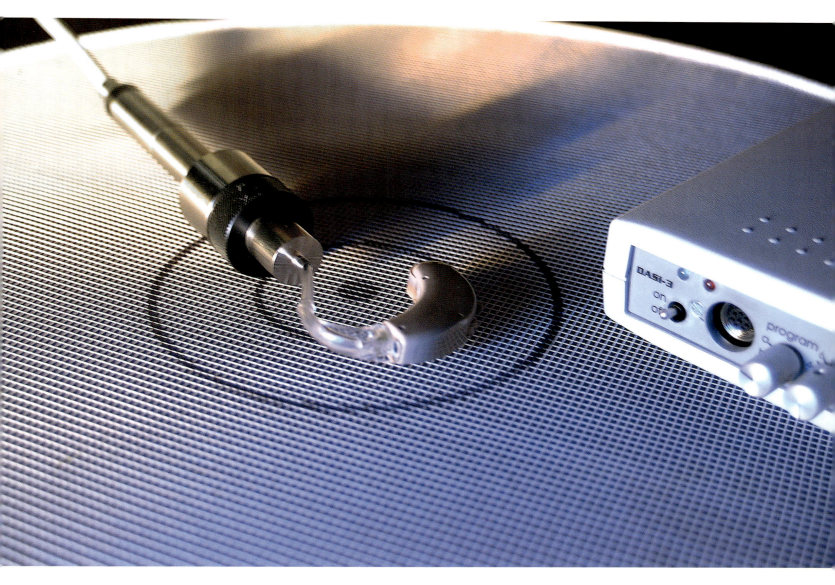

Das „Ohm" ist die forschungsintensivste der 17 bayerischen Hochschulen. Nicht zuletzt aufgrund der hervorragenden technischen Ausstattung der Labors ist die Fachhochschule bereits mit zahlreichen Innovationspreisen ausgezeichnet worden.

The "Ohm" is the most intensive in research of the 17 Bavarian universities. Not least by reason of the excellent technical equipment in the laboratory, the university of applied sciences has already been awarded countless innovation prizes.

Doch nicht nur die Weiterbildung erfuhr höchste Anerkennung. Zahlreiche weitere Preise zeugen von der exzellenten Qualität von Lehre und Forschung: So gingen bereits mehrere Innovationspreise nach Nürnberg; Auszeichnungen für gute Lehre oder die gelebte Internationalität bestätigen die hervorragende Arbeit. Derweil heimsen die Designer in den letzten Jahren Film- und Medien-Preise in Serie ein: Von Auszeichnungen bei Festivals oder bedeutenden Wettbewerben bis hin zu zwei Oscar-Prämierungen für Absolventen der Hochschule reicht hier die Palette.

Mit den Nachbarhochschulen bestehen enge Vernetzungen. Die gemeinsame Entwicklung der Curricula mit anderen Hochschulen sowie intensive Kooperationen mit der Nachbaruniversität Erlangen-Nürnberg kennzeichnen die vielfältigen Kontakte. So etwa im „KONWIHR"-Projekt für wissenschaftliches Höchstleistungsrechnen, in dem der Fachbereich Verfahrenstechnik und der Lehrstuhl für Strömungsmechanik im Bereich von Strömungssimulation zusammenarbeiten und gemeinsam funktionale Lösungen für die Wirtschaft anbieten. Damit schlägt das „Ohm" die wichtige Brücke zwischen Grundlagen- und Anwendungsforschung.

Überhaupt ist die Hochschule im Bereich des Wissens- und Technologietransfers ein kompetenter Partner für die Wirtschaft. Sie bietet Technologie- und Innovationsberatung, angewandte Forschung und Entwicklung, Verbundpartnerschaften, Mess- und Prüfservice oder liefert Gutachten und Studien. Für die Energieregion Nürnberg hält das „Ohm" ein breit gefächertes Themenpaket parat; zum Beispiel im hochschuleigenen Institut für Energie und Gebäude (ieg), das kompetente und intelligente Lösungen für hoch effizientes Energie- und Facility-Management zur Verfügung stellt.

Schließlich ist das Haus von der gemeinnützigen Hertie-Stiftung als familiengerechte Hochschule offiziell zertifiziert und bietet damit Studierenden wie Mitarbeitern optimale Bedingungen für die Verbindung von Job, Studium und Privatleben. Um in Zukunft stark zu bleiben, vergrößert sich die Georg-Simon-Ohm-Fachhochschule stetig: Nach den jüngsten Bauprojekten für Betriebswirtschaft und Sozialwesen in der Bahnhofstraße (1999) und den neuen Zentralwerkstätten mit Mensateria (2002) entsteht seit Sommer 2005 ein modernes Gebäude für die Angewandte Chemie und die Zentralen Dienste, das bis 2008 in Betrieb genommen werden wird.

grammes or specialised further training programmes for engineers, as well as many others, are just some examples of the wide range on offer.

However, it is not only for further education that some of the highest honours have been received. Numerous other prizes bear witness to the excellence of education and research: Several innovation prizes have also been awarded to Nuremberg; awards for the quality of the education or the internationality experienced serve to confirm the excellence of the work. In the past few years, designers have accumulated whole series of film and media prizes ranging from awards during festivals or significant competitions through to two Oscars for graduates of the university of applied sciences.

The links with neighbouring universities are close. Mutual development of curricula with other universities as well as intensive cooperation with the neighbouring university in Erlangen-Nuremberg characterise the manifold contacts. Typical of these is the "KONWIHR" project for scientific high-powered calculation, in which the faculty of process engineering and the chair for current mechanics in the sector of current simulation work together to find common functional solutions to offer to the industry. The "Ohm" thereby significantly bridges the gap between basic research and application research.

The university of applied sciences is in general a competent partner for the industry in the sector of scientific and technological transfer. It provides advisory services for questions of technology and innovation, applied research and development, associate partnerships, measuring and testing services and supplies expertises and studies. For the energy region of Nuremberg the "Ohm" has a wide spread range of subjects on hand; for example, in the university's own Institut für Energie und Gebäude (ieg), competent and intelligent solutions for highly efficient energy and facility management are available.

Finally, the institution has received official certification from the charitable Hertie-Stiftung as a family-friendly university/college and offers students and employees alike optimal conditions for combining job, study course and private life. In order to remain strong in the future the Georg-Simon-Ohm University of applied sciences expands constantly: following the latest building projects for economics and social studies in the Bahnhofstraße (1999) and the new central workshops with mensateria (2002) a modern building for applied chemistry and central services was begun in the summer of 2005 which should be finalised in 2008.

Forschung und Technologie
Research and Technology

Versuchsanordnung zur Solarenergie im Fachbereich Maschinenbau und Versorgungstechnik der Fachhochschule Nürnberg

Set-up of an experiment for solar energy in the Faculty of Machine Construction and Service Technology at the university of applied sciences in Nuremberg

Zukunftsweisend – die Forschungsinstitute

Professor Dr. Heinz Gerhäuser

Mit ihren Universitäten, den Fachhochschulen und den beiden Fraunhofer-Instituten verfügt die Metropolregion Nürnberg über leistungsfähige Forschungseinrichtungen. Zahlreiche Kooperationen und Netzwerke der Einrichtungen untereinander sowie mit Wirtschaftspartnern der Region ermöglichen ein breites Kompetenzspektrum von der Grundlagenforschung bis hin zu praktischen Umsetzungen.

Das Fraunhofer-Institut für Integrierte Schaltungen IIS betreibt seit 20 Jahren erfolgreich angewandte Forschung für die Mikroelektronik sowie für die Informations- und Kommunikationstechnik. Unser Potenzial sind Ideen, unser Ziel ist die Nutzung von Wissenschaft und Forschung für innovative Technologien und neue Produkte. Unsere Dienstleistungen und Entwicklungen werden in der ganzen Welt genutzt und eingesetzt. Das am Fraunhofer IIS entwickelte und mittlerweile weltweit angewandte Audiocodierverfahren MP3 ist ein sichtbarer – und hörbarer – Erfolg für die Fraunhofer-Gesellschaft und die Metropolregion Nürnberg.

Unsere Forscher entwickeln zukunftsorientierte elektronische Geräte, die das Leben und Arbeiten der Menschen im 21. Jahrhundert unterstützen. Wir forschen auf den Gebieten Audiocodierung, digitale Rundfunksysteme, Kamera- und Bildverarbeitungstechnologien, Prüfsysteme, Funkortung und Navigation sowie Medizintechnik. Ein grundlegender Forschungsbereich des Fraunhofer IIS sind integrierte Schaltungen und Sensoren.

Das Jubiläumsjahr 2005 war für uns nicht nur ein Jahr des Rückblicks und des Feierns, sondern auch ein Jahr der Vorbereitungen auf zukünftige Entwicklungen. Im Dezember des Jahres erfolgte die Grundsteinlegung für den zweiten Bauabschnitt des Hauptsitzes in Erlangen-Tennenlohe. Mit dem Erweiterungsbau wird sich die Büro- und Laborkapazität des Fraunhofer IIS nach etwa zweijähriger Bauzeit fast verdoppeln.

With its universities, universities of applied sciences and the two Fraunhofer-Institutes, the metropolitan region of Nuremberg has several extremely efficient research institutions at its disposal. Countless cooperations and networking of institutions amongst each other as well as with the region's industrial partners enable a wide range of competences ranging from basic research through to practical application.

The Fraunhofer-Institute for Integrated Circuits IIS has successfully worked on applied research for microelectronics as well as for information and communication technology for more than 20 years. Our potential lies in ideas; our target is the utilisation of science and research for innovative technologies and new products. Our services and developments are applied and utilised all over the world. The audio coding process MP3 developed at the Fraunhofer IIS which, in the meantime, is used all over the world, has been a visible – and audible – success for the Fraunhofer-Gesellschaft and the metropolitan region of Nuremberg.

Our researchers develop future-oriented electronic equipment which supports the life and work of people in the 21st century. We carry out research on the sectors of audio coding, digital radio systems, camera and image processing technologies, testing systems, radio location and navigation as well as medicine technology. One of the basic research sections of the Fraunhofer IIS is dedicated to integrated circuits and sensors.

For us the jubilee year of 2005 was not only a year of retrospect and celebration, it was also a year of preparing for future developments. In December of that year the foundation stone was laid for the second stage of the head office in Erlangen-Tennenlohe. With the completion of the building extension, which will take almost two years to construct, the office and laboratory capacity of the Fraunhofer IIS will be almost doubled.

The Fraunhofer IIS installations in Nuremberg and Fürth will also be significantly extended and will, in time, be developed into independent Fraunhofer-Institutes.

Future-oriented – Research Institutions

Forschung und Technologie
Research and Technology

Antennenmesshalle am Fraunhofer-Institut für Integrierte Schaltungen IIS in Erlangen

Antenna measuring hall at the Fraunhofer-Institute for Integrated Circuits IIS in Erlangen

Auch in Nürnberg und Fürth werden die Einrichtungen des Fraunhofer IIS signifikant ausgebaut und langfristig zu eigenen Fraunhofer-Instituten entwickelt.

In der Forschungsfabrik im Nürnberger Nordostpark wird das Thema „Informations- und Kommunikationstechnik für die Lokalisierung und Navigation" ein neuer Forschungsschwerpunkt. Es gewinnt vor allem für autonome und energieautarke Systeme zunehmend an Bedeutung.

Das Fraunhofer-Entwicklungszentrum Röntgentechnik EZRT widmet sich seit dem Jahr 2000 am Standort Fürth der industriellen Röntgentechnik. Neben Forschung und Entwicklung bieten die Wissenschaftler und Techniker der Industrie auch Röntgendienstleistungen für die Qualitätssicherung an. Weitere Chancen ermöglicht das neue, mit europäischen Mitteln geförderte „Entwicklungszentrum für neue zerstörungsfreie Prüfmethoden an neuen Materialien für die Luft- und Raumfahrt". Im Rahmen dieses Projekts

The theme of "Information and communication technology for localising and navigation" will become a new focal point of research in the research factory in the Nuremberg Northeast Park. It is increasingly gaining in significance primarily for autonomous and self-sufficient energy systems.

At the Fürth location the Fraunhofer development centre X-ray technology EZRT has been dedicated to industrial X-ray technology since the year 2000. Alongside research and development, scientists and technicians offer to the industry also X-ray services for application in quality assurance. Further opportunities are provided with the new "Development centre for new nondestructive testing methods on new materials for aerospace" which also receives European financial support. Within the framework of this project, other testing technologies such as ultra-sound and eddy current will be applied in Fürth alongside X-ray technology.

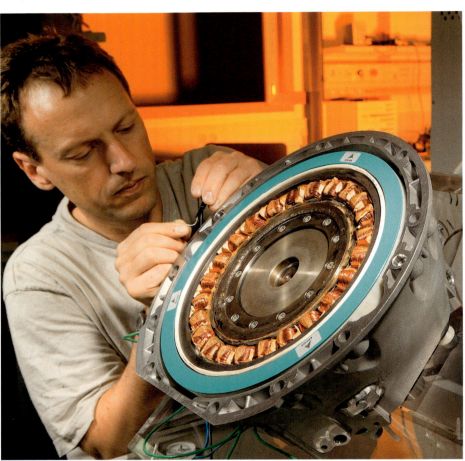

Im Zentrum für Kfz-Leistungselektronik und Mechatronik (ZKLM) in Nürnberg werden leistungselektronische Systeme für die Autos von morgen entwickelt.

Power switching systems for the cars of the future are developed in the centre for automobile power electronics and mechatronic (ZKLM) in Nuremberg.

Forschung und Technologie
Research and Technology

Blick in das Reinraumlabor des Fraunhofer-Instituts für Integrierte Systeme und Bauelementetechnologie: Untersuchung von Oberflächen mit einem Massenspektrometer im Nanobereich

A glimpse in the clean room laboratory of the Fraunhofer Institute for Integrated Systems and Component Technology: examining surfaces with a mass spectrometer in the nano range

werden in Fürth neben der Röntgentechnik auch andere Prüftechniken wie Ultraschall und Wirbelstrom zum Einsatz kommen.

Für den Standort Erlangen, die Region Erlangen-Nürnberg-Fürth und darüber hinaus für den gesamten Großraum markieren die Begriffe Medizin, Medizintechnik und Pharmazie wichtige Kompetenzbereiche. Zahlreiche Kooperationen zwischen medizintechnischen, klinischen und forschungsorientierten Partnern auf der ganzen Welt zeugen von der Qualifikation des Großraums Erlangen-Nürnberg-Fürth. Die Bedeutung von Stadt und Region im Bereich Medizintechnik („Medizinstadt Erlangen", „Medical Valley") wird von kommunaler, landes- und bundespolitischer Seite anerkannt und unterstützt. Die medizintechnischen Schwerpunktbereiche des Fraunhofer IIS liegen auf medizinischer Bildgebung, deren Auswertung und Visualisierung, auf medizinischer Endoskopie und mikroskopiebasierten Bildauswertesystemen sowie auf drahtloser Patientenbeobachtung und Gesundheitstelematik.

Vorangetrieben wird beim Fraunhofer IIS auch die Forschung im digitalen Medienbereich. Musikangebote im Internet sind schon heute ohne das in den neunziger Jahren vom Fraunhofer IIS vorgestellte Format MP3 nicht mehr denkbar. Weitere Audio-

The terms medicine, medicine technology and pharmacy are important competence areas for the whole of the area, for the business location of Erlangen, the region of Erlangen-Nuremberg-Fürth and beyond. Countless cooperations between medicine-technical, clinical and research-oriented partners everywhere in the world bear witness to the qualification of the conurbation area of Erlangen-Nuremberg-Fürth. The importance of town and region in the sector of medical technology ("medicine city of Erlangen", "Medical Valley") has been recognised and supported by community, country and national bodies. The Fraunhofer IIS's medicine technology department's interests are mainly focused on medical imaging as well as its evaluation and visualisation, medical endoscopy and microscopy-based image evaluation systems as well as cordless patient monitoring and health telemetry.

Research in the digital media sector is also being pushed forwards by the Fraunhofer IIS. Music offered today in the internet would be unthinkable without the MP3 format introduced by the Fraunhofer IIS in the nineties. Other audio developments such as advanced audio coding AAC enable countless new applications. The digital radio system Digital Radio Mondiale DRM brings improvements such as disturbance-free reception, optimal hearing quality and additional data serv-

entwicklungen wie zum Beispiel Advanced Audio Coding AAC ermöglichen zahlreiche neue Anwendungen. Das digitale Rundfunksystem Digital Radio Mondiale DRM bringt Verbesserungen wie störungsfreien Empfang, optimale Hörqualität und Datenzusatzdienste auf der fast schon vergessenen Kurzwelle. Mit Digital Audio Broadcasting DAB ist Radiohören sogar im Surround-Sound möglich. Die Technologie DVB-H (Digital Video Broadcasting Handheld) schließlich verwirklicht Fernsehen auf mobilen Endgeräten wie Handys oder persönlichen digitalen Assistenten (PDAs). Ein anderes Forschungsfeld des Fraunhofer IIS ist die Digitalisierung der gesamten Kinokette. Der Kinofilm der Zukunft im digitalen Format ist damit einfacher zu produzieren, zu verteilen und zu archivieren.

Zusammen mit seinen Partnern aus Wirtschaft und Wissenschaft hat auch das Fraunhofer-Institut für Integrierte Systeme und Bauelementetechnologie IISB die Entwicklung der Mikroelektronik aktiv mitgestaltet. Die Wissenschaftler arbeiten an Aufgabenstellungen von den Grundlagen der Kristallzüchtung über Prozesse und Fertigungsgeräte für die Nanotechnologie bis hin zur Systementwicklung für die Leistungselektronik. Als sehr fruchtbar hat sich insbesondere die Zusammenarbeit mit der regionalen Wirtschaft und Wissenschaft erwiesen. Vielfältig ist die Kooperation mit der Universität Erlangen-Nürnberg und mit zahlreichen Unternehmen in der Metropolregion. 2005 wurde die Außenstelle „Zentrum für Kfz-Leistungselektronik und Mechatronik ZKLM" in Nürnberg eröffnet.

Der Aufbau von weiteren, zukunftsweisenden Forschungsstätten in der Metropolregion wird vorangetrieben. Die Ansiedlung von Fraunhofer-Projektgruppen in Bayreuth hat begonnen. Der Start für die erste Projektgruppe „Prozessinnovation für Unternehmen des ostbayerischen Raumes PRINZ" des Fraunhofer-Instituts für Produktionstechnik und Automatisierung IPA in Stuttgart erfolgte am 2. März 2006. Die Projektgruppe „Röntgengestützte Materialcharakterisierung" vom Fraunhofer IIS in Erlangen wird folgen.

Die Einrichtungen zur Forschung und Entwicklung in der Metropolregion treiben Themen voran, die weit in die Zukunft reichen. Sie stärken damit auf lange Sicht die Wirtschaft im Großraum und tragen zu seiner Attraktivität als Wirtschaftsstandort und als Lebensraum bei.

Information

Europäische Metropolregion Nürnberg
European Metropolitan Region of Nuremberg
Forschungs- und Entwicklungseinrichtungen außerhalb der Hochschulen
Research and Development institutions outside of Universities

Fraunhofer-Institut für Integrierte Schaltungen (IIS), Erlangen
www.iis.fraunhofer.de

Fraunhofer-Institut für integrierte Systeme und Bauelementetechnologie (IISB), Erlangen
www.iisb.fraunhofer.de

Fraunhofer-Institut für Silikatforschung (ISC), Würzburg
www.isc.fraunhofer.de

Max-Planck-Forschungsgruppe Optik, Information, Photonik, Erlangen
http://kerr.physik.uni-erlangen.de/mpf/php/

Heinrich-Hertz-Institut, Terabitlabor, Nürnberg
www.hhi.fraunhofer.de

Zentrum für Angewandte Energieforschung (ZAE Bayern) mit Sitz in Würzburg und Erlangen, Würzburg
www.zae-bayern.de

Süddeutsches Kunststoffzentrum (SKZ), Würzburg
www.skz.de

Zentrum für Werkstoffanalytik Lauf, Lauf a. d. Pegnitz
www.werkstoffanalytik.de

FuE-Einrichtung Neue Materialien Nordbayern Technika in Bayreuth, Fürth und Würzburg, Bayreuth
www.nmngmbh.de

Bayerisches Laserzentrum, Erlangen
www.blz.org

Forschungs- und Entwicklungszentrum für Sondertechnologien (FES), Schwabach und Rednitzhembach
www.fes-schwabach.de

atz Entwicklungszentrum, Sulzbach-Rosenberg
www.atz.de

EBA-Zentrum zur verstärkten Nutzung von Biomasse, Weidenbach
www.triesdorf.de/eba

Bayerisches Landesamt für Gesundheit und Lebensmittelsicherheit (LGL), Erlangen
www.lgl.bayern.de

Bayerisches Landesamt für Umwelt (LfU), Kulmbach und Marktredwitz (Boden- und Gesteinsanalytik, Landesaufnahme Geologie und Boden)
www.lfu.bayern.de

Bundesforschungsanstalt für Ernährung und Lebensmittel (BFEL), Kulmbach
www.bfa-fleisch.de

Institut für Arbeitsmarkt- und Berufsforschung der Bundesagentur für Arbeit, Nürnberg
www.iab.de

Forschungseinrichtung der Leibniz-Gemeinschaft, Germanisches Nationalmuseum, Nürnberg
www.gnm.de

Forschung und Technologie
Research and Technology

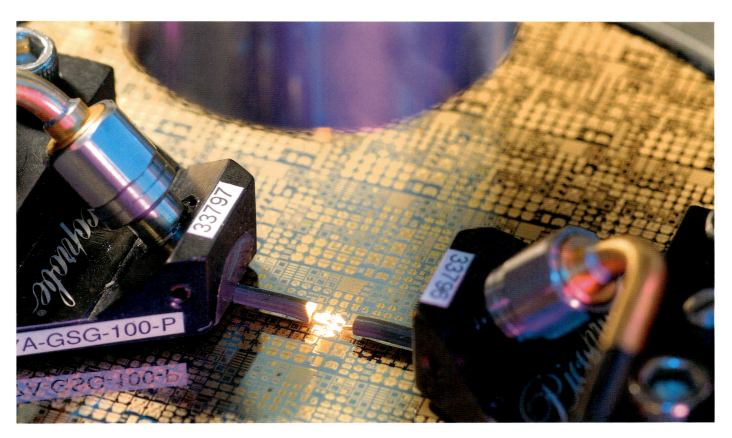

Schaltungsentwicklung für hochbit-ratige Übertragungssysteme

Circuit development for high bit-rated transmission systems

ices to the almost forgotten short wave. With Digital Audio Broadcasting DAB, listening to the radio is even possible in surround-sound. And DVB-H (Digital Video Broadcasting Handheld) technology enables one to watch television on mobile units such as cell phones or personal digital assistants (PDAs). One other important research field of the Fraunhofer IIS is the digitalisation of the entire cinema chain. The cinema film of the future in digital format is thereby easier to produce, to distribute and to file.

Together with its partners from industry and science, the Fraunhofer-Institute for Integrated Systems and Component Technology IISB has also actively helped to fashion the development of microelectronics. Scientists are working on types of problems from the basics of the cultivation of crystals via processes and production equipment for nanotechnology through to system development for power electronics. Cooperation with the university of Erlangen-Nuremberg and with numerous undertakings in the metropolitan region is diverse. In 2005 the branch "Centre for vehicle power electronics and mechatronics ZKLM" was opened in Nuremberg.

The expansion of further, future-oriented research institutes in the metropolitan region is being pushed ahead. The settlement of Fraunhofer-project groups in Bayreuth has already begun. The start for the first project group "Process innovation for undertakings of the East Bavarian Area PRINZ" of the Fraunhofer-Institute for Production Engineering and Automation IPA in Stuttgart was on the 2nd of March 2006. The project group "X-ray supported material characterisation" from the Fraunhofer IIS in Erlangen will follow.

The institutions of research and development in the metropolitan region are pushing ahead with subjects which reach well into the future. In the long term, they strengthen the industry in the area and contribute towards its attraction as a business and residential location.

Das Nationalmuseum der deutschen Kultur steht in Nürnberg

Professor Dr. G. Ulrich Großmann

Mit 1,3 Millionen Sammlungsstücken ist das Germanische Nationalmuseum das größte kulturgeschichtliche Museum in Mitteleuropa und eines der größten weltweit. 1852 auf Initiative des fränkischen Adligen Hans von und zu Aufseß gegründet, wurde es 1853 als das Nationalmuseum des Deutschen Bundes anerkannt und ist damit ein typischer Vertreter der föderalen Struktur der deutschen Kultur. Das Nationalmuseum befindet sich nicht in der Hauptstadt, sondern an einem der historisch wichtigsten Orte, in Nürnberg. Der Name des Museums leitet sich von dem durch die Brüder Grimm eingeführten Begriff für die Erforschung deutscher Sprache und Kultur ab: Germanistik, heute noch die Bezeichnung für das Lehrfach für deutsche Literatur und Sprache.

Das Museum im Kloster

1857 erhielt das Germanische Nationalmuseum, das zunächst provisorisch im Tiergärtner Turm untergebracht war und mit Coburg und der Wartburg über Räumlichkeiten verhandelte, als Standort das im Jahr 1830 gegründete ehemalige Kartäuserkloster in Nürnberg. Die Präsentation der Sammlung in einem mittelalterlichen Kloster entsprach dem Geschichtsbezug des Museumsauftrags. Der große Kreuzgang umschließt weiträumig die Klosterkirche; drei Flügel sind davon heute noch erhalten, ebenso drei der alten Mönchshäuser, obwohl das Kloster mit Einführung der Reformation 1525 aufgelöst wurde.

Die Vielfalt der Sammlung

Das Germanische Nationalmuseum zeigt die Kulturgeschichte des deutschsprachigen Raumes. Das Museum leistet einen Vergleich über die Kunstgattungen hinweg. Einzigartig in Deutschland ist, dass Gemälde, Skulpturen, Kunsthandwerk, Waffen, wissenschaftliche Instrumente und Textilien einer Epoche in engem Zusammenhang gezeigt werden.

With 1.3 million articles in the collection, the Germanic National Museum is the largest cultural history museum in Central Europe and one of the largest worldwide. Founded in 1852 on the initiative of the Franconian aristocrat Hans von und zu Aufseß, it was acknowledged in 1853 as the National Museum of the German Confederation thereby becoming a typical representative of the federal structure of German culture. The National Museum is not located in the capital, but in Nuremberg, one of the most important historical locations. The name of the museum can be traced back to the phrase introduced by the Grimm Brothers: Germanistics, meaning research of the German language and culture, today still the title of the subject dealing with German literature and language.

The Museum in a Cloister

In 1857 the Germanic National Museum, at that time located provisionally in the Tiergärtner Tower although negotiations with Coburg and the Wartburg were under way concerning premises, received the former Carthusian cloister in Nuremberg which had been founded in 1830 as residence. The presentation of the collection in a medieval cloister was most suitable considering the museum commission's historical reference. The large cloister spaciously enclosed the cloister church; three wings of which are still preserved today as well as three of the old monk's houses, even though the cloister was dissolved with the introduction of the Reformation in 1525.

The Variety of the Collection

The Germanic National Museum shows the cultural history of the German speaking area and has made a comparison beyond its artistic forms. The fact that paintings, sculptures, crafts, weapons, scientific instruments and textiles from one epoch are displayed in close relationship to one another is unique in Germany.

The National Museum of German Culture is located in Nuremberg

Kulturglanzlichter
Cultural Highlights

Das „Schlüsselfelder Schiff" entstand um 1500 als Tafelaufsatz aus knapp 6 kg vergoldetem Silber. Das Schiff mit Takelage, Besatzung und Waren ist bis in alle Einzelheiten detailgetreu ausgearbeitet.

The "Schlüsselfelder Schiff" was created about 1500 as part of the table top piece made of almost 6 kg gold-plated silver. The ship with tackle, crew and goods is elaborately worked, true to the last detail.

Ursprünglich konzentrierte sich die Sammeltätigkeit des Museums auf das Mittelalter und die frühe Neuzeit. Erst später erweiterte man den Sammelauftrag auf die Vor- und Frühgeschichte, aus dem heute der Goldkegel von Etzelsdorf-Buch (um 1000 bis 800 v. Chr.) und der Schatz aus Domagnano (San Marino, um 500 n. Chr.) herausragende Werke sind. Das entgegengesetzte Ende der Sammel- und Ausstellungstätigkeit wird durch Namen wie Joseph Beuys, dessen Filzmantel das Museum zeigt, vertreten, aber auch durch Nam June Paik, die „Straße der Menschenrechte" von Dani Karavan und den berühmten Radio-Plattenspieler der Firma Braun („Schneewittchensarg").

Die Sammeltätigkeit des Museums umfasste alle Bereiche der „materiellen" Kultur, reicht also von Gegenständen des täglichen Gebrauchs über Objekte

Originally, the collecting activities of the museum concentrated themselves on the medieval and the early modern times. It was only later that the collection commission was extended to the prehistoric and early historic times, of which the golden ball from Etzelsdorf-Buch (about 1000 to 800 B.C.) and the treasure from Domagnano (San Marino, about 500 A.D.) are exceptional works.

The opposite end of the collecting and exhibiting activities is represented with names such as Joseph Beuys, whose felt coat is displayed in the museum, together with Nam June Paik, the so-called street of human rights ("Straße der Menschenrechte") from Dani Karavan and the well-known radio-record player from Messrs Braun ("Schneewittchensarg") Snow White's coffin.

Straße der Menschenrechte und Eingang des Germanischen Nationalmuseums in Nürnberg

The street of human rights and entrance to the Germanic National Museum in Nuremberg

der religiösen Verehrung bis zu Werken der bildenden Kunst. Die umfangreiche Sammeltätigkeit war nur durch das außerordentliche Bürgerengagement möglich, denn viele originale Werke der Kunst und Kultur wurden von privaten Stiftern und Leihgebern, darunter viele Nürnberger Familien und Unternehmen, dem Museum übergeben. Gemälde, Skulpturen und Kunsthandwerk, vor- und frühgeschichtliche Grabungsfunde, volkskundliche Keramik und Möbel, aber auch Musikinstrumente, Objekte der Zunft, der Rechtsaltertümer und des Handels sollten das Leben der Menschen in den vergangenen Epochen dokumentieren. Selbst Aspekte des Hausbaus und der Architektur blieben dabei nicht ausgespart.

International bekannt ist das Museum durch seine schier unerschöpflichen Bestände zur deutschen Kulturgeschichte. So finden sich hier die ältesten Schulbücher, Rechenbücher nebst Rechenpfennigen, aber auch die Originalhandschrift des Struwwelpeter. Mit dem Echternacher Codex (um 1000 n. Chr.) stellt das Museum eines der wichtigsten Bücher der europäischen Buchmalerei aus. Der weltweit älteste Globus, der Behaim-Globus, entstand unmittelbar vor der Entdeckung Amerikas und ist mit seinen zahlreichen Ortsangaben eine Fundgrube zum Wissen und zur Mobilität des endenden Mittelalters. Von der ältesten deutschen Eisenbahn besitzt das Museum einen Wagen, der als Leihgabe in den Haupträumen des DB-Museums ausgestellt ist. In der Sammlung zum 19. Jahrhundert zeigen eine Guillotine, die Erstfassung von Carl Spitzwegs „Armer Poet", eines der berühmtesten deutschen Gemälde, der Schreibtisch von Wilhelm Grimm sowie zahlreiche Werke der Malerei, Skulptur und des Kunsthandwerks die Bandbreite jener Epoche, mit der die Industrialisierung und Technisierung ihren Lauf nahm.

The collecting activities of the museum encompasses all areas of "material" culture, stretches then from objects of daily use via objects of religious worship through to works of fine arts. The extensive collecting activity was only possible thanks to citizens' exceptional commitments as many original works of art and culture were handed over to the museum by private donators and lenders, amongst them being many Nuremberg families and firms. Paintings, sculptures and articles of craft, archaeological finds from pre-historical and early modern history, folkloric ceramics and furniture, as well as musical instruments, objects from the Guilds, objects of law and trade are meant to document the lives of people in past epochs. Even aspects of house building and architecture were displayed.

The museum is internationally known for its almost inexhaustible stock of German cultural history. Thus, we can find the oldest school books, arithmetic books alongside arithmetic pennies, and also the original hand-written story of Struwwelpeter. With the Echternacher Codex (about 1000 A.D.) the museum displays one of the most important books containing European book illustrations. The world's oldest globe, the Behaim-Globe, was created shortly before the discovery of America and is, with its countless names of places, a treasure trove of knowledge and of mobility in the closing Middle Ages. The museum also possesses a coach of the oldest German railways which is currently displayed as a loan in the main rooms of the DB museum. In the collection on the 19th century there is a guillotine, the first edition of Carl Spitzweg's "Armer Poet" (Poor Poet) one of the best known German paintings, Wilhelm Grimm's writing desk as well as innumerable works of painting, sculpture and crafts covering the range of the epoch with which industrialisation and mechanisation began.

Kulturglanzlichter
Cultural Highlights

Der Behaim-Globus entstand kurz vor der Entdeckung Amerikas und gilt als ältester erhaltener Globus der Welt.

The Behaim globe was created just before America was discovered and is considered to be the oldest globe existing in the world.

Für das 16. und frühe 17. Jahrhundert hingegen stehen Namen wie Peter Henlein, der als Schöpfer der ältesten Taschenuhr der Welt gilt, und Albrecht Dürer, von dem allein acht Werke ausgestellt sind – nach Wien und München die größte Zahl originaler Dürer-Werke, die man in einem Museum betrachten kann. Auch Albrecht Altdorfer ist mit einem Werk vertreten, dessen Urheberschaft erst jüngst entdeckt wurde. Zwei bedeutende Rembrandt-Gemälde ergänzen die Sammlungsbestände. Auf 25 000 Quadratmetern werden rund 25 000 Werke der Kunst und Kultur dauerhaft gezeigt; im Jahr 2006 runden Dauerausstellungen zum Hohen Mittelalter und zur Vor- und Frühgeschichte die Präsentation ab. Weitere 900 000 Werke sind über Bibliothek und Graphische Sammlung für den Besucher erreichbar. Ein weit gefächertes Programm von Sonderausstellungen widmet sich darüber hinaus Themen, die Wissenschaft und Publikum bewegen, von der „Faszination Meisterwerk" über die Frage „Was ist deutsch?" bis hin zu Albrecht Dürer und seiner Kunst.

The 16th and early 17th century, however, are represented by names such as Peter Henlein considered to be the creator of the oldest pocket watch in the world and Albrecht Dürer, eight of whose works are exhibited – after Vienna and Munich the largest number of original Dürer works to be observed in one museum. Albrecht Altdorfer is also represented with one of his works, the provenance of which has only recently been discovered. Two important Rembrandt paintings supplement the collection. Some 25,000 works of art and culture are on permanent display in 25,000 square metres; in the year 2006 permanent exhibitions on the peak of the middle ages and on prehistory and early modern will complete the presentation. Another 900,000 works are attainable for the visitor in the Library and Graphics Collection. A widespread programme of special exhibitions are dedicated to themes which concern science and public alike, from the "Fascination of Masterpieces" via the question "What is German?" through to Albrecht Dürer and his art.

Bayreuth – internationale Festspielstadt Richard Wagners

Dr. Dieter Mronz* / Dr. Michael Hohl

*von 1988 bis Mai 2006 Oberbürgermeister der Stadt Bayreuth und Geschäftsführer der Richard-Wagner-Stiftung

Die Stadt Bayreuth präsentiert sich in der Metropolregion Nürnberg als internationale Festspielstadt Richard Wagners, nordbayerische Universitätsstadt und oberfränkische Regierungshauptstadt.

Bayreuths internationaler Ruf als Kulturstadt beruht vor allem auf der Festspielidee Richard Wagners. Über 60 000 Opernbesucher erleben während der jährlichen Festspielzeit die Stars der Wagner-Szene in richtungweisenden Inszenierungen. Die Bayreuther Festspiele haben die Stadt weltweit bekannt gemacht, ebenso wie ihre Sänger, Dirigenten, Regisseure und Bühnenbildner. Jahr für Jahr strömt ein internationales Publikum zum Festspielhaus auf den Grünen Hügel, dessen Grundstein dort 1872 gelegt wurde, und das mit seiner unvergleichlichen Akustik die Besucher in seinen Bann zieht. Ein Opernhaus mit der künstlerischen Identität des Erbauers und des Komponisten der aufgeführten Werke wie dieses gibt es sonst nirgendwo.

Die ungebrochene Attraktivität der Bayreuther Festspiele als bundesdeutsches kulturelles Großereignis spiegelt sich nicht zuletzt in einem immer größer werdenden Medienaufgebot wider, das in allen Facetten und Schattierungen über die künstlerischen Aspekte der Festspielinszenierungen, aber auch über Glanz und Glamour des Festspielpublikums berichtet.

Richard Wagner ist ein ganz besonderer Glanzpunkt in der Geschichte der Kulturstadt Bayreuth – aber nicht ihr Ausgangspunkt. Schon weit früher zog es bedeutende Künstler hierher. Der Straßburger Baumeister Michael Mebart prägte im 17. Jahrhundert mit seinen repräsentativen Bauten das Stadtbild. Und als 1619 in der von ihm wiederaufgebauten Stadtkirche die 35-stimmige Orgel eingeweiht wurde, lud Markgraf Christian die bedeutendsten Organisten seiner Zeit ein. Auch die Baumeister Charles Philipp Dieussart und Leonhard Dientzenhofer ebenso wie der Hofbildhauer Elias Räntz arbeiteten in der Residenzstadt. Georg Philipp Telemann komponierte für den Bayreuther Hof.

The city of Bayreuth presents itself in the metropolitan region of Nuremberg as Richard Wagner's international festival city, North Bavarian university city and Upper Franconian governing capital.

Bayreuth's international reputation as a cultural city rests primarily on Richard Wagner's idea of a festival. More than 60,000 opera visitors watch and hear the stars of the Wagner scene in forward-looking productions during the annual festival period. The Bayreuth Festival has made the city well known all over the world, equally so the singers, conductors, directors and stage designers. Year after year an international public streams into the festival opera house on the green hill, the foundation for which was laid in 1872, with its unique acoustics holding visitors spellbound. An opera house such as this with the artistic identity of the builder and the composer of the works produced can be found nowhere else.

The unbroken attraction of the Bayreuth Festival as a major national and cultural event is reflected not least in an increasingly large media crowd reporting on all the artistic aspects of the festival productions in all their facets and shades and also reporting on the splendour and glamour of the festival public.

Richard Wagner is a particular highlight in the history of the cultural city of Bayreuth – but it does not begin with him. Important artists were drawn here much earlier. Michael Mebart, the master builder from Strasbourg marked the 17th century cityscape with his representative buildings. And when, in 1619, the 35-voice organ was inaugurated in the city church that he had reconstructed, Margrave Christian invited all the most important organists of the time. The master builders Charles Philipp Dieussart and Leonhard Dientzenhofer as well as the court sculptor Elias Räntz also worked in the residency while Georg Philipp Telemann composed for the Bayreuth Court.

In the middle of the 18th century Margravine Wilhelmine, favourite sister of Friedrich der Große

Bayreuth – Richard Wagner's International Festival City

Sein Ruf ragt in die Welt: das Festspielhaus in Bayreuth.
Im Bild unten:
Familie Wagner auf dem Roten Teppich

Its reputation is worldwide: the Festspielhaus (festival opera house) in Bayreuth
In the picture below:
The Wagner family on the red carpet

Mitte des 18. Jahrhunderts brachte Markgräfin Wilhelmine, Lieblingsschwester Friedrichs des Großen, neue Impulse in die Stadt. Sie malte, komponierte und pflegte Kontakte zu geistigen Größen ihrer Zeit. Mit dem französischen Philosophen Voltaire spielte sie gar gemeinsam Theater in Bayreuth.

Wilhelmine berief ausgezeichnete Künstler aus Italien, Frankreich und Deutschland nach Bayreuth. Neben exzellenten Musikern, Sängern, Tänzern und Schauspielern konnte der Hof die berühmten Architekten Joseph Saint-Pierre und Carl Philipp von Gontard verpflichten, den Bildhauer Johann David Räntz, die Maler Wilhelm Wunder und Johann Benjamin Müller. Die Stuckarbeiten von Jean Baptiste Pedrozzi zeugen heute noch von der künstlerischen Qualität des Bayreuther Rokoko. Guiseppe und Carlo Bibiena, Vater und Sohn, schufen das Markgräfliche Opernhaus, das bis heute als das schönste erhaltene Barocktheater Europas gilt und auf der Vorschlagsliste für die Aufnahme ins UNESCO-Weltkulturerbe steht.

Die Gartenkünste jener Epoche sind im Hofgarten am Neuen Schloss lebendig, vor allem aber in der Eremitage, einem der bedeutendsten Beispiele europäischer Gartenkultur.

Markgräfin Wilhelmine war es auch, die mit ihrem fürstlichen Opernhaus, das damals als das größte in Europa galt, die Voraussetzungen schuf, dass sich im 19. Jahrhundert Richard Wagner für Bayreuth interessierte. Bei seinem Besuch stellte er zwar fest, dass es für seinen Traum vom „Gesamtkunstwerk" immer noch zu beengt war, doch weitsichtige Stadtväter stellten dem Komponisten ein exponiertes Grundstück für den Bau seines Festspielhauses kostenlos zur Verfügung – ein in heutiger Zeit aufgrund der unternehmerischen Risiken wohl kaum wiederholbarer Vorgang.

Dank Richard Wagner hielt sich auch der Vater seiner Frau Cosima, der Komponist Franz Liszt, wiederholt in Bayreuth auf. Bei seinem Festspielbesuch 1886 starb er und wurde in einer eigenen Grabkapelle auf dem Bayreuther Stadtfriedhof beerdigt. Prominente Mitglieder der Wagner-Familie haben hier ebenfalls ihre letzte Ruhe gefunden.

Das ehemalige Wohnhaus Richard Wagners – „Wahnfried" – beherbergt heute als viel besuchte Attraktion das großartige Richard-Wagner-Museum mit Nationalarchiv und Forschungsstätte. Und im benachbarten Sterbehaus von Franz Liszt bewahrt ein weiteres Museum das Andenken an den Klaviervirtuosen. Gleich nebenan befinden sich das Deutsche Freimaurermuseum und das Jean-Paul-Museum: Vier museale Kostbarkeiten, auf die die Stadt zu Recht stolz ist. Die reiche Bayreuther Museumslandschaft zählt inzwischen 25 unterschiedliche Einrichtungen, denen Experten teilweise europäische Ausstrahlung bescheinigen.

(Frederick the Great), gave the city new impulses. She painted, composed and maintained contact with the intellectual personalities of her time. She even played theatre in Bayreuth with the French philosopher Voltaire.

Wilhelmine summoned distinguished artists from Italy, France and Germany to Bayreuth. Alongside excellent musicians, singers, dancers and actors the Court was able to engage the famous architects Joseph Saint-Pierre and Carl Philipp von Gontard, the sculptor Johann David Räntz, the painters Wilhelm Wunder and Johann Benjamin Müller. The stucco works by Jean Baptiste Pedrozzi still demonstrate the artistic qualities of the Bayreuth Rococo. Guiseppe and Carlo Bibiena, father and son, created the Margrave's opera house, considered even today as one of the best maintained Baroque theatres in Europe and which is up for acceptance on the UNESCO world cultural heritage list.

The gardening arts of that epoch are alive in the Hofgarten of the Neues Schloss, but principally in the Eremitage, one of the most important examples of European garden culture.

It was also Margravine Wilhelmine who, with her princely opera house considered at that time to be the largest in Europe, created the conditions under which Richard Wagner became interested in Bayreuth in the 19th century. It is true that during his visit he had decided that it was still too confined for his dream of a "Gesamtkunstwerk", but far-sighted city fathers put a suitable piece of land at his disposal for the construction of a Festival house free of charge – a procedure that could hardly be repeated today due to the entrepreneurial risks.

Thanks to Richard Wagner, the composer Franz Liszt who was the father of his wife Cosima visited Bayreuth several times. He died in 1886 during a visit to the Festival and was interred in his own burial chapel on the municipal cemetery in Bayreuth. Prominent members of the Wagner family also have their final resting place here.

The former residence of Richard Wagner – "Wahnfried" – today accommodates the splendid Richard-Wagner-Museum, a well-visited attraction with national archive and research establishment. And in the neighbouring house where Franz Liszt died a further museum preserves the memorabilia of the piano virtuoso. Next door are the German Freemason Museum and the Jean-Paul-Museum: Four museum rarities of which the city is proud, and rightly so. In the meantime the rich Bayreuth museum scene totals 25 different establishments with a certain amount of European charisma as experts are pleased to document.

The cultural highlights in Bayreuth form and characterise the course of the entire year: the concert series

Kulturglanzlichter
Cultural Highlights

Szenenbild aus „Der fliegende Holländer" nach einer Inszenierung von Claus Guth, 2005

A scene from "The Flying Dutchman" in a production by Claus Guth, 2005

Die kulturellen Highlights in Bayreuth gestalten und prägen den gesamten Jahresverlauf: die Konzertreihe „Musica Bayreuth", Gastspiele der Bayerischen Staatstheater im Rahmen der Fränkischen Festwoche, das Bayreuther Osterfestival oder die Veranstaltungsreihe „Bayreuther Barock". Abwechslungsreiche Konzertangebote privater Veranstalter runden diese attraktive Palette das ganze Jahr über ab. Aber auch an der Basis wird auf musikalischem Gebiet viel geleistet, so in der groß ausgebauten städtischen Musikschule, im Orchesterverein und im Philharmonischen Chor Bayreuth. Und die Hochschule für Evangelische Kirchenmusik bietet mit ihren Studiengängen akademisches Niveau und viel beachtete Angebote der sakralen Musik.

Bayreuth, die Festspielstadt im Grünen, hat ebenso Jazzkonzerte, Kabarett und Open-Air-Konzerte zu bieten. In der Oberfrankenhalle treten regelmäßig bekannte Rock- und Popgrößen auf. Kammermusik-Ensembles lassen die Musik vom Hofe der Markgrafen neu erklingen. Volkstümliche Bräuche und Gegenwartskunst runden ein anspruchsvolles kulturelles Repertoire ab, das ausgehend vom Werk Richard Wagners bundesweit einen ersten Rang einnimmt. □

"Musica Bayreuth", guest performances by the Bavarian State Theatre within the framework of the Franconian Festival Week, the Bayreuth Easter Festival or the "Bayreuth Baroque" series of events. A varied selection of concerts by private organisers the whole year round completes this attractive range. At base level too, much is done on the musical side: in the widely extended municipal Music School, in the Orchestral Association and in the Bayreuth Philharmonic Choir. The study courses offered by the College of Protestant Church Music have a high academic level and a noteworthy selection of religious music.

Bayreuth, festival city of green spaces, also has jazz concerts, cabaret and open-air concerts on offer. Well-known rock and pop stars appear regularly in the Oberfrankenhalle. Chamber music ensembles give a new sound to the music from the courts of the Margrave. Traditional customs and modern art round off a demanding cultural repertoire, which, beginning with works by Richard Wagner, has achieved great national significance. □

Facetten einer Kulturregion

Professor Dr. Julia Lehner

Die Indikatoren und Faktoren, die für die Charakterisierung einer europäischen Metropolregion als ausschlaggebend erachtet werden, sind hinlänglich bekannt. Primär werden hier ökonomische und infrastrukturelle, statistische und demographische, aber auch prognostische Kriterien herangezogen. Dass Kultur, Tourismus und Sport Standortfaktoren von nationaler und internationaler Bedeutung sind, bedarf keiner besonderen Erwähnung. Der nüchternen und objektiven Faktizität den anderen Indikatoren gegenüber, benötigt der Stellenwert der Kultur allerdings immer besondere Beachtung. In regionaler Verantwortung dem europäischen Leitbild der Polyzentralität verpflichtet, wird es das Ziel aller die Metropolregion bildenden Partner sein, gerade durch die Kultur die begonnene Entwicklung zu einem „Europa der Regionen" fortzusetzen und weiter zu verstärken. Hierzu zählen die Pflege der regionalen Charakteristika zur Wahrung der kulturellen Vielfalt, der kulturelle Austausch, das Interesse an unbekannten Kulturen und die Auseinandersetzung mit der eigenen kulturellen Identität.

Die kulturelle Topographie der Europäischen Metropolregion Nürnberg ist das Ergebnis historisch gewachsener Strukturen. Die Region ist in verschiedener Hinsicht durch Gegensätzlichkeiten gekennzeichnet und nimmt historisch, mentalitäts- oder sprachgeschichtlich eine Brückenfunktion ein. Diese Vielschichtigkeit fügt sich dennoch zu einem Ganzen zusammen, das mit Recht als „Patchwork" bezeichnet wurde.

Eine Perlenschnur historischer Ereignisse belegt das Bild. So mag man beispielsweise an die Nachbarschaft der Städte Erlangen und Bamberg denken. Erstere war ein ehemaliges Refugium für die verfolgten Hugenotten und universitäres Zentrum für evangelische Theologie. Letztere – 40 Kilometer davon entfernt – erzbischöflicher Sitz und katholisches Zentrum.

In wirtschaftshistorischer Hinsicht war die Region, vor allem aber Nürnberg, eine Art „Silicon Valley", wo über lange Zeiträume hinweg ausgeprägte technische Innovationskraft sich mit ökonomischer Um- und

The indicators and factors considered to be decisive for characterisation as a European metropolitan region are sufficiently well-known. They are primarily economic and infrastructural, statistical and demographic, but prognostication is also a criterion. The fact that culture, tourism and sport are business location factors of national and international significance need not be particularly mentioned. Because of its sober and objective actuality in comparison with the remaining indicators however, the status of culture always needs particular attention. With the region's responsibility committed to Europe's role model of poly-centralism, it will be the target of all of the partners forming the metropolitan region to continue – especially through culture – the development and to strengthen it to become a "Europe of Regions". This includes the care and maintenance of regional characteristics in order to safeguard cultural variety, cultural exchange, interest in unknown cultures and the analysis of one's own cultural identity.

The cultural topography of the European metropolitan region of Nuremberg is the result of structures with their growth in history. In various respects, the region has been characterised by contrariness, taking on the function of bridge-building historically, concerning mentality and in the history of languages. However, this ability to be multi-layered blends together to a whole which, justifiably, could be considered as "Patchwork".

A necklace of historical events supports the picture. Thus one could consider for instance the neighbourly relations between the towns of Erlangen and Bamberg. The former was a one-time refuge for the persecuted Huguenots and a universal centre for protestant theology. The latter – some 40 kilometres removed – residence of the archbishop and Roman Catholic centre.

From an economic-historical view the region, but above all Nuremberg, was a type of "Silicon Valley", where, for many years, distinctive technical innovative power paired with economical prudence and farsightedness. The metropolitan region however, not only enjoys a reputation as highly economical and cultural with regard to its past. It is a cultural landscape radi-

Facets of a Cultural Region

Kulturglanzlichter
Cultural Highlights

Projektion auf der Fassade der Lorenzkirche während der „Blauen Nacht" in Nürnberg

A projection onto the façade of "Blaue Nacht" (blue night) in Nuremberg

Das Poetenfest in Erlangen gehört zu den Highlights im kulturellen Veranstaltungskalender der ganzen Region.

The poets' festival in Erlangen is one of the highlights of the region's cultural events calendar.

Weitsicht paarte. Die Metropolregion ist aber durchaus nicht nur in Bezug auf ihre Vergangenheit von hohem wirtschaftlichem und kulturellem Ansehen. Sie ist eine Kulturlandschaft mit internationaler Strahlkraft. Eine ganze Reihe von kulturellen Einrichtungen, wiederkehrenden Ereignissen und innovativen Neuerungen in den einzelnen Kommunen liefern hierfür eindrucksvolle Belege. Stellvertretend und beispielhaft seien einige davon charakterisiert:

Mit der Einrichtung des Dokumentationszentrums Reichsparteitagsgelände hat sich die Stadt Nürnberg der drückenden Erblast ihrer jüngeren Vergangenheit gestellt. Die verantwortungsvolle Auseinandersetzung mit den historischen Gegebenheiten auf der einen Seite und die Schaffung eines bewussten Gegen-

ating international power. A whole series of cultural institutions, recurring events and innovative reforms in the individual communities document this quite impressively. Some of them are characterised in a representative and exemplary manner:

With the setting up of the documentation centre Reichsparteitagsgelände the city of Nuremberg is facing up to the heavy legacy of its recent past. The responsible examination of historical reality on the one hand and the creation of a conscious counterweight by the rewarding of an international human rights prize on the other, has found enormous international recognition.

Things are looking well for Nuremberg's museum landscape. This applies for the communal institutions as well as for the state's New Museum for Art and Design and the Germanic National Museum which enjoys an international reputation. Further facets are various temporary events such as the International Organ Week, the continuously held meeting of bards within the sector of "Weltmusik" or the recently initiated Gluck-Festspiele accompanied by an international symposium.

Kulturglanzlichter
Cultural Highlights

Gepflegtes Brauchtum: Kirchweih im Knoblauchsland im Norden Nürnbergs

A well-maintained custom: a fair in the garlic country in the North of Nuremberg

gewichtes durch die Auslobung eines Internationalen Menschenrechtspreises auf der anderen, hat international große Anerkennung gefunden.

Die Museumslandschaft Nürnbergs ist bestens bestellt. Dies trifft sowohl für die kommunalen Häuser zu wie auch für das staatliche Neue Museum für Kunst und Design und das Germanische Nationalmuseum, das weltweite Bedeutung genießt. Weitere Facetten sind verschiedene temporäre Ereignisse wie die Internationale Orgelwoche, das kontinuierlich stattfindende Bardentreffen im Bereich der „Weltmusik" oder die jüngst initiierten Gluck-Festspiele, die ein internationales Symposion begleitete.

Der Einzugsbereich des Staatstheaters Nürnberg geht weit über die Metropolregion hinaus, und das Dreisparten-Haus ist Theaterzentrum für ganz Nordbayern. Gastspiele tragen den Ruf der Region in die Welt, wie die erste Aufführung des gesamten „Ring des Nibelungen" von Richard Wagner in China deutlich unterstrich. Das internationale Renommee und die Ausstrahlung der Ansbacher Bachwoche sind ebenso ein besonderes kulturelles Ereignis wie der in vielen Ländern der Erde gastierende Windsbacher Knaben-

The Nuremberg State Theatre's catchment area reaches far beyond the metropolitan region and the Dreisparten House is a theatre centre for the whole of Northern Bavaria. Guest performances carry the region's reputation out into the world, as clearly emphasised by the first performance of the entire "Ring des Nibelungen" by Richard Wagner in China. Its international reputation and the aura surrounding the Ansbach Bach Week are an equally special cultural event as is the Windsbach Boys Choir giving performances in many countries around the globe. Fürth, Nuremberg's neighbour, maintains special cultural institutions organising events which confirm the cultural topography of the metropolitan region in its uniqueness. At the moment it accommodates the most

chor. Fürth, Nürnbergs Nachbarstadt, verfügt über spezielle Kultureinrichtungen und richtet typische Veranstaltungen aus, die die kulturelle Topographie der Metropolregion in ihrer Einmaligkeit bestätigen. Sie beherbergt derzeit das bedeutendste Museum zu jüdischem Leben in Bayern, und die Dependance des Hauses im unweit entfernten Schnaittach stellt mit einer Synagoge aus dem 16. Jahrhundert, dem Rabbinerhaus und einem Ritualbad ein in Deutschland einmaliges Ensemble dar. Die Fürther Michaelis-Kirchweih ist weit mehr als ein beliebiges Volksfest, sondern Markt, Handelsplatz und Forum für Traditionen. Das Fest besitzt damit auch einen bedeutenden Stellenwert zur regionalen Identifikation.

Erlangen richtet das Poetenfest aus, das turnusmäßig Autoren, Publizisten und Literaturkritikern aus Deutschland und seinen Nachbarstaaten ein gern genutztes und weithin beachtetes Forum bietet. Das Internationale Theaterfestival Arena ebenso wie der Internationale Comic-Salon seien als weitere Beispiele kultureller Besonderheiten der Universitätsstadt genannt.

Aus dem umfangreichen kulturellen Angebot genügt bereits dieser kleine Ausschnitt, um seine Vielfältigkeit und Bedeutung zu zeigen. Auch in kleineren Kommunen wie in Schwabach finden Kulturveranstaltungen wie die „Goldschläger-Nacht" oder die „Ortungen", eine zweiwöchige Kunstbiennale, statt, die in der gesamten Region eine große Resonanz haben. Roth mit seinen international besetzten Bluestagen ist an dieser Stelle zu erwähnen, auch Forchheim als eine Kommune, die von der mittelalterlichen Geschichte ebenso geprägt ist wie heute von High-Tech-Industrie. Als Weltkulturerbe und urbanes Gesamtkunstwerk nimmt Bamberg in der Kulturregion eine Sonderstellung ein. Der Ruf der Stadt und damit auch der Ruf der Metropolregion werden durch das Renommee der Bamberger Symphoniker in die ganze Welt getragen.

Kaleidoskopartig vielschichtig und im bunten Wechsel stellt sich das kulturelle Profil der Metropolregion dar. Trotz teilweiser großer räumlicher Nähe und unmittelbarer Nachbarschaft zeichnen sich die Partner der Region durch zahlreiche, scharf umrissene Alleinstellungsmerkmale aus. Die Kultur ist eine tragende Säule der Europäischen Metropolregion Nürnberg, bestimmt wesentlich deren Strukturen und ist zugleich Kristallisationspunkt und Brücke für internationale kulturelle Transfers.

significant museum on Jewish life in Bavaria and its annex located in nearby Schnaittach represents an ensemble with a synagogue from the 16th century, a Rabbi's house and a ritual bath, unique in Germany. The Fürth Michaelis-Kirchweih is much more than a popular public festival, but a market, trading place and forum for tradition. The festival has thereby achieved significance in regional identification.

Erlangen organises the Festival of Poets which, at regular intervals, offers authors, publicists and literary critics from Germany and its neighbouring states a well-used and widely-known forum. The international theatre festival Arena, as the International Comic-Salon, are mentioned as further examples of cultural features of the university town.

This small excerpt from the blanketing cultural assortment will suffice to show its versatility and importance. Cultural events such as the "Goldschläger-Nacht" or the "Ortungen" a two-week art exhibition are also to be found in smaller communities such as Schwabach, events which find enormous response in the entire region. Roth, with its internationally booked Blues Days should be mentioned at this point and Forchheim too, as a community just as marked by its medieval history as it is from its present-day high-tech industries. Bamberg enjoys a very special place as a world cultural heritage and urban "Gesamtkunstwerk" (overall work of art) in the cultural region. The city's reputation and thereby the reputation of the metropolitan region is carried out into the whole world by the good name of the Bamberg Symphonic Orchestra.

The cultural profile of the metropolitan region is represented like a kaleidoscope, multi-layered and colourfully changing. In spite of their being direct and, to a certain extent, close neighbours, the partners of the region are characterised by countless, sharply defined and outlined exclusive features. Culture is a pillar of the European metropolitan region of Nuremberg, has considerable influence on its structure and is simultaneously a point of crystallisation and a bridge for international cultural transfers.

Kulturglanzlichter
Cultural Highlights

Sherlock Holmes hoch zu Strauß: eigentümliche Szene auf dem Internationalen Figurentheater Festival

Sherlock Holmes on an ostrich: a strange scene at the international figure theatre festival

Eindrucksvolle Goldhasen-Installation anlässlich der Goldschlägernacht 2004 in Schwabach

Impressive Goldhasen installation on the occasion of the gold beaters' night in Schwabach in 2004

Innovation – Neue Kunst und Design

Dr. Lucius Grisebach

Bis zum Jahr 2000 war Nürnberg – eine der geschichtsträchtigsten Städte Europas und von alters her Sitz des größten Museums deutscher Kunst und Kultur – die einzige deutsche Halbmillionenstadt ohne ein Museum für moderne und zeitgenössische Kunst. Aber mit der Eröffnung des Neuen Museums, des Staatlichen Museums für Kunst und Design in Nürnberg, am 15. April 2000 änderte sich das schlagartig. Heute verfügt die Stadt Dürers über eines der attraktivsten Museen für Gegenwartskunst, das sich inzwischen auch hinsichtlich seiner Resonanz beim Publikum zur Spitzengruppe dieser Museumsgattung in Deutschland rechnen darf.

Errichtet und gegründet wurde es in den neunziger Jahren im Rahmen der „Offensive Zukunft Bayern", einem Investitionsprogramm der bayerischen Staatsregierung, aus dem neben zahlreichen Institutionen der industriebezogenen wissenschaftlichen Forschung verschiedene weltweit beachtete Museumsneubauten hervorgegangen sind. Der preisgekrönte Entwurf des jungen Berliner Architekten Volker Staab – inzwischen einer der namhaftesten Architekten seiner Generation in Deutschland – zeichnete sich durch eine vorbildliche Integration modernster Bauformen in den historischen Grundriss der Nürnberger Altstadt aus und macht das Museum nicht nur zu einem idealen Standort für Werke der Kunst und des Designs, sondern zu einer Pilgerstätte der Architekten und Architekturfreunde.

Gegenüber den anderen Museen für Gegenwartskunst widmet sich das Neue Museum in Nürnberg nicht nur den freien, sondern mit gleicher Ausführlichkeit auch den angewandten Künsten. Es folgt damit einem offeneren und moderneren Kunstbegriff, der Kunst und Design verbindet und die Aufmerksamkeit auf deren vielfältige Wechselbeziehungen lenkt. Hinter der großen Glasfassade entfalten sich auf zwei Etagen zwei Sammlungen: Designobjekte aus den fünfziger Jahren bis heute im Erdgeschoss und Werke der bildenden Kunst aus der gleichen Zeit im Obergeschoss, beides in internationaler Vielfalt. Ein großer Saal in einem benachbarten Bauteil bietet Platz für wechselnde Ausstellungen.

Up to the year 2000 Nuremberg – one of Europe's most historic cities and, as it has always been, the residence of the largest museum of German Art and Culture – was the only German City with a population of half a million without a museum for modern and contemporary art. But with the opening of the New Museum, the state museum for art and design in Nuremberg on 15th April 2000 this changed suddenly. Today, Dürer's city can boast of one of the most attractive museums for contemporary art, one which in the meantime can count as one of the top museums of its sort in Germany, certainly also as far as public response is concerned.

It was organised and founded in the nineties within the framework of the "Bavaria's Offensive for the Future", an investment programme of the Bavarian government, from whence various globally acknowledged new museums have arisen, as well as numerous institutions of industry-related scientific research. The prize winning design by the young Berlin architect Volker Staab – in the meantime one of the best known architects of his generation in Germany – is quite remarkable for its ideal integration of modern building form within the historical outline of Nuremberg's old city, making the museum not only an ideal location for works of art and design, but also a place of pilgrimage for architects and friends of architecture.

In contrast to other museums for contemporary art, the New Museum in Nuremberg is dedicated not only to the free arts, but also, and with the same fullness of detail, to the applied arts. It follows a more open and modern meaning of art, one which combines art and design, directing attention to their manifold interrelationships. Behind the large glass facade two collections unfold on two floors: design objects from the fifties up until today on the ground floor and works of fine art from the same period on the first floor, both of them in international diversity. A large hall in a neighbouring part of the building offers room for changing exhibitions.

Two skeins of museum development are linked in this house: The stock of the Design Collection originate from the New Collection, the State Museum for Applied

Innovation – New Art and Design

Kulturglanzlichter
Cultural Highlights

Das Neue Museum – Staatliches Museum für Kunst und Design in Nürnberg – wurde im April 2000 eröffnet.

The New Museum – state-owned museum for art and design in Nuremberg – was opened in April 2000.

Zwei Stränge der Museumsentwicklung verbinden sich in diesem Haus: Die Bestände der Sammlung Design stammen aus der Neuen Sammlung, dem staatlichen Museum für angewandte Kunst in München, und werden von dort aus auch betreut. Grundstock der Sammlung Kunst hingegen ist die in das Neue Museum eingebrachte Sammlung internationaler zeitgenössischer Kunst der Stadt Nürnberg, die jetzt mit staatlichen Mitteln fortgeführt wird.

In den Museumskomplex einbezogen sind zwei Institutionen, die sich auf je eigene Art für Kunst und Design engagieren: Die Bayern Design gGmbH, die sich der Förderung von Design als Wirtschaftsfaktor widmet, und das Institut für moderne Kunst Nürnberg,

Arts in Munich and are supervised from there. The foundation of the Art Collection, however, is the collection of international contemporary art of the city of Nuremberg brought into the New Museum and which is now continued with the help of state funding.

Included in the museum complex are two institutions that commit themselves to art and design, each in its own way: The Bayern Design gGmbH, dedicated to the support of design as an economic factor, and the Institute of Modern Art in Nuremberg, an association existing since the sixties maintaining Germany's only documentation institute for contemporary art. With its library, this institute, which is open to the public, serves the museum at the same time as a specialist library.

> **Information**
>
> **Akademie der Bildenden Künste Nürnberg:**
> Die 1662 gegründete Akademie der Bildenden Künste in Nürnberg ist die älteste Kunstschule im deutschsprachigen Raum. Die freien und angewandten Künste bilden seitdem die zentralen Lehrbereiche, wenn sich auch die Gewichtung über die Jahrhunderte in die eine oder andere Richtung verschoben hat. Heute kennzeichnet interdisziplinäres Agieren den Dialog zwischen den freien und den angewandten Künsten, gestützt durch neue Studiengänge und die Ergänzung durch medientechnologische Ausbildung. Die Akademie bildet derzeit etwa 350 Studierende aus.
> www.adbk-nuernberg.de
>
> **Weitere Kunst- und Musikhochschulen:**
> Hochschule für Musik Nürnberg-Augsburg, Nürnberg
> www.kubiss.de/bildung/info/musikhochschule/
>
> Hochschule für Musik Würzburg
> www.hfm-wuerzburg.de
>
> Hochschule für evangelische Kirchenmusik, Bayreuth
> www.hfk-bayreuth.de

Das Neue Museum in Nürnberg ist eines der attraktivsten Häuser der Gegenwartskunst in Deutschland.

The New Museum in Nuremberg is one of the most attractive exhibitions of modern art in Germany.

ein seit den sechziger Jahren bestehender Verein, der Deutschlands einziges Dokumentationsinstitut für zeitgenössische Kunst betreibt. Mit seiner Bibliothek dient dieses der Öffentlichkeit zugängliche Institut zugleich dem Museum als Fachbibliothek.

Mit seinen Sammlungen, Ausstellungen und knapp tausend Kunstvermittlungsveranstaltungen pro Jahr hat das Neue Museum in Nürnberg in den sechs Jahren seiner öffentlichen Wirksamkeit ein komplexes Netz von Angeboten für die Auseinandersetzung mit Kunst und Design der Gegenwart ausgelegt.

„Vornehmste Aufgabe des Museums ist die Vermittlung von Wissen und Verständnis, von Aufgeschlossenheit und Begeisterung im Umgang mit Kunst und Design", heißt es im „Mission Statement" dieser Institution. Der Zuspruch des Publikums von nah und fern bekräftigt, dass diese Bemühungen Früchte tragen.

With its collections, exhibitions and almost one thousand art-appreciation events every year the New Museum in Nuremberg has, in the six years of its public effectiveness, laid out a complex network of offers dealing with the analysis of present day art and design.

"The primary task of the museum is to impart knowledge and understanding, to encourage openness and enthusiasm in dealing with art and design", is said in the "Mission Statement" of this institution. Encouragement from the public both near and far confirms that these efforts are bearing fruit.

> **Information**
>
> **Academy of Fine Arts in Nuremberg:**
> The Academy of Fine Arts founded in 1662 in Nuremberg is the oldest art school in the German speaking area. Since that time the free and applied arts have formed the central teaching area, even though the emphasis has been moved from one direction to the other over the centuries. Today, interdisciplinary actions characterise the dialogue between the free and the applied arts, supported by new study subjects and supplemented by media-technological training. At the moment the academy educates some 350 students.
> www.adbk-nuernberg.de
>
> **Further Colleges of Art and Music:**
> College of Music Nuremberg-Augsburg, Nuremberg
> www.kubiss.de/bildung/info/musikhochschule/
>
> College of Music Würzburg
> www.hfm-wuerzburg.de
>
> College of Evangelical Music, Bayreuth
> www.hfk-bayreuth.de

Kulturglanzlichter
Cultural Highlights

Bretter, die die Welt bedeuten – Oper, Schauspiel, Tanz

Professor Dr. Wulf Konold

Die alte Reichsstadt Nürnberg ist seit Jahrhunderten auch ein wichtiger Ort der theatralischen Künste. Nicht nur, dass die erste erhaltene Oper auf deutschem Boden, Theophil Stadens „Seelewig", 1645 in Nürnberg das Licht der Welt erblickte; auch die Verbindung von Kunst und Handwerk, zum Beispiel bei den weltberühmten Gold- und Silberschmieden, hat eine große Rolle gespielt – etwa beim frühen Notendruck oder bei der Entwicklung von Musikinstrumenten. So baute Christoph Denner im frühen 18. Jahrhundert hier die erste Klarinette.

Heute verfügt die nordbayerische Metropole über eines der größten Dreispartentheater Deutschlands, seit dem 1. Januar 2005 das einzige bayerische Staatstheater außerhalb der Landeshauptstadt. Gerade erst hat man feierlich den 100. Geburtstag des Opernhauses am Ring gefeiert. Dieses Haus war in seiner Geschichte Schauplatz künstlerischer Triumphe, aber auch der kulturpolitischen Propaganda der Nationalsozialisten, die mit Wagners „Meistersingern von Nürnberg" ihre Reichsparteitage eröffneten. Heute beherbergt es die Sparten Musiktheater und Tanztheater – für das Schauspiel wurde nach dem Krieg am Richard-Wagner-Platz ein eigenes Haus errichtet. Mit gut 500 Mitarbeitern, knapp 700 Vorstellungen pro Jahr, davon allein etwa 25 Premieren, und etwa 300 000 Besuchern ist das Staatstheater Nürnberg das kulturelle Flaggschiff der Metropolregion. Der Spielplan bietet für alle Geschmäcker etwas; das hohe künstlerische Niveau hat dazu geführt, dass vor allem das Musiktheater inzwischen international unterwegs ist – allein in der Saison 2005/06 mit dem ersten Gesamtgastspiel von Wagners „Ring des Nibelungen" in Peking und mit Mozarts „Don Giovanni" beim Hongkong Arts Festival. Ebenfalls 2005 wurde in der Oper Nürnberg das weltweit einzige internationale Gluck-Festival aus der Taufe gehoben – der große Opernreformer und Mozart-Zeitgenosse Gluck, 1714

The old free city of Nuremberg has been an important location for the theatrical arts for centuries. Not only because the first preserved opera on German soil, Theophil Staden's "Seelewig", first saw the light of day in Nuremberg in 1645; but also the combination of handicraft and art, for example the world-renowned gold and silver smiths, had played a large role – for instance in the early printing of musical notes or in the development of musical instruments. Christoph Denner built the first clarinet here in the early 18th century.

Today, the North Bavarian metropolis has at its disposal one of the largest three-branch theatres in Germany, the only Bavarian State Theatre outside the capital since the 1st of January 2005. The 100th birthday of the Opernhaus am Ring was formally celebrated only recently. This house has been the showplace of many artistic triumphs but also of the politico-cultural propaganda of the National Socialists who opened their Reichsparteitage with Wagner's "Meistersinger von Nürnberg" (The Mastersingers of Nuremberg). Today the building accommodates the branches of musical theatre and dance theatre – the drama theatre's own building was erected on the Richard-Wagner-Platz after the war. With more than 500 employees, almost 700 performances each year, of which 25 of them alone are opening nights, and approximately 300,000 visitors, the State Theatre in Nuremberg is the cultural flagship of the metropolitan region. The programme contains something to suit all tastes; in the meantime the high artistic level has led to the Music Theatre being on the road a lot, nationally and internationally – in the 2005/06 season alone with the first entire guest performance of Wagner's "Ring des Nibelungen" (The Ring of the Nibelung) in Beijing and with Mozart's "Don Giovanni" at the Hong Kong Arts Festival. In 2005 too, the Nuremberg Opera was godfather to the only international Gluck Festival in the world – Gluck, born in 1714, the great opera reformer

The Stage: Boards that represent the World – Opera, Theatre, Dance

Das traditionsreiche Opernhaus ist jeweils im September Schauplatz des Nürnberger Opernballs.

The traditional opera house is the venue for the Nuremberg opera ball held every September.

geboren, gehört neben Albrecht Dürer zu den international erfolgreichsten Künstlern der Region und findet künftig alle drei Jahre seinen zentralen Platz in der Noris. Apropos Dürer: Der neben dem Wiener Opernball wohl erfolgreichste und stimmungsvollste Opernball trägt den Namen Albrecht Dürer und versammelt jedes Jahr im September über 3000 prominente Gäste zu einem gesellschaftlichen Ereignis erster Güte.

Aber auch das Tanztheater unter der Leitung von Daniela Kurz gehört zu den renommiertesten Compagnien Deutschlands. Innovative Regiehandschriften prägen das Schauspiel unter Klaus Kusenberg, das mit seinem attraktiven Mix von neuen Stücken und Klassikern in modernem Gewand außerordentlich erfolgreich ist. Und das Philharmonische Orchester – bis 2005 von Philippe Auguin geleitet, seitdem ist Christof Prick Chefdirigent – sorgt in der Meistersingerhalle, aber auch auf Tourneen für abwechslungsreiche, qualitätvolle Konzerterlebnisse.

Die Metropolregion Nürnberg verfügt über zwei

and Mozart contemporary and together with Albrecht Dürer one of the internationally most successful artists of the region – that will be held every third year in the Noris. Apropos Dürer: The most successful and entertaining opera ball next to the Vienna Opera Ball carries the name of Albrecht Dürer and each year in September draws more than 3,000 prominent guests to a social event of the first order.

But the Dance Theatre too, under the leadership of Daniela Kurz, is one of the best-known companies in Germany. Innovative directions distinguish the stage plays under Klaus Kusenberg, which, with their attractive mixture of new pieces and classics in modern costume, are extraordinarily successful. And the Philharmonic Orchestra – until 2005 directed by Philippe Auguin, Christof Prick having been head conductor ever since – produces varied and top quality concert events, not only in the Meistersingerhalle, but also on tour.

The metropolitan region of Nuremberg maintains

Das Tanztheater zählt zu den renommiertesten Compagnien Deutschlands.

The Tanztheater counts as one of the best known companies in Germany.

weitere kommunale Theater: Das Stadttheater in Fürth sorgt, verbunden mit dem neu errichteten Kulturforum Schlachthof, für attraktive Gastspiele und abwechslungsreiche Eigenproduktionen. Das Markgrafentheater in Erlangen, das älteste regelmäßig bespielte Barocktheater Deutschlands, bietet in der Hugenottenstadt lebendiges Schauspiel und – in Zusammenarbeit mit dem Staatstheater Nürnberg – jährlich eine Barockoper in historischem Ambiente.

Selbstverständlich verfügt die Metropolregion auch über eine außerordentlich lebendige freie Theaterszene. Vor allem die Kindertheater – zum Beispiel „Mummpitz" und „Pfütze" – haben sich mit ihrer fantasievollen Arbeit für die jungen Besucher deutschlandweit durchgesetzt.

So zeigt die vermeintliche Theaterprovinz Nordbayern, dass sie hinter den vermeintlichen Metropolen Berlin, Hamburg und München kaum zurücksteht – ein gutes Gefühl für alle theaterbegeisterten Besucher aus der Region und von außerhalb.

two further communal theatres: The Municipal Theatre in Fürth combined with the newly organised culture forum "Schlachthof" provides attractive guest performances as well as their own varied productions. The Markgrafentheatre in Erlangen, the oldest regularly used baroque theatre in Germany, offers lively plays in the Huguenot city and – in cooperation with the State Theatre in Nuremberg – once a year a baroque opera in historical ambience.

Naturally the metropolitan region also has an extremely vivid free stage. Primarily the children's theatre – for example "Mummpitz" and "Pfütze" – have become generally accepted with their imaginative work for young audiences all over Germany.

In this way, the supposedly theatre province of North Bavaria shows that it hardly takes second place to the so-called metropolises of Berlin, Hamburg and Munich – a good feeling for all theatre fans in the region and elsewhere.

Albrecht Dürer – Geniestreiche des Nürnberger Weltkünstlers

Eva Schickler

Albrecht Dürer (1471–1528) ist der berühmteste Sohn Nürnbergs. Schon zu Lebzeiten wurde er als nördliches Pendant zu Leonardo da Vinci gesehen und als „Apelles Germaniae" gerühmt. Die „Betenden Hände" und der „Feldhase" haben sich dem Kollektivgedächtnis der Menschheit eingeprägt. Sein Werk steht für virtuose Qualität, intensive Präsenz, Neuschöpfung und Innovation. Bis heute zieht es in Ausstellungen ein Massenpublikum an und vergegenwärtigt uns, welche Impulse, kommunikative Kraft und mobilisierende Energie von innovativen künstlerischen Konzeptionen ausgehen können.

Albrecht Dürer wurde am 21. Mai 1471 als Kind des Goldschmieds Albrecht Dürer d. Ä. und Barbara Dürer, geb. Holper, in Nürnberg geboren. Bei seinem Vater absolvierte der junge Dürer eine Goldschmiedelehre. Sein großer Traum jedoch war die Malerei. So setzte er sich durch und lernte anschließend in der Werkstatt des renommierten Nürnberger Künstlers Michael Wolgemut. Aus eigenem Antrieb hat sich Dürer zu einem der vielschichtigsten Intellektuellen entwickelt. Kein geringerer als Christus, aber auch die größten Künstler aller Zeiten waren Dürers Leitbilder. Trotz zahlreicher Reisen, die ihm wesentliche Impulse gaben, verbrachte er die meiste Zeit seines Lebens in seiner Heimatstadt. Nürnberg war in der Renaissance, an der Wende zur Neuzeit, als Zentrum des Humanismus eine der wirtschaftlich am weitesten entwickelten Städte Europas und für seine vielfältigen, bahnbrechenden Erfindungen berühmt.

In vielerlei Hinsicht hat Dürer Bedeutendes geleistet – als Künstler, als Forscher, als Humanist und als Unternehmer. Er war der Prototyp, der sich über konventionelle Zunftschranken hinwegsetzte. Zu einem Zeitpunkt, als nördlich der Alpen eigenständige Selbstporträts noch nicht üblich waren, zeichnete er sich im Alter von dreizehn Jahren. Es ist die früheste erhaltene Kinderzeichnung. Sein radikales Selbstbildnis als Akt (1500–05) ist die erste Darstellung dieser

Albrecht Dürer (1471–1528) is Nuremberg's most famous son. Even during his lifetime he was known as the North's counterpart of Leonardo da Vinci and famous as "Apelles Germaniae". The "Betenden Hände" (The Praying Hands) and the "Feldhase" (The Brown Hare) have embedded themselves in man's collective memory. His work stands for virtuoso quality, intensive presence, new creation and innovation. Still today, his exhibitions draw a mass public and make us realise which impulses, communicative power and mobilising energy can radiate from innovative artistic conceptions.

Albrecht Dürer was born on 21st May 1471 as child of the goldsmith Albrecht Dürer d. Ä. (senior) and Barbara Dürer, nee Holper, in Nuremberg. The young Dürer completed his apprenticeship as goldsmith with his father. However, his great dream was to paint. He managed to get his own way and eventually began lessons in the workshop of the well-known Nuremberg artist Michael Wolgemut. On his own initiative Dürer developed into one of the most multilayered intellectuals. His idols were no less than Christ and some of the most famous artists of all times. In spite of countless journeys which gave him significant impulses he spent most of his life in his home city. In the Renaissance, on the cusp of the modern age, Nuremberg was, as the centre of humanism, one of the furthest economically developed cities in Europe well known for its manifold, ground-breaking inventions.

Dürer accomplished much of significance in many ways – as an artist, researcher, as humanist and as an entrepreneur. He was the prototype who disregarded the conventional limits set by the Guilds. At a time when independent self portraits were not yet customary North of the Alps he drew his own portrait at the age of thirteen. It is the earliest preserved child's drawing. His radical self-portrait as nude (1500–05) is the first reproduction at all of this sort. It remained singular in art for a long time. No other artist before him left so many self-

Albrecht Dürer – Nuremberg's Global Artist's Strokes of Genius

Kulturglanzlichter
Cultural Highlights

Wurde zur Ikone des modernen Menschen: der christusähnliche Dürer im „Selbstbildnis", 1500, München, Bayerische Gemäldesammlungen, Alte Pinakothek

The Christ-like Dürer in "Self portrait", 1500, Munich, Bavarian painting collections, in the Alte Pinakothek has become the icon of modern times

Revolutionäre Landschaften: „Weiher im Walde", um 1496, London British Museum

Revolutiony Landscapes: "Pond in the Forest", around 1496, London British Museum

„Das große Hasenstück" hieß in Anlehnung an zwei berühmte Dürer-Gemälde die eindrucksvolle Installation des Künstlers Ottmar Hoerl im August 2003 auf dem Nürnberger Hauptmarkt.

The impressive installation by the artist Ottmar Hoerl "Das große Hasenstück", named in imitation of the two famous Dürer paintings, was erected in August 2003 on the Nuremberg main market.

Art überhaupt. Sie blieb lange Zeit singulär in der Kunst. Kein anderer Künstler vor ihm hinterließ so viele Selbstbildnisse. So hat Dürer u. a. als erster die Gattung des Selbstporträts und der Bildniszeichnung zur künstlerischen Selbstständigkeit erhoben. Die ersten eigenständigen Baumporträts in der europäischen Kunstgeschichte stammen ebenso von seiner Hand wie das erste authentische Bildnis eines Schwarzafrikaners und die ersten gedruckten Sternkarten. Seine atemberaubenden Landschaftsaquarelle waren der Beginn der selbstständigen modernen Landschaftsmalerei. Erst von jetzt an gibt es in der europäischen Kunstgeschichte moderne Aquarellkunst in einer Weise wie sie erst wieder im 19. Jahrhundert aufgegriffen wurde. Innerhalb kurzer Zeit erneuerte er die graphischen Künste und inspirierte Kollegen und Kunsthandwerker in vielen Ländern der Welt. Laut Erwin Panofsky erreichte Deutschland durch Albrecht Dürer auf dem Gebiet der graphischen Kunst die Position einer Großmacht. Dürers Streben war beseelt von der Suche nach Schönheit, von dem Wunsch nach Erkenntnis, Unabhängigkeit und schöpferischer Freiheit. Immer wieder stellte er höchste Ansprüche an sich. Sein Monogramm entwickelte er zu einem beispiellosen Label. Er war der erste mit einer globalen

portraits. Thus Dürer, amongst others, was one of the first to raise the genre of self-portraits and portrait drawing to artistic independence. The first independent tree portraits in the history of European art originated from his hand as did the first authentic portrait of a negro (black African) and the first printed star maps. His breathtaking landscape watercolours were the beginning of independent modern landscape painting. It is only from this point onwards that there was in European history modern watercolour art as it was picked up again in the 19th century. Within a short period of time he renewed graphic art giving inspiration to colleagues and artistic craftsmen in many countries around the world. According to Erwin Panofsky, Germany achieved the position of a major power on the sector of graphic arts thanks to Albrecht Dürer. Dürer's strivings were inspired by the search of beauty, by the desire for insight, independence and creative freedom. Time and again he made heavy demands of himself. He developed his monogram into a exemplary label. He was the first with global vision, producing for an anonymous market. His workshop which included publishing and a sales structure was quite unique and introduced considerable changes with respect to the commercialisation of art. In literature on the subject he is named

---

Information

Jedes Jahr bietet die „Dürer-Stadt" Nürnberg eine Palette von Veranstaltungen, Ausstellungen, Kunstaktionen, Führungen und Vorträgen, die weit über die Metropolregion hinausstrahlen und dazu einladen, den Weltkünstler immer wieder neu zu entdecken. Der Dürer-Weg, das alljährliche Dürer-Fest und „das weltgrößte Rasenstück" zur Fußball-Weltmeisterschaft 2006 sind solche Glanzlichter.

Each year the "Dürer city" of Nuremberg offers a selection of events, exhibitions, art campaigns, tours and lectures radiating far beyond the metropolitan region and inviting one to rediscover the global artist. The Dürer-Way, the yearly Dürer festival and "the world's largest piece of lawn" for the Football-World Championships 2006 are such highlights.

Kulturglanzlichter
Cultural Highlights

Vision, der für einen anonymen Markt produzierte. Seine Werkstatt mit Verlags- und Vertriebsstruktur war einzigartig und leitete wesentliche Veränderungen im Hinblick auf die Kunstkommerzialisierung ein. In der Fachliteratur wird er als „Erfinder des Markenartikels" bezeichnet. Dürer war sich seiner historischen Bedeutung bewusst. Auch nachfolgende Generationen sollten von seinen Erfahrungen profitieren. So war es Dürer, der als erster Künstler eine deutschsprachige Kunsttheorie publizierte und autobiographische Schriften verfasste.

Ob Aktdarstellung, Tierstücke, Porträtmalerei, Kunsthandwerk oder Graphik, ob Proportionslehre, Mathematik, Marketing, Selbstdarstellung, Sprache oder Urheberrecht: Wir haben Dürer auf verschiedensten Gebieten vieles zu verdanken. Die Liste mit seinen Pionierleistungen und Weiterentwicklungen ist lang. So bedeutet die spannende Auseinandersetzung mit diesem Weltkünstler auch eine Chance für die Zukunft, für individuellen Erkenntnisgewinn ebenso wie für kulturelle Highlights. ☐

"inventor of the brand article". Dürer was fully conscious of his historical significance. Future generations were meant to profit from his experience. And so it was Dürer who was the first artist to publish a German speaking theory of art and who wrote autobiographical scripts.

Whether nude painting, animal works, portraiture, artistic craftwork or graphics, whether teaching proportions, mathematics, marketing, self-portraits, language or copyright: on many territories we have much to thank Dürer for. The list of his pioneer performances and developments is long. Thus the thrilling analysis of this global artist also demonstrates the opportunity for the future, for individual gain of insight as well as for cultural highlights. ☐

Eine Hommage an die Natur: „Das große Rasenstück", 1503, Aquarell und Deckfarben auf Pergament, Wien, Albertina

Homage to nature: „Das große Rasenstück" (The Great Piece of Turf), 1503, watercolour and opaque colour on parchment, Vienna, Albertina

Intelligenz für Verkehr und Logistik

Dr. Hans-Joachim Lindstadt

Nürnberg war schon immer Verkehrsdrehscheibe mit europäischer Dimension und Raum für innovative Verkehrstechnik. Mit der Wiedervereinigung und der Öffnung der Grenzen nach Osteuropa ist die Region Anfang der neunziger Jahre erneut in das Zentrum eines gesamteuropäischen Wirtschaftsraumes gerückt.

Die besondere Rolle, die ihr dabei zukommt, verdeutlichen zwei Prädikate: Von der EU wurde Nürnberg als eine von zwei Gateway-Regionen eingestuft, denen eine Ausnahmestellung mit Blick auf die EU-Osterweiterung zukommt. Zudem wurde die Region im vergangenen Jahr in den Kreis der europäischen Metropolregionen in Deutschland aufgenommen.

Um diesen Aufgaben gerecht werden zu können, braucht man neben der wirtschaftsgeographischen Lage eine hervorragende Verkehrsinfrastruktur und ein hohes verkehrstechnologisches Know-how. Beides besitzt die Metropol- und Gateway-Region Nürnberg in hohem Maße.

Mit 80 täglichen Flugverbindungen ist Nürnberg mit allen europäischen Wirtschaftsmetropolen direkt verbunden. Das trimodale Güterverkehrszentrum Hafen Nürnberg ist mit rund 260 Logistikunternehmen und über 5000 Beschäftigten eines der größten Logistikzentren in Deutschland. Außerdem ist Nürnberg Schnittpunkt des ICE-Hochgeschwindigkeitsnetzes der Bahn und hat einen sechsstrahligen Autobahnstern im Schnittpunkt wichtiger europäischer Autobahnverbindungen.

Aber nicht nur die Verkehrsinfrastruktur entspricht europäischen Dimensionen. Die Region ist auch ein Kompetenzzentrum für Verkehrstechnologie. Eines der sechs Kompetenzfelder, die im Entwicklungsleitbild der Region herausgearbeitet wurden, ist der Bereich Verkehr und Logistik.

Die technologische Grundlage bilden rund 800 Unternehmen mit rund 75 000 Beschäftigten, die die

Nuremberg has always been a traffic hub of European dimensions and an area of innovative transport technology. With reunification and the opening of the borders to East Europe at the beginning of the nineties the Region once again moved back into the centre of a pan-European economic area.

The special role which it has taken over can be explained with two predicates: The EU classified Nuremberg as one of the two gateway regions to which an exceptional position has been attached, especially when seen from the angle of the EU's extension eastwards. The region was also accepted into the circle of European Metropolitan Regions in Germany last year.

To be able to do justice to these tasks an excellent transport infrastructure will be needed in addition to the economic-geographic location and a large amount of transport-technological know-how. The metropolitan and gateway region possesses both to a high degree.

With 80 flight connections daily, Nuremberg is directly connected with all European industrial metropolises. The tri-mode Güterverkehrszentrum Hafen Nürnberg is one of the largest logistic centres in Germany with some 260 logistics concerns employing more than 5,000 people. Nuremberg is also at the intersection of the ICE high speed railway network and has a six-point motorway junction at the intersection of important European motorways.

But not only the transport structure is of European dimensions. The region is also a competence centre for transport technology. One of the six fields of competence set up in the region's development model is the sector of transport and logistics.

Its technological foundation is formed by some 800 companies with approximately 75,000 employees, making clear the innovative power of industry in this competence field. To this, the exceptional scientific competence created by a large number of transport-relevant researchers and developers at the Friedrich-Alexander-University, the universities of applied

Intelligence for Transport and Logistics

Kompetenzfelder
Fields of Competence

High-Tech-Produkte aus der Metropolregion für die ganze Welt: Computeranimation des Transrapid

High-tech products from the metropolitan region for the whole world: computer animation of the Transrapid

Die Convoi Deutschland GmbH ist ein Tochterunternehmen des niederländischen Konzerns Convoi Europe B.V. – einem internationalen Spezialisten für Umzüge und Verlagerungen kompletter Industrieanlagen und technische Dienstleistungen. Convoi Deutschland verfügt trotz Neugründung über ein 20-jähriges Verlagerungs-Know-how und hat mit Verlagerungen einer Trafofabrik (von Schottland nach Indien) sowie eines Fermacellplattenwerkes (von Spanien nach Deutschland) bereits wenige Wochen nach Unternehmensgründung Großaufträge in Millionenhöhe realisiert und seine außerordentliche Kompetenz eindrucksvoll dokumentiert.

Convoi Deutschland GmbH is a subsidiary of the Dutch concern Convoi Europe B.V. – an international specialist for removals and relocations of complete industrial plants and technical services. In spite of being newly established, Convoi Deutschland has more than 20 years of know-how in relocation and, with the removal of a transformer factory (from Scotland to India) and a Fermacell board works (from Spain to Germany) completed orders to the order of many millions within a few weeks of company foundation thus impressively documenting their extreme competence.

Eine Fabrik zieht um: In nur etwa sechs Wochen demontierte Convoi Deutschland eine komplette Fabrik in Schottland. Die eingesetzten Krananlagen – mit bis zu 400 t Hubkraft – mussten die einzelnen Elemente teilweise durch Dachöffnungen nach draußen heben.

A factory is moved: In only six weeks Convoi Deutschland dismantled a complete factory in Scotland. The crane equipment used – up to 400 t lifting power – had to partially lift the single elements through holes in the roof to get them outside.

Information

Gründungsjahr: 2005

Mitarbeiter: etwa 50

Leistungsspektrum: industrielle Verlagerungen und technische Dienstleistungen weltweit

Umsatz: ca. 6 Mio. Euro (Stand 2005)

Year founded: 2005

Employees: some 50

Range of services: industrial removals and technical services worldwide

Turnover: about 6 million Euro (as at 2005)

Convoi Deutschland GmbH, Nürnberg

Kompetenzfelder
Fields of Competence

innovative Wirtschaftskraft in diesem Kompetenzfeld verdeutlichen. Hinzu kommt eine hervorragende wissenschaftliche Kompetenz, die durch eine Vielzahl von verkehrsrelevanten Forschern und Entwicklern an der Friedrich-Alexander-Universität, den Fachhochschulen, den Fraunhofer-Instituten und vielen weiteren Forschungseinrichtungen der Region geschaffen wird.

Die Bündelung dieser wirtschaftlichen und wissenschaftlichen Verkehrskompetenz erfolgt über das „Center for Transportation and Logistics Neuer Adler (CNA)", das seit zehn Jahren sehr erfolgreiche Netzwerke in fünf verkehrlichen Schwerpunktbereichen aufgebaut hat. In diesen Netzwerken arbeiten die verkehrstechnologischen Unternehmen der Region und die Bereiche Forschung und Wissenschaft eng zusammen und befördern damit Technologietransfer und Innovation. Die technologischen Schwerpunkte der Region liegen vornehmlich in den Bereichen Antriebstechnik (u. a. Siemens, A & D, MAN), Automotive (u. a. INA, Leoni, Bosch, Federal Mogul), Telematik (u. a. Siemens I & S, VDO) und Bahntechnik (u. a. Siemens TS, Bögl, Pfleiderer). Hinzu kommt ein ausgesprochener Schwerpunkt im Bereich der Logistik-Dienstleistungswirtschaft.

Die erfolgreiche Vernetzung der vorhandenen Verkehrskompetenz hat eine Vielzahl hervorragender Ergebnisse gebracht. So verdeutlicht heute ein regionaler Wertschöpfungsanteil von 30 Prozent am Transrapid in Shanghai die Innovationskraft der Metropolregion Nürnberg. Das dynamische Verkehrsleitsystem im Süden Nürnbergs gehört europaweit zu den innovativsten Projekten der effizienten Verkehrssteuerung. Bereits diese wenigen Beispiele dokumentieren die hohe Verkehrskompetenz in der Region, die sich aus vielen sehr gut funktionierenden Netzwerken zwischen innovativen Unternehmen und der breit gefächerten wissenschaftlichen Kompetenz entwickelt hat. Zusammen mit der wirtschaftsgeographischen Gateway-Funktion ist die Metropolregion Nürnberg heute ein europäisches Kompetenzzentrum für Verkehr und Logistik.

sciences, the Fraunhofer-Institutes and many other research establishments in the region must be added.

This economic and scientific transport competence is concentrated in the "Center for Transportation and Logistics Neuer Adler (CNA)", which has built up a very successful network in five transport-emphasised areas in the last ten years. The transport-technological undertakings and the sectors of research and science of the region work closely together within these networks thereby encouraging technology transfers and innovation. Technological emphasis in the region lies principally in the sectors of drive engineering (among them Siemens, A & D, MAN), automotive (among them INA, Leoni, Bosch, Federal Mogul), telematic (among them Siemens I & S, VDO) and rail engineering (among them Siemens TS, Bögl, Pfleiderer). One particular point of emphasis within the sector of logistics must be mentioned – the service supply industry.

The successful meshing of existing transport competence has given a large number of excellent results. Thus a regional added value share of 30 percent in the Transrapid in Shanghai demonstrates the innovative powers of the metropolitan region of Nuremberg. The dynamic traffic guidance system in the south of Nuremberg is one of the most innovative projects of efficient traffic control in the whole of Europe. These few examples document the high transport competence in the region which has developed from very many well functioning networks of innovative concerns and widely spread scientific competence. Together with the economic-geographic gateway function, the metropolitan region of Nuremberg is today a European competence centre for transport and logistics.

Der Transrapid wurde in der Metropolregion Nürnberg entwickelt und fährt heute in Schanghai in China.

The Transrapid, developed in the metropolitan region of Nuremberg, today runs in Shanghai in China.

Kompetenzfelder
Fields of Competence

Hightech in Information und Kommunikation

Michael Nordschild

Wo steht die größte Denkfabrik der für ihre Nobelpreisträgerriege berühmten Bell Laboratories außerhalb der USA? Wo werden die modernsten RFID-Chips entwickelt, wo ist die härteste Konkurrenz von Bill Gates zuhause? Wo wurde MP3 erfunden? Wo waren Mobilfunklösungen der 3. Generation lange vor dem offiziellen UMTS-Start live zu erleben? Viele Fragen, eine Antwort, und die lautet: in der Metropolregion Nürnberg.

Dem drohenden Abstieg des Forschungs- und Entwicklungsstandorts Deutschland steuert man hier vor allem in der Informations- und Kommunikationstechnik konsequent entgegen. Entstanden sind F+E-Zentren und innovative Anwenderunternehmen von Weltruf. Ihre Produkte und Dienstleistungen gehen in die ganze Welt. Kommunikationstechnik, Softwarelösungen mit dem Fokus Open Source, Automatisierung, Medizin, Unternehmensanwendungen oder eGovernment heißen die Wachstumsträger. Sogar die ansonsten von der deutschen Landkarte getilgte Unterhaltungselektronik hat hier wieder Tritt gefasst. Premium-Geräte von Loewe aus Kronach, Metz aus Fürth oder GRUNDIG Intermedia aus Nürnberg zeugen davon, dass TV und Internet zusammenwachsen.

Nürnberg ist auch einer der führenden Mobilfunkstandorte Europas. Netzausrüster, -betreiber und F+E-Spezialisten entwickeln hier Chips, Soft- und Hardware-Intelligenz fürs Mobile Business. „Best brains", die besten Köpfe habe man hier gefunden, begründete der US-Konzern Lucent Mitte der Neunziger den Erwerb der Philips Kommunikations Industrie. Andere sind offenbar der gleichen Meinung, denn auch T-Mobile, Ericsson, Philips Semiconductors, Comneon, Qualcomm und Teleca haben in Nürnberg wichtige Entwicklungszentren. Lucent betreibt hier das erwähnte Bell Lab, einen futuristischen „Think Tank" mit weltweiter Verantwortung für TK-Innovation.

Stichwort Open Source: Die Linux-Welt blickt auf die zu Novell gehörenden Labs der SuSE Linux. Ihre Entwickler zählen zu den Vordenkern des alternativen

Fortsetzung Seite 163

Where is the largest think-tank famous for its Nobel prize-winner Bell Laboratories outside the USA? Where are the cutting-edge RFID-chips developed, where is Bill Gates' hottest competitor? Where was the MP3 invented? Where could mobile telecommunication solutions of the 3rd generation be enjoyed live long before the official UMTS start? Lots of questions but only one answer and that one is: in the metropolitan region of Nuremberg.

The threatened decline of Germany as a research and development location has been and continues to be consistently counter-steered here, particularly in the information and communication engineering sectors. Research and development centres and innovative application concerns of global reputation have been created spreading their products and services all over the world. The names of the growth carriers are communication engineering, software solutions with the focus on open sourcing, automation, medicine, applications for undertakings and eGovernment. Even entertainment electronics, otherwise erased from the German map, has once again gained a foothold here. Premium equipment from Loewe in Kronach, Metz in Fürth or GRUNDIG Intermedia in Nuremberg bears witness to the fact that TV and internet are growing ever closer.

Nuremberg is also one of the leading locations for mobile telecommunication in Europe. Network equippers, operators and research and development specialists are busy developing chips, soft- and hardware-intelligence for mobile business. That the "best brains", were to be found here was the US-concern Lucent's justification for acquisition of the Philips Communication Industry in the middle of the nineties. Others obviously share their opinion because T-Mobile, Ericsson, Philips Semiconductors, Comneon, Qualcomm and Teleca also maintain important development centres in Nuremberg. Lucent operates the aforementioned Bell Lab here, a futuristic "think-tank" with global responsibility for telecommunication innovation.

Continued on page 163

High-tech in Information and Communication

LEONI AG – Die Drahtzieher sitzen in Franken

Als 1917 durch den Zusammenschluss dreier traditionsreicher Firmen aus Roth und Nürnberg die Leonische Werke Roth-Nürnberg AG entstand, hatten die Gründer mit Elektrotechnik noch nicht viel im Sinn. Das Fertigungsprogramm umfasste damals ausschließlich feinste Gold- und Silberdrähte sowie Gespinste für kostbare Stickereien und Webprodukte – die so genannten „Leonischen Waren".

Als die Nachfrage nach Leonischen Waren in den 1920er Jahren stark zurückging, verlegte man sich zunehmend auf die Produktion von Kupferdrähten und wenig später auch von isolierten Kabeln, denn mit dem damaligen Einzug der Elektrotechnik stieg der Bedarf an solchen Produkten rasant an. Von Anfang an hatte man dabei vor allem vergleichsweise dünne und flexible Kabel im Visier. Diese Art der Spezialisierung wurde bis heute beibehalten und macht einen großen Teil des Erfolgs der LEONI AG aus.

In den fünfziger Jahren übernahm LEONI als zusätzliche Fertigungsstufe die Konfektionierung. Gemeint ist damit die Weiterverarbeitung zur einbau- bzw. montagefertigen Leitung insbesondere für Haushaltsgeräte und – das Anwendungsgebiet schlechthin – im Automobilbau.

In den neunziger Jahren wuchs das Unternehmen rasant und entwickelte sich zu einem Weltkonzern mit inzwischen über 34 000 Mitarbeitern an rund 60 Standorten in 23 Ländern.

Der Name LEONI steht heute als Synonym für Qualität und Innovation sowie hochkomplexe Spezialitäten auf dem Gebiet der Kabeltechnik. So zählt LEONI zu den weltgrößten Anbietern von Leitungen für den Automobilbau sowie von Spezialkabeln und Energiezuführungssystemen für Industrieroboter, elektromedizinische Geräte und Schienenfahrzeuge. Bei Bordnetz-Systemen gehört LEONI zu den weltweit führenden Herstellern. Mit innovativen Produkten hat LEONI immer wieder Maßstäbe gesetzt. So wurden bereits in den siebziger Jahren Platz sparende und gewichtsreduzierte Fahrzeugleitungen entwickelt, die heute weltweiter Standard für die gesamte Automobilbranche sind.

LEONI ist seinen Kernkompetenzen Draht, Kabel und Bordnetz-Systeme treu geblieben und hat sich gleichzeitig schrittweise zum Entwicklungs- und Systemlieferanten weiterentwickelt. Dies macht das Erfolgsrezept der ursprünglich nur in Franken ansässigen Drahtzieher aus, die heute in aller Welt präsent sind.

Luftaufnahme vom LEONI-Werk Roth. Das Werk Roth ist eine der „Keimzellen" der heutigen LEONI-Gruppe.

Arial view of the LEONI works in Roth. The Roth works is one of the "nuclei" of the present-day LEONI group.

Kompetenzfelder
Fields of Competence

Auf dieser modernen Walzmaschine werden spezielle Kupferleiter für flache Fahrzeugleitungen (LEONIexFC®) hergestellt.

Special copper conductors for flat automotive cables (LEONIexFC®) are manufactured on this modern rolling machine.

Information

Gründungsjahr: 1917

Mitarbeiter:
in der Region Nürnberg ca. 1000;
im Konzern 34 000

Auszubildende: 60

Umsatz: 1,5 Mrd. Euro (Stand 2005)

Produktspektrum:
– Drähte
– Kabel
– Bordnetz-Systeme

Year founded: 1917

Employees:
about 1,000 in the Nuremberg region;
34,000 in the concern

Apprentices: 60

Turnover: 1.5 billion Euro (as at 2005)

Range of products:
– wires
– cables
– on-board wiring systems

☐
LEONI AG
Nürnberg

LEONI AG – The quality connectors have their headquarters in Franconia

In 1917, when the Leonische Werke Roth-Nürnberg AG was created by the amalgamation of three traditional firms from Roth and Nuremberg, the founders did not yet have electrical engineering in mind. The production program at that time was chiefly occupied with producing the finest gold and silver wires as well as gossamer for expensive embroideries and woven products – the so-called "Leonische Waren".
As the demand for Leonische Waren in the 1920's dropped heavily, production was increasingly directed towards copper wire and, somewhat later, to insulated cables. The appearance of electrical engineering at that time swiftly increased the demand for such products. But from the very beginning, care was taken that relatively thin and flexible cables were produced.
This sort of specialisation has been maintained until today thus forming a large part of LEONI AG's success.
In the fifties, LEONI started processing goods as additional manufacturing stage, meaning the onward processing into ready-to-fit and ready-to-assemble wiring, especially for domestic equipment and automobile construction – the ultimate utilizer.
During the nineties the concern grew swiftly, developing into a global concern, and has in the meantime more than 34,000 employees and some 60 locations in 23 different countries.
The name of LEONI stands today as a synonym for quality and innovation in addition to highly complex specialities in the sector of cable engineering. Thus LEONI counts as one of the world's largest suppliers of cable and wiring for automobile construction as well as special cables and energy feeding systems for industrial robots, electromedical equipment and rail transport vehicles. In the sector of on-board wiring systems, LEONI has become one of the world's leading manufacturers.
LEONI's innovative products have set standards time and again. As early as the seventies for example, space-saving and weight-reduced vehicle cables were developed, which are today a global standard for the entire automobile branch.
While remaining faithful to its core competences of wire, cable and on-board wiring systems LEONI has simultaneously expanded step by step and finally become a supplier of developments and systems – a result of the recipe for success developed by the quality connector who was originally only located in Franconia but who is now to be found all over the world.

Das IZB Informatik-Zentrum München – Frankfurt GmbH & Co. KG wurde 1994 als Unternehmen der Sparkassen-Finanzgruppe gegründet. Die Kunden können entweder ihre komplette IT-Infrastruktur oder einzelne Teilbereiche wie den Betrieb der Server, die Datenspeicherung, den Betrieb des Rechenzentrums oder die Telefonie auslagern. Das Unternehmen betreibt in Nürnberg eines der leistungsfähigsten Rechenzentren Deutschlands. Das IZB Informatik-Zentrum beschäftigt am Hauptsitz in Aschheim bei München und an den Standorten Nürnberg und Offenbach rund 650 Mitarbeiter. Der Outsourcing-Spezialist erwirtschaftet einen jährlichen Gesamtumsatz von ca. 200 Mio. Euro. Zu den Kunden des IT-Dienstleisters zählen u. a. die BayernLB, die Landesbank Hessen-Thüringen, Hauck & Aufhäuser, IZB Soft, der Sparkassenverband Bayern, die Deka Bank, die Deutsche Kreditbank AG sowie State Street.

The IZB Informatik-Zentrum München – Frankfurt GmbH & Co. KG was founded in 1994 as a company of the Savings Bank Financial Group (Sparkassen-Finanzgruppe). Customers are able to either transfer their entire IT-infrastructure or individual sections such as the operation of the server, data storage, operating the computer centre or telephony to another site. In Nuremberg the company operates one of the most efficient computer centres in Germany. In its headquarters in Aschheim near Munich and in its locations in Nuremberg and Offenbach the IZB Informatik-Zentrum employs some 650 people. This outsourcing specialist achieves an annual turnover of about 200 million Euro. Amongst the customers of the IT service supplier are the BayernLB, the Landesbank Hessen-Thüringen, Hauck & Aufhäuser, IZB Soft, the Sparkassenverband Bayern, the Deka Bank, the Deutsche Kreditbank AG, as well as State Street.

Information

Gründungsjahr: 1994

Mitarbeiter: etwa 650

Leistungsspektrum: Aufbau, Betrieb und Betreuung von IT-Systemen in den Bereichen
– Client/Server
– Mainframe
– Netzwerke
– Kommunikation

– technische Plattform für über 21 Mio. Bankkonten
– über 2,5 Mrd. Transaktionen für Bayerische Sparkassen im Jahr
– tägliche Spiegelung von über 50 TeraByte Daten in Echtzeit

Year founded: 1994

Employees: some 650

Range of services: setting up, operating and maintaining IT systems in the sectors
– client/server
– mainframe
– networks
– communication

– technical platform for more than 21 million bank accounts
– more than 2.5 billion transactions for Bavarian savings banks annually
– daily reflecting more than 50 terabytes data in real time

☐ IZB Informatik-Zentrum Standort Nürnberg

Kompetenzfelder
Fields of Competence

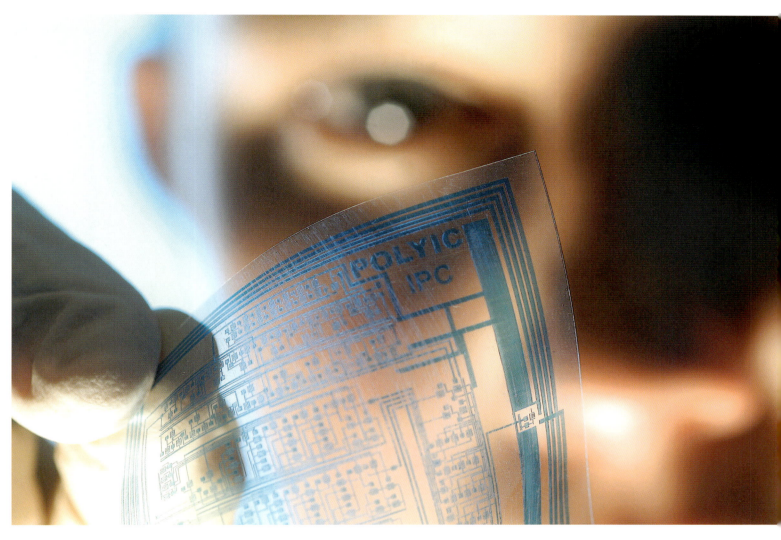

Polymerer RFID-Chip: die Funketiketten sind eine Neuentwicklung der Firma PolyIC und sollen künftig in Produktion, Handel, Logistik und Medizin eingesetzt werden.

Polymer RFID chip: the radio labels are a new development of Messrs PolyIC and it is planned to utilise them in future production, trade, logistics and medicine.

Betriebssystems, das auch Microsoft-Chef Bill Gates mehr als ernst nimmt. Nicht umsonst spricht man bereits von Nürnberg als Europas Linux Valley.

eGovernment ist oft nur ein Schlagwort, in Kommunen der Metropolregion wird es gelebt: Interessenten aus ganz Europa und eine Kooperation mit Russlands High-Tech-Zentrum Moskau zeigen, dass dies der Pilotraum für praktiziertes und praktikables eGovernment ist.

Stichwort „Best Brains": Auf die Bevölkerung umgerechnet, arbeiten hier die meisten Ingenieure in Deutschland. Allein Siemens beschäftigt 32 000 Mitarbeiter. Sieben Bereichszentralen steuern weltweit das Geschäft in Medizintechnik, Energie, Verkehr und Industrie. IT und Telekommunikation sorgen dort für

Apropos open source: the Linux world is watching the labs of SuSE Linux which belong to Novell. Their developers count as some of the most progressive thinkers of the alternative operating system and even Microsoft boss Bill Gates takes them more than seriously. Not without reason is Nuremberg already spoken of as Europe's Linux Valley.

die Technologiesprünge. Aktuelles Highlight sind die modernsten RFID-Chips der Welt.

Moderne Kommunikationstechnik und Software-Intelligenz sind nicht nur auf der Schiene möglich. Beim Online-Banking war Nürnberg Pionier. Mit Cortal Consors, ING DiBa und der Norisbank sitzen auch heute hier Trendsetter. Und die DATEV ist nicht nur Deutschlands Dienstleister Nummer 1 für Steuerberater und Wirtschaftsprüfer, sondern mit 1250 Entwicklern eines der größten deutschen Softwarehäuser. Für die GfK, die unter den Top Five der internationalen Marktforscher rangiert, sind Internet & Co. Wachstumsmotoren.

All diese Unternehmen bauen auf die ausgezeichnete Forschungslandschaft mit den Unis Erlangen-Nürnberg, Bamberg und Bayreuth, Fachhochschulen in Amberg, Ansbach, Coburg, Hof und Nürnberg, dem Heinrich-Hertz-Institut oder der Max-Planck-Forschungsgruppe Optik, Information und Photonik. Nicht zu vergessen den erfolgreichsten Fraunhofer-Stützpunkt, das Institut für Integrierte Schaltungen IIS, an dem der Weltstandard MP3 geboren wurde.

Information

Die Nürnberger Initiative für die Kommunikationswirtschaft e. V. (NIK) zählt 90 führende Unternehmen, Forschungseinrichtungen, Hochschulen und Institutionen zu ihren Mitgliedern. Sie wurde 1994 gegründet und ist heute die Kooperations- und Innovationsplattform für die Informations- und Kommunikationstechnologie in der Metropolregion Nürnberg, dem wirtschaftlichen Zentrum Nordbayerns.
Der NIK gehören international operierende Unternehmen ebenso wie mittelständische Spezialisten an. Ihre Mitglieder vertritt die NIK gegenüber der Öffentlichkeit unter der Politik. Sie initiiert innovative Projekte, sie bietet Informationsveranstaltungen zu I&K Themen an, berät die regionale Wirtschaft und unterstützt innovative junge Unternehmen der Informations- und Kommunikationstechnologie.

Information

The Nürnberger Initiative für die Kommunikationswirtschaft e. V. (NIK) can count 90 leading undertakings, research institutions, high schools and institutions as their members. It was founded in 1994 and is today the cooperation and innovation platform for information and communication technology in the metropolitan region of Nuremberg, the industrial centre of Northern Bavaria. Internationally operating undertakings belong to the NIK as do other medium-sized specialists. The NIK represents its members towards the public according to this policy. It initiates innovative projects; it provides informative events on information and communication subjects, acts as advisor to regional industry and supports young innovative concerns in information and communication technology.

In other places eGovernment is frequently a mere cliché, in the communities of the metropolitan region it is lived: interested people from all over Europe and co-operation with Russia's high-tech centre in Moscow show that this is the pilot area for practiced and practicable eGovernment.

Apropos "Best Brains": calculated per head, this is where most of Germany's engineers work. Some 32,000 people are employed in Siemens alone. Seven departmental centres globally control their business of medicine engineering, energy, transport and industry whilst IT and telecommunication take care of leaps in technology. Current highlight are the RFID chips, the most modern in the world.

Modern communication engineering and software-intelligence are not only possible on the rails. Nuremberg was a pioneer in online-banking. Even today, trendsetters such as Cortal Consors, ING DiBa and the Norisbank can be found here. And DATEV is not only Germany's number 1 service supplier for tax consultants and auditors, but is one of the largest German software companies employing 1,250 developers. In the opinion of GfK, which ranks amongst the top five international market researchers, internet & Co. are the drive behind expansion.

All these concerns rely on the excellence of the research landscape which includes the universities of Erlangen-Nuremberg, Bamberg and Bayreuth, the universities of applied scineces in Amberg, Ansbach, Coburg, Hof and Nuremberg, the Heinrich-Hertz-Institute or the Max-Planck-Research Group Optics, Information and Photonic. Not to be forgotten is the most successful Fraunhofer-Support Group, the Institut für Integrierte Schaltungen IIS (Institute for Integrated Circuits), where the world's standard MP3 was born.

Kompetenzfelder
Fields of Competence

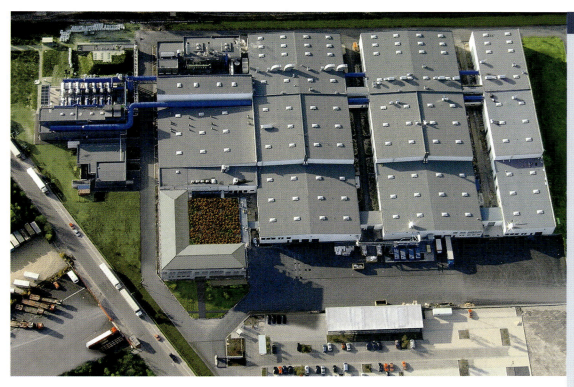

u.e. sebald – ein Unternehmen der schlott gruppe AG

u.e. sebald ist einer der modernsten Illustrationstiefdruckbetriebe in Europa, eingebunden in die schlott gruppe AG, die zu den drei größten Druck- und Direktmarketingdienstleistern in Europa zählt. Mit den beiden Leistungsbereichen schlott print und meiller direct deckt die schlott gruppe alle Leistungen rund um die Prozesse digitaler und gedruckter Kommunikation ab. In enger Zusammenarbeit mit dem Kunden entwickelt das Unternehmen vernetzte, integrierte Print- und Direktmarketinglösungen.

u.e. sebald – a concern of the schlott gruppe AG

u.e. sebald is one of the most modern illustrations intaglio printing works in Europe, integrated in the schlott gruppe AG which counts as one of the three largest printing and direct marketing service suppliers in Europe. With both these service areas, schlott print and meiller direct, the schlott gruppe covers all the services surrounding the processes of digital and printed communication. In close cooperation with the customer, the concern develops linked, integrated print and direct marketing solutions.

Information

Gründungsjahr: 1658

Mitarbeiter: 550 am Standort Nürnberg

Produktionsspektrum:
– Mediendatenverarbeitung
– Illustrationstiefdruck

Produkte:
– aktuelle und hochauflagige Produktion von Zeitschriften
– hochauflagige Wirtschafts- und Sportmagazine
– hochauflagige Kataloge

Year founded: 1658

Employees: 550 at the Nuremberg location

Range of products:
– media data processing
– illustrations intaglio printing

Products:
– production of topical magazines with a large circulation
– business and sports magazines with large circulations
– catalogues with large circulations

☐
u.e. sebald druck GmbH, Nürnberg

FrankenData ist seit Firmengründung ein stetig wachsendes, international tätiges Softwareunternehmen. Aufgabe der 100-prozentigen Siemens-Tochter ist es, für ihre Kunden aus der Energiewirtschaft innovative IT-Lösungen und Service-Leistungen für den Netzbetrieb zu konzipieren und zu implementieren.

Seit dem Jahr 2000 ist FrankenData für das weltweite Service- und Aftersales-Geschäft der Energieautomatisierung innerhalb der Siemens PTD (Power Transmission and Distribution) verantwortlich.

FrankenData versteht sich als Partner, der neben der klassischen Serviceaufgabe den Kunden über Jahre hinweg begleitet und mit ihm zusammen langfristig technisch und kommerziell abgesicherte Lösungen entwickelt – seien es Erweiterungen in der vorhandenen IT-Landschaft, gezielte Upgrades oder Migrationen auf die neuesten technologischen Standards.

Darüber hinaus bietet FrankenData in seinem Trainingscenter Standard- bzw. kundenindividuelle Schulungen für Siemens-Netzleitsysteme an.

FrankenData has been a steadily growing, internationally active software company since its foundation. It is the task of this 100 percent Siemens subsidiary to plan and implement innovative IT solutions and services for networking on behalf of their customers in the energy industry.

Since the year 2000, FrankenData has been responsible for the global service and after-sales business of the energy automation within the Siemens PTD (Power Transmission and Distribution).

FrankenData sees itself as a partner who, alongside the classical service tasks, accompanies customers for many years developing long-term technically and commercially safeguarded solutions – be they as expansions in the present IT landscape, purposeful upgrades or migration to the latest technological standards.

FrankenData also offers standard and/or customer individual training courses for Siemens network control in its training centre.

Information

Gründungsjahr: 1984

Mitarbeiter: 75

Leistungsspektrum:
Konzeptionierung und Implementierung von IT-Lösungen und Serviceleistungen für Kunden aus der Energiewirtschaft weltweit

Standorte:
Erlangen
Stuttgart
Mannheim

Year founded: 1984

Employees: 75

Range of services:
planning and implementation of IT solutions and services for customers in the global energy industry

Locations:
Erlangen
Stuttgart
Mannheim

☐
FrankenData
Softwareengineering
GmbH & Co. KG
Erlangen

Kompetenzfelder
Fields of Competence

Erlangen – Hauptstadt der Medizintechnik

Dr. Siegfried Balleis

Für wissenschaftliche Zusammenarbeit spielt heute der Standort der Beteiligten eigentlich keine Rolle mehr. Und doch bilden sich gerade im High-Tech-Bereich immer wieder regionale Schwerpunkte. So auch in Erlangen. Hier schlägt das Herz des medizintechnischen Fortschritts.

Das Stichwort für Wachstumsdynamik lautet heute Clusterbildung. Erlangen ist ein solch ausgezeichnetes Cluster für die Medizintechnik. Nirgendwo sonst findet man eine größere medizintechnische Kompetenzdichte als in der 100 000-Einwohner-Stadt. Beinahe jeder vierte Arbeitnehmer verdient heute sein Brot in den Bereichen Medizintechnik und Gesundheit.

Eine äußerst leistungsfähige Infrastruktur, enorme Innovationskraft und hohe Lebensqualität machen die Stadt zu einem attraktiven Standort für Industrie- und Dienstleistungsunternehmen und zu einem national wie international anerkannten Wirtschafts- und For-

Fortsetzung Seite 173

Das Innovationszentrum für Medizintechnik und Pharma (IZMP) in Erlangen

The Innovation centre for Medical Technology and Pharmaceuticals (IZMP) in Erlangen

Nowadays, the location of the participants in scientific cooperation does not matter any more. And yet, regional focal points are formed in the high-tech sector time and again. Such is the case in Erlangen. This is where the heart of medical technology's progress beats.

The keyword for growth dynamic today is cluster forming and Erlangen is such an excellent cluster for medical technology. Nowhere else can one find a greater density of medical engineering competence than in the city of 100,000 inhabitants. Almost every fourth employee today earns his daily bread in the sectors of medical engineering and health.

An extremely productive infrastructure, enormous innovative power and a high quality of life make the city an attractive business location for industry and service supply concerns and into a nationally as internationally recognised centre of industry and research. Medicine

Continued on page 173

Erlangen – Medical Technology Capital

BIOTRONIK GmbH & Co. KG

Zentrum für Technologie und Service in Erlangen.

Leben retten.
Sicherheit geben.

BIOTRONIK® ist ein führendes europäisches Unternehmen der Medizintechnik. Die Konzentration liegt auf den Geschäftsfeldern Elektrotherapie des Herzens und Vaskuläre Intervention. BIOTRONIK Produkte helfen dem Arzt, Leben zu retten und die Lebensqualität der Patienten zu verbessern.

Centre for Technology and Service in Erlangen.

*Saving life.
Giving assurance.*

BIOTRONIK® is a leading European company in the field of medical engineering. BIOTRONIK concentrates on the business units of cardiac electrotherapy and vascular intervention. BIOTRONIK products help the physician to save life and to improve the patient's quality of life.

Schrittmacher und Defibrillator für Herzinsuffizienz-Patienten:

Das Implantat der neuesten Generation kann den gestörten Pumpablauf mit Hilfe von drei Elektroden wieder resynchronisieren und so die Arbeitslast des Herzens verringern. Bei auftretendem Kammerflimmern gibt das Gerät einen Hochspannungspuls ab, der das Herz zurück in den Sinusrhythmus holt. Über den BIOTRONIK Home Monitoring Service versendet es automatisch per Mobilfunk Informationen zum Therapieverlauf. Eine engmaschige Überwachung und Therapiekontrolle des Patienten ist so ohne zusätzliche Arztbesuche möglich.

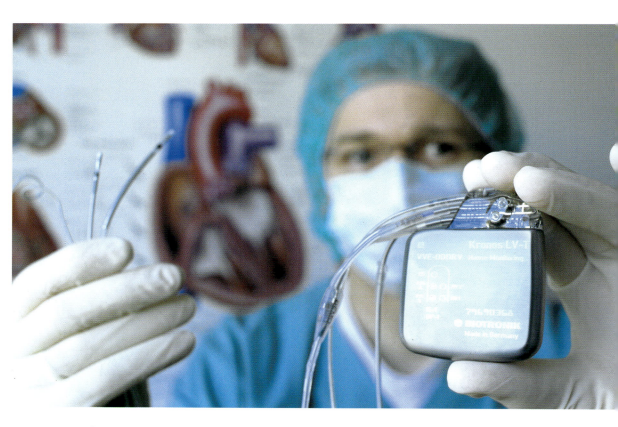

Pacemaker and defibrillator for chronic heart failure patients:

The latest generation of implants can resynchronise the disturbed pump process by means of three electrodes thus reducing the heart's workload. Should ventricular fibrillation arise, the device applies a high voltage pulse which brings the heart back into sinus rhythm. Using the BIOTRONIK Home Monitoring Service it automatically sends out information on the progress of therapy via the cellular phone network. Seamless monitoring and therapy control of the patient is possible without additionally visiting a physician.

Kompetenzfelder
Fields of Competence

Technologien für's Herz: Forschungsstandort in Erlangen.

Am Erlanger Zentrum für Technologie und Service arbeiten 130 Mitarbeiter an den Grundlagen für neue Therapiekonzepte und deren Evaluation im Rahmen klinischer Studien. Zwei Schwerpunkte stehen aktuell im Fokus: Um die Behandlung von Herzinsuffizienzpatienten zu optimieren, wird die Kardiale Resynchronisationstherapie per Herzschrittmacher-Implantat mit den Vorteilen der automatischen Fernüberwachung (BIOTRONIK Home Monitoring®) kombiniert. Zur Behandlung verengter Blutgefäße erforscht und entwickelt das Unternehmen einen neuartigen biodegradierbaren Metallstent – ein kleines Stützgitter, das sich im Körper vollständig auflöst.

Technology for the heart: research site in Erlangen.

At the Erlangen Centre for Technology and Service 130 employees work on the basis for new therapy concepts and their evaluation within the scope of clinical studies.
At present, the focus is on two main topics: In order to optimise treatment of chronic heart failure patients, cardiac resynchronisation therapy using a pacemaker implant is combined with the advantages of automatic tele-monitoring (BIOTRONIK Home Monitoring®). For treating narrowed blood vessels, the company carries out research and development on a new type of biodegradable metal stent – a small support grid which completely dissolves in the body.

Der Absorbierbare Metallstent:

Diese revolutionäre Technologie wurde maßgeblich von dem jungen Forschungs- und Entwicklungsteam am Standort Erlangen in Zusammenarbeit mit europäischen Kooperationspartnern vorangetrieben. Der neuartige Stent verbindet in idealer Weise die Vorteile des klassischen Stents mit denen der Ballonangioplastie, bei welcher kein Fremdkörper im Blutgefäß verbleibt.
Zu den größten technologischen Herausforderungen dieses innovativen Therapiekonzepts gehören die Ermittlung der mechanischen Eigenschaften und die Kinetik des Abbaus.

The absorbable metal stent:

This revolutionary technology was decisively pushed ahead by the young research and development team in Erlangen in cooperation with European partners. The new type of stent combines in an ideal way the advantages of the classic stent with those of balloon angioplasty, i.e. no foreign body remaining in the blood vessel. Determining the mechanical characteristics and the kinetics of absorption are one of the biggest technological challenges presented by this innovative therapy concept.

Information

Gründungsjahr: 1963
Mitarbeiter: weltweit 2800; am Standort Erlangen 130
Produktspektrum: Elektrotherapie des Herzens/Vaskuläre Intervention; Herzschrittmacher, Implantierbare Defibrillatoren, Elektroden, Externe Geräte, Katheter, Stentsysteme, Health Services
Standorte:
– Berlin (Unternehmenszentrale)
– Erlangen
– Berg
– Rostock-Warnemünde
– Pirna
– Lake Oswego (USA)
– Bülach (Schweiz)

Year founded: 1963
Employees: 2,800 worldwide; at the Erlangen location 130
Range of products: electrotherapy of the heart/vascular intervention; pacemakers, implantable defibrillators, electrodes, external devices, catheters, stent systems, Health Services
Locations:
– Berlin (Headquarter)
– Erlangen
– Berg
– Rostock-Warnemünde
– Pirna
– Lake Oswego (USA)
– Bülach (Switzerland)

BIOTRONIK GmbH & Co. KG

In der Unternehmenszentrale Nürnberg finden intensive internationale Produkt- und Serviceschulungen statt.

Intensive international product and service training is held in the undertaking's headquarters in Nuremberg.

Das Unternehmen Ziehm Imaging entstand 2004 aus der Fusion der Ziehm GmbH, Nürnberg, und der Ziehm Riverside Inc. aus Kalifornien (USA). Ziehm Imaging ist auf Entwicklung, Produktion, Vertrieb und Service digitaler Röntgenbildgebungssysteme spezialisiert und ist damit seit zehn Jahren unbestrittener Marktführer Deutschlands.

Die mobilen C-Bögen von Ziehm Imaging setzen von Beginn an Maßstäbe in der Branche – bei Röntgen-, Video- und digitaler Bildverarbeitungstechnologie ebenso wie bei der mechanischen Präzision. Markenzeichen aller Produkte ist ihre enorme Vielseitigkeit und einfache Handhabung in einer breiten Palette medizinischer Anwendungen sowie ihre mühelose, leichte Integration in bestehende IT-Umgebungen.

Seit mehr als 30 Jahren arbeitet Ziehm eng mit seinen weltweiten Kunden zusammen, reagiert flexibel auf veränderte Anwendungsprofile und liefert modernste technische Produktqualität – zum Vorteil des Patienten, des Bedieners und des Arztes. Jedes neue Produkt von Ziehm Imaging bringt eine deutliche Innovation und somit intelligente und effiziente Bildgebungslösungen für den Kunden.

Kompetenzfelder
Fields of Competence

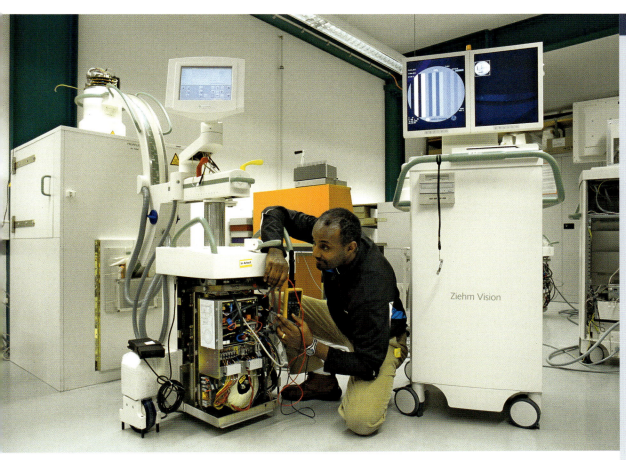

The Ziehm Imaging undertaking was created in 2004 from the fusion of Ziehm GmbH, Nuremberg, and the Ziehm Riverside Inc., from California (USA). Ziehm Imaging is specialised in the development, production, sales and service of digital x-ray imaging systems and has been the unquestioned market leader in Germany for ten years.

From the very beginning the mobile c-arms from Ziehm Imaging set standards in the branch – in x-ray, video and digital picture processing technology as well as with mechanical precision. The benchmark of all their products is the enormous versatility and easy handling in a wide range of medical sectors as well as their effortless integration in existing IT environments.

For more than 30 years, Ziehm has worked closely with its worldwide customers, has reacted flexibly to altered consumer profiles and has supplied cutting-edge technical product quality – to the advantage of the patient, the operator and the physician. Each new product from Ziehm Imaging brings with it a clear innovation, hence intelligent and efficient solutions for picture reproduction for the customer.

Die strengen Qualitätsrichtlinien im hauseigenen Systemtest garantieren höchste Qualität und Zuverlässigkeit der Geräte beim Kunden.

The strict quality guidelines in the concern's own system test guarantee top quality and reliability of the units on the customer's premises.

Information

Gründungsjahr: 1971

Mitarbeiter: ca. 250

Leistungsspektrum: Entwicklung, Produktion, Vertrieb und Service digitaler Röntgenbildgebungssysteme

Produkte:
- Ziehm Vision 5 + Vision R 6
- Ziehm Vista 2 + Vision FD 7
- Ziehm Vista Endo 3
- Ziehm Compact 1
- Ziehm Vario 3D 4

Year founded: 1971

Employees: about 250

Range of products: development, production, sales and service of digital x-ray imaging systems

Products:
- Ziehm Vision 5 + Vision R 6
- Ziehm Vista 2 + Vision FD 7
- Ziehm Vista Endo 3
- Ziehm Compact 1
- Ziehm Vario 3D 4

Ziehm Imaging GmbH
Nürnberg

Seit mehr als 70 Jahren fertigt PAUSCH Geräte für die Medizintechnik, insbesondere Röntgensysteme, und ist heute ein gefragter Partner für innovative Produkte. Als PAUSCH technologies entwickelt und fertigt das Unternehmen individuelle Serien im Kundenauftrag, prüft nach internationalen Standards und bietet einen weltweiten Support und Versand an.
Mit Eigen- und Exklusiventwicklungen beliefert PAUSCH weltweit alle führenden Medizingerätehersteller. Die Palette reicht von Einzelkomponenten bis hin zu komplett softwaregesteuerten Anlagen zur Anwendung in der konventionellen als auch in der digitalen Radiographie.
Seit 1994 ist PAUSCH nach ISO 9001 und seit 2005 nach ISO 13485 zertifiziert.
Der Bau von innovativen Röntgensystemen und medizintechnischen Anlagen erfordert höchste Präzision, viel Erfahrung und eine Menge Know-how.

Wandstativ für Röntgenaufnahmen am stehenden oder sitzenden Patienten

Wallstands for X-rays of sitting or standing patients

*For more than 70 years, PAUSCH has been manufacturing equipment for medical technology, and for X-ray systems in particular. Today, it is a much sought-after partner for innovative products. PAUSCH technologies develops and manufactures individual series to customer orders. The company inspects all products according to international standards and offers a worldwide support and despatch service.
With its own and exclusive developments, PAUSCH is a global supplier to all leading manufacturers of medical equipment.
The range stretches from individual components through to complete software-controlled plants for use in conventional as well as digital radiography.
Since 1994, PAUSCH has been certified in accordance with ISO 9001 and since 2005 in accordance with ISO 13485.
The construction of innovative X-ray systems and medico-technical equipment requires the utmost precision, a wealth of experience and a great deal of know-how.*

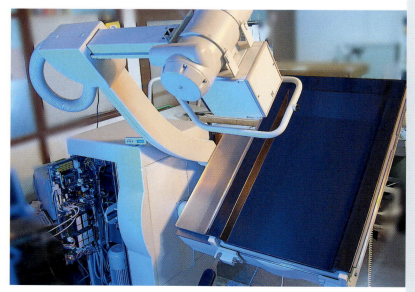

Spezialarbeitsplatz für die Urologie

Special workplace for Urology

Information

Gründungsjahr: 1932

Mitarbeiter: rund 330

Leistungsspektrum:
- Entwicklung von mechanischen und mechatronischen Produkten
- Fertigung und Montage
- weltweiter Vertrieb von medizintechnischen Geräten

Standorte:
Erlangen (Deutschland)
Tapsony (Ungarn)
New Jersey (USA)

Produkte:
Urologietische
Wandstative
Deckenstative
Buckytische
Röhrenstative
Universalgeräte

Year founded: 1932

Employees: about 330

Range of services:
- development of mechanical and mechatronical products
- manufacture and assembly
- worldwide sale of medico-technical devices

Locations:
Erlangen (Germany)
Tapsony (Hungary)
New Jersey (USA)

Products:
urology tables
wallstands
ceiling suspensions
buckytables
tubestands
universal positioning devices

☐
PAUSCH technologies
Hans Pausch
GmbH & Co.
Erlangen

Kompetenzfelder
Fields of Competence

Information
Gründungsjahr: 1902
Mitarbeiter: 40
Produktspektrum: – Heilmittel – Wickel – Pflegepräparate
Year founded: 1902
Employees: 40
Range of products: – healing preparations – packings/compresses – care products
Retterspitz GmbH Schwaig

Seit über 100 Jahren steht der Name Retterspitz für sicher wirkende und gut verträgliche Heil- und Pflegepräparate. Außerdem ist Retterspitz der größte Hersteller medizinischer und kosmetischer Wickel-Flüssigkeiten. Mit Retterspitz Äußerlich bietet das Unternehmen das zweitälteste (seit 1902), in Apotheken erhältliche Produkt in Deutschland an.

For more than 100 years the name of Retterspitz has stood for healing and care preparations which are safe and effective. In addition, Retterspitz is the biggest manufacturer of medicinal and cosmetic packing fluids. Retterspitz Äußerlich is the second-oldest (since 1902) product produced by the undertaking which is available in chemist's shops in Germany.

schungszentrum. Medizin hat Tradition in Erlangen. Davon zeugen zahlreiche Pionierleistungen. So waren es ein Erlanger Ordinarius, der 1847 erstmals im deutschsprachigen Raum eine Äthernarkose durchführte, und Erlanger Ingenieure, die die ersten Röntgengeräte bauten. Aber auch die moderne Medizin wird maßgeblich von hiesigen Errungenschaften beeinflusst. Anfang der sechziger Jahre entwickelte die damalige Firma Pfrimmer zusammen mit der NASA die „Astronautenkost", das erste Retortenbaby zwischen Alpen und Nordsee wurde in der fränkischen Universitätsstadt geboren, hier arbeitete weltweit auch der erste Operationssimulator.

Und dennoch waren es nicht nur diese Spitzenleistungen, die Erlangen heute zur Vorzeigestadt

has a long tradition in Erlangen, as countless pioneering works bear witness. Thus it was a professor from Erlangen who used ether as an anaesthetic for the first time in a German-speaking country in 1847, and it was Erlangen engineers who built the first x-ray machines. Modern medicine too has been decisively influenced by local achievements. At the beginning of the sixties Messrs. Pfrimmer, as the firm was then known, together with NASA, developed "astronauts food", the first test-tube baby between the Alps and the North See was born in the Franconian university city, and the world's first operation simulator was put into operation here.

Nevertheless, it was not only these first-rate performances that made Erlangen today's model town.

Pfrimmer Nutricia kann auf eine lange Tradition als Spezialist bei der Entwicklung von klinischer Ernährung zurückblicken. Nach Gründung der Firma Pfrimmer Pharmazeutische Werke & Co. KG im Jahr 1919 wurde bereits 1925 in Zusammenarbeit mit der Universitätsklinik Erlangen die erste industriell hergestellte Infusionslösung möglich. 1969 entwickelte Pfrimmer im Auftrag der NASA die erste so genannte Astronautenkost und erlangte damit Weltruf. Für den Bereich der klinischen Ernährung wurde diese Astronautenkost weiterentwickelt. 1974 brachte die Firma die erste vollbilanzierte Diät zur enteralen Ernährung auf den Markt. Heute leisten diese Produkte in der Medizin wertvolle Dienste. Sie verbessern als Sonden- oder Trinknahrung die Lebensqualität vieler Menschen, die aus medizinischen Gründen nicht essen können oder dürfen. Etwa 100 000 Menschen in Deutschland sind auf eine Ernährung per Sonde angewiesen.
Die Pfrimmer Nutricia GmbH ist seit ihrer Gründung 1991 ein Unternehmen der niederländischen Royal Numico Gruppe. Als Spezialist auf dem Gebiet krankheitsbedingter Ernährungsstörungen und deren Therapien ist die Pfrimmer Nutricia GmbH in Deutschland einer der Marktführer für enterale Ernährung.

Pfrimmer Nutricia can look back on a long tradition as specialist for the development of clinical nutrition. Following the founding of Messrs Pfrimmer Pharmazeutische Werke & Co. KG in the year 1919, the first industrially produced infusion solution became possible as early as 1925 in cooperation with the Erlangen University Clinic. In 1969 Pfrimmer, by order of NASA, developed the first so-called astronaut food and became world famous. This astronaut food was developed further for the sector of clinical nutrition. In 1974 the company introduced the first fully balanced diet for enteral feeding. Today these products serve the medical sector well. As liquid nutrition or tube-nutrition they improve the quality of the lives of many people who, for medical reasons, cannot or may not eat. Some 100,000 people in Germany rely on their nutrition by tube. Since its foundation in 1991, the Pfrimmer Nutricia GmbH has been an undertaking of the Dutch Royal Numico Group. As specialist on the sector of eating disturbances caused by illness and their therapies, the Pfrimmer Nutricia GmbH in Germany is one of the market leaders for enteral feeding.

Information

Gründungsjahr: 1991

Mitarbeiter: 291

Leistungsspektrum:
Produkte und Dienstleistungen aus den Bereichen Medizinische Diätetik und Ernährungstherapie
– Trinknahrungen
– Sondennahrungen
– Ernährungssonden und Überleitgeräte
– Ernährungspumpen
– Ernährungsteam Pfrimmer (etp): Dienstleistung zur Versorgung von künstlich ernährten Patienten in der häuslichen Umgebung

Year founded: 1991

Employees: 291

Range of services:
products and services in the sectors of medical dietetics and eating therapies
– liquid nutrition
– tube nutrition
– gravity feeding tubes and feeding pump sets
– feeding pumps
– Pfrimmer nutrition team (etp): services surrounding the care of patients needing tube feeding in their own surroundings

Pfrimmer Nutricia GmbH, Erlangen

Akkomodierende Intraokularlinse von der HumanOptics AG, einem der vielen innovativen Unternehmen aus dem „Medical Valley" im Raum Erlangen.

Accommodating intraocular lenses from HumanOptics AG, one of the many innovative concerns based in "Medical Valley" in the Erlangen area.

machen. Das besondere ökonomische Profil der Stadt wird durch das enge Zusammenwirken von Wissenschaft, Wirtschaft und Kommune geprägt. Die unmittelbare Nähe von hervorragender Wissenschaft sowie ein Mix aus Weltkonzern und Mittelstand bilden den Nährboden für die dynamische Entwicklung Erlangens. Mit der zweitgrößten bayerischen Alma Mater, deren Medizinische Fakultät zu den angesehensten in Deutschland zählt, sowie über 100 mittelständischen Unternehmen mit den Schwerpunkten medizinische Forschung, Produktion und Dienstleistung und dem Global Player Siemens Medical Solutions an der Spitze zählt die Hugenottenstadt mittlerweile zu den Topregionen Europas.

Die Vernetzung der vorhandenen Aktivitäten, die Schaffung von Synergieeffekten und der Austausch von Erfahrungswerten auf kurzen Wegen schaffen ein hochkreatives Milieu, das freie Räume für Visionen und innovative Geschäftsideen lässt. Die Stadtverwaltung schlüpft dabei in die Rolle des Moderators, der die Strukturen für eine enge Kooperation von Wirtschaft und Wissenschaft ausbaut. So unterstützt und initiiert die Kommune Kooperationsprojekte wie die Kompetenzinitiative „Medizin-Pharma-Gesundheit", die den Kontakt zwischen regionalen Firmen, Forschungseinrichtungen und Kliniken knüpft und fördert. Die Vernetzung der vorhandenen Aktivitäten schließt auch die Existenzgründer ein, die optimale Voraussetzungen für ihre Firmen finden.

Der Erfolg lässt sich messen. Über 60 Firmen haben sich seit 1996 neu gegründet, darunter auch mit bedeutenden Preisen ausgezeichnete Unternehmen

The especially economic city image is influenced by the close cooperation between science, industry and community. The close proximity of first-rate science as well as the mixture of global concerns and small and medium-sized enterprises provides the breeding ground for Erlangen's dynamic development. With the second-largest Bavarian Alma Mater, whose medical faculty counts as one of the most respected in Germany together with more than 100 medium-sized undertakings centred around medicinal research, production and service supply and the global player Siemens Medical Solutions at the tip, the Huguenot city counts in the meantime to the top regions of Europe.

The networking of existing activities, the creation of synergy effects and the exchange of experiences in the shortest possible way provides a highly creative milieu allowing plenty of free space for visions and innovative business ideas. The city administration has taken over the role of a presenter, one who extends the structures for the close cooperation between industry and science. In this way the community supports and initiates cooperative projects such as the competence initiative "Medizin-Pharma-Gesundheit", (medicine-pharma-health) which links and promotes the contact between regional companies, research institutions and clinics. The networking of existing activities also includes founders of new businesses who here find optimal conditions for their companies.

The success can be measured. More than 60 firms have been founded since 1996 amongst them undertakings which have also been awarded significant prizes such as november AG, WaveLight and

wie november AG, WaveLight oder HumanOptics. Nach einer Studie des Forschungsinstituts empirica Delasasse von 1999 zählt Erlangen sogar zu den vier gründerfreundlichsten Städten Deutschlands, und das Handelsblatt hat Erlangen zur Innovationshauptstadt erhoben.

Erlangen ist Sitz des Bayerischen Laserzentrums, zweier Fraunhofer-Institute und jüngst auch der Max-Planck-Forschergruppe „Optik, Information und Photonik". Ein weiterer Meilenstein auf dem Weg Erlangens zur „Medizinhauptstadt" wurde mit dem Bau des Innovationszentrums für Medizintechnik und Pharma (IZMP) gesetzt. Auf 4000 Quadratmetern Nutzfläche stehen Mietern modernste Büroräume und Laborflächen zur Verfügung. In dem seit 2003 im Betrieb befindlichen Innovationszentrum wurden in den zurückliegenden Jahren mehr als 30 Unternehmen mit über 150 Mitarbeitern angesiedelt. Mit einer Auslastung von fast 100 Prozent gehört es zu den erfolgreichsten Gründerzentren in Bayern. Und der nächste Meilenstein steht in Kürze ins Haus: Mit der bereits eingeleiteten Erweiterung des Gebäudekomplexes dürfte die Erfolgsgeschichte der Medizinstadt Erlangen eine weitere erfreuliche Fortsetzung finden.

HumanOptics. According to a study by the research institute empirica Delasasse in 1999, Erlangen even counts as one of the four founder-friendliest cities in Germany and the Handelsblatt elevated Erlangen to innovative capital.

Erlangen is the headquarters of the Bavarian Laser Centre, two Fraunhofer-Institutes and recently the Max-Planck-Research group "Optic, Information and Photonic". Another milestone on Erlangen's way to being "Medicine capital" was set with the construction of the Innovation Centre for Medical Technology and Pharmaceuticals (IZMP). 4,000 square metres of usable ground are available for the tenants of extremely modern offices and laboratory areas. In the innovation centre which has been in operation since 2003 more than 30 companies with over 150 employees have settled in the past few years. With the utilisation at almost 100 percent it belongs to the most successful founder centres in Bavaria. And the next milestone will soon be set: With the extension of the building complex already begun, the success story of the medicine city of Erlangen will find a welcome continuation.

Information

Gründungsjahr: 1994
Mitarbeiter: 265
Leistungsspektrum:
– Werk- und Objektschutz
– Ermittlungsdienst
– Empfangsservice
– Personenschutz
– Sicherheitsberatung
– Veranstaltungsdienst
– Hundestaffel

Year founded: 1994
Employees: 265
Range of services:
– works and property protection
– investigating services
– reception service
– body-guards
– safety counselling
– event services
– canine teams

ESS – Erlanger Sicherheits-Service GmbH, Erlangen

Die ESS – Erlanger Sicherheits-Service GmbH ist seit über zehn Jahren an verschiedenen Standorten in Nordbayern als Dienstleister aktiv.
Besonders ausgewähltes und qualifiziertes Personal setzt die gemeinsam mit den Kunden erarbeiteten Sicherheitskonzepte zuverlässig und hoch professionell um.

The ESS – Erlanger Sicherheits-Service GmbH has been active as a service supplier for more than ten years at various locations in North Bavaria.
Specially chosen and well-qualified personnel put the safety concepts which have been previously drawn up together with the customer into effect in a reliable and highly professional manner.

Kompetenzfelder
Fields of Competence

Schlüssel zum Erfolg – neue Materialien

Dr. Thomas Jung

Erfolgreicher Test unter Extrembedingungen: Sportbrille von UVEX im Einsatz beim Klettern am gefrorenen Wasserfall.

A successful test under extreme conditions: sports spectacles by UVEX used while climbing a frozen waterfall.

Neue Werkstoffe, neue Materialien und ihre Prüfung sind die Grundlage für neue Produkte. Geschätzt 70 Prozent des Bruttosozialproduktes der westlichen Industriestaaten stehen unmittelbar oder mittelbar mit Werkstoffen in Zusammenhang.

Die Stadt Fürth bekennt sich ausdrücklich zur Zukunft der Produktion und der produzierenden Industrie neben einem starken Dienstleistungssektor. Dazu entwickelt in Fürth das Zentralinstitut für Neue Materialien und Prozesstechnik (ZMP) der Friedrich-Alexander-Universität (Erlangen-Nürnberg) die erforderliche Zukunftstechnologie. Ergänzt wird die Entwicklung neuer Materialien und Prozesstechnologien durch die Arbeit des in der Fürther Uferstadt ebenfalls angesiedelten Entwicklungszentrums für Röntgentechnik des Fraunhofer-Instituts.

Die Entwicklung neuer Materialien und die zerstörungsfreie Materialprüfung gewinnt bei den industriellen Fertigungstechniken eine immer größere Bedeutung. Dem wird die Stadt Fürth mit ihren Forschungseinrichtungen im internationalen Maßstab gerecht.

New materials and their testing are the basis for new products. An estimated 70 percent of the gross national product of Western industrial countries is directly or indirectly connected with materials.

The city of Fürth has expressly committed itself to supporting the future of production and the producing industry alongside a strong service supply sector. To do this, the Central Institute for New Materials and Process Technology (ZMP) of the Friedrich-Alexander-University (Erlangen-Nuremberg) is developing the necessary future technology in Fürth. The development of new materials and processing technologies is supported by the work of the Fraunhofer-Institute's development centre for x-ray engineering which is also settled in the Fürth riverside city.

The development of new materials and destruction-free material tests in industrial manufacturing technologies is continuously gaining in importance. The city of Fürth does it justice with its research institutes of international standards.

The interdisciplinary research themes within the framework of the ZMP, which have established them-

The Key to Success – New Materials

Einer der faszinierendsten Werkstoffe unserer Zeit: Hochleistungskeramik. Basierend auf über 100 Jahren Entwicklungs- und Produktions-Know-how setzt CeramTec hier mit innovativen Ideen und Lösungen weltweit Maßstäbe. Am Standort Lauf fertigen drei Geschäftsbereiche Bauteile aus Technischer Keramik für unterschiedlichste Anwendungen:
Der Geschäftsbereich Multifunktionskeramik stellt Isolierbauteile für die Elektro-, Heiz- und Lichttechnik sowie keramische Bauteile für die Umwelt-, Wärme-, Präzisions- und Messtechnik her.
Der Geschäftsbereich Piezotechnik produziert piezokeramische Bauteile für alle Industriezweige von der Fahrzeugtechnik bis zum Anlagenbau sowie metallisierte Aluminiumoxidkeramik für die Elektronik.
Der Geschäftsbereich Systemtechnik fertigt Dicht- und Regelscheiben für Armaturen, Gleitringe für Pumpen aller Art und eine breite Palette an Bauteilen für die Automobiltechnik.

*One of the most fascinating materials of our times: high-performance ceramics. Based on more than 100 years of development and production know-how, CeramTec has set global standards with their innovative ideas and complete solutions. At their Lauf location three business divisions manufacture technical ceramic components for a wide variety of applications:
The Multifunctional Ceramics Division produces insulating components for electro, heating and light engineering as well as ceramic components for environmental, heating, precision and measuring technologies.
The Piezo Applications Division produces piezo ceramic components for all branches of industry ranging from automotive engineering through to plant construction as well as metallised alumina ceramics for the electronics industry.
The Mechanical Systems Division produces seal and regulator discs for sanitary fittings, face seal rings for pumps of all kinds and a wide selection of components for automotive engineering.*

Information

Gründungsjahr: 1903

Mitarbeiter:
weltweit 3000;
am Standort Lauf 550

Leistungsspektrum:
Entwicklung und Herstellung von Technischer Keramik für die Branchen
– Automotive
– Elektronik
– Medizintechnik
– Maschinen- und Gerätebau

Standorte:
Deutschland;
Tochterunternehmen in Großbritannien, Spanien, Italien, Tschechien, China, Südkorea, Malaysia, USA

Year founded: 1903

Employees:
worldwide 3,000;
550 at the Lauf location

Range of services:
Development and manufacture of technical ceramics for the branches
– automotive
– electronic
– medical technology
– machine and plant construction

Sites:
Germany;
Subsidiary firms in Great Britain, Spain, Italy, Czech Republic, China, South Korea, Malaysia, USA

☐
CeramTec AG
Innovative Ceramic Engineering
Lauf a. d. Pegnitz

Kompetenzfelder
Fields of Competence

Entwicklung von Metallschaum bei der Neue Materialien Fürth GmbH in Zusammenarbeit mit dem Institut für Werkstoffwissenschaften der Universität Erlangen-Nürnberg

Developing metal foam at Neue Materialien Fürth GmbH in cooperation with the Erlangen-Nuremberg University

Die interdisziplinären Forschungsthemen im Rahmen des ZMP, die zwischen Werkstoffwissenschaften, Maschinenbau, Chemie und Physik angesiedelt sind, führen zur Entwicklung innovativer neuer Verfahren, die beispielsweise innovative Verfahren zur Herstellung leichterer Bauteile entstehen lassen. Aus der Grundlagenforschung heraus werden die in Fürth engagierten Lehrstühle der Universität eine Entwicklung neuer Formteile bis ins Prototypenstadium gewährleisten. Die Neue Materialien Fürth GmbH hat im Mittelpunkt ihrer Tätigkeit die Entwicklung innovativer Fertigungsverfahren zur Herstellung von Bauteilen, Metallen, Kunststoffen und Verbundwerkstoffen. Auf modernsten Fertigungsanlagen entstehen Prototypenbauteile und Kleinserien aus neuen Werkstoffen und Verbundwerkstoffen. Die Bereiche Kohlenstoffwerkstoffe und Leichtbaufertigung stehen dabei besonders im Fokus.

Bei Kohlenstoffwerkstoffen werden neue Herstellungsverfahren für Werkstoffe aus Mesophasenpulvern entwickelt. Bei der Leichtbaufertigung liegt ein Schwer-

selves somewhere between material sciences, mechanical engineering, chemistry and physics, lead to the development of innovative new processes, which in turn allow, for instance, the creation of innovative processes for the manufacture of lighter components. The institutes of the Fürth University guarantee that from basic research new structural parts right through to the prototype stage will be developed. At the centre of the Neue Materialien Fürth GmbH's activities is the development of innovative processes for the manufacture of components, metals, synthetics and composite materials. Prototype components and small series made of new materials and composite materials are created on modern manufacturing equipment. The focus is on the sectors of carbon materials and light-weight manufacture.

New manufacturing processes for materials made of mesophase powders are developed in the carbon materials sector. In the light-weight manufacturing sector, the focus is on the development of the laser

Versuchsanlage zum Metallisieren von Kunststoffen

Experimental plant for metallising synthetics

punkt auf der Entwicklung von Laserstrahlschweißen bei Aluminium oder Magnesiumschäumen. Auch die Spritzgusstechnologie und die Technologie zur Beschichtung von metallischen Substraten mit Diamanten sind von Bedeutung.

Heutige Unternehmen mit Spitzenstellungen auf dem Weltmarkt werden diese Technologien auch im 21. Jahrhundert in der Region umsetzen. Weltmarktführer wie Kurz, Mekra-Lang, Uvex und Ecka-Granulate sind hier besonders zu nennen.

Neue Materialien sind Grundlage vieler Schlüsseltechnologien, insbesondere in der Automobiltechnik, Informationstechnik, Medizintechnik, Umwelttechnik, aber auch in der Energietechnik sowie Verkehrs- und Fertigungstechnologie. Für die Wirtschaftsregion Nürnberg sind diese Bereiche von entscheidender Bedeutung.

Mit ihren mittelständischen Unternehmen und innovativen Forschungseinrichtungen wird die Stadt Fürth ihre Stellung als einer der führenden produktionsnahen Technologiestandorte in Deutschland und Europa, insbesondere auf dem Feld der neuen Materialien, weiter ausbauen.

welding of aluminium or magnesium foams. Injection moulding technology and the technology for coating metal substratum with diamonds are also of importance.

Modern concerns with top positions on the global market will put these technologies into practice in the region also in the 21st century. World market leaders such as Kurz, Mekra-Lang, Uvex and Ecka-Granulate should at this point receive special mention.

New materials are the basis of many key technologies, especially in automobile engineering, information technology, medicine technology, environmental technology as well as in energy technologies and transport and manufacturing technologies. These sectors are of decisive importance for the economic region of Nuremberg.

With its medium-sized concerns and innovative research institutions the city of Fürth will be able to further consolidate its position as one of the leading production-friendly technological locations in Germany and Europe especially in the field of new materials.

Kompetenzfelder
Fields of Competence

Das Firmenmotto „Wir geben Ihrer Idee Form" ist für die HBW-Gubesch Anspruch und Auftrag zugleich. Ob im Bereich Design, in der Entwicklung und Produktion von Kunststoffteilen und Baugruppen für Autos und Unterhaltungselektronik, technischen Teilen für sonstige Konsumgüter, Lichtleitern, in der Folienhinterspritzung sowie Insert- und Inmouldtechnologie oder von Kunststoffen für die Medizintechnik – durch seine breiten Kapazitäten im Werkzeugbau, Formenbau und Spritzguss und einem kreativen Ideenreichtum ist HBW-Gubesch ein anerkannter und geschätzter Partner für seine weltweiten Kunden.

The company motto "We form your ideas" is a claim and at the same time a commandment for HBW-Gubesch. Whether in the sector of design, in the development and production of synthetic parts and assemblies for vehicles and entertainment electronics, technical parts for other consumer goods, light conductors, in film insert moulding or in the insert and inmould engineering or of synthetics for medicine technology – its wide capacities in tool making, mould making and injection moulding and a creative wealth of ideas makes HBW-Gubesch an acknowledged and appreciated partner for its worldwide customers.

Information

Gründungsjahr:
2005 durch Fusion der beiden Kooperationspartner HBW und Gubesch;
Gründung HBW: 1981;
Gründung Gubesch: 1990

Mitarbeiter: 200

Leistungsspektrum:
– Produktdesign und Baugruppenentwicklung
– Rapid-Prototyping
– Formenbau
– Spritzguss
 · 2-Komponenten
 · Lichtleitertechnologie
 · Folienhinterspritzung
 · Insert- und Inmouldtechnologie

Umsatz: 16 Mio. Euro

Year founded:
2005 by amalgamating both cooperation partners HBW and Gubesch;
year HBW founded: 1981;
year Gubesch founded: 1990

Employees: 200

Range of services:
– product design and assembly group development
– rapid-prototyping
– mould-making
– injection moulding
 · 2-component
 · light-conductor engineering
 · film insert moulding
 · insert and inmould engineering

Turnover:
16 million Euro

☐
HBW-Gubesch
Kunststoff-Engineering
GmbH, Emskirchen

Metropolregion Nürnberg – Energie- und Umwelttechnologien für den Weltmarkt

Dr. Robert Schmidt

Die Metropolregion Nürnberg gehört zu den sechs größten Wirtschaftsräumen in Deutschland mit bedeutenden wirtschaft- und wissenschaftlichen Potenzialen im Kompetenzfeld „Energie und Umwelt".

Im Energiebereich nimmt die Region mit 500 Unternehmen und über 50 000 Arbeitsplätzen europaweit eine Spitzenposition ein. Ein wichtiger Produktschwerpunkt ist der Turbinen- und Kraftwerksbau – getragen vom Bereich „Power Generation" (PG) der Siemens AG sowie der ANP Framatome. Auch im Segment „Elektrizitätsverteilungs- und Schalteinrichtungen" ist die Region führend. Eine Leitfunktion kommt hier dem Bereich „Power Transmission and Distribution" (PTD) der Siemens AG zu. Eine Vielzahl internationaler Großprojekte wie der Bau hoch effizienter Kraftwerke oder die Errichtung von neuen verlustarmen Übertragungssystemen wird von der Metropolregion Nürnberg aus geplant und umgesetzt.

In der Leistungselektronik besitzt die Region ein europaweites Alleinstellungsmerkmal durch ihre hohe Kompetenz in der gesamten Wertschöpfungskette, angefangen bei F+E über Produktion von leistungselektronischen Komponenten und Systemen bis hin zur Anwendung in den Bereichen Industrie-, Kfz- und Konsumelektronik sowie Gebäudetechnik. Deshalb wurde vor wenigen Jahren in Nürnberg das European Center for Power Electronics (ECPE) gegründet.

Im Solarsektor verfügt die Region mit dem „solid-Zentrum" in Fürth über einen Kristallisationskeim für ein dichtes Solarhändlernetz. Das Energietechnologische Zentrum (etz) in Nürnberg bietet innovativen Projekten und jungen Energietechnikunternehmen ein attraktives Umfeld. Zudem besteht im Westen der Metropolregion eine hohe Kompetenz im Sektor Photovoltaik, Wasserkraft und Biomasse. Deutsch-

The metropolitan region of Nuremberg is one of the six largest industrial areas in Germany with significant economic and scientific potential in the competence fields of "Energy and Environment".

In the energy sector, the region's 500 concerns and more than 50,000 workplaces take on a top position in Europe. One important sector of production is the turbine and power plant construction – carried by the "Power Generation" (PG) division of Siemens AG as well as the ANP Framatome. The region also leads in the segment of "electricity distribution and switchgears". The sector "Power Transmission and Distribution" (PTD) of the Siemens AG has here a guiding function. A large number of international major projects such as the construction of highly efficient power plants or the erection of new low-leakage transmission systems are planned and put into effect from the metropolitan region of Nuremberg.

In power electronics, the region has a characterising feature unique in Europe thanks to its extreme competence in the entire added value chain, beginning with research and development via the production of power electronic elements and systems through to application in the sectors of industry, vehicle and consumer electronics as well as building technology. Which is why the European Centre for Power Electronics (ECPE) was founded in Nuremberg a few years ago.

In the solar sector, with the "solid-Zentrum" in Fürth the region has a crystallisation nucleus for a dense network of solar dealers. The Energietechnologische Zentrum (energy technological centre) (etz) in Nuremberg provides an attractive sphere for innovative projects and young energy-technology concerns. There is also a large amount of competence in the sectors of photo-

Metropolitan Region of Nuremberg – Energy- and Environmental Engineering for the Global Market

Kompetenzfelder
Fields of Competence

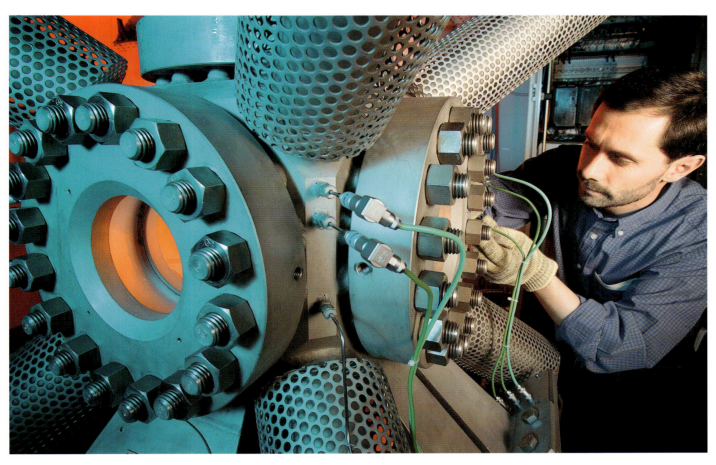

Praktische Forschung an einer Diesel-Einspritzkammer bei der Firma ESYTEC aus Erlangen in Kooperation mit der Universität Erlangen-Nürnberg	*Practical research on a diesel injection chamber at Messrs ESYTEC in Erlangen in cooperation with the Erlangen-Nuremberg University*

lands erste großtechnische Bioabfallvergärungsanlage mit angeschlossener Nahwärmeversorgung wurde bereits vor zehn Jahren in Schwabach errichtet. Gemeinsam mit Partnern realisiert die Erlanger Solar Millennium AG eine Vision: den Bau solarthermischer Kraftwerke in den Ländern des Sonnengürtels der Erde.

Innovative Energietechnik bietet neben Wirtschaftlichkeit und Versorgungssicherheit daher auch die Basis für Lösungen bei Energieeffizienz und Umweltschutz. Hierfür stehen mehr als 1000 Unternehmen und Institutionen und über 20 000 Arbeitsplätze mit Schwerpunkten in den Bereichen Wassertechnik, Luftreinhaltung, Recycling sowie produkt- und produktionsintegrierter Umweltschutz.

Fortsetzung Seite 188

voltaic, water power and biomass in the West of the metropolitan region. Germany's first large technical biological waste fermenting plant with connecting local heat supply was erected in Schwabach ten years ago. Together with their partners, the Erlangen Solar Millennium AG has realised a vision: the construction of solar-thermal power plants in those countries of the world which are in the sun zone.

Continued on page 188

Vom Versorger zum Dienstleister: So lässt sich die Erfolgsgeschichte der Ferngas Nordbayern GmbH am treffendsten charakterisieren.
Lag die Aufgabe noch in den sechziger Jahren vor allem im Aufbau eines umfassenden Gasleitungsnetzes im nordbayerischen Raum, entwickelte sich die FGN schon bald zu einem modernen Energiedienstleistungsunternehmen mit einem differenzierten Angebot für ihre Kunden. Heute reicht das Leistungsspektrum von der Beratung eines Hausbesitzers, der seine Heizung modernisieren möchte, bis zur Übernahme von komplexen Aufgaben in Verbindung mit der Kraft-Wärme-Kopplung.
Die FGN in Nürnberg zählt zu den größeren Ferngasgesellschaften in Deutschland und ist die zweitgrößte in Bayern.

*From supplier to service supplier: This is how one could best characterise the success story of the Ferngas Nordbayern GmbH.
Although in the sixties their main task lay primarily in building up an all-encompassing gas pipe network in the North Bavarian area, the FGN soon developed itself into a modern energy service supply with differentiated offers for its customers. Today, the range of services reaches from advising house owners who wish to modernise their heating system through to taking over complex tasks in connection with combined heat and power generation.
The FGN in Nuremberg counts as one of the largest distribution companies for natural gas in Germany and is the second largest in Bavaria.*

Information

Gründungsjahr: 1962

Leistungsspektrum:
Versorgung von Städten, Gemeinden und Industriebetrieben in Nordbayern mit Erdgas; umfassende Beratung für Industrie-, Gewerbe- und Privatkunden; Wärme- und emissionstechnische Untersuchungen; Seminare; Erstellung effizienter Energiekonzepte

Absatzgebiet:
rund 27 000 km²

Year founded: 1962

Range of services:
supplying towns, communities and industrial concerns in North Bavaria with natural gas; encompassing advisory service for industry, commercial and private customers; heat and emission technical examinations; seminars; elaboration of efficient energy concepts

Sales area:
about 27,000 km²

☐
Ferngas Nordbayern GmbH, Nürnberg

Kompetenzfelder
Fields of Competence

N-ERGIE für die Region

Das Unternehmen ging im Jahr 2000 aus den fränkischen Energieversorgern EWAG Energie und Wasserversorgung AG, Fränkisches Überlandwerk AG (FÜW) und MEG Mittelfränkischer Erdgas GmbH hervor. Mit einem Stromabsatz von 6,9 Mrd. Kilowattstunden an Endkunden im Jahr 2004 zählt die N-ERGIE zu den größten zehn Stromversorgern Deutschlands und ist in ihrem Netzgebiet, das weite Teile von Mittelfranken und angrenzende Gebiete umfasst, klare Marktführerin. Das Erdgas-Verteilnetz ist annähernd 4000 Kilometer lang. Für die Stadt Nürnberg ist die N-ERGIE auch Lieferant für Fernwärme und Wasser. Die rund 2800 Mitarbeiter setzen jährlich über eine Mrd. Euro um.

Mit ihren Dienstleistungsangeboten, wie Contracting oder Facility Management, eroberte sich das Unternehmen einen neuen Markt. Entscheidend für die gute Marktposition der N-ERGIE ist die Entwicklung innovativer Produkte und Energielösungen. Damit erwirtschaftet sie bereits 30 Prozent des Stromabsatzes außerhalb ihres Netzgebietes. Mit jährlichen Investitionen in Höhe von über 80 Mio. Euro ist die N-ERGIE treibender Motor der Region und sorgt für einen hohen Grad an Versorgungssicherheit – eine Grundvoraussetzung für den wirtschaftlichen Erfolg der Region.

N-ERGIE for the region

The company resulted from the merging of the Franconian energy suppliers EWAG Energie and Wasserversorgung AG, Fränkisches Überlandwerk AG (FÜW) and MEG Mittelfränkische Erdgas GmbH in 2000. With a power sale of 6.9 billion kilowatt-hours to the consumer in 2004, N-ERGIE counts as one of the largest ten power suppliers in Germany and is clear leader in its network area which covers a large amount of Middle Franconia and surroundings. The natural gas distributor network is almost 4,000 kilometres long. For the city of Nürnberg, N-ERGIE is also supplier of long-distance thermal energy and water. A staff of some 2,800 employees make an annual turnover of more than a billion Euro.

With the services offered, such as contracting or facility management, the company has conquered a new market. The development of innovative products and energy solutions is decisive for N-ERGIE's good position on the market and 30 percent of the power sales have already been made outside its network area. With annual investments amounting to more than 80 million Euro, N-ERGIE is the driving force of the region and provides a high degree of security of supply – one of the basic prerequisites for the economic success of the region.

Information

Gründungsjahr: 2000

Gesellschafter:
Städtische Werke Nürnberg GmbH (60,2 %);
Thüga AG (39,8 %)

Mitarbeiter: rund 2800

Leistungsspektrum:
– Strom
– Erdgas
– Wasser
– Fernwärme
– weitere Dienstleistungen wie Contracting, Facility Management, Betriebsführung, regenerative Energien usw.

Umsatz: über 1 Mrd. Euro jährlich

Year founded: 2000

Shareholders:
Städtische Werke Nürnberg GmbH (60.2 %);
Thüga AG (39.8 %)

Employees: some 2,800

Range of services:
– power
– natural gas
– water
– long-distance thermal energy
– additional services such as contracting, facility management, management, regenerative energies etc.

Turnover: more than 1 billion Euro annually

☐ N-ERGIE
Aktiengesellschaft
Nürnberg

Die Max Aicher Recycling GmbH (MAR) ist ein kompetenter Partner von Industrieanlagen in allen Fragen der Ver- und Entsorgung.

An den Standorten Nürnberg und Amberg betreibt MAR zwei Schrottbehandlungsanlagen. In Meitingen, in unmittelbarer Nähe zu den Lech-Stahlwerken, unterhält MAR außerdem eine Anlage zur Herstellung von Baustoffen aus Rückständen der Stahlproduktion. Aus der Schlacke des Schmelzprozesses von Schrott werden u. a. hochwertige Produkte hergestellt, die als Straßenbaustoff zugelassen sind.

Der bei Lech-Stahlwerke GmbH produzierte Stahl wird in der Baubranche und der Automobilindustrie europa- und weltweit vermarktet. Die Jahresproduktion in Meitingen liegt bei rund einer Million Tonnen.

Aus Schrotten unterschiedlichster Anlaufstellen produziert MAR Schrottsorten – gemäß Europäischer Schrottsortenliste – für die Nachfrage am Stahlmarkt und verwandter Branchen. Der Standort von MAR im Hafen Nürnberg mit angeschlossener Betriebsstätte in Amberg ist direkt an das Straßen-, Bahn- und Wassernetz angebunden und bietet damit ideale Voraussetzungen nahtloser logistischer Abläufe.

Darüber hinaus ist MAR nach dem Altfahrzeuggesetz anerkannt als Annahmestelle, Demontagebetrieb sowie Shredderanlage und damit kompetenter und zuverlässiger Ansprechpartner der Automobilindustrie für die Altautoentsorgung.

Weitere Geschäftsaktivitäten von MAR sind der Vertrieb von aufbereiteter Schlacke des Müllheizkraftwerks Burgkirchen sowie die umweltstrategische Betreuung von Industrieanlagen.

Die MAR ist Teil der international operierenden Unternehmensgruppe Max Aicher mit Standorten in Deutschland, Tschechien, der Slowakei, Ungarn und Rumänien rund um die Geschäftsfelder Bau, Immobilien, Stahl und Umwelt.

Kompetenzfelder
Fields of Competence

The Max Aicher Recycling GmbH (MAR) is a competent partner for industrial plants in all questions of supply and disposal. At their locations in Nuremberg and Amberg, MAR operates two scrap metal treatment plants. In Meitingen, in close proximity to the Lech steelworks, MAR also operates a plant for producing building materials from the residue of steel production. Amongst others, high-quality products are produced from the slags resulting from the scrap metal melting process, products which are licensed to be used as road building materials. The steel produced by the Lech-Stahlwerke GmbH is sold all over the world to the building industry and the automobile industry. The annual production in Meitingen lies around 1 million tons.

From scrap metal accumulated from various places, MAR produces different types of scrap metal – in accordance with the European scrap metal list – to cover the demands from the steel market and related branches. The MAR location in the Nuremberg port with its affiliated works in Amberg is directly linked with the road, rail and water networks offering ideal conditions for seamless logistical processes.

In addition, MAR is a recognised receiving office, dismantling point and shredding plant in accordance with the end-of-life-vehicle laws and is thereby a competent and reliable partner for the automobile industry and scrap car disposal.

Further business activities of MAR are the sales of recycled slag from the refuse incineration power station in Burgkirchen as well as the environment-strategic supervision of industrial plants.

MAR is part of the internationally operating concern group of Max Aicher which has locations in Germany, the Czech Republic, Slovakia, Hungary and Romania around the business fields of construction, property, steel and the environment.

Information

Gründungsjahr: 1996

Mitarbeiter: 55

Leistungsspektrum:
- Behandlung von Schrott
- Herstellung und Vertrieb von SE-Stein 4.0 aus Elektroofenschlacke
- Vertrieb von HMV-Schlacke
- umweltstrategische Unternehmensbetreuung

Year founded: 1996

Employees: 55

Range of services:
- scrap metal treatment
- manufacturing and selling SE-Stein (rare earth stone) 4.0 from electric furnace slag
- selling HMV slag
- environment-strategic concern counselling

Max Aicher Recycling GmbH, Nürnberg

Zentrale Standortfaktoren in der Forschung sind die Friedrich-Alexander-Universität Erlangen-Nürnberg mit dem Schwerpunkt „Ökosystemare Forschung und Umwelttechnik", die Universität Bayreuth mit dem Fokus „Ökologie und Umweltwissenschaften", das Fraunhofer-Institut IISB mit dem Thema Leistungselektronik sowie die Fachhochschulen in Ansbach, Amberg-Weiden, Coburg, Nürnberg und Triesdorf, die mit ihrem breiten Spektrum und bundesweiten thematischen Alleinstellungen in der Aus- und Weiterbildung das Kompetenzfeld „Energie und Umwelt" stärken. Dieses Umfeld wird ergänzt durch zahlreiche weitere technologieorientierte Einrichtungen wie zum Beispiel das Forschungs- und Entwicklungszentrum für Sondertechnologien (FES) in Schwabach, das EBA-Zentrum in Triesdorf zur verstärkten energetischen Nutzung von Biomasse, das ATZ Entwicklungszentrum für Energieverfahrens- und Umwelttechnik in Sulzbach-Rosenberg bzw. das Zentrum für Angewandte Energieforschung (ZAE Bayern) in Erlangen und Würzburg.

Mit Energiefachmessen wie der ENKON dezentral, den Weltleitmessen IKK BioFach sowie der weltweit führenden Leistungselektronikmesse PCIM verfügt Nürnberg über wirksame Plattformen für ein internationales Marketing. Die Vernetzung erfolgt durch den EnergieRegion Nürnberg e. V., im Umweltsektor durch die Initiative Umweltkompetenz Nordbayern sowie in zahlreichen technologischen Clustern der nordbayerischen IHKn Bayreuth, Coburg, Nürnberg, Regensburg und Würzburg-Schweinfurt.

In der Summe ihrer Stärken darf sich die Metropolregion Nürnberg zu Recht als europäisches Kompetenzzentrum in Sachen Energie und Umwelt betrachten.

Innovative energy technology, alongside its being economical and providing supply assurance, also provides the basis for solutions of efficient energy and in environmental protection. To accomplish this, there are more than 1,000 undertakings and institutions and more than 20,000 workplaces centred on the sectors of water technology, anti air pollution, recycling as well as product and production integrated environment protection.

The central business location factors in research are the Friedrich-Alexander-University Erlangen-Nuremberg with the focal points on "Eco-system-relevant Research and Environment Technology", the university of Bayreuth with the focus on "Ecology and Environmental Sciences", the Fraunhofer-Institute IISB with the subject of power electronics as well as the universities of applied sciences in Ansbach, Amberg-Weiden, Coburg, Nuremberg and Triesdorf, which, with their wide range and thematic national uniqueness in education and professional training, strengthen the competence field of "energy and environment". This sphere is supplemented by countless additional technology-oriented institutions such as the Research and Development Centre for Special Technologies (FES) in Schwabach, the EBA centre in Triesdorf for increased energetic utilisation of biomass, the ATZ development centre for energy processes and environmental technology in Sulzbach-Rosenberg and/or the Centre for Applied Energy Research (ZAE Bavaria) in Erlangen and Würzburg.

With special energy trade fairs such as the ENKON dezentral, the world's leading trade fairs IKK, BioFach as well as the worldwide leading power electronics fair PCIM Nuremberg maintains effective platforms for international marketing. Networking is done through the EnergieRegion Nürnberg e. V., in the environmental sector through the initiative Environmental Competence North Bavaria as well as in a large number of technological clusters of the North Bavarian Chambers of Commerce in Bayreuth, Coburg, Nuremberg, Regensburg and Würzburg-Schweinfurt.

In the sum of their strengths, the metropolitan region of Nuremberg may justifiably consider itself a European competence centre in questions of energy and environment.

Kompetenzfelder
Fields of Competence

LOOS INTERNATIONAL zählt heute zu den führenden Herstellern von Heißwasser- und Dampfkesselanlagen. Das Einsatzspektrum der Qualitätserzeugnisse ist breit gefächert. Es reicht von der Heizwärmeerzeugung in Fernwärmekraftwerken bis hin zur ökonomischen Bereitstellung von Prozesswärme für unzählige gewerbliche und industrielle Anwendungen. Die Erfüllung höchster Umweltanforderungen ist dabei selbstverständlich.

Innovation beginnt bei LOOS INTERNATIONAL schon bei der Auftragsannahme. Jedes Projekt wird von einem verantwortlichen Systemspezialisten geleitet. Für den Kunden bedeutet dies einen Ansprechpartner in allen Realisierungsphasen des Auftrags. So sind Innovation und Produktionsverbesserung ein ständiger Prozess und immanenter Teil des Gesamtunternehmens zum Nutzen des Kunden. Dabei spielt die Entwicklung der Modultechnik für Kesselhauskomponenten eine große Rolle. Dies sieht LOOS INTERNATIONAL als Bestandteil der strategischen Ausrichtung zur Partnerschaft mit Planern und Anlagenbauern mit größerem Nutzen für den Betreiber. Im computergesteuerten Logistik-Center sind Ersatzteile rund um die Uhr abrufbar. Ein engmaschiges Netz an Servicegebieten und die Nutzung des LOOS-Teleservice stellt kürzeste Reaktionszeiten sicher.

LOOS INTERNATIONAL today counts as one of the leading manufacturers of hot water and steam generating plants. The application spectrum of its quality products is wide. It reaches from generating heat in long-distance thermal power plants through to the economic preparation of process heat for countless commercial and industrial applications. Fulfilling the exacting demands set by environmental protection is a matter of course. According to LOOS INTERNATIONAL, innovation begins with order acceptance. Each project is managed by a responsible system specialist. For the customer this means that he has a contact person in all realisation phases of the order. Thus innovation and production improvement are a continuous process and an immanent part of the entire concern, for the benefit of the customer. At the same time, the development of modular technology for boilerhouse components plays an important role. LOOS INTERNATIONAL considers this to be an essential part of the strategic orientation towards partnership with planers and plant constructors providing enormous benefits also to the operating company.
Spare parts can be called up round the clock in the computer-controlled logistics centre. A closely meshed network of service areas and the use of the LOOS-teleservice guarantee the shortest possible reaction times.

Information

Gründungsjahr: 1865
Mitarbeiter: 620
Leistungsspektrum: Entwicklung und Fertigung von Kesselsystemen sowie von Kesselhauskomponenten für alle gewerblichen und industriellen Anwendungen
Produktion: Deutschland und Österreich
Niederlassungen und Tochtergesellschaften in: Frankreich, Griechenland, Italien, Österreich, Polen, Russland, Skandinavien, Slowakei, Spanien und Portugal, Südostasien, Tschechische Republik und China
Vertretungen: weltweit

Year founded: 1865
Employees: 620
Range of services: development and production of boiler systems as well as of boilerhouse components for all commercial and industrial applications
Production: Germany and Austria
Branches and affiliates in: France, Greece, Italy, Austria, Poland, Russia, Scandinavia, Slovakia, Spain and Portugal, Southeast Asia, Czech Republic and China
Agencies: worldwide

LOOS INTERNATIONAL
Loos Deutschland GmbH
Gunzenhausen

Auf eine inzwischen 100-jährige Firmengeschichte blickt die OSSBERGER GmbH + Co in Weißenburg zurück.
Im Laufe der Jahrzehnte hat sich Ossberger drei Geschäftsfelder erschlossen: Hydro (Erzeugung elektrischer Energie aus Wasserkraft), Plastics Technology (Bau von Kunststoff verarbeitenden Maschinen) und Coli-Cleaner (industrielle Reinigung von Werkstücken). Heute befindet sich in Weißenburg auf einem Firmengelände von 26 000 Quadratmetern eine Produktionsfläche von 7000 Quadratmetern.
85 Prozent seiner Produkte exportiert Ossberger in die ganze Welt.
Seit Jahrzehnten gehört das Unternehmen zu den Weltmarktführern bei der Herstellung von Turbinen, die auf umweltfreundliche Weise elektrische Energie aus Wasserkraft erzeugen. Über 9500 Ossberger-Turbinen mit bis zu 2 MW sind in über 100 Ländern der Erde in Betrieb.
Mit dem PRESSBLOWER-Spritzblasautomaten gehört die Firma ebenfalls zur Weltspitze der Branche. Auf den Maschinen aus Weißenburg werden zum Beispiel Tuben und Ampullen mit hauchdünner Wandstärke sowie Rund- und Ovalflaschen gefertigt; darüber hinaus werden Lenkungsfaltenbälge für alle gängigen Fahrzeugtypen auf den PRESSBLOWER-Automaten hergestellt.
Die neueste Entwicklung wurde vor kurzem zur Serienreife gebracht. In enger Zusammenarbeit mit dem Fraunhofer-Institut entwickelte Ossberger den „Coli-Cleaner", ein System zur automatischen industriellen Reinigung von Werkstücken, das ohne chemische Reinigungsmittel und mit geringem Energieeinsatz auskommt. Mit dieser Innovation hat Ossberger erneut Maßstäbe gesetzt und ist seiner Philosophie treu geblieben, Umweltschutz und Technologie zu vereinen.

*The OSSBERGER GmbH + Co in Weißenburg can look back over a history of meanwhile 100 years. Over the last decades, Ossberger has developed three fields of business: hydro (creating electrical energy from water power), plastics technology (constructing plastic-processing machines) and coli-cleaner (industrial cleaning of worked pieces).
In Weissenburg today, there is a production area of 7,000 square metres standing on company ground covering 26,000 square metres.
85 percent of its products is exported by Ossberger all over the world. For decades, the undertaking has been one of the world's market leaders in manufacturing turbines, creating electrical energy from water power in an environmentally friendly manner.
More than 9,500 Ossberger turbines with up to 2 MW are operating in more than 100 countries all over the world.
With the PRESSBLOWER automatic injection-blow moulding machine, the firm also counts as one of the branch's world leaders. For instance, tubes and ampoules with wafer-thin wall thickness are produced on machines from Weißenburg as well as round and oval bottles; in addition to that steering fold bellows for all common vehicle types are manufactured on the automatic PRESSBLOWER machines. Their latest development has recently become ready for series production. In close cooperation with the Fraunhofer Institute, Ossberger developed the "Coli-Cleaner", a system for automatically, industrially cleaning worked pieces, without the need for chemical cleansing agents and using extremely low energy. With this innovation, Ossberger has once again set high standards and has remained true to its philosophy of combining environmental protection and technology.*

Information

Gründungsjahr: 1906

Mitarbeiter: 120

Leistungsspektrum:
– Hydro
– Plastics Technology
– Coli-Cleaner

Umsatz: 19 Mio. Euro jährlich

Year founded: 1906

Employees: 120

Range of services:
– hydro
– plastics technology
– coli-cleaner

Turnover: 19 million Euro annually

☐ OSSBERGER GmbH + Co Weißenburg

Kompetenzfelder
Fields of Competence

Hoch spezialisiert – Automation und Produktionstechnik

Professor Dr. Klaus Feldmann

Für eine zukunftsfähige Wirtschaftsregion sind moderne Automatisierungstechnik und effiziente Produktionssysteme entscheidende Schlüsseltechnologien. Seit Jahrhunderten ist Nürnberg ein Schwerpunkt in der Produktion unterschiedlicher Güter. Mit intelligenten Mechanisierungslösungen wurden bereits früh wettbewerbsfähige Produktionsstrukturen geschaffen. Aus der Tradition einer großen Industrieregion hat sich heute in der Metropolregion Nürnberg ein breites Netzwerk mit global wirkenden Industriefirmen, technologiespezifischen Zulieferern und zahlreichen Forschungseinrichtungen entwickelt.

Leistungsfähige Antriebe und Steuerungen sind maßgebliche Komponenten für Industrieroboter und Werkzeugmaschinen. Bereits 1975 wurde in Nürnberg das erste Montagesystem in Deutschland mit einem integrierten Industrieroboter entwickelt und in Erlangen in der Montage medizinischer Geräte erprobt. Später wurde in einem Fürther Unternehmen mit einem kreativen Antriebskonzept eine neue Generation von Industrierobotern begründet.

Die führenden Unternehmen der Region haben sich von Antriebslieferanten längst zu Anbietern kompletter Systemlösungen für die Automatisierungsaufgaben bei den Anlagenherstellern entwickelt. Mit Leistungselektronik, digitaler Technik und speziellen Motorkonstruktionen sind mechatronische Automatisierungskonzepte verfügbar, die in allen Zielanwendungen die Wettbewerbsfähigkeit nachdrücklich verstärken können.

Dieses erfolgreiche Kompetenzfeld setzt auf hoch qualifizierte Mitarbeiter – die zukunftsorientierte Ausrichtung dieses Fachgebietes stärkt wiederum den regionalen Arbeitsmarkt. Inzwischen sind im Großraum Nürnberg rund 20 000 Beschäftigte in etwa 200 Unternehmen im Bereich Automatisierungstechnik engagiert. Ein maßgeblicher Standortvorteil der Region liegt in der engen Vernetzung von Industrie und vielfältigen leistungsfähigen Einrichtungen in Forschung und

Fortsetzung Seite 197

When an economic region is to be competent for the future then modern automation and efficient production systems are decisive key technologies. Nuremberg has been a main centre for the production of various kinds of goods for many centuries. Competitive production structures were created relatively early by using intelligent mechanisation solutions. In the metropolitan region of Nuremberg a wide network of global-playing industrial firms, technology-specific suppliers and numerous research institutions has evolved from the traditions of a major industrial region.

Powerful drives and controls are significant components for industrial robots and machine tools. As early as 1975 Germany's first assembly system was developed in Nuremberg with an integrated industrial robot and tested in Erlangen in the assembly of medical equipment. Later a new generation of industrial robots with a creative drive concept was founded in a Fürth concern.

Leading concerns of the region have long since evolved from being mere drive suppliers to being suppliers of complete system solutions for automation on plant manufacturers' premises. Mechatronic automation concepts are available with power electronics, digital engineering and special engine construction, which can firmly strengthen competitiveness regardless of the purpose aimed at.

This successful field of competence relies on highly qualified employees – and then again, this specialised sector's orientation towards the future strengthens the regional labour market. In the meantime approximately 20,000 people are employed in some 200 companies in the automation technology sector in Nuremberg's conurbation area. One of the region's considerable locational advantages lies in the close links between industry and various efficient research and training institutions. Which is why the training of qualified specialised engineers for electro-technology and automation has long been a particular strong point of the Georg-

Continued on page 197

Highly specialised – Automation and Production Technology

Baumüller ist einer der weltweit führenden Spezialisten für Automatisierungslösungen und intelligente Antriebssysteme. Getreu der Unternehmensphilosophie „be in motion" setzt die Baumüller Gruppe Maßstäbe in der Betreuung der Maschinenbauer sowie bei Forschung und Entwicklung. In enger Zusammenarbeit mit seinen Kunden plant und realisiert der Global Player innovative Automatisierungs- und Antriebssysteme und bietet außerdem ein Komplettangebot aus Engineering, Service und Dienstleistungen, das auf die individuellen Bedürfnisse der einzelnen Kunden abgestimmt wird. Diese werden von der Planung über die Montage und Installation bis hin zur Inbetriebnahme der Maschinen und Anlagen von erfahrenen Mitarbeitern begleitet. Auch anschließender Service und Wartung gehören zum Leistungsspektrum des Systempartners. Durchgängige, konfigurierbare und ausgereifte Systemlösungen für die Automatisierung sind für die Baumüller Gruppe selbstverständlich. Optimale Branchenkenntnisse sowie die Betreuung über den gesamten Lebenszyklus der Maschine runden das Dienstleistungspaket der Baumüller Gruppe ab. Mit über 40 Standorten weltweit garantiert das Unternehmen außerdem eine optimale Kundenbetreuung vor Ort.

Kompetenzfelder
Fields of Competence

Baumüller is one of the world's leading specialists for automation solutions and intelligent drive systems. True to the company's philosophy of "be in motion", the Baumüller Group sets standards in taking care of the demands and needs of machine builders as well as in research and development. In close cooperation with its customers the global player designs and implements innovative automation and drive systems backed by a complete range of engineering skills and services which are tailored to the individual needs of the customer.
Universal, configurable and technically matured automation system solutions are a matter of course for the Baumüller Group. Expertise in the sectors of mechanical engineering together with the support offered throughout the lifecycle of the machine round off the benefits provided by the Baumüller Group.
With more than 40 locations worldwide the company also ensures optimal on site customer care.

Information

Gründungsjahr: 1930

Mitarbeiter:
etwa 1800

Leistungsspektrum:
– Automatisierungs- und Antriebssysteme bestehend aus Steuerungen, Umrichtern und Motoren für alle Bereiche des Maschinenbaus
– Service und Wartung über den gesamten Lebenszyklus der Maschine
– weltweite Montage und Installation von Maschinen und Anlagen

Niederlassungen:
weltweit über 40

Year founded: 1930

Employees:
approx. 1,800

Range of activities:
– automation and drive systems consisting of controllers, converters and motors for all sectors of mechanical engineering
– service and maintenance throughout the machine's lifecycle
– worldwide assembly and installation of machines and plants

Branches:
more than 40 worldwide

☐
Baumüller Holding
GmbH & Co. KG
Nürnberg

Das Qualitätsmanagement/-sicherungssystem ist integraler Bestandteil des Managementsystems. Es zielt nicht nur auf die Sicherung und Verbesserung der Produktqualität ab, sondern darauf, alle externen und internen Kundenerwartungen zu verstehen und zu erfüllen.

The quality management/assurance system is an integral part of their management system. This aims not only at assuring and improving product quality, but also in comprehending and fulfilling all external and internal customer expectations.

Das Druckguss Werk Nürnberg der HONSEL GMBH & CO. KG besteht aus 30 Druckgießmaschinen mit einer Schließkraft zwischen 400 und 4500 Tonnen, verketteten Fertigungsstraßen (CNC-Bearbeitung) und hochmodernen Messanlagen. Die Kernkompetenzen des Unternehmens liegen in der Herstellung von Getriebegehäusen und Getriebesteuerteilen sowie von Fahrwerks- und Strukturteilen. Auf Wunsch liefert HONSEL einbaufertig bearbeitete und montierte Produkte just-in-time an die Fertigungslinie seiner Kunden, wie zum Beispiel DaimlerChrysler, ZF-Saarbrücken, ZF-Friedrichshafen, Deutz, Ford und MAN.

Die Basis zur Weiterentwicklung des Standortes ist die Beherrschung des operativen Geschäfts. Hauptthemen dabei sind die sichere Bewältigung von Serienanläufen bei Neuprojekten – insbesondere im Getriebegehäuse-, Schaltschieber- und Fahrwerksbereich. Dabei setzt HONSEL auf hochmoderne Technologien und Simulationsverfahren zur Produktentwicklung und zur strukturierten Arbeitsweise.

Kompetenzfelder
Fields of Competence

Im Bereich Prozessentwicklung liegen die Schwerpunkte in neuen Verfahren, hier am Beispiel der Wärmebehandlung von Druckgießteilen.

In the process development area, the emphasis is on new processes as can be seen here in the example of the heat treatment of die-cast parts.

The Nuremberg die-casting works of HONSEL GMBH & CO. KG comprise 30 die-casting machines with a mould clamping force of between 400 and 4,500 tons, linked production lines (CNC processed) and highly modern measuring equipment.
The cores of the company's competence are in the manufacture of gear housings and gear controlling parts together with chassis and structural parts. On request, HONSEL can supply ready-for-installation processed and assembled parts just-in-time into the production lines of customers such as Daimler-Chrysler, ZF-Saarbrucken, ZF-Friedrichshafen, Deutz, Ford and MAN.
The basis for the further development of their location is their mastery of strategic business, the main themes being their coping securely with series starts for new projects – especially in the areas of gear housing, transfer valves and chassis. HONSEL rely on top-of-the-line technology and simulation processes for their product development and the structured working methods.

Information

Gründungsjahr: 1908

Mitarbeiter:
773, davon 47 Auszubildende
(Stand: Oktober 2005)

Leistungsspektrum:
– Anbauteile (Türen, Hauben)
– großflächige Strukturgussteile
– Fahrwerksteile (Integralteile)
– Getriebegehäuse
– Ecosplitgehäuse
– Front-Schalt-Getriebe
– Wandlerglocken
– Ventilgehäuse
– Schaltschieber

Year founded: 1908

Employees:
773, of which 47 are apprentices
(as at October 2005)

Range of services:
– add-on components (doors, hoods)
– large structural die-cast parts
– chassis parts (integral parts)
– gear housings
– ecosplit housings
– front shift transmissions
– converter housings
– valve boxes
– transfer valves

Die Unternehmen der HONSEL INTERNATIONAL TECHNOLOGIES S. A. verfügen über alle wesentlichen Gießverfahren und fertigen die Gussteile in dem für den jeweiligen Anwendungsfall optimalen Verfahren.

The undertakings of the HONSEL INTERNATIONAL TECHNOLOGIES S. A. have all essential die-casting processes at their disposal and produce the cast parts using the best process for each individual case.

☐ HONSEL
GMBH & CO. KG
Druckguss
Werk Nürnberg

Der Name E-T-A steht seit mehr als fünf Jahrzehnten weltweit als Synonym für Geräteschutz und Sicherheit. Das global agierende Familienunternehmen mit Stammsitz in Altdorf bei Nürnberg bietet seinen Kunden als Weltmarktführer die umfassendste Palette an Geräteschutzschaltern ebenso wie ein umfangreiches Produkt-Portfolio im Bereich Mess- und Regelungstechnik sowie Sensorik.
1300 hoch qualifizierte Mitarbeiter sind weltweit für E-T-A im Einsatz und sorgen dafür, dass die Qualitätsprodukte stets die entscheidende Innovation voraus sind.

E-T-A ist Global Player und denkt deshalb grenzüberschreitend. So ist es selbstverständlich, dass Produkte von E-T-A in vielen Ländern der Erde zugelassen sind und national wie international eine Vielzahl von Zulassungen und Prüfzeichen tragen.

*For over five decades E-T-A has been a synonym for circuit protection, safety and reliability throughout the field of circuit protection. The headquarters of the family-owned company is located in Altdorf near Nuremberg. As a world market leader E-T-A offers its customers a wide range of circuit breakers for equipment protection as well as a choice of electronic process sensors and products for electronic switching and control.
Over 1,300 highly qualified personnel working for E-T-A worldwide ensure that E-T-A remains at the forefront of technology and innovation. As a global player E-T-A has a globe-spanning network of representatives and subsidiaries and its products are approved by internationally respected authorities.*

Information

Gründungsjahr: 1948

Mitarbeiter:
weltweit rund 1300, ca. 850 in Deutschland

Produktschwerpunkte:
– Geräteschutzschalter
– Mess- und Regelungstechnik
– Sensorikprodukte

Produktionsstandorte:
– Altdorf
– Hohenfels
– Akouda (Tunesien)
– Surabaya (Indonesien)
sowie zehn Vertriebsniederlassungen in Europa, Amerika, Asien und Australien

---

Year of foundation: 1948

Employees:
about 1,300 worldwide, about 850 in Germany

Major products:
– circuit breakers for equipment
– electronic process sensors
– electronic switching and control

Production locations:
– Altdorf
– Hohenfels
– Akouda (Tunesia)
– Surabaya (Indonesia)
as well as ten subsidiaries in Europe, America, Asia and Australia

E-T-A
Elektrotechnische
Apparate GmbH
Altdorf

Kompetenzfelder
Fields of Competence

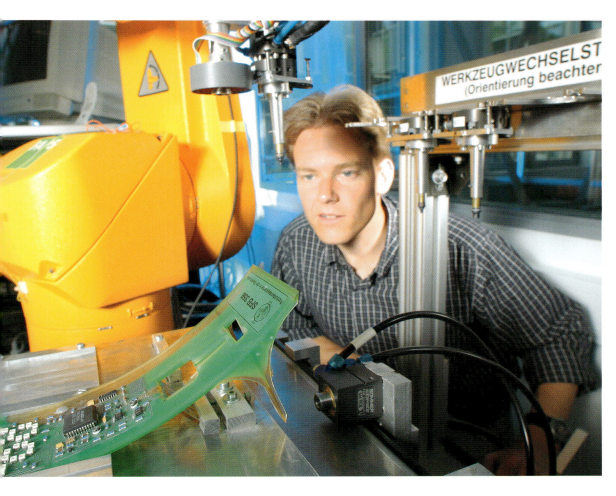

Demonstration einer Werkzeugwechselstation in der Forschungsfabrik Nürnberg im Nordostpark

Demonstrating a tool changing station in the research factory in Nuremberg in the Nordostpark

Lehre. So ist die Ausbildung qualifizierter Fachingenieure für Elektrotechnik und Automatisierung seit langem eine besondere Stärke der Georg-Simon-Ohm-Fachhochschule Nürnberg. An der Technischen Fakultät der Friedrich-Alexander-Universität Erlangen-Nürnberg ist ein international beachteter Schwerpunkt zu mechatronischen Systemen entstanden, der ein breites Forschungsnetzwerk zu industriellen Partnern aufgebaut hat. Der besondere Anspruch dieses Erlanger Modells liegt in der engen Vernetzung von Fachgebieten der Elektrotechnik, des Maschinenbaus und der Informatik. Zur Förderung dieser zukunftsorientierten Ausbildung wurde von der Firma Baumüller, Nürnberg, ein Studienpreis für Mechatronik gestiftet und 2005 erstmalig verliehen.

Mit der neuen Forschungsfabrik im Nordostpark Nürnberg wird der regionale Schwerpunkt zur Mechatronik nachdrücklich verstärkt. In diesem Gebäudekomplex hat neben einem Fraunhofer-Institut der Lehrstuhl für Fertigungsautomatisierung und Produktionssystematik (FAPS) ein Schwerpunktlabor zur Elektronikproduktion und Mikromechatronik eingerichtet.

Zahlreiche Partnerschaften zwischen Industrie und

Simon-Ohm University of applied sciences in Nuremberg. In the technical faculty of the Friedrich-Alexander-University Erlangen-Nuremberg an internationally acknowledged focal point for mechatronic systems has been created and a wide research network with industrial partners has been built up. The particular advantage of this Erlangen model lies in the close networking of specialised areas of electro-technology, mechanical engineering and informatics. To express their support of this future-oriented training Messrs Baumüller, Nuremberg donated a prize for mechatronic studies which was awarded for the first time in 2005.

The new research plant in the Nuremberg Northeast Park firmly strengthens the regional focal point of mechantronics. Alongside a Fraunhofer-Institute the building complex accommodates a laboratory installed by the institute for manufacturing automation and production systematic (FAPS) that focuses on electronic production and micro-mechatronics.

In the meantime numerous partnerships between industry and research strengthen the international aura of the metropolitan region of Nuremberg in the automation and mechatronics sector. One outstanding cooperation network is 3-D MID e. V., a research associa-

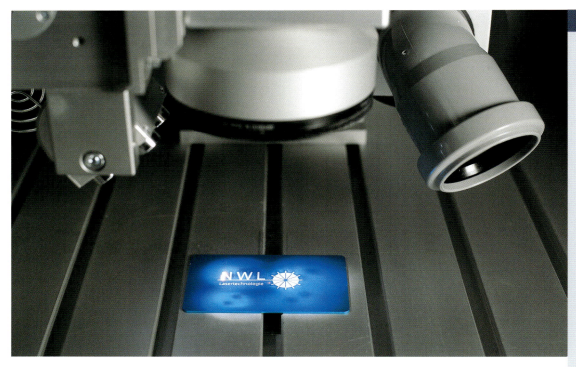

Im Jahr 1990 gründeten Alfred Neubert und Erich Weimel die Firma NWL Laser-Technologie GmbH. Mit der Herstellung eines Argon-Ionen-Lasers zur Behandlung von Patienten mit Grünem Star wurde der erste Meilenstein in der Firmengeschichte gelegt. Zielstrebig konstruierte das Team von NWL weitere Laserprodukte und brachte 1991 den ersten kompakten Laserbeschrifter „DALI" auf den Markt. Beide Produktlinien – medizinische wie industrielle Lasersysteme – wurden in den nachfolgenden Jahren intensiv aufgebaut. Stetiges Unternehmenswachstum und steigende Umsätze führten 1995 zum Bau eines neuen Produktionswerks in Pressath (Oberpfalz). Im Zuge einer geschäftlichen Neuausrichtung wurde die Sparte medizinische Laser einige Jahre später an die Mutterfirma der NWL – die WaveLight AG – abgegeben.
Heute hat sich NWL eine Marktposition als Spezialist und Hersteller von industriellen Lasern für Materialbearbeitung erarbeiten können und sorgt für neue Wege in der Lasertechnologie.

*Alfred Neubert and Erich Weimel founded the company NWL Laser-Technologie GmbH in the year 1990. With the manufacture of an argon-ion-laser for the treatment of patients with glaucoma the first milestone in the firm's history was laid. The NWL team carried on purposefully constructing further laser products and brought the first compact laser label-writer "DALI" on the market in 1991.
Both product lines – medicinal as industrial laser systems – were intensively extended over the following years. Constant concern growth and increasing turnover led in 1995 to the construction of new product works in Pressath (Upper Palatinate). In the course of taking a new business direction, the sector of medicinal laser*

*was handed over to the parent company of NWL – WaveLight AG – several years later.
Today NWL has achieved a market position as specialist and producer of industrial lasers for material processing and provides new routes in laser technology.*

Information

Gründungsjahr: 1990

Mitarbeiter: insgesamt 36; davon 28 am Hauptsitz in Ottensoos und 8 im Werk Pressath

Leistungsspektrum: Lasersysteme für die einfache technische Beschriftung industrieller Bauteile und Werkzeuge, über die Massenproduktion von Industriegütern bis hin zu individuellen Designbeschriftungen auf Sichtteilen umfassen das Produktportfolio von NWL.

Year founded: 1990

Employees: altogether 36; of which 28 are at headquarters in Ottensoos and 8 in the Pressath works

Range of services: The product range of NWL encompasses laser systems for easy technical lettering of industrial components and tools, via mass production of industrial goods through to individual designer markings on visible parts.

NWL Laser-Technologie GmbH
Ottensoos

Kompetenzfelder
Fields of Competence

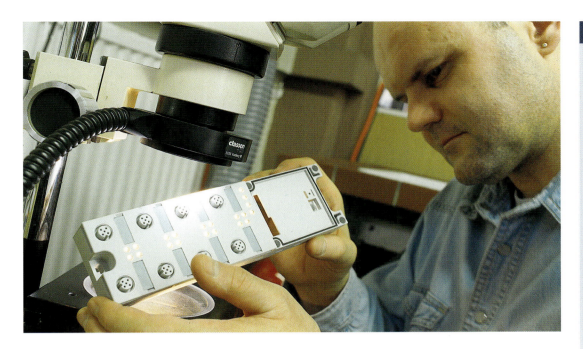

Seit 1934 steht der Name Joseph Müller für hochwertige technische Kunststoffteile. Die Erfahrung bei der Herstellung von bisher weit über 4000 Werkzeugen fließt in alle Projekte und Prozesse ein.
Das Unternehmen verarbeitet Thermoplaste und Duroplaste bestehend aus einer Auswahl von über 200 Werkstoffen.

The name of Joseph Müller has stood for top-quality technical synthetics since 1934. The experience gained in the manufacture of far more than 4,000 tools flows into all their projects and processes.
The concern processes thermoplasts and duroplasts which consist of an assortment of more than 200 materials.

Information

Gründungsjahr: 1934
Mitarbeiter: 55
Leistungsspektrum: Entwicklung und Formenbau; Verarbeitung von Thermoplasten und Duroplasten; Baugruppen-Montage; Fertigung von Spulenkörpern mit Draht; Einspritzen von Dichtungen in Kunststoffteile

Year founded: 1934
Employees: 55
Range of services: development and mould making; processing thermoplasts and duroplasts; component assembly; manufacture of spools with wires; injection of sealants in synthetic parts

☐
Joseph Müller GmbH & Co. Press- und Spritzgusswerk KG Nürnberg

---

Forschung verstärken inzwischen die internationale Ausstrahlung der Metropolregion Nürnberg zu Automatisierung und Mechatronik. Ein herausragendes Kooperationsnetzwerk ist die 1992 gegründete Forschungsvereinigung 3-D MID e. V., die sich der Entwicklung und Produktion innovativer mechatronischer Baugruppen widmet. Mit diesem Cluster sind insbesondere alle technologiespezifischen Aspekte der alternativen Wertschöpfungsketten für mechatronische Baugruppen besetzt. Viele der beteiligten Unternehmen haben ihren Firmensitz in der Metropolregion Nürnberg.

Für die volkswirtschaftlich zentralen Felder der Automation und der Produktionstechnik verfügt die Metropolregion Nürnberg über eine leistungsfähige und zukunftsorientierte Basis: Die erfolgreiche Vernetzung von unterschiedlich strukturierten Unternehmen mit leistungsfähiger Forschung und Lehre an den regionalen Hochschulen sind Garanten für weitere Innovationen und Wettbewerbsfähigkeit im globalen Markt. ☐

tion founded in 1992 and dedicated to the development and production of innovative mechatronic assemblies. This cluster covers in particular all the technology-specific aspects of alternative added value chains for mechatronic assemblies. Many of the concerns involved have their headquarters in the metropolitan region of Nuremberg.

The metropolitan region of Nuremberg has an efficient and forward-looking basis for automation and production technology, fields which are so central to the economy: The successful linking of flourishing, differently structured concerns with efficient research and teaching centres on regional colleges are guarantees for further innovation and competitiveness on the global market. ☐

Die AVL Gruppe als weltweit größtes privates und unabhängiges Unternehmen für die Entwicklung von Motoren sowie Mess- und Prüftechnik besitzt das Kfz-technische Know-how aus über 50 Jahren Entwicklungsarbeit.

Die AVL DiTEST rüstet als Gruppenunternehmen im Rahmen dieser Zielsetzung Werkstätten und Prüfzentren mit Testsystemen und Diagnosetechnik der gehobenen Klasse aus.

Neben dem Verkauf und der Entwicklung der Fahrzeugdiagnose ist Fürth auch der weltweite Servicestandort für die Prüfgeräte. Inzwischen nutzen viele namhafte Automobilhersteller, Prüforganisationen und Werkstätten auf der ganzen Welt die Test- und Prüfgeräte von AVL DiTEST.

As the world's largest private and independent undertaking for the development of motors, measuring and testing technology, the AVL Group possesses the vehicle- technical know-how gained over more than 50 years of development work.
As group concern and within the scope of this target, the AVL DiTEST equips workshops and testing centres with testing systems and diagnosis technology of the better class.
Alongside sales and development of vehicle diagnosis, Fürth is also the world's service location for testing equipment. In the meantime, many renowned automobile manufacturers, testing organisations and workshops all over the world use testing equipment from AVL DiTEST.

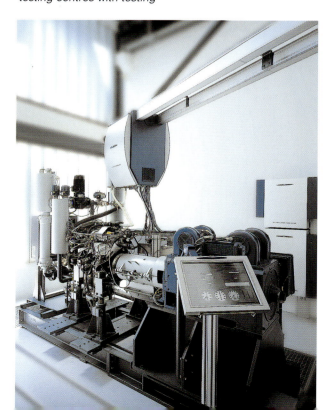

Information

Gründungsjahr: 1980

Mitarbeiter: ca. 200

Leistungsspektrum:
– Entwicklung, Fertigung, Vertrieb und Service für Abgasmessgeräte, Diagnosemessgeräte, bordnetzunabhängige Drehzahlmessgeräte und Motortester/Scopes
– Dienstleistungen und Hotline rund um die Fahrzeugdiagnose

Year founded: 1980

Employees: some 200

Range of services:
– development, production, sales and service for exhaust measuring units, diagnosis measuring units, revolution measuring units independent of on-board supply and engine testers/scopes
– services and hotline encompassing vehicle diagnostic

AVL DiTEST GmbH
Fürth

Kompetenzfelder
Fields of Competence

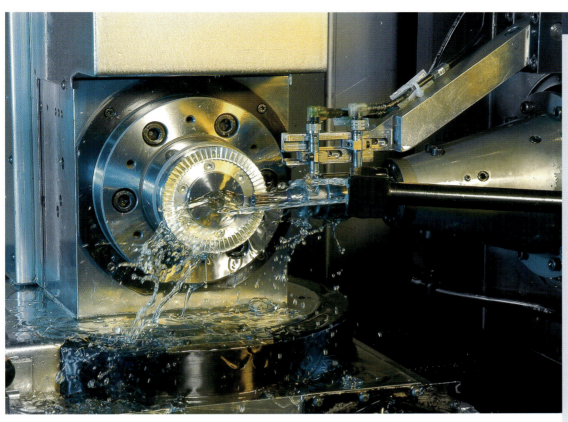

„ZEITLAUF® – it's time for tomorrow" ist die kurzgefasste Unternehmensphilosophie des innovativen Global Players auf dem Gebiet der Antriebstechnik. Seit vier Jahrzehnten ist ZEITLAUF® mit präzisen und erstklassigen Lösungen, die immer auf die Bedürfnisse seiner Kunden ausgerichtet sind, am Markt präsent. Die intelligenten Antriebslösungen zeichnen sich insbesondere durch eine hervorragende technologische Kompetenz sowie durch zielorientiertes und vor allem zukunftsgerichtetes Handeln aus.

In jeder Stufe der Prozesskette ist ZEITLAUF® Partner, der mitdenkt und das Gesamte im Blick behält. Mit seinem breit gefächerten und produktspezifischem Wissen entwickelt das Unternehmen für jede Kundenanforderung die passende Antriebslösung. Ob Getriebemotoren aus dem Standardprogramm – natürlich inklusive der elektrischen Komponenten – oder individuelle Komplettlösungen: ZEITLAUF® liefert alles aus einer Hand. Abgerundet wird das Leistungsspektrum des Unternehmens durch ein Servicepaket, das von der ersten Beratung über die Produktion und Anwendungsphase bis hin zum Remanufacturing eine Rundumbetreuung bietet.

"ZEITLAUF® – it's time for tomorrow" is the byword of the company philosophy of this innovative global player in the sector of motive power engineering. For almost half a century ZEITLAUF® has been present in the market with precise, first class solutions, always oriented to meet the needs of their customers. Their intelligent motive power solutions distinguish themselves in particular through exceptional technological competence as well as purposeful and forward-looking negotiations.
At every stage of the process chain ZEITLAUF® is a partner that understands and retains the whole picture in their mind. With wide ranging and product specific knowledge, the undertaking develops a fitting drive solution to suit every demand made by the customer. Whether gear motors from the standard programme – naturally including the electric components – or individual complete solutions: ZEITLAUF® supplies everything from one source.
The company's range of products is further enhanced by a service packet which offers the customer an all-round service, from the first advisory meeting via production and application phase through to manufacturing.

Information

Gründungsjahr: 1957
Mitarbeiter: 180
Produktspektrum:
- Stirnradgetriebemotoren
- Planetengetriebemotoren
- Planradgetriebemotoren
- Systemtechnik

Anwendungsbereiche:
- Medizin- und Rehatechnik
- Fördertechnik
- Türtechnik
- Verpackungstechnik
- Bürogeräte
- Schaltertechnik
- Textilmaschinen
- Fahrzeugtechnik
- Drucktechnik

Standorte:
Deutschland und Großbritannien

Year founded: 1957
Employees: 180
Range of products:
- spur gear motors
- planetary gear motors
- crown gear motors
- system engineering

Application areas:
- medical and rehab technology
- materials handling technology
- door technology
- packaging engineering
- office equipment
- switch engineering
- textile machines
- vehicle engineering
- printing technology

Locations:
Germany and Great Britain

ZEITLAUF®
GmbH antriebstechnik & Co KG
Lauf a. d. Pegnitz

Wachstumsmotor Innovative Dienstleistungen

Dr. Roland Fleck

Keiner kann es bestreiten: Der Wandel von der Industrie- zur Dienstleistungsgesellschaft ist einer der großen globalen Entwicklungstrends. Dieser Prozess hat auch in der Wirtschaftsregion Nürnberg zu massiven Umschichtungen geführt: Waren vor 30 Jahren noch über 60 Prozent der Arbeitnehmer in der Industrie beschäftigt und knapp 40 Prozent im Dienstleistungssektor, so ist dieses Verhältnis heute umgekehrt. Konkret verzeichnete der Ballungsraum Nürnberg 2004 über 390 000 Beschäftigte im Dienstleistungsbereich und 235 000 im produzierenden Gewerbe – eine Zunahme im Dienstleistungssektor von 77 Prozent in 30 Jahren. Gleichzeitig hat in Nürnberg die industrielle Bruttowertschöpfung kontinuierlich zugenommen – wenn auch mit weniger Dynamik. Ein überaus wichtiger Punkt, denn der Erhalt der industriellen und technologischen Leistungsfähigkeit ist für den Standort Nürnberg von strategischer Bedeutung, da sie die innovativen unternehmensnahen Dienstleistungsbereiche in hohem Maße fördert.

Unter Innovativen Dienstleistungen werden Leistungsangebote vereint, die im Strukturwandel aufgrund neuer gesellschaftlicher Entwicklungen sowohl demographischer und kultureller als auch technologischer und betriebswirtschaftlicher Art entstehen. Sie bilden sich in klassischen Servicebranchen (zum Beispiel Handel, Tourismus, Gesundheitswesen, Finanzwesen) ebenso heraus wie in der High-Tech-Industrie oder im Handwerk. Dabei entstehen völlig neue Geschäftsfelder (zum Beispiel Multimedia, Internetdienste, Customer Care) mit neuen Berufsbildern wie Multimedia-Designer oder Call-Center-Agents.

Für die Europäische Metropolregion Nürnberg sind die Innovativen Dienstleistungen aus verschiedenen Gründen von großer Bedeutung:
– Sie bieten gute und hochwertige Beschäftigungspotenziale.
– Sie ergänzen, verstärken und verbreitern Entwicklungsimpulse, die von neuen Technologien angestoßen wurden.
– Sie sind Wachstumsmärkte der Zukunft.

Fortsetzung Seite 210

No-one can deny it: The changeover from an industrial to a service supplier society is one of the most significant global trends. This process has also led to massive restructuring in the industrial region of Nuremberg: Whereas 30 years ago more than 60 percent of employees were still employed in industry and little less than 40 percent in the service supply sector, this relationship is today reversed. Specifically speaking, Nuremberg's conurbation area had more than 390,000 employees in the service supply sector in 2004 and 235,000 in productive trades – an increase in the services sector of 77 percent over 30 years. Simultaneously the industrial gross product in Nuremberg has steadily increased – even if it was with less dynamic. This is an extremely important point, because retaining industrial and technological productivity is of strategic significance for the business location of Nuremberg as it strongly promotes the innovative concern-close service supply sectors.

Services are combined under innovative services supply; services which in the structural changeover have been created as a result of new social developments as well as developments in the demographic and cultural and technological and economic sectors. They are developed from classical service branches (for instance trade, tourism, the health sector, the financial sector) as well as from high-tech industries and in handicrafts. Thus entirely new business fields are created (for instance multimedia, internet services, customer care) with new careers such as multimedia-designer or call-centre-agents.

For the European metropolitan region of Nuremberg the innovative services are extremely important for various reasons:
– They offer excellent and top-quality employment potential.
– They supplement, strengthen and expand development impulses set into motion by new technologies.
– They are the growing markets of the future.

Because of its economic strengths, Nuremberg as a business location is virtually predestined for the settle-

Continued on page 210

Innovative Services as the Drive behind Expansion

Kompetenzfelder
Fields of Competence

Der Dienstleistungssektor bringt auch in der Metropolregion Nürnberg immer neue Geschäftsfelder und Beschäftigungsformen hervor (im Bild ein Call-Center eines großen Marketingunternehmens).

The service supply sector also continuously produces new business fields and forms of employment (in the picture is the call-centre of a major marketing concern).

Der „Business Tower Nürnberg" ist mit 135 Metern der höchste Büroturm Bayerns und Sitz der Nürnberger Versicherungsgruppe.

The "Business Tower Nürnberg" is with 135 metres the highest office tower in Bavaria and is headquarters of the Nürnberger Versicherungsgruppe.

Das Medien-Systemhaus infowerk ag bietet umfassende Dienstleistungen für alle Aspekte der Medien-Produktion im Print- und Onlinebereich. Das Portfolio reicht von der kreativen und technischen Konzeption über die Gestaltung bis zur Realisation; von Öffentlichkeitsarbeit bis zum Event; von der Programmierung über CMS und Datenmanagement bis Prepress und individualisiertem Digitaldruck mit integrierter Logistik.

Aus dem Zusammenspiel der fünf Geschäftsbereiche im infowerk entstehen intelligente Systemlösungen. Am Ende der effizienten Prozesse bieten Digitaldruck und Digitaler Großdruck hochmoderne Ausgabetechniken. Dabei garantiert ein durchgängiges Farbmanagement gleichbleibende Farbwiedergabe und brillante Qualität. Flexibilität bei Format, Material und Inhalt der gedruckten Kommunikation ermöglichen die personalisierte und individualisierte Ansprache unterschiedlicher Zielgruppen.

The media system house infowerk ag offers the whole range of services covering all aspects of media production in the print and online sectors. Their portfolio reaches from the creative and technical conception via design through to realisation; from public relations work to the event; from programming via CMS (content management systems) and data management to prepress and individualised digital print with integrated logistics. Intelligent system solutions arise from the interaction of the five business sectors in infowerk. At the end of the efficient processes, digital print and digital large print provide highly modern issue techniques. Constant colour management guarantees consistent colour reproduction and brilliant quality. Flexibility in format, material and content of the printed communication enables addressing various target groups in a personalised and individualised manner.

Information

Gründungsjahr: 1977 als HeszSatzRepro; 1994 Umfirmierung in infowerk nürnberg; seit 2000 Aktiengesellschaft

Mitarbeiter:
171 (Stand 2005)

Geschäftsbereiche:
- Kreativ-Service
- Medien-Consulting
- System-Entwicklung
- Medien-Produktion
- Digitaldruck-Zentrum

Produkte:
Systemlösungen:
- Medien-Datenbank
- Print-On-Demand
- Online-Produktion
- Content-Management-Systeme

Umsatz:
ca. 15,5 Mio. Euro jährlich (Stand 2005)

Year founded: 1977 as HeszSatzRepro; 1994 renaming the company into infowerk nürnberg; since 2000 limited company

Employees:
171 (as at 2005)

Business sectors:
- creative service
- media consulting
- system development
- media production
- digital print centre

Products:
system solutions:
- media data bank
- print-on-demand
- online production
- content management systems

Turnover:
about 15.5 million Euro annually (as at 2005)

infowerk ag
Nürnberg

Kompetenzfelder
Fields of Competence

Telefonbuch Verlag Hans Müller GmbH & Co. KG, Verlagsgebäude in Nürnberg (Bayern)

Telefonbuch Verlag Hans Müller GmbH & Co. KG, Publishing House in Nuremberg (Bavaria)

MüllerVerlag ist der zuverlässige Partner für das medienübergreifende Suchen und Finden hochwertiger Kontakte. Als innovativer Medien-Experte trägt der MüllerVerlag mit seinen Leistungen zu hoher Kontaktstärke, spürbaren Werbeerfolgen und zur Umsatzsicherung der Unternehmen vor Ort bei.

MüllerVerlag is a reliable partner for comprehensive media searches and finding top quality contacts. As an innovative media expert MüllerVerlag's services contribute toward strong contacts, noticeable advertising success and to the increase of turnover in local concerns.

Kompetente und engagierte Mitarbeiterinnen im modernen Customer Care Center pflegen den persönlichen und vertrauensvollen Kundenkontakt.

Competent and committed employees in the modern customer care centre maintain personal and trusting contacts with the customers.

Information

Gründungsjahr: 1950

Mitarbeiter: 350

Produktionsspektrum:
die bekannten Verzeichnismarken
– GelbeSeiten
– DasÖrtliche
– DasTelefonbuch
in print, online und mobile

Standorte:
Nürnberg/Fürth,
Oberfranken,
Oberpfalz,
Mittelfranken,
Unterfranken,
teilweise Niederbayern

Year founded: 1950

Employees: 350

Production program:
the well-known directory names
– Yellow Pages
– DasÖrtliche
– DasTelefonbuch
in print, online and mobile

Locations:
Nuremberg/Fürth,
Upper Franconia,
Upper Palatinate,
Middle Franconia,
Lower Franconia,
parts of Lower Bavaria

☐ Telefonbuch Verlag Hans Müller GmbH & Co. KG Nürnberg

CSC JÄKLECHEMIE GmbH & Co. KG begann 1886 als Firma Wilhelm Jäkle in Nürnberg mit dem Handel von Chemikalien. Heute versorgt das Chemiehandelshaus tausende von Kunden in aller Welt. Die seit Jahrzehnten in der Branche tätigen Gesellschafter haben dem Unternehmen eine breite Basis für solides Wachstum in West- und Osteuropa geschaffen. Die Metropolregion Nürnberg bietet hierfür die besten logistischen Voraussetzungen. In der Vielfalt der Dienstleistungen, wie zum Beispiel Beratung in der Anwendungstechnik, Entsorgungs- und Recyclingkonzepte, Umfüllen, Mischen, Lagermanagement, produktgerechte internationale Transporte oder Single Sourcing zeigt sich die Flexibilität des mittelständischen Unternehmens.

Am Firmensitz in Nürnberg werden höchste Maßstäbe hinsichtlich Sicherheit und Umweltbewusstsein gesetzt. In hervorragender Zusammenarbeit mit den Behörden vor Ort wird das vorbildliche Lager- und Umschlagszentrum stets nachhaltig weiterentwickelt.

Das Unternehmen ist zertifiziert nach ISO 9001, ISO 14001 sowie als Entsorgungsfachbetrieb, es wurde dem Assessment der europäischen Chemieverbände SQAS ESAD II unterzogen und nimmt teil am Responsible Care Programm des Verbands Chemiehandel e. V. und dem Umweltpakt Bayern.

Der direkte Draht zu den Herstellern der Produkte schafft das notwendige Vertrauen bei den Kunden. Das breite Sortiment reicht von Rohstoffen für die Lackindustrie über Säuren, Laugen und Lösungsmittel bis zu Spezialitäten für die Oberflächentechnik oder die Abwasserbehandlung.

Kompetenzfelder
Fields of Competence

CSC JÄKLECHEMIE GmbH & Co. KG began with chemical trading in Nuremberg in 1886 as Messrs Wilhelm Jäkle. Today, the chemical distributor supplies thousands of customers all over the world.

The shareholders, active in the branch for decades, have given the undertaking a wide base for solid growth in West and East Europe. The metropolitan region of Nuremberg provides the best logistic conditions. The flexibility of this medium sized company can be seen from the variety of services it offers, for example an advisory service in application technology, disposal and recycling concepts, transfusing, mixing, warehouse management, international product-specific transport or single sourcing.

In the firm's headquarters in Nuremberg, the highest standards regarding safety and environmental awareness have been set. In excellent cooperation with local government, the exemplary warehouse and trans-shipment centre is under constant development.

The company has been certified in accordance with ISO 9001, ISO 14001 and as waste disposal specialists as well, it has undergone the assessment of the European Chemical Association SQAS ESAD II and participates in the Responsible Care Program of the Verband Chemiehandel e. V. and the Umweltpakt Bayern (Bavarian Environmental Pact). Direct links with product manufacturers creates the confidence necessary for the customer. The wide assortment reaches from raw materials for the lacquer industry via acids, alkalis and solvents through to specialities for surface technology or sewage treatment.

Information

Gründungsjahr: 1886
Mitarbeiter: 105
Standorte:
Firmensitz Nürnberg mit Lager und Umschlagszentrum; Verkaufsbüro Hamburg
Produktspektrum:
Industriechemikalien:
– Lösungsmittel
– Säuren und Laugen
– Feststoffe
Rohstoffe für:
– Farben
– Lacke
– Klebstoffe
– Beschichtungen
Spezialchemikalien für:
– Oberflächenreinigung
– Umwelttechnik
– Behandlung von Trinkwasser, Abwasser und Brauchwasser
– Pharma und Kosmetik
Umsatz: 70 Mio. Euro

Year founded: 1886
Employees: 105
Locations:
headquarters Nuremberg with warehouse and trans-shipment centre; sales office Hamburg
Range of products:
industrial chemicals:
– solvents
– acids and alkalis
– solids
raw materials for:
– paints
– lacquers
– adhesives
– coatings
special chemicals for:
– surface cleaning
– environmental technology
– treatment of drinking water, waste water and industrial water
– pharmaceuticals and cosmetics
Turnover:
70 million Euro

CSC JÄKLECHEMIE GmbH & Co. KG
Nürnberg

Information
Gründungsjahr: 1935
Mitarbeiter: 350
Leistungsspektrum: – Entsorgungsdienstleistungen aller Art – Miettoiletten – Aktenvernichtung – Straßenreinigung – Winterdienst – Kompostverkauf – Sinkkästenreinigung – Wertstoffhofbetreuung – Mülltonnenreinigung „To-wash"
Überwachungszertifikat als Entsorgungsfachbetrieb für Büchenbach und Erlangen

Hofmann denkt. Hinter der Unternehmensphilosophie „Ideenquelle für Umweltlösungen sein" verbirgt sich nicht zuletzt ein starkes soziales und kulturelles Engagement Hofmanns für die Region. Damit Gegenwart und Zukunft lebenswert sind und bleiben.

Das Unternehmen Friedrich Hofmann GmbH & Co. in Büchenbach hat an seinem Standort im Landkreis Roth eine lange Tradition. Angefangen als allgemeiner Transportbetrieb, entwickelte sich der Betrieb schnell zu einem innovativen Dienstleister im Bereich Städtereinigung. Heute ist Hofmann im gesamten mittelfränkischen Raum und in Bayern eine der besten Adressen für flächendeckende und innovative Entsorgungstechnologien mit einem stetig wachsenden Kundenkreis aus öffentlicher Hand, Industrie und privaten Haushalten.

Hofmann thinks. Behind the concern's philosophy of "Ideenquelle für Umweltlösungen sein" (being the source of ideas for solving environmental problems) hides Hofmann's strong social and cultural commitment to the region – that the present and future are and remain worth living.

The undertaking Friedrich Hofmann GmbH & Co., in Büchenbach has a long tradition at its location in the administrative district of Roth. Beginning as a general transport company, the firm developed quickly into an innovative service supplier in the sector of city cleaning. Today, Hofmann is one of the best addresses for innovative waste disposal technologies covering needs in the entire middle-Franconian area as well as in Bavaria with a steadily increasing circle of customers from the municipal sector, industry and private households.

Year founded: 1935
Employees: 350
Range of services: – all kinds of disposal services – rental toilets – document shredding – street cleaning – winter services – compost sales – gully hole cleaning – recycling centre supervision – dustbin cleaning "To-wash"
surveillance certificate as specialised disposal works for Büchenbach and Erlangen

☐
Friedrich Hofmann GmbH & Co.
Büchenbach

Kompetenzfelder
Fields of Competence

serviceLogiQ – Partner für innovative Fulfillmentlösungen

Seit mehr als 10 Jahren entwickelt und realisiert die KarstadtQuelle-Tochter serviceLogiQ erfolgreich innovative Fulfillment- und Logistiklösungen für die Endkundenbelieferung im Versand- und Onlinehandel.
Als zuverlässiger Outsourcing-Partner bietet serviceLogiQ interessierten Unternehmen quasi ein komplettes „Versandhaus zum Mieten" an und übernimmt für seine Kunden alle Leistungen rund um Kundenservice, Zahlungsmanagement, Lagerung, Versand, Retourenmanagement bis hin zum After-Sales-Service.
Genau abgestimmt auf die Wünsche seiner Kunden „schnürt" der Dienstleistungsspezialist dann jeweils ein individuelles „Leistungspaket".
Ein besonderer Vorteil ist es, dass serviceLogiQ am Standort Nürnberg über rund 200 000 Quadratmeter moderne Lager- und Kommissionierflächen sowie ein eigenes Paketumschlagszentrum verfügt. So können kurze Lieferzeiten und die weltweite Auslieferung inkl. Zollabwicklung garantiert werden.
Namhafte Kunden unterschiedlichster Branchen – darunter Bogner Homeshopping, Christ Juweliere und Uhrmacher oder Audi quattro – setzen inzwischen erfolgreich auf eine Zusammenarbeit mit serviceLogiQ.

serviceLogiQ – Partner for innovative fulfilment solutions

For more than 10 years, the KarstadtQuelle subsidiary serviceLogiQ developed and realised successful innovative fulfilment and logistic solutions for deliveries to end consumers in mail order and online trading.
As a reliable outsourcing partner, serviceLogiQ provides interested companies an almost complete "mail-order firm for rent" and takes over all the services surrounding customer service, payment management, warehousing, dispatch, returns management through to after sales service on behalf of its customers.
Precisely coordinated to the desires of his customers, the service specialist ties up an individual "performance parcel".
One particular advantage is that at its Nuremberg location, serviceLogiQ has some 200,000 square metres of modern storage and consignment areas as well as their own parcel transfer centre. So short delivery periods and global deliveries including customs clearance can be guaranteed.
In the meantime, renowned customers from the most diverse branches – amongst them Bogner Homeshopping, Christ Jewellers or Audi quattro – rely on successful cooperation with serviceLogiQ.

Information

Gründungsjahr: 1995

Mitarbeiter: 1000

Leistungsspektrum:
Integrierte Logistik- und Fulfillmentlösungen
– Kundenservice
– Zahlungsmanagement
– Logistik
– Retourenmanagement
– E-Commerce
– Beschaffungslogistik

Lagerkapazität: 200 000 m²

Umsatz: 72 Mio. Euro

Handlingvolumen:
38 Mio. Sendungen
120 Mio. Warenstücke

Year founded: 1995

Employees: 1,000

Range of services:
integrated logistics and fulfilment solutions
– customer service
– payment management
– logistics
– returns management
– e-commerce
– acquisition logistics

Storage capacity: 200,000 m²

Turnover: 72 million Euro

Dealing volumes:
38 million dispatches
120 million pieces of goods

serviceLogiQ GmbH
Nürnberg

Zukunft braucht Herkunft

Die Nürnberger Wach- und Schließgesellschaft mbH als eines der ältesten Sicherheitsunternehmen Deutschlands entwickelte sich in über 100 Jahren Firmengeschichte zu einer der größten und bedeutendsten Firmen dieser Branche.
Das moderne Dienstleistungsunternehmen, welches sich in seinen 24-Stunden-Notruf- und Serviceleitstellen sowie Videozentralen einer äußerst aufwändigen Technik bedient, verfügt über ein eigenes Schulungszentrum und steht seinen überwiegend langjährigen Kunden mit den Geschäftsfeldern Notruf- und Serviceleitstelle (VdS), Objektsicherheit und Gebäudemanagement, Bahndienste, Passagier- und Flugsicherheit, Revier- und Streifendienste sowie Kommunale Verkehrsüberwachung als qualitativ hochwertiger und zuverlässiger Geschäftspartner zur Verfügung.

Future needs an origin

As one of the oldest security concerns in Germany and in more than 100 years of company history the Nürnberger Wach- und Schließgesellschaft mbH has developed into one of the largest and most important companies of its branch.
The modern service supplier, which uses extremely lavish technology in its 24-hour emergency and service directing centres as well as video centres, maintains its own training centre and supports its mostly long-standing customers as a top-quality and reliable business partner in the sectors of emergency and services directing centre (VdS), object security and building management, railway services, passenger and flight security, area and patrol services as well as communal traffic control.

Information

Gründungsjahr: 1902

Mitarbeiter: ca. 1000

Year founded: 1902

Employees: about 1,000

☐ Nürnberger Wach- und Schließgesellschaft mbH, Nürnberg

Aufgrund seiner wirtschaftlichen Stärken ist der Standort Nürnberg für Ansiedlungen und Gründungen im Bereich Innovative Dienstleistungen geradezu prädestiniert. Die Region bietet beste Voraussetzungen für Systemgeschäfte aus industriellen Produkten und komplementären Dienstleistungen. Untermauert wird dies von der herausragenden Dienstleistungsdichte von 229 Beschäftigten je 1000 Einwohner im Dienstleistungssektor in der Region Nürnberg. Zum Vergleich: In ganz Deutschland liegt die durchschnittliche Dienstleistungsdichte bei 211.

Essenzielle Entwicklungsträger Innovativer Dienstleistungen sind in Nürnberg die Bereiche Marktforschung, Rechts- und Wirtschaftsberatung, Technikberatung/Software und Datenverarbeitung/Datenbanken, Technischer Service, Facility Management, Kommunikationsdienstleistungen (Messe- und Kongresswesen, Call-Center) sowie Finanzdienstleistungen (u. a. Internet-Broker und Direktbanken).

Das vorhandene Wachstum basiert – neben dem Kreativpotenzial vieler mittelständischer Unternehmen

Fortsetzung Seite 216

ment and foundation of businesses in the sector of innovative service supply. The region can offer excellent conditions for system businesses arising from industrial products and complementary services. The exceptional density of services supplied by 229 employees per 1,000 inhabitants working in the service supply sector in the Nuremberg region supports this. In comparison: In the whole of Germany, the density of service suppliers lies at 211 (per 1,000 head).

Essential development carriers of innovative services in Nuremberg are the sectors of market research, legal and economic advisors, technology advisors/software and data processing/databases, technical services, facility management, communication services (trade fair and congresses, call-centres) as well as financial services (amongst them internet-brokers and direct banks).

Present growth is based – in addition to the creative potential of many medium-sized concerns – on the successful national and international market processing of major resident service supply concerns such as

Continued on page 216

Kompetenzfelder
Fields of Competence

Das Hofmann-Team

The Hofmann team

Das Jobmobil vor der Hauptverwaltung in Nürnberg-Langwasser

The job mobile in front of the headquarters in Nuremberg-Langwasser

Die Firma I. K. Hofmann GmbH, auch Hofmann Personal Leasing genannt, ist eine der großen unternehmerischen Erfolgsgeschichten in der Metropolregion Nürnberg. Ingrid Hofmann gründet 1985 eine Zeitarbeitsfirma, die heute mit rund 6500 Mitarbeitern in bundesweit 56 Niederlassungen und Tochterunternehmen in Österreich, England und Tschechien zu den größten Zeitarbeitsunternehmen in Deutschland gehört.
Damit zählt Ingrid Hofmann zu den Pionieren dieser Branche. Die Kombination aus beruflichem Erfolg, Qualitätsbewusstsein sowie konsequenter Kunden- und Mitarbeiterorientierung der Unternehmensgründerin führten die I. K. Hofmann GmbH an die Spitze eines Wirtschaftszweiges, der sich im 21. Jahrhundert in der Branchenlandschaft einen festen Platz erobert hat. Das Unternehmen erhielt unterschiedlichste Auszeichnungen, darunter den Nürnberger Nachhaltigkeitspreis und den Bayerischen Qualitätspreis. Hofmann Personal Leasing wurde zudem als eines der 50 wachstumsstärksten Unternehmen Bayerns geehrt. Ingrid Hofmann selbst war „Unternehmerin des Jahres 2002". In ihrer Eigenschaft als Geschäftsführerin und Präsidiumsmitglied der Bundesvereinigung Deutscher Arbeitgeberverbände (BDA) setzt sie sich besonders für die Belange des Mittelstands und die Vereinbarkeit von Familie und Beruf ein.

Messrs I. K. Hofmann GmbH, also known as Hofmann Personal Leasing, is one of the largest entrepreneurial success stories in the metropolitan region of Nuremberg. In 1985 Ingrid Hofmann founded a temporary employment agency which today, with some 6,500 employees in 56 branches all over Germany and subsidiaries in Austria, England and the Czech Republic, belongs to the major temporary employment agencies in Germany.

Ingrid Hofmann is considered to be a pioneer in this branch. The undertaking founder's combination of professional success, quality consciousness and consequent customer and employee orientation has lead I. K. Hofmann GmbH to the peak of an industrial branch which has conquered a firm position for itself in the branch landscape of the 21st century. The undertaking has received many varied awards amongst them the Nürnberger Nachhaltigkeitspreis and the Bayerischer Qualitätspreis. Hofmann Personal Leasing has also been honoured as one of the 50 undertakings with the strongest growth in Bavaria. Ingrid Hofmann herself was "Unternehmerin des Jahres 2002" (woman entrepreneur of the year 2002). In her function as business manager and member of the committee of the Bundesvereinigung Deutscher Arbeitgeberverbände (BDA) (National Federation of German Employer Associations) she takes special interest in the concerns of small and medium-sized firms as well as the compatibility of family and profession.

Information

Gründungsjahr: 1985
Mitarbeiter: rund 6500
Leistungsspektrum: Arbeitnehmerüberlassung von gewerblichem, technischem und kaufmännischem Personal, Ingenieursdienstleistungen, sowie private Arbeitsvermittlung insbesondere in den Bereichen Automotive, Elektro, Dienstleistung, Aviation und Handel
Umsatz: 155 Mio. Euro (in 2005)

Year founded: 1985
Employees: some 6,500
Range of services: Providing commercial, technical and clerical personnel, engineering services, as well as private employment agency work especially in the sectors of automotive, electro, service supply, aviation and trade
Turnover: 155 million Euro (in 2005)

I. K. Hofmann GmbH
Nürnberg

Das Unternehmen BERG Zeitarbeit GmbH sieht sich als Human Resources Partner gegenüber seinen Kunden und Mitarbeitern. In der Praxis bedeutet das, flexibel, schnell und effektiv auf Kundenanfragen zu reagieren und Mitarbeiter qualifikationsentsprechend einzusetzen. Neben dem professionellen Personalrecruitment wird sehr viel Wert auf Betreuung und Entwicklung der Mitarbeiter gelegt. Von Beginn an hat sich das Unternehmen auf Office-, Call-Center- und IT-Personal spezialisiert und damit auf eine starke Konzentration in seiner Personaldienstleistung gesetzt.

BERG Zeitarbeit hat sich seit 1987 kontinuierlich und innovativ ein hohes Maß an Fachwissen und Kompetenz innerhalb der Branche erarbeitet. Zu dem fachlichen Know-how kommt die wirtschaftliche Stabilität des Unternehmens und ein entwicklungsstarkes, beständiges Betreuungsteam – von diesen Faktoren profitieren die Partner des Unternehmens auf Kunden- und Mitarbeiterseite. In wirtschaftlichen Spitzenzeiten wechseln bis zu 31 Prozent der Mitarbeiter in ein Angestelltenverhältnis zum Kundenbetrieb.
Gezielt und erfolgreich besetzt BERG Zeitarbeit personelle Lücken in Unternehmen, die durch Krankheit, Urlaub, Elternzeit, konjunktur- oder projektbedingte Auftragsspitzen entstehen. Das Spektrum ist groß und reicht von den Bereichen Datenerfassung, Sachbearbeitung und Sekretariat über Buchhaltung und Call-Center bis hin zur PC-Technik, Netzwerkadministration, Multimedia, Technische Redaktion und Softwareentwicklung. Kunden der BERG Zeitarbeit sind nationale und internationale Unternehmen unterschiedlichster Branchen.

Kompetenzfelder
Fields of Competence

The BERG Zeitarbeit GmbH concern sees itself as a human resources partner for its customers and employees alike. In practice, this means being able to react flexibly, quickly and effectively to customer requests, utilising the most suitably qualified employee for the occasion. In addition to professional personnel recruitment, emphasis is placed on caring for and developing the abilities of each employee. From the very beginning, the concern has specialised in office, call-centre and IT personnel, putting thus a high concentration on personnel services.

Since 1987 BERG Zeitarbeit has continually and innovatively accrued a large amount of specialised knowledge and competence within the branch. The economic stability of the concern and a strongly developed, steady team of attendants can be added to this specialised know-how – from which the concern's partners, whether customer or employee, equally benefit. In peak economic periods, up to 31 percent of the employees change over to employment in the customer's business. Well directed and successful, BERG Zeitarbeit fills personnel gaps in concerns which have been caused by illness, holidays, maternity leave, business or project-related order peaks. The range is wide and reaches from the areas of data processing, employees in charge of particular subject matters and secretarial duties via bookkeeping and call-centres through to PC technology, network administration, multimedia, technical editing and software development. Customers of BERG Zeitarbeit are national and international concerns from widely differing branches.

Information

Gründungsjahr: 1987

Mitarbeiter:
Interne Verwaltung: 14 Mitarbeiter
Extern eingesetzte Mitarbeiter: zwischen 400 und 600 je nach konjunkturbedingter Auftragslage

Schwerpunkte:
Mitarbeiter für die Bereiche
– Office (Büro/Verwaltung)
– Call-Center (Kundenmanagement)
– Information Technology (IT/EDV)

Leistungsspektrum:
– Personalüberlassung
– Personalvermittlung
– Outsourcing
– Outplacement
– On-Site-Management
– Projektdienstleistung (Werk- und Dienstverträge)

Year founded: 1987

Employees:
internal administration: 14 employees
employees used externally: between 400 and 600 depending on the state of the business order book

Emphasis:
employees for the sectors
– office (office/administration)
– call-centres (customer management)
– information technology (IT/EDP)

Range of services:
– temporary placement service
– personnel mediation
– outsourcing
– outplacement
– on-site management
– project services (works and service contracts)

BERG Zeitarbeit GmbH
Nürnberg

ADAC sichert Lebensqualität durch Mobilität

Der Allgemeine Deutsche Automobilclub (ADAC) e. V. ist mit über 15 Millionen Mitgliedern Europas größter Automobilclub und hat sich im Laufe von über hundert Jahren zum führenden Mobilitätsdienstleister Deutschlands entwickelt. Gegründet wurde der Verein von Motorradfahrern 1903 in Stuttgart. Nach wie vor ist der Motorsport eine wichtige Aufgabe des ADAC. In Nordbayern organisieren 170 Ortsclubs pro Jahr an die 300 motorsportliche Veranstaltungen. Zu den bedeutendsten Motorsport-Events gehört zweifelsfrei das berühmte Norisring-Rennen. Deutschlands einziges und nach Monaco traditionsreichstes Stadtrennen der Welt zieht jedes Jahr über 100 000 Besucher auf die Ränge der Steintribüne im Süden Nürnbergs.
Heute vertrauen in Nordbayern über 880 000 Mitglieder auf die Leistungen des ADAC. Die Mitglieder schätzen vor allem die Kerndienstleistung Pannenhilfe und profitieren von zahlreichen zusätzlichen Serviceleistungen. Was vor 50 Jahren mit Motorrädern und einer Ausrüstung, die in zwei Seitentaschen Platz hatte, anfing, hat sich zu vollelektronischer Fehlererkennung mit Laptops und kleinen Werkstätten auf vier Rädern entwickelt. Die modernen Gelben Engel sorgen im 24-Stunden-Service dafür, dass die Autofahrer in über 84 Prozent der Fälle ihre Fahrt wieder aufnehmen können.

Das Auto ermöglicht individuelle Mobilität, die heute ganz selbstverständlich ist, aber auch Gefahren birgt. Der ADAC bietet daher zahlreiche Verkehrssicherheitsprogramme an. Dazu gehören Fahrsicherheitstrainings für Auto- und Motorradfahrer, Verkehrserziehungsprogramme wie „Kind und Verkehr", „Hallo Auto", „Mobil mit Köpfchen" und die bekannten Fahrradturniere, die der ADAC schon seit den siebziger Jahren zusammen mit großen Kooperationspartnern durchführt.
Die flächendeckende Betreuung der ADAC-Mitglieder wird durch ein dichtes Filialnetz von Geschäftsstellen gewährleistet. Allein in der Region Nürnberg unterhält der ADAC ServiceCenter in Fürth, Erlangen, Ansbach sowie zwei in Nürnberg und weitere in Coburg, Bayreuth, Bamberg, Amberg, Schweinfurt, Würzburg, Aschaffenburg und Weiden. Neben Beratung sind auch Reisen, Versicherungen und ein breites Warensortiment im Angebot. Im Prüfzentrum in Fürth und mit mobilen Prüfdiensten werden kostenlose Autoprüfungen durchgeführt, die der Sicherheit der Autofahrer dienen.
In jüngster Zeit ist der ADAC mit einem multifunktionalen Truck auf vielen Festen und Veranstaltungen in Nordbayern unterwegs und steht Mitgliedern und Interessierten auch in ihrer Freizeit mit vielen Informationen rund um die Mobilität zur Verfügung.

ADAC secures quality of life through mobility

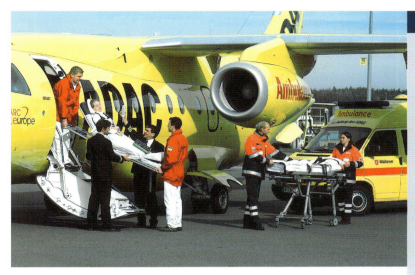

With more than 15 million members, the Allgemeiner Deutscher Automobilclub (ADAC) e. V. is Europe's largest automobile club and has, in the course of more than a hundred years, developed into the leading mobility service supplier in Germany. The club was founded by motorbike fans in Stuttgart in 1903. The motor sport is, and has always been, an important task of the ADAC. In North Bavaria, some 170 local clubs organise something like 300 motor-sporting events per year. One of the most important ones is, without doubt, the famous Noris-Ring race. Germany's only city race, running a close second to Monaco as the most traditional one in the world, attracts more than 100,000 visitors each year to the places on the stone stand in the south of Nuremberg.

Today more than 880,000 members in North Bavaria rely on the products of the ADAC. Members appreciate above all the core service of breakdown assistance at the same time profiting from countless additional services. What began 50 years ago with motorbikes and as much equipment as could be packed into two saddle-bags, has developed into fully-electronic error-detection with laptops and a small workshop on four wheels. The modern yellow angels make sure, in a 24-hour service, that in more than 84 percent of the cases car drivers are able to carry on with their journeys.

The automobile enables individual mobility, something that is today taken as a matter of course, but also one which carries risks. The ADAC therefore offers numerous traffic safety programmes. Amongst them are road safety training for car and motorbike drivers, traffic instruction programmes such as "Kind und Verkehr" (Child and Traffic), "Hallo Auto", "Mobil mit Köpfchen" and famous bicycle tournaments which the ADAC, together with major cooperating partners, has organised since the seventies.

The dense network of branch offices guarantees that all ADAC members are well looked after. In the region of Nuremberg alone the ADAC maintains service centres in Fürth, Erlangen, Ansbach and two in Nuremberg and further ones in Coburg, Bayreuth, Bamberg, Amberg, Schweinfurt, Würzburg, Aschaffenburg and Weiden. Alongside counselling travel services, insurances and a wide range of goods are also provided. Car tests are carried out free-of-charge in the test centre in Fürth and on mobile test services, serving to secure driver safety.

Recently the ADAC, together with its multifunctional truck, visited many festivities and events in North Bavaria, giving members and interested members of the public a chance to obtain information on mobility even in their leisure time.

Information

(Nordbayern)
Gründungsjahr: 1905
Mitarbeiter:
insgesamt 138, davon 46 in der Verwaltung in Nürnberg und 90 in insgesamt 13 Geschäftsstellen im Raum Nordbayern, 2 im Prüfzentrum

Regionale Infrastruktur:
- 13 Geschäftsstellen
- 17 Vertretungen
- 1 Prüfzentrum (in Fürth)
- 1 Fahrsicherheitsgelände (in Sigritzau bei Forchheim)

Leistungsspektrum:
Pannenhilfe, Versicherungen, Verlagsprodukte wie Karten, touristische Beratung, Beratung zu allen Mobilitätsthemen (Mitgliedsleistungen, Versicherungen, Finanzierung, Verkehrssicherheit etc.)

(North Bavaria)
Year founded: 1905
Employees:
a total of 138, of which 46 are in administration in Nuremberg and 90 in a total of 13 branch offices in the North Bavarian area and 2 in the test centre

Regional infrastructure:
- 13 branch offices
- 17 agencies
- 1 test centre (in Fürth)
- 1 driving safety site (in Sigritzau near Forchheim)

Range of services:
breakdown assistance, insurances, published products such as maps, tourism advice, counselling on all subjects of mobility (benefits for members, insurances, financing, traffic safety etc.)

ADAC Nordbayern e. V.
Nürnberg

Die Firma Hüttinger wurde vor über 80 Jahren in Fürth gegründet. Das Familienunternehmen besteht bis heute in seinen Wurzeln fort. Ab 1949 begann die Firma mit der Planung und Fertigung von technischen Modellen, Vorführungen und Funktionsschaubildern. Später verlagerte sich der Schwerpunkt vom Einzelmodell zur Ausstattung kompletter Ausstellungen und Informationszentren, insbesondere für die Bereiche Energietechnik, Kommunikationstechnologie und Automobil. Heute ist Hüttinger ein weltweit agierender Anbieter von hochwertigen Museen, Science Centern und Erlebnisausstellungen.

Hüttinger was founded more than 80 years ago in Fürth. The family business continues today at its roots. In 1949 the company started planning and manufacturing of technical models, interactive exhibits and functional diagrams. Later on, the focus was shifted from individual models to the delivery of complete exhibitions and information centres, especially for energy suppliers, IT companies and the automotive industry. Today, Hüttinger is a globally active supplier of museum and science centre exhibits and themed experience exhibitions.

Information

Leistungsspektrum:
Konzeption und Realisation von Erlebnissen, die Besucher in eine lebendige und be„greifbare" Erfahrungswelt entführen, wie zum Beispiel Besucherzentren, Museen und interaktive Science Center sowie Kindermuseen

Range of services:
the conception and implementation of experiences leading visitors through a world of tangible experiences such as guest centres, museums and interactive science centres as well as museums for children

☐

Kurt Hüttinger GmbH
Schwaig

– auf der erfolgreichen nationalen und internationalen Marktbearbeitung ansässiger großer Dienstleistungsunternehmen wie DATEV, GfK, Nürnberger Versicherung, Rödl & Partner oder Sellbytel.

Die technologischen Kernkompetenzen der Region bieten zudem viele Ansatzpunkte und Schnittstellen für Anbieter innovativer Dienstleistungen. So schöpfen technikorientierte Beratungs- und Serviceunternehmen unterschiedlichste Entwicklungsimpulse aus der industriellen Tradition der Region Nürnberg. So ist zum Beispiel die Informations- und Kommunikationstechnik eine unverzichtbare Grundlage für Wissensproduktion und -umschlag. Weitere Schnittstellen und Ansatzpunkte gibt es im Bereich Verkehr und Logistik sowie in den industriellen Kernbereichen Maschinenbau, Elektrotechnik, Energie und Automatisierungstechnik.

Die überwiegend mittelständische Struktur des Dienstleistungssektors gewährleistet hohe Flexibilität und Innovationsfreude. Zudem bieten Innovative Dienstleistungen ein breites Feld an Geschäftsideen und Marktchancen für Neugründungen und Ausgründungen. Chancen, die in Nürnberg wahrgenommen und von der Wirtschaftsförderung der Stadt mit allen Kräften unterstützt werden.

DATEV, GfK, Nürnberger Versicherung, Rödl & Partner and Sellbytel.

The region's technological core competences also provide many starting points and interfaces for suppliers of innovative services. In this way technically-oriented advisory and service companies create various impulses for development from the industrial traditions of the Nuremberg region and in their turn, information and communication technology become an essential base for the production of knowledge and its realisation. There are further parallels and starting points in the sectors of transport and logistics as well as in the industrial core sectors of mechanical engineering, electro-technology, energy and automation technology.

The predominantly medium-sized structure of the service supply sector guarantees high flexibility and pleasure in innovation. Innovative services also provide a wide range of business ideas and marketing chances for new companies and spin-offs. Chances which are taken advantage of in Nuremberg and which are strongly supported by the city's economic development service.

Kompetenzfelder
Fields of Competence

Das Berufsförderungswerk Nürnberg ist ein außerbetriebliches Zentrum der beruflichen Rehabilitation mit 13 Geschäftsstellen im gesamten nordbayrischen Raum.
Seine Hauptaufgabe ist die Wiedereingliederung von Erwachsenen, die ihren bisherigen Beruf aus gesundheitlichen Gründen nicht mehr ausüben können. Seit Bestehen wurden 7500 Absolventen zu ca. 80 Prozent erfolgreich in den ersten Arbeitsmarkt integriert.
Das modulare Dienstleistungsangebot „RehaAssessment®" bietet die umfassende Klärung der beruflichen Eignung von Rehabilitanden/-innen. Anwendung findet es in den Bereichen Prävention, Diagnostik und Orientierung.
Kompetente Ausbildungsfachkräfte unterstützen eigenverantwortliches und mitgestaltendes Lernen. Durch praxisgerechtes Arbeiten in modernen Ausbildungsräumen wird die berufliche Handlungskompetenz trainiert, um den aktuellen Anforderungen der Wirtschaft und Verwaltung Rechnung zu tragen.
RehaAssessment® ist eine eingetragene Marke der Arbeitsgemeinschaft Deutscher Berufsförderungswerke.

*The Berufsförderungswerk Nuremberg is an out-of-house centre of professional rehabilitation with 13 branches in the entire North Bavarian area.
Its main task is the re-integration of adults who are not able to carry on in their previous profession for health reasons. Since establishment, almost 80 percent of the 7,500 graduates have been successfully integrated in the first employment market.
The modular services offered by "RehaAssessment®" provides an encompassing clarification of professional suitability for people in rehabilitation. Its application can be found in the sectors of prevention, diagnostic and orientation.
Competent training experts support the students in designing the courses and learning on their own account. By working in a practice-oriented manner in modern training rooms, professional competence in acting on one's own is trained to enable the student to cope with the current demands of industry and administration. RehaAssessment® is a registered trademark of the Arbeitsgemeinschaft Deutscher Berufsförderungswerke.*

Information

Gründungsjahr: 1974
Mitarbeiter: 230
Geschäftsfelder:
- 24-monatige Vollqualifizierungen in 25 Berufen aus Wirtschaft, Verwaltung, Industrie und Handwerk
- betriebliche Qualifizierungen in über 80 Berufen
- Weiterbildungen/Teilqualifizierungen
- berufsbegleitende Schulungen und Firmenschulungen
- Bildungspartnerschaften SAP, CISCO, AKDB und BRK
- Abklärung der beruflichen Eignung
- Integrationsunterstützung
- Individualmaßnahmen/Casemanagement

Year founded: 1974
Employees: 230
Business fields:
- 24-month full qualification in 25 professions within industry, administration and the trades
- internal qualifications in more than 80 professions
- further-education/partial qualification
- training courses in tandem with work and company training
- educational partnerships SAP, CISCO, AKDB and BRK
- clarification of professional suitability
- integration support
- individual measures/case management

Berufsförderungswerk Nürnberg gGmbH

Lokale Verbundenheit und Nähe zu den Kunden kennzeichnen die Philosophie der VR Bank Nürnberg. Mit 18 Geschäftsstellen und drei SB-Stellen ist das Institut in und um Nürnberg immer in Kundennähe vor Ort.
Für einen optimalen Vermögensaufbau, die Vermögensabsicherung und Zukunftsvorsorge bietet die VR Bank Nürnberg – gemeinsam mit ihren starken Partnern im Finanzverbund – maßgeschneiderte Anlage-, Spar- und Vorsorgeformen sowie Finanzierungen aller Art. Als mittelständische Genossenschaftsbank fühlt sich die VR Bank Nürnberg traditionell dem Mittelstand in der Region verbunden. Ob erfahrener Geschäftsführer oder Neugründer – zu den Themen Finanzierung und Leasing, betriebliche Altersvorsorge, Existenzgründung, Unternehmensnachfolge und Riskmanagement ist die VR Bank ein kompetenter Ansprechpartner.

Unity with the local area and customer-closeness is characteristic of the philosophy of the VR Bank Nuremberg. With its 18 branches and three self-service points, the institute is in and around Nuremberg always close to its customers and on the spot when needed. To optimally increase and protect assets and to secure the future, the VR Bank Nuremberg offers – together with its efficient partners in the financial combine – tailor-made investments, savings and contingency plans as well as all kinds of financing. As a medium-sized co-operative bank, the VR Bank Nuremberg considers itself traditionally linked to the small and medium-sized firms of the region. Whether experienced manager or starting up a new business – the VR Bank is a competent partner on the subjects of financing and leasing, company pension scheme, establishment of new business enterprises, company successions and risk management.

Vorstand der VR Bank Nürnberg: (v. l.) Hans-Peter Lang, Dirk Helmbrecht, Brigitte Baur, Bernhard Link

Chair people of the VR Bank Nuremberg: (from the left) Hans-Peter Lang, Dirk Helmbrecht, Brigitte Baur, Bernhard Link

Information

Gründungsjahr: 1893

Mitarbeiter: 235

Bilanzsumme 2005: 799 Mio. Euro

Year founded: 1893

Employees: 235

Balance sheet total 2005: 799 million Euro

Volksbank Raiffeisenbank Nürnberg eG

Kompetenzfelder
Fields of Competence

Die HypoVereinsbank in Nürnberg (Nordbayern) positioniert sich als regional tief verwurzelter Bankpartner, andererseits als leistungsfähige internationale europäische Großbank für Privat- und Firmenkunden. Mit rund 1350 Mitarbeitern in 53 Filialstandorten in der Region ist die HypoVereinsbank flächendeckend vertreten. Gerade der Mittelstand ist eine Kernzielgruppe der HypoVereinsbank; hier ist sie mit hohen Marktanteilen regelmäßig als Haupt- oder Kernbank mit ihren Kunden aktiv. Egal, ob individuelle oder maßgeschneiderte Finanzierungslösungen, komplexe Zahlungsverkehrsfragen, Problemlösungen für internationale Handelstransaktionen oder das Zins- und Devisengeschäft, die Beratungs- und Betreuungsleistungen sind auf die Bedürfnisse der Kunden eng ausgerichtet. Auch die bedürfnisorientierte Beratung von Privatkunden steht im Mittelpunkt des Handelns. Hier vor allem die Bereiche Wertpapier- und Geldanlage, Vorsorge und Baufinanzierungen sowie individuelle Lösungen der betrieblichen und individuellen Altersvorsorge.

The HypoVereinsbank in Nuremberg (North Bavaria) has positioned itself not only as a deeply rooted regional banking partner but also as an efficient international European major bank for private and commercial customers. With some 1,350 employees in 53 branch locations in the region, the HypoVereinsbank is widely and well represented. It is precisely the medium-sized companies that are the core target group of the HypoVereinsbank; on this sector it is regularly active on behalf of its customers as a main or core bank with a large share of the market. Regardless of whether individual or tailor-made financing solutions, complex questions of payment transactions, solving the problems of international trading transactions or the interest and foreign exchange business, their counselling and care services are closely directed towards the needs of their customers. Also the need-oriented advisory service for private customers stands in the centre of their dealings, primarily in the sectors of securities and investments, provisions and construction finance as well as individual solutions for company and individual pensions schemes.

Information

Gründungsjahr:
seit 1896 in der Region vertreten

Mitarbeiter: rund 1350

Filialen:
53 in der Region, über 650 bundesweit

Leistungsspektrum:
komplettes Angebot in allen Vermögens-, Vorsorge- und Finanzierungsfragen; spezielle Ausrichtung auf den europäischen Markt

---

Year founded:
represented in the region since 1896

Employees:
some 1,350

Branches:
53 in the region, more than 650 nationally

Range of services:
complete offers covering all assets, provision and financing questions; specially directed towards the European market

HypoVereinsbank AG
Nürnberg

„Made in Nürnberg": Hier ist die Heimat von Deutschlands bekanntestem und wachstumsstärkstem Ratenkredit.

"Made in Nuremberg": This is the home of Germany's best known and strongest growing credit to be repaid in instalments.

Die norisbank AG gehört seit 2003 als Tochter der DZ BANK zum genossenschaftlichen FinanzVerbund. Mit seinem innovativen Produkt, dem easyCredit, ist das Nürnberger Institut der Ratenkreditspezialist der Volksbanken und Raiffeisenbanken in Deutschland und hat sich den Ruf als Wachstums-Marktführer erworben.
Motor dieser Entwicklung in den letzten Jahren sind die rund 900 Genossenschaftsbanken, die sich für den Verkauf des Markenartikels easyCredit entschieden haben. Die in der Region verwurzelte Bank setzt damit nationale Maßstäbe, die auch den internationalen Vergleich nicht zu scheuen brauchen.
Ein weiteres Novum: Seit Jahren bewirbt die norisbank ausschließlich ihr Produkt easyCredit und betreibt keine andere Unternehmenswerbung. Die anhaltende Erfolgsgeschichte der norisbank ist auch Grundlage für das gesellschaftliche, soziale und kulturelle Engagement. Sie initiierte das Projekt „Finanz-ABC" zur finanziellen Aufklärung Jugendlicher im Großraum sowie eine Spendenaktion zu Gunsten eines vom Tsunami verwüsteten Dorfs auf Sri Lanka im Rahmen einer Patenschaft der Stadt Nürnberg. Außerdem engagiert sich die norisbank als Gründungsmitglied der Nürnberger Bürgerstiftung u. a. alljährlich für gemeinnützige Zwecke beim Albrecht-Dürer-Opernball. Daneben fördert die Bank die Deutsche Akademie für Fußball-Kultur mit Sitz am WM-Standort Nürnberg.

Die norisbank ist stolz auf die motivierteste Mannschaft im deutschen Bankenmarkt.

The norisbank AG has been a subsidiary of the DZ BANK since 2003 and belongs to the cooperative FinanzVerbund.
With its innovative product easyCredit, the Nuremberg institute is the expert for credits to be repaid in instalments of the Volksbanks and Raiffeisenbanks (industrial and agricultural credit cooperatives) in Germany and has earned itself the reputation as growth-market leader.
The motor of this development in the few last years has been the 900 cooperative banks which have decided to sell the branded article of easyCredit. The bank, which is strongly rooted in the region, has thereby set national standards and need not shy from international comparisons.
An additional new factor: the norisbank has only advertised its easyCredit for years and carries out no other concern advertising.
The continuing success story of the norisbank is also the basis for its social and cultural commitment. It initiated the "Finanz-ABC" project for financial clarification of young people in the area and, within the scope of a sponsorship by the city of Nuremberg, a donation programme for the benefit of a village in Sri Lanka destroyed by the tsunami. As a founding member, the norisbank is also very committed to the Nürnberger Bürgerstiftung, amongst others for the annual charity at the Albrecht-Dürer opera ball. The bank also supports the Deutsche Akademie für Fußball-Kultur with headquarters at the world championship's location of Nuremberg.

The norisbank is proud of the most motivated team on the German banking market.

Information

Gründungsjahr: 1998

Mitarbeiter:
knapp 1200, davon über 600 im Großraum Nürnberg

Filialen:
99, davon 7 in der Region; zusätzlich 2 easyCredit-Shops in Nürnberg

Leistungsspektrum:
Finanzdienstleistungen mit Schwerpunkt auf dem Konsumentenkredit easyCredit

---

Year founded: 1998

Employees:
almost 1,200, of which more than 600 in the greater Nuremberg area

Branches:
99, of which 7 are in the region; additionally 2 easyCredit shops in Nuremberg

Range of services:
financial services centring on consumer credit easyCredit

☐
norisbank
Aktiengesellschaft
Nürnberg

Kompetenzfelder
Fields of Competence

Der Hauptsitz, Königstorgraben 9, Nürnberg

Head Office, Königstorgraben 9, Nuremberg

Die J. L. Orth GmbH Assekuranzmakler ist mit einer Firmentradition von über zwei Jahrhunderten einer der ältesten und bekanntesten Versicherungsvermittler und gehört mittlerweile zur Ecclesia Gruppe, dem größten deutschen inhabergeführten Versicherungsmaklerverbund. Etwa 70 qualifizierte Mitarbeiter setzen sich für ihre Kunden ein und helfen, Versicherungsprobleme kreativ und gezielt zu lösen. Gemeinsam mit den Kunden erfassen und bewerten die Experten sämtliche Risiken und untersuchen die bestehenden Versicherungsverträge des Unternehmens.

Die J. L. Orth GmbH Assekuranzmakler erarbeitet daraufhin individuell auf das Unternehmen zugeschnittene Versicherungskonzepte und legt diese entscheidungsreif vor. Sie realisiert den erforderlichen Versicherungsschutz mit leistungsstarken Gesellschaften und berücksichtigt dabei bestehende Geschäftsverbindungen zu den bisherigen Versicherern. Die internationalen Aktivitäten werden durch die neue Zugehörigkeit zum Ecclesia Verbund über das weltweite EOS RISQ-Netz abgesichert. Auch im Schadensfall steht das Unternehmen seinen Kunden bei der Durchsetzung der Ansprüche aktiv und kompetent zur Seite.

With a company tradition dating back over two centuries, J. L. Orth GmbH Assekuranzmakler is one of the oldest and best-known Insurance Brokers in Germany. Today J. L. Orth belongs to the Ecclesia Group, Germany's largest insurance brokerage group managed by the owners. Approximately 70 experts and specialists in all areas of the insurance business are committed to meet the various and ever increasing insurance requirements of its clients. With the clients' support, experts evaluate the potential risks and analyse the clients' current insurance contracts. J. L. Orth develops industrial, commercial and international insurance concepts individually tailored to the customers' requirements and by taking into acount the corporate culture and personal preferences. The insurance concept is then presented for the client's approval.

The necessary insurance protection will be placed by J. L. Orth with reputable national and international insurers, considering the clients' long-term business relationships with certain insurance companies. Global activities of the customers are well cared for through the worldwide EOS RISQ network, an affiliate of the Ecclesia Group. J. L. Orth's main office is the access to global coverage.

J. L. Orth's competence, experience and reliability are just as important when a claim has occurred. Especially in this case can the quality of the client's insurance coverage and the claim handling of J. L. Orth be truly appreciated.

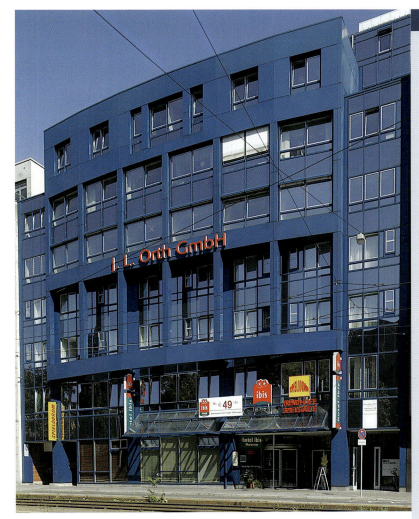

Information

Gründungsjahr: 1798

Mitarbeiter: 70

Leistungsspektrum: Vermittlung und Abschluss von Versicherungen aller Art inklusive Schadensregulierung vorwiegend im industriellen Bereich

Niederlassungen: Augsburg, Düsseldorf, Jena, Stuttgart

Beteiligungsgesellschaften:
- Industrie-Assekuranz Augsburg Versicherungsmakler GmbH, Augsburg
- Industrie- und Handels-Assekuranz Versicherungsmakler GmbH, Ransbach-Baumbach

Year of foundation: 1798

Employees: 70

Scope of services: Brokerage of all types of insurance including claims settlement, primarily in the industrial sector

Branches: Augsburg, Düsseldorf, Jena, Stuttgart

Affiliated companies:
- Industrie-Assekuranz Augsburg Versicherungsmakler GmbH, Augsburg
- Industrie- und Handels-Assekuranz Versicherungsmakler GmbH, Ransbach-Baumbach

J. L. Orth GmbH Assekuranzmakler, Nürnberg – ein Unternehmen der Ecclesia Gruppe

Ein Blick zurück – die Geschichte Mittelfrankens

Professor em. Dr. Rudolf Endres

Es waren wohl geopolitische und verkehrsstrategische Gründe, die um 1040 König Heinrich III. veranlassten, in dem weitgehend siedlungsleeren Raum des königlichen Bannforstes an der Pegnitz einen Stützpunkt zu errichten. Schon bald liefen die herausragende Burg „Norenberc" und die Siedlung, die erstmals 1050 urkundlich erwähnt wird, den benachbarten älteren Siedlungen den Rang ab. Allen voran dem alten Königshof Fürth, der 1007 an das Bamberger Domkapitel verschenkt worden war, aber auch dem karolingischen Ansbach. Nürnberg lag im Schnittpunkt wichtiger Straßen, sodass der Ort bald als „Spinne im Netz" des europäischen Fernhandelssystems zu überregionaler Bedeutung aufstieg. Schwabach und Erlangen waren im Mittelalter noch unbedeutende Dörfer mit nur wenigen Häusern.

Unter den Staufern trat das Königtum im Raum um die Reichsburg und die Königsstadt Nürnberg entscheidend in Erscheinung. Denn in der Reichslandpolitik der Stauferkönige, die das zerstreute Reichsland zwischen Schwaben und dem Egerland wieder zusammenfassen wollten, spielte Franken eine wichtige Rolle. Hier sollten die Grundlagen eines mittelalterlichen deutschen Königsstaates entstehen, getragen von Reichsstädten und Reichsmärkten und vor allem von ritteradeligen Reichsministerialen auf ihren Burgen im Königsland. So wurde Rothenburg mit der Pfalz Mittelpunkt des umfangreichen Reichsgutes, und auch Windsheim bildete eine Bastion gegen Würzburg. Vor allem aber sollte Nürnberg zum Mittelpunkt des Reichslandes in Franken werden, mit dem Reichsbutigler und dem Burggrafen auf der Reichsburg und der stetig wachsenden Stadt um St. Sebald und St. Lorenz.

Doch mit dem Zusammenbruch der staufischen Reichslandpolitik 1268 ging der Weg zu einer staatlichen Vereinheitlichung verloren, und es setzte sich die territoriale Vielfalt durch, der typische fränkische „Flickenteppich". Es entstanden die drei Hochstifte, die

The reasons that induced King Henry III about 1040 to set up a base in the practically non-settled area of the royal Bannforst (Protection forest) on the Pegnitz were no doubt geopolitical and strategic for traffic. But it wasn't long before the outstanding castle "Norenberc" and the settlement, which was first documented in 1050, overtook the neighbouring older settlement in significance. In front of all of them, however, the old royal court of Fürth, which had been given to the Bamberg Cathedral Chapter in 1007 as well as the Carolingian Ansbach. Nuremberg lay at the hub, at the crossing of strategic roads, so that the place was soon elevated to having significance beyond the region as the "spider in the web" of the long-distance trading system in Europe. In the Middle Ages, Schwabach and Erlangen were still unimportant villages with only a few houses.

Under the Staufer Dynasty the kingdom surrounding the Reichsburg and royal city of Nuremberg made a decisive appearance because in the Reich's land policy of the Staufer kings, who wanted to reunite the widespread imperial land between Swabia and Egerland, Franconia played an important role. The foundation for a medieval German royal state was to be created here borne by imperial cities and imperial markets but above all by knight noblemen's imperial ministries in their castles in the king's country. Thus Rothenburg with the Palatinate became the centre point of the extensive imperial estates with Windsheim also forming a bastion against Würzburg. But above all, Nuremberg was to become the centre of imperial land in Franconia, with the Reichsbutigler (a bailiff with royal rights who supervised the imperial forest) and the Burgrave on the Reichsburg as well as the steadily growing town around St. Sebald and St. Lorenz.

With the collapse of the Staufer Reich's land policy in 1268, however, the way to a stately standardisation was lost and territorial diversity, the typical Franconian "rag rug" was installed. Three bishoprics were created,

A Look Back – the History of Middle Franconia

Lebensqualität pur
The Pure Quality of Life

Nürnberg mit der Kaiserburg: Um 1040 wurde mit dem Bau von Burg und Siedlung auf Anordnung von Heinrich III., König von Italien und Burgund, begonnen.

Nuremberg with the Kaiserburg: about 1040 building commenced on the castle and settlement on the orders of Heinrich III., King of Italy and Burgundy.

Die 800 Jahre alte Burg Rabenstein im Herzen der Fränkischen Schweiz wird heute als Hotel genutzt.

The 800 year old castle Rabenstein in the heart of Franconian Switzerland is today used as a hotel.

Fürstentümer Ansbach und Kulmbach der Hohenzollern, die Grafen und die vielen freien Reichsritter sowie die fünf Reichsstädte. Nürnberg errang im 13./14. Jahrhundert die Reichsunmittelbarkeit, doch bis 1427 mussten die Hohenzollern auf der Burggrafenburg erduldet werden. Die Hohenzollern, die 1363 in den Reichsfürstenrang erhoben worden waren, bauten als Erben des staufischen Bannwaldes ein umfangreiches Territorium um die Reichsstadt auf und übten wichtige Hoheitsrechte bis an die Tore Nürnbergs aus. Stützpunkte der burggräflichen bzw. seit 1415 markgräflichen Macht der Hohenzollern waren die Städte Cadolzburg, Ansbach und Gunzenhausen, Schwabach, Windsbach und Uffenheim, die zumeist im 14. Jahrhundert käuflich erworben wurden. In dem Marktflecken Fürth beanspruchten die Dompröpste von Bamberg, die Markgrafen von Ansbach und die Reichsstadt Nürnberg zugleich die Herrschaft. Diese Zersplitterung konnten die bedrängten Juden nutzen, die in Fürth ihre wichtigste Gemeinde in Oberdeutschland gründeten, nachdem sie aus Nürnberg, Rothenburg und anderen Städten vertrieben worden waren. Erlangen wurde von Bamberg an Kaiser Karl IV. vertauscht, der als König von Böhmen sein „Neuböhmisches Reich" von der Oberpfalz bis nach Lauf und Erlenstegen verschob. Doch dieses „Neuböhmen" zerfiel unter seinem Sohn Wenzel.

Zu dieser Zeit war Nürnberg das wirtschaftliche Zentrum Frankens. In Kaiser Ludwig dem Baiern hatte die Stadt einen großen Förderer und Gönner gefunden. Wichtig war auch der Ausbau der Wirtschaftsbeziehungen zur Montanindustrie in der Oberpfalz, dem „Ruhrgebiet des Mittelalters". Denn Nürnberg war das Zentrum der Metallverarbeitung und der Waffenindustrie in Europa. Zur „heimlichen Hauptstadt des Reiches" aber wurde die Reichsstadt an der Pegnitz

the principalities of Ansbach and Kulmbach of the Hohenzollern, the counts and the many free imperial knights as well as the five imperial cities. In the 13th/14th centuries Nuremberg gained immediacy, but the Hohenzollern had to be endured on the Burggrafenburg until 1427. The Hohenzollern, who had been elevated to the rank of Reich princes in 1363, built up, as heirs of the Staufer Bannwald, a widespread territory surrounding the Reichsstadt and practiced important rights of sovereignty right up to the gates of Nuremberg. The cities of Cadolzburg, Ansbach and Gunzenhausen, Schwabach, Windsbach and Uffenheim, which had mostly been bought in the 14th century, formed the centres of power of the Hohenzollern's Burgrave and from 1415 onwards, Margrave. In the market town of Fürth the cathedral provosts of Bamberg, the Margraves of Ansbach and the Reichsstadt of Nuremberg claimed sovereignty at the same time. This fragmentation was able to be utilised by the Jews who

Burg und Wallfahrtskirche („Balthasar-Neumann Basilika") bestimmen das Bild des idyllischen Ortes Gößweinstein in der Fränkischen Schweiz.

Castle and pilgrimage church ("Balthasar-Neumann Basilika") determine the picture of the idyllic village of Gößweinstein in Franconian Switzerland.

Die Burgruine Pappenheim im malerischen Altmühltal

The ruined castle of Pappenheim in the picturesque Altmühl valley

als beliebter Tagungsort für Reichstage und als Aufbewahrungsort der Reichsinsignien und Heiligtümer. Weiterhin war Nürnberg Nachrichtenzentrum und eine „Wiege der europäischen Technik". Hinzu kam noch die Rolle als „Vorort der lutherischen Reformation" seit 1525. Auch besaß die Reichsstadt seit 1505 das größte Landgebiet mit den Städten Lauf, Hersbruck, Altdorf und Gräfenberg und eine eigene Universität.

Nach den schweren Schäden des Dreißigjährigen Krieges verlor Nürnberg an wirtschaftlicher und politischer Bedeutung, wenn es auch kulturell noch immer große Leistungen vorweisen konnte. Wirtschaftlich wurde die erstarrte Reichsstadt nicht zuletzt von den Hugenotten in Erlangen und Schwabach überholt, die neue Fertigkeiten, Produkte und Produktionsweisen mitbrachten. Die Hugenottenstadt „Christian-Erlang" war so erfolgreich, dass 1743 hier auch die Landesuniversität errichtet wurde.

were under pressure and who had founded their most important community of Upper Germany in Fürth after their ejection from Nuremberg, Rothenburg and other cities. Erlangen was exchanged by Bamberg and went to the Emperor Charles IV who, as King of Bohemia, moved his "New Bohemian Kingdom" from the Upper Palatinate to beyond Lauf and Erlenstegen. However, this "New Bohemia" disintegrated under his son Wenzel.

At that time Nuremberg was the economic centre of Franconia. In Kaiser Ludwig der Baier the city had found a generous supporter and patron. Important too, was the strengthening of the economic relationship to the coal and steel industry in the Upper Palatinate, the "Ruhr area of the middle ages", because Nuremberg was Europe's centre of metal processing and the weapons industry. However, the Reichsstadt on the Pegnitz became the "secret imperial capital" as a favourite conference venue for imperial conferences and as place of safekeeping for imperial insignia and holy articles. Nuremberg was still the centre of news an information and a "cradle of European technology". To this was added the role as "suburb of the Lutheran Reformation" after 1525. From 1505 onwards the Reichsstadt had also possessed the largest area of

Das Bamberger Domkreuz in der Landesausstellung „200 Jahre Franken in Bayern" im Centrum Industriekultur in Nürnberg

The Bamberg cathedral cross in the county exhibition "200 years of Franconia in Bavaria" in the centre for industrial culture in Nuremberg

Die „Flurbereinigung" unter Napoleon zerschlug den alten territorialen „Flickenteppich" und Franken wurde Bayern zugeschlagen, das seit 1806 Königreich war. Unter Montgelas wurde das moderne, zentralistisch regierte Bayern auf den Weg gebracht, während sich in Franken im Vormärz die Kämpfer für Einheit und Freiheit sammelten. 1837 bewilligte König Ludwig I. die Bezeichnung „Mittelfranken" für den Regierungsbezirk, doch blieb die Verwaltung in Ansbach. Dafür wurde Nürnberg zum Zentrum der Industrialisierung, die 1835 ihren Anfang mit dem Eisenbahnbau zwischen Nürnberg und Fürth nahm. Die Führungsrolle im Industrialisierungsprozess übernahmen die Nürnberger Maschinenbaufirmen Spaeth und Kramer-Klett, die vor allem Eisenbahnwaggons fertigten. Beherrschender Industrieller in der weltberühmten Bleistiftindustrie war Lothar von Faber. In der zweiten Hälfte des 19. Jahrhunderts rückten die Zweiradindustrie und die Elektroindustrie unter Sigmund Schuckert in den Vordergrund. Maßgeblichen Anteil am Aufstieg zur Industriemetropole hatten jüdische Mitbürger, denen es auch zu verdanken war, dass Nürnberg zum größten Hopfenhandelsplatz weltweit wurde. Fürth lebte von der Spiegelglasindustrie, und Erlangen war eine verträumte Universitätsstadt mit vielen Brauereien.

land with the towns Lauf, Hersbruck, Altdorf and Gräfenberg together with its own university.

Following the heavy damage incurred by the thirty-year war Nuremberg lost in economic and political significance, even though it could still show outstanding cultural work. Economically, the congealed Reichsstadt was overtaken not least by the Huguenots in Erlangen and Schwabach who brought new skills, products and production methods with them. The Huguenot town of "Christian-Erlang" was so successful that in 1743 the county university was also founded here.

The "reallocation of agricultural land" under Napoleon destroyed the old territorial "rag rug" and Franconia was annexed to Bavaria, which had been a kingdom since 1806. Under Montgelas, the modern, centralist governed Bavaria was introduced whilst in Franconia the fighters for unity and freedom collected in Vormärz (on the eve of the 1848 German revolution). In 1837 King Louis I granted the name "Middle Franconia" for the administrative district, although local government remained in Ansbach. In return, Nuremberg became the centre of industrialisation, which began with the construction of the railway between Nuremberg and Fürth in 1835. The leading role in the industrialisation process was taken over by the Nuremberg machine construction companies Spaeth and Kramer-Klett, who produced primarily railway carriages. The ruling industrialist in the world-famous pencil industry was Lothar von Faber. In the second half of the 19th century the bicycle industry and the electro industry moved into the foreground under Sigmund Schuckert. Jewish citizens had a decisive share in the elevation to an industrial metropolis and they also had to be thanked for the fact that Nuremberg became the world's largest trade centre for hops. Fürth lived from the mirror glass industry, and Erlangen was a sleepy university town with many breweries.

Besonderes Schmuckstück im Schloss Ratibor in Roth ist der Prunksaal

The state room in castle Ratibor in Roth is a particular masterpiece

Das änderte sich erst, als sich die „Erba-Baumwollindustrie" in Erlangen niederließ und die Firma „Reiniger, Gebbert und Schall" gegründet wurde, die medizinische Geräte herstellte. Sie wurde in der Weimarer Republik von Siemens übernommen. In Schwabach dominierte die Feinmetallindustrie, wohingegen Westmittelfranken weitgehend agrarisch strukturiert blieb.

Im „Dritten Reich" erlangte Nürnberg als „Stadt der Reichsparteitage" und der rassistischen „Nürnberger Gesetze" traurige Berühmtheit und wurde nach dem Krieg durch die „Nürnberger Kriegsverbrecherprozesse" weltweit bekannt, während die Bevölkerung eine fast völlig zerstörte Stadt wieder aufbauen musste. Das unzerstörte Erlangen hingegen profitierte von der Verlagerung der zentralen Verwaltung der Siemens-Schuckert AG aus Berlin.

In den zurückliegenden 60 Jahren hat die ehemalige Industrieregion Mittelfranken einen tief greifenden Umstrukturierungsprozess vom traditionellen Produktionsstandort zum modernen Industrie- und Dienstleistungszentrum erfolgreich bewältigt und darf heute zu Recht das Prädikat „Metropolregion" tragen.

This only changed when the "Erba-Baumwollindustrie" (Erba cotton industry) settled in Erlangen and the firm "Reiniger, Gebbert und Schall" was founded, a company which manufactured medical equipment and which was later taken over by Siemens in the Weimar Republic. In Schwabach the fine metal industry dominated, whereas Western Middle Franconia remained mostly agrarian structured.

In the "Third Reich" Nuremberg sadly became famous as "City of the Reichsparteitage" and the racist "Nuremberg Laws" and becoming known all over the world after the war for the "Nuremberg War Crimes Trials", while the population had to rebuild an almost totally destroyed city. In contrast, the city of Erlangen, which had not been destroyed, profited from moving the central administration of the Siemens-Schuckert AG from Berlin.

In the past 60 years the former industrial region of Middle Franconia has very successfully overcome a far-reaching process of restructuring from a traditional production location to a modern industry and services centre and may today, with justification, carry the title of "metropolitan region".

Faszination und Gewalt – das Dokumentationszentrum Reichsparteitagsgelände

Dr. Franz Sonnenberger

Noch heute zeugen auf dem ehemaligen Reichsparteitagsgelände im Süden Nürnbergs gigantische Baureste vom Größenwahn des nationalsozialistischen Regimes. Auf elf Quadratkilometern – ein Vielfaches der Fläche der Nürnberger Altstadt – sollte eine monumentale Kulisse für die Selbstinszenierung der NSDAP entstehen. Nürnberg wurde zur „Stadt der Reichsparteitage" und damit geradezu zu einem Symbolort des Nationalsozialismus.

Nach 1945 nutzte man die baulichen Überreste auf dem Gelände lange Zeit rein pragmatisch, zum Beispiel als Lagerhallen oder als Szenerie für Autorennen oder sonstige Massenveranstaltungen. Wie auch an anderen Orten mit vergleichbaren Hinterlassenschaften der NS-Zeit verbreitete sich erst nach und nach die Überzeugung, dass es sich bei dem Gelände um einen wichtigen historischen Ort handelte, der entsprechend präsentiert werden musste. Auf Initiative der museen der stadt nürnberg entstand 1994 das Projekt einer Dauerausstellung im Torso der für 50 000 Menschen ausgelegten Kongresshalle, das von allen demokratischen Parteien unterstützt wurde. Spenden von privater und öffentlich-rechtlicher Seite sowie Zuschüsse von Bund, Freistaat Bayern, der Stadt Nürnberg und des Bezirks Mittelfranken stellten die Finanzierung sicher.

Ein Architektenwettbewerb, den Professor Günther Domenig (Graz) für sich entschied, verlieh dem Vorhaben eine überzeugende, mittlerweile vielfach preisgekrönte Gestalt. So entstand im nördlichen der beiden Kongresshallen-Kopfbauten die bauliche Hülle des Dokumentationszentrums. Ein 130 Meter langer, gläserner „Pfahl" bohrt sich diagonal durch das massive Gebäude und stört nachhaltig dessen rechtwinkelige Geometrie. Dieses begehbare Zeichen aus Stahl und Glas bildet zugleich ein wichtiges Element der

Gigantic ruins bearing witness to megalomania of the national socialist regime can still be seen on the former Reichsparteitagsgelände in the south of Nuremberg. On eleven square kilometres – many times the size of the Nuremberg old city – a monumental backdrop was to be erected for the self-aggrandizement of the NSDAP (National socialist German workers' party). Nuremberg became the "city of the Reich's party congresses" a truly symbolic place of national socialism.

For a long time after 1945 the structural remains were used purely pragmatically, for example as storage warehouses and as a backdrop for car races and other mass events. As in other places with similar ruins left over from the NS period, the conviction that the grounds were of historical signification and should be suitably presented arose only little by little. On the initiative of the museums of the city of nuremberg the project of a permanent exhibition was created in 1994 in the skeleton of the congress hall which, incidentally, had been built to accommodate 50,000 people. The project was supported by all democratic parties. Contributions from private and public purses as well as subsidies from the Federation, the Free State of Bavaria, the city of Nuremberg and the region of Middle Franconia assured the financing.

A competition between architects which was won by Professor Günther Domenig (Graz) lent the plans a convincing design, one which has since won many prizes. And so the structural shell of the documentation centre was erected in the northerly of the two congress hall head (quarters) buildings. A 130 metre long, glass "post" was driven diagonally through the massive building – causing a lasting disturbance to its right-angled geometry. At the same time this accessible symbol of steel and glass forms an important element of guided tours for visitors around the permanent exhibition and

Fascination and Power – the Reichsparteitagsgelände Documentation Centre

Lebensqualität pur
The Pure Quality of Life

Das Dokumentationszentrum Reichsparteitagsgelände beschäftigt sich mit der Rolle Nürnbergs im Nationalsozialismus als „Stadt der Reichsparteitage".

The documentation centre in the Reichsparteitagsgelände concerns itself with the role of Nuremberg during the National Socialism period as the "City of Reichs Party Conresses".

Besucherführung durch die Dauerausstellung, aber auch durch ansonsten unzugängliche Bereiche des Gebäudes. Deutlich sichtbar auf dem Dach des Kopfbaus befindet sich das Studienforum, in dem ein vertiefendes pädagogisches Programm für Schulklassen, Jugend- und Erwachsenengruppen angeboten wird. Das kühn in den Luftraum des Foyers eingehängte Kino präsentiert vor allem Interviews mit Zeitzeugen der Reichsparteitage.

Mit durchschnittlich etwa 180 000 Besuchern pro Jahr hat das Dokumentationszentrum im Kreis der deutschen Gedenk- und Erinnerungsstätten an die NS-Zeit einen festen Platz eingenommen. Unter dem Titel „Faszination und Gewalt" informiert das Dokumentationszentrum Reichsparteitagsgelände über die Geschichte der Parteitage und dokumentiert das Vorhaben der Nationalsozialisten, ein ganzes Volk für sich zu vereinnahmen. Das Dokumentationszentrum setzt sich sehr bewusst mit der von vielen Zeitgenossen als attraktiv empfundenen Schauseite des Dritten Reichs auseinander, macht aber zugleich die verbrecherischen Konsequenzen deutlich, die dessen Politik zeitigte. Den Schwerpunkt der Dauerausstellung bilden die Reichsparteitage selbst sowie das in Nürnberg

Die Fassadengestaltung der Kongresshalle erinnert stark an das antike Collosseum in Rom. Die Kongresshalle blieb unvollendet und gilt heute als der größte erhaltene Bau und Sinnbild des Größenwahns der NS-Herrschaftsarchitektur.

The facade of the Congress Hall reminds one strongly of the antique Coliseum in Rome. The Congress Hall remained unfinished and is today considered to be the largest kept building and symbol of the megalomania of the NS-power architecture.

for tours through the normally inaccessible parts of the building. Clearly visible on the roof of the head building is the study forum, in which an absorbing pedagogic programme is provided for schoolchildren and groups of youths and adults. The boldly hanging cinema in the airspace in the foyer presents primarily interviews with contemporary witnesses of the Reich's party congresses.

With its average of some 180,000 visitors per year, the documentation centre has taken over a firm position in the circle of German memorials and reminders of the NS period. Under the title "Fascination and Power" the documentation centre on the Reichsparteitagsgelände gives information on the history of party

Lebensqualität pur
The Pure Quality of Life

Unter dem Titel „Faszination und Gewalt" informiert das Dokumentationszentrum über die Geschichte der Parteitage und zeigt die propagandistischen Methoden der Gleichschaltung, um ein ganzes Volk für sich zu vereinnahmen.

Under the title of "Fascination and Terror" the documentation centre provides information on the history of party congresses and shows the propaganda methods of elimination of all opposition in order to collect a whole nation for itself.

von den Nationalsozialisten in Gang gesetzte Bauprogramm.

Der Ausstellungsrundgang setzt in den zwanziger Jahren ein, in denen Nürnberg infolge der Reichsparteitage von 1927 und 1929 bereits ein Veranstaltungsort für die NS-Bewegung geworden war. Nach 1933 fanden hier alle sechs Reichsparteitage des Dritten Reichs statt, an denen jeweils bis zu einer Million Menschen teilnahmen. Unter Gesamtleitung von Albert Speer wurde ein gigantisches Bauprogramm in die Wege geleitet, das unter anderem auch die Errichtung des „Deutschen Stadions" mit einem Fassungsvermögen von über 400 000 Zuschauern vorsah. Fertig gestellt wurden zwischen 1934 und 1937 indes nur die Zeppelin-Tribüne und das Zeppelin-Feld. Für die im Entstehen begriffenen Bauten lieferten ab 1940 auch Steinbrüche in Konzentrationslagern Granit. Aufgrund der unmenschlichen Bedingungen kamen Abertausende von Häftlingen dabei ums Leben. Der Rundgang schließt mit einer ausführlichen Darstellung der Nürnberger Prozesse, die im heutigen Saal 600 des Justizgebäudes an der Fürther Straße stattfanden.

Aufgrund seiner welthistorischen Bedeutung bieten die museen der stadt nürnberg seit dem Jahr 2000 Führungen im Saal 600 des Nürnberger Justizgebäudes an. Am Geburtsort des modernen Völkerstrafrechts, das letztlich zur Gründung des Internationalen Gerichtshofs in Den Haag führte, soll künftig das geplante „Memorium Nürnberger Prozesse" Besucher aus aller Welt empfangen und eine Brücke von der Vergangenheit in die Gegenwart schlagen.

congresses and documents the plans of the national socialists to absorb an entire folk into its party. The documentation centre analyses very consciously the showy side of the Third Reich, found to be attractive by many contemporaries, while at the same time making perfectly clear the criminal consequences which resulted from their politics. The focal point of the permanent exhibition is the Reich's party congresses themselves as well as the construction programme set into operation in Nuremberg by the national socialists.

The exhibition tour begins in the twenties when Nuremberg had already become a location for events of the NS movement as a result of the Reich's party congresses in 1927 and 1929. After 1933 all six Reich's party congresses of the Third Reich were held here, to which as many as one million people attended each time. A gigantic programme of building was introduced under the overall management of Albert Speer which included, amongst others, the erection of the "German Stadium" with a capacity of more than 400,000 spectators. Between 1934 and 1937, though, only the Zeppelin tribune and the Zeppelin field were completed. From 1940 onwards quarries in concentration camps delivered granite for the buildings under construction. While doing so, and because of the inhuman conditions, thousands upon thousands of prisoners forfeited their lives. The tour finishes with a detailed reproduction of the Nuremberg processes which took place in today's hall 600 of the court house on Fürth Street.

Because of its globally historical significance the museum of the city of nuremberg has organised guided tours in hall 600 of the Nuremberg court house since the year 2000. For the future, plans have been made for visitors to the "Nuremberg Processes Memorium" coming from all over the world to be received at the birthplace of modern international criminal law, which in the long run led to the foundation of the International Court of Justice in the Hague, forming a bridge between the past and the present.

Tourismus in der Metropolregion Nürnberg – vom Guten das Beste

Michael Weber

Die hohe Lebensqualität in der Metropolregion Nürnberg, begründet durch geschichtsträchtige Städte, erholsame Landschaften und Naturparks sowie ein reiches Kulturleben, ist die Basis für einen florierenden Fremdenverkehr. Dieser hat drei starke Säulen – Urlaubstourismus, Städtereisen, Kur- und Gesundheitswesen, gepaart mit einem renommierten Messe- und Kongressgeschehen – und zeichnet sich wie das übrige Wirtschaftsleben durch Exzellenz und hohe internationale Bedeutung aus. Das hat in Franken eine lange Tradition. Wobei die Metropolregion Nürnberg mit ihrem Kern sowie ihrem anschließenden Netz den größten Teil Frankens und partiell auch die Oberpfalz abdeckt.

Hatten einst die Romantiker solche Städte wie Nürnberg und Rothenburg ob der Tauber oder die Höhlen und Felsen der Fränkischen Schweiz als Seele des deutschen Gemüts entdeckt, so sind es inzwischen weit reisende Gäste aus Deutschland, Europa und Übersee, die als Urlauber, Kultur- und Bildungstouristen sowie Messe- und Kongressbesucher den Fremdenverkehr wachsen lassen und beispielsweise dafür sorgen, dass die Stadt Nürnberg mit ihren rund zwei Millionen Übernachtungen (Stand: 2005) zu den Top Ten im deutschen Städtetourismus zählt. So haben Wanderkongresse die jedes Jahr in einer anderen Stadt gastieren, in Nürnberg stets mehr Teilnehmer als anderswo. Hier ist, wie die Veranstalter bestätigen, der Rahmen ganz einfach attraktiver und bietet für Begleitprogramme viele Anregungen. Auch andere Städte im Umkreis ziehen mit ihren Kongresshallen internationales Publikum an, zum Beispiel Fürth, Erlangen, Bamberg, Hof und Würzburg.

Gleich zwei Weltkulturerbe bereichern den Kern der Region: der Limes bei Weißenburg und das Gesamtensemble der Domstadt Bamberg. Im so genannten Netz kommt noch die fürstbischöfliche Residenz in Würzburg hinzu. Außerdem besteht hier bundesweit die größte Dichte historischer Städte und

The basis for the flourishing tourist trade is the high quality of life in the metropolitan region of Nuremberg which is founded on historical towns, relaxing landscapes and nature parks, as well as a rich cultural life. Tourism has three strong pillars – holiday makers, city tours, cure and health regeneration paired with well-known trade fair and congress events – and is characterised by its excellence and international significance, as indeed is the remainder of commercial life. These factors have a long tradition in Franconia and the metropolitan region of Nuremberg with its core and its neighbouring network covers the largest part of Franconia and part of the Upper Palatinate.

Whereas it was once the romantics who discovered the heart of German sentiment in cities like Nuremberg and Rothenburg ob der Tauber or the caves and cliffs of the Franconian nature parks (Franconian Switzerland), it is in the meantime the far-travelled guests from Germany, Europe and overseas who encourage the growth of tourism as holiday-makers, cultural and educational tourists as well as visitors to trade fairs and congresses, allowing the city of Nuremberg with its approximately two million overnight guests (as at: 2005) to count as one of the top ten in German city tourism. It is a fact that wandering congresses making a guest appearance in a different city each year always have more participants when they are in Nuremberg than anywhere else. As the organisers can confirm, the framework is simply more attractive here and supplies more stimulus for accompanying programmes. Other cities in the area also draw an international public with their congress halls, for example Fürth, Erlangen, Bamberg, Hof and Würzburg.

Two world cultural heritages enrich the core of the region: the Limes (Roman wall) near Weißenburg and the entire ensemble of the cathedral town of Bamberg. Still to be mentioned in the so-called network is the princebishop's residence in Würzburg. The densest number of historical towns and cities in Germany must

Tourism in the Metropolitan Region of Nuremberg – the Best of the Best

Weltkulturerbe Bamberger Altstadt mit dem Bamberger Dom, dem Alten Rathaus und der Klosteranlage St. Michael im Hintergrund

The world cultural heritage of the Bamberg old city with the Bamberg cathedral, the old town hall and the cloisters of St. Michael in the background

Sehenswertes Naturdenkmal: Steinerner Beutel bei Burg Zwernitz im Landkreis Kulmbach

A natural monument well worth seeing: the Steinerner Beutel near the castle Zwernitz in the district of Kulmbach

Eine ideale Kombination von Entspannung und Aktivität bietet das 5-Sterne-Seminar- und Wellnesshotel Residenz Bad Windsheim. Der hoteleigene Wellness- und Fitnessbereich steht dem Gast kostenfrei zur Verfügung. Nur wenige Minuten vom Hotel entfernt gibt es ein in Europa einmaliges touristisches Highlight: die Franken-Therme. Ein ganzjährig auf 32 °C beheizter Salz-Sole-See bietet ein Badeerlebnis wie am Toten Meer. Das vielfach ausgezeichnete Hotel Residenz Bad Windsheim bietet eine erstklassige Küche mit fränkischen und internationalen Spezialitäten.

The 5-star Seminar and Wellness Hotel Residenz Bad Windsheim offers the ideal combination of relaxation and action. The wellness and fitness area owned by the hotel is at the guests' disposal, free of charge. The Franken-Therme, a touristic highlight unique in Europe, is only a few minutes from the hotel. Heated to 32 °C all the year round, the salt-brine-lake offers a bathing experience similar to that of the Dead Sea. The award-winning Hotel Residenz Bad Windsheim offers first-class cuisine with Franconian and international specialities.

Information

Zimmer: 116 mit 185 Betten; 4 Suiten
Tagungen: 14 Funktionsräume für Veranstaltungen bis 600 Personen
Gastronomie: Restaurants „Brücke" und „Charlize"; Café mit Terrasse; Wein- und Bierbar; Lobbybar

Rooms: 116 with 185 beds; 4 suites
Conferences: 14 function rooms for events of up to 600 people
Gastronomy: restaurants "Brücke" and "Charlize"; café with terrace; wine and beer bar; lobby bar

☐ Seminar- und Wellnesshotel Residenz Bad Windsheim

Städtchen. Dazu zählen in unmittelbarer Nürnberger Nachbarschaft Fürth, Erlangen und Schwabach sowie Hersbruck, Neumarkt, Amberg und Bayreuth, aber auch Ansbach, Feuchtwangen und Dinkelsbühl.

Sie alle liegen eingebettet in Landschaftsgebieten mit herrlicher, zum größten Teil als Parks geschützter Natur: Fränkische Schweiz, Fichtelgebirge, Frankenalb, Oberpfälzer Wald, Oberes Maintal-Coburger Land, Steigerwald, Fränkisches Weinland, Romantisches Franken, Fränkisches Seenland, Naturpark Altmühltal. Durch sie führen mehrere Themenstraßen wie die Burgenstraße, die Deutsche Spielzeugstraße und der Klassiker unter den deutschen Ferienrouten, die Romantische Straße, die bereits ein Gegenstück im fernen Japan gefunden hat.

Heilbäder und Kurorte stellen wertvolle Perlen in der Kette der Naturparks dar und sorgen für die Gesundheit von Bewohnern und Besuchern. Zwei sind es im Kern der Metroporegion, Bad Windsheim und Treuchtlingen; weitere sechs im Netz. Sich hier einzu-

also be added, amongst them, in Nuremberg's immediate proximity, are Fürth, Erlangen and Schwabach as well as Hersbruck, Neumarkt, Amberg and Bayreuth as well as Ansbach, Feuchtwangen and Dinkelsbühl.

They are all embedded in magnificent landscapes many of which are protected as parks: the Franconian Switzerland, Fichtel mountains, Frankenalb, Upper Palatinate Forest, Upper Main valley/Coburg land, Steiger Forest, Franconian Wineland, romantic Franconia, Franconian lake district, the Altmühltal nature park. They are criss-crossed with several theme routes such as the castle route, the German toy route and, the classic amongst the Germany holiday routes, the romantic route which already has its counterpart in far-off Japan.

Health resorts and spas are valuable pearls in the chain of nature parks, caring for the health of inhabitants and visitors alike. Two of them are in the core of the metropolitan region, Bad Windsheim and Treuchtlingen; a further six in the network. To book oneself in

Lebensqualität pur
The Pure Quality of Life

buchen, bedeutet willkommene Entspannung, Heilung und Prävention zugleich.

Es sind vor allem die herausragenden Dinge auf den Gebieten der Geschichte und der Kultur, die die Menschen als Touristen in die Metropolregion bringen. Dass die Hohenzollern von der Nürnberger Burg aus Preußen in Besitz genommen haben, ist da genauso interessant wie ihre Markgrafenresidenz in Ansbach oder ihre Grablege im nahen Münster von Heilsbronn. Der begnadete Architekt Balthasar Neumann hat in zahlreichen Orten seine Spuren hinterlassen wie auch der Bildhauer Tilman Riemenschneider, der mit naturgetreuer Menschendarstellung nicht nur in den Lindenholzaltären von Rothenburg und Detwang verewigt ist.

means welcome relaxation, healing and prevention all at once.

It is the particularly exceptional things in the areas of history and culture which bring people as tourists into the metropolitan region. The fact that the Hohenzollern took possession of Prussia from the Nuremberg castle is just as interesting as the Margrave residence in Ansbach or their graves in the nearby Heilsbronn Minster. The talented architect Balthasar Neumann left his traces in countless places as did the sculptor Tilman Riemenschneider, who with his lifelike statues, is immortalised not only in the limewood altars of Rothenburg and Detwang. Numerous castles in the Franconian Switzerland bear witness to the unbend-

Der Playmobil FunPark in Zirndorf ist eine Spieloase für Jung und Alt.

The Playmobil FunPark in Zirndorf is an oasis of amusement for young and old.

Die zahlreichen Burgen der Fränkischen Schweiz zeugen vom unbeugsamen Willen ihrer einstigen Besitzer, und der Stolz fleißiger Bürger und Kaufleute ist in den ehemals Freien Reichsstädten Nürnberg, Weißenburg, Schweinfurt, Bad Windsheim, Rothenburg und Dinkelsbühl heute noch spürbar. Bischöfe und Fürstbischöfe haben in und um Würzburg wie Bamberg Residenzen und Kirchen errichten lassen, die Weltrang genießen.

Nicht minder erwähnenswert ist die reich bestückte Museumsszene. Mit dem Germanischen Nationalmuseum in Nürnberg, dem Verkehrsmuseum mit DB-Museum und Museum für Kommunikation und dem

able wills of their former owners and the pride of diligent citizens and tradesmen can still be traced in the former free imperial cities of Nuremberg, Weißenburg, Schweinfurt, Bad Windsheim, Rothenburg and Dinkelsbühl. Bishops and princebishops had residences and churches erected in and around Würzburg and Bamberg which today enjoy world status.

No less worth mentioning is the richly equipped museum landscape. One or two of the most important ones are the Germanic National Museum in Nuremberg, the Transport Museum with DB-Museum (Federal Railways Museum) and Museum for Commu-

Dokumentationszentrum Reichsparteitagsgelände seien hier nur einige der wichtigsten genannt. Die städtischen Museen verstehen sich als „historische Theater", in denen Persönlichkeiten vergangener Jahrhunderte wieder lebendig werden, den Besucher an die Hand nehmen und unterhaltsam in ferne Zeiten entführen. Nicht weniger Interessantes auch in den anderen Städten: In Weißenburg etwa künden Römermuseum, Kastell und Thermen von römischer Geschichte in diesem Teil des Landes. In Bad Windsheim zeugt das Fränkische Freilandmuseum vom Leben vergangener Zeiten. Kulmbach beherbergt in seiner Plassenburg eine der größten Zinnfigurensammlungen, und im Schweinfurter Museum Georg Schäfer sind unter anderem so viele Spitzweg-Bilder zu besichtigen wie sonst nirgendwo.

Über die zahllosen Veranstaltungen musikalischer Art wird in einem anderen Beitrag ausführlich berichtet.

Wer das Sprechtheater der Musik vorzieht, der geht zu den Kreuzgangspielen nach Feuchtwangen, zu den Calderón-Freilichtspielen nach Bamberg, zu den Luisenburg-Festspielen in Wunsiedel oder ins Bergwaldtheater nach Weißenburg.

Weihnachten, so könnte man meinen, ist in der Metropolregion zu Hause. Nicht nur, dass der wohl berühmteste Weihnachtsmarkt Deutschlands, der Christkindlesmarkt, ein Nürnberger Markenartikel ist – er macht auch den Dezember zum übernachtungsstärksten Monat im Nürnberger Tourismusjahr. Zahlreich sind auch die adventlichen Veranstaltungen in den anderen Städten der Region: beispielsweise der Krippenweg in Bamberg, der größte Adventskalender Deutschlands in Forchheim, der Reiterlesmarkt in Rothenburg.

Auch der Spitzensport kann in der Metropolregion Nürnberg mit einer breiten Vielfalt aufwarten. Zwar gibt der 1. FCN durch schwankende Leistungen immer wieder Anlass zu Herzattacken seiner Anhänger, aber der Fußball hat in der Region eine große Tradition. Nürnberg ist Austragungsort für die Fußball-WM im Jahr 2006, die Deutsche Tourenwagenmeisterschaft zieht am Norisring über 100 000 Motorsportfans an, beim Internationalen Radkriterium rund um die Nürnberger Altstadt kämpft die Radsport-Elite beiderlei Geschlechts um den Sieg, während in Roth mit dem Quelle Challenge alljährlich ein Weltklasse-Triathlon stattfindet.

Und was wäre eine touristische Region ohne kulinarische Genüsse? So abwechslungsreich wie die Landschaften sind die Speisen. Zahlreiche Spitzen-

nication and the Documentation Centre Reichsparteitagsgelände. The municipal museums see themselves as "historic theatres", in which personalities of past centuries come to life once again, who take visitors by the hand and take them on entertaining journeys into the past. Of no less interest in other cities: In Weißenburg the Roman Museum, Fort and thermal baths bear witness to the Roman history in this part of the country. In Bad Windsheim the Franconian Open Air Museum testifies to life in past ages. Kulmbach accommodates one of the largest tin figure collections in the Plassenburg, and in the Schweinfurt Museum Georg Schäfer, amongst other things, there are more Spitzweg paintings to be seen than can be found anywhere else.

The numerous musical events held have been reported upon in detail in another contribution.

Whoever prefers speaking theatre to music, he should attend the cloister plays in Feuchtwangen, the Calderón-open-air theatre in Bamberg, the Luisenburg-Festival in Wunsiedel or the Bergwald theatre in Weißenburg.

One would assume that the metropolitan region is the home of Christmas. Not only because the most famous Christmas market in Germany, the Christkindlesmarkt is a trade mark of Nuremberg – it also makes December the strongest month for overnight stays in the Nuremberg tourism year. Many and varied are also the events in Advent in the other cities of the region: for example the Krippenweg in Bamberg, Germany's largest Advent calendar in Forchheim and the Reiterlesmarkt in Rothenburg.

The top sports offer a wide selection in the metropolitan region of Nuremberg too. Although it is true that the fluctuating performances of the 1. FCN occasionally give its fans reasons for heart attacks; football has a long tradition in the region. Nuremberg is one venue for the Football-WM in the year 2006, the German touring car championships attract more than 100,000 motor sport fans to the Norisring, in the International Radkriterium round the Nuremberg old city the cycling elite of both sexes fights for victory, while a world-class triathlon is held in Roth each year – the Quelle Challenge.

Just what would a touristic region be without culinary enjoyments? The food is as varied as the landscape. Numerous top chefs exert themselves to do justice to the claims of the metropolitan region: "Franken kulinarisch erleben." (Experience Franconia from a culinary angle). The same applies to Franconian

Lebensqualität pur
The Pure Quality of Life

Paddelvergnügen auf der Wiesent

Paddling fun on the Wiesent

Der Christkindlesmarkt in Nürnberg gilt als der berühmteste Weihnachtsmarkt der Welt.

The Christkindlesmarkt in Nuremberg is considered to be the most famous Christmas fair in the world.

köche strengen sich an, um dem Anspruch in der Metropolregion gerecht zu werden: „Franken kulinarisch erleben." Gleiches gilt für den fränkischen Wein, der zum Besten gehört, was unsere Keller und Weinfeste zu bieten haben.

Bleibt noch nachzutragen, dass Nürnberg den schönsten Landschaftszoo Europas (mit dem einzigen Delphinarium Süddeutschlands) hat und dort Städteurlaubern eine Mischung aus Erholung und Bildung offeriert. Große Erlebnisparks wie der Playmobil FunPark in Zirndorf, der Freizeitpark Schloss Thurn bei Forchheim, das Fränkische Wunderland in Plech und das Freizeit-Land Geiselwind runden das breite Spektrum für abwechslungsreiche Familienunterhaltung ab. Am besten, man überzeugt sich selbst von alledem; die Metropolregion heißt ihre Gäste jederzeit herzlich willkommen!

wine, some of the best, which our cellars and wine festivals have to offer.

It simply remains to say that Nuremberg has the most beautiful landscape zoo in Europe (with the only Delphinarium in Southern Germany) offering holidaymakers from the cities a mixture of relaxation and education. Major theme parks such as the Playmobil FunPark in Zirndorf, the Freizeitpark Schloss Thurn near Forchheim, the Franconian Wunderland in Plech and the Leisure-Land Geiselwind round off the wide range of varied family entertainments. The best would be to convince yourself; the metropolitan region gives its guests a hearty welcome at any time!

Zur Architektur-Geschichte Frankens

Dr. Oscar Schneider

Franken sei hier als historisch-geographischer Begriff verstanden. Deshalb kann es sich bei dieser skizzenhaften Darstellung nicht nur um den fränkischen Baustil – das hohe Giebeldach, die Fachwerkmauer, die Komposition der Dörfer und Städte, der Straßen und Plätze und das innere Ordnungsgefüge der Gesellschaft – handeln.

Die frühen fränkischen Baudenkmäler gehen auf die karolingische Zeit zurück. Es waren die Mönche des Heiligen Benedikt und der Zisterzienser, die in Franken vor der Renaissance, vor Barock und Rokoko Bauwerke schufen, die noch heute unsere Beachtung, das baugeschichtliche Interesse und auch unsere Bewunderung finden. Allem Fränkischen haftet eine gewisse Schlichtheit an, eine formale Strenge: Nach außen wie nach innen tritt das handwerklich Notwendige und Dauerhafte in Erscheinung.

Selbstverständlich finden sich in Franken Bauwerke der Weltarchitektur, große und großartige Beispiele der fürstlichen und kirchlichen Repräsentation und selbstbewusster Machtgewissheit. Der Bamberger Dom ist ein Zeugnis abendländischer Baukunst; französische Ursprungsdetails an ihm sind unverkennbar.

Die Würzburger Residenz, das Ansbacher Schloss, das Münster von Heilsbronn oder die Nürnberger gotischen Stadtkirchen gehören der europäischen Baukultur an, wie Franken selbst eine europäische Vergangenheit hat und eine ebenso europäische Zukunft haben wird.

Zur fränkischen Baukultur gehören Rothenburg und Dinkelsbühl, Prichsenstadt und Coburg, die Deutsche Ordensballei in Ellingen und gewiss auch Ansbach, Kulmbach und Bayreuth mit ihren zollerischen Residenzen. Überall verströmen Plätze und Straßenfluchten, winkelige Vertrautheit und versteckte Kostbarkeiten eine Atmosphäre bürgerlicher Geborgenheit und urbaner Kultur. Burgen überragen Städte, erheben sich über Flussläufe, bekrönen Bergkuppen, bezeugen Kriege und Brandschatzungen.

Es gibt eine fränkische Polyphonie des Schönen, eine vielstimmige Harmonie der Formen und Stile; es

On the Architectural History of Franconia

Franconia is to be understood here as a historical geographic term. Which is why this roughly sketched representation cannot only cover the Franconian architectural style – the high gable roof, the half-timbered building, the composition of the towns and villages, the streets and places and the internal structures of society.

The early Franconian architectural monuments go back to Carolingian times. It was the monks of Saint Benedict and the Cistercians who created buildings in Franconia before the Renaissance, before the Baroque and Rococo, which still today attract our attention and even the admiration of those interested in the history of buildings. Certain simplicity is attached to all that is Franconian, a formal severity: From the outside as well as on the inside, the essentials and permanence of handwork make their appearance.

Naturally Franconia has buildings of world-class architecture, large and magnificent examples of princely and ecclesiastical representation and the self-confident certainty of their power. The cathedral in Bamberg is a testimonial to occidental architecture; the French details of origin are unmistakable.

The Würzburg Residence, the Ansbach Castle, the Minster of Heilsbronn and the Nuremberg gothic town churches belong to European architectural culture, just as Franconia itself has a European past and will have an equally European future.

Rothenburg und Dinkelsbühl, Prichsenstadt and Coburg, the seat of the Commanders of the Teutonic Order in Ellingen and certainly the Zollern residences of Ansbach, Kulmbach and Bayreuth belong to Franconian architectural culture. Everywhere squares and street lines, twisty familiarity full of nooks and crannies and hidden treasures, radiate an atmosphere of bourgeois security and urban culture. Castle buildings loom over towns, elevate themselves above river courses, crown mountain tops and give evidence of wars, sackings and pillaging.

There is a Franconian polyphony of the beautiful, a harmony of many voices of shapes and styles; but there

gibt auch den Kontrapunkt der Zeiten und Geschichte, worin sich die politischen Machtverhältnisse eingeprägt haben, wo geistige Gegensätze sichtbar werden.

In der karolingischen Renaissance erstrebte man die Renovatio Imperii, die Erneuerung des Römischen Reiches. Die Macht des Kaisers wurde durch die Krönung durch den Papst ins Sakrale erhoben, aufgehoben in den Sinnzusammenhang der Erlösungstheologie. Den Formen der kirchlichen Bauten sind religiöse Bedeutungen immanent: Der römische Bogen, die Kuppel des Pantheon, die Säulen auf den Foren dienten den monastischen Baumeistern zum Vorbild. Von Fulda aus nahm die Missionierung Frankens ihren wirkungsvollen Ausgang. Mit den Missionaren kamen Handwerker und Bauleute ins Land. So auch die Kunstfertigkeit, Kirchen auf Krypten zu errichten, wie dies am Basilikabau in Solnhofen in Erscheinung tritt.

Die Rundkapelle in Nürnberg-Altenfurt stammt aus der zweiten Hälfte des 12. Jahrhunderts. Beispiele von frühen romanisch-karolingischen Architekturen und Bildhauereien finden sich in Heidenheim, Forchheim und in den meisten fränkischen Klöstern aus dieser Zeit. Der Dom zu Eichstätt, der dem fränkischen Kulturkreis angehört, ist ein Denkmal vieler Baustile.

Als man begann, die Dampfkraft in den Lokomotiven der Eisenbahnen zu nutzen, entstanden die ersten Bahnhöfe und Eisenbahnbrücken in Nürnberg und in Franken. Die Architektur der Zweckmäßigkeit und rationalen Ästhetik veränderte das vielfach noch mittelalterliche, biedermeierliche Bild unserer Städte.

Hat man dem München im 19. Jahrhundert ein griechisch-römisches Antlitz verliehen, blieb man in Franken deutsch, altdeutsch – eben fränkisch. Es gibt keine fränkische Monotonie im Erscheinungsbild unserer Städte, keine uniforme Stileinheit: Die Vielfalt findet im Ensemble ihre Einheit und das Neue nimmt Maß an der Tradition. Man vermeidet den Bruch mit der Vergangenheit, ohne sich durch die Geschichte der Freiheit der neuen Formen und Wagnisse berauben zu lassen. In allen Baustilen, von der Romanik bis zur funktionalen Rationalität der Glas- und Stahlarchitektur der Gegenwart, befinden sich Beispiele hoher Vollendung und missratener Kühnheit in fränkischen Städten und Dörfern.

Der erste deutsche Bahnhof wurde auf dem Nürnberger Plärrer in gotischem Hallenstil erbaut. Im 19. Jahrhundert huldigte man bei den Bahnhofsbauten und Amtsgebäuden häufig dem gotischen Historismus. Doch zu Beginn des 20. Jahrhunderts baute man ganz modern: Der Jugendstil hat in Nürnbergs Archi-

is also a counterpart to time and history, where political balance of powers have left their mark and where spiritual opposites become visible.

In the Carolingian Renaissance the striving was towards the Renovatio Imperii, the renewal of the Roman Empire. The emperor's power was elevated through crowning by the Pope into a sacred act, elevated to being a link in the sense of the theory of redemption. Religious significance is immanent in the forms of ecclesiastical buildings: roman arches, the cupola of the Pantheon, the columns on the Forum served the monastic architects as models. The missionary work in Franconia began its effective work in Fulda. Craftsmen and builders travelled with the missionaries into the area bringing with them the skill to build churches on top of crypts as can be seen in the Basilica in Solnhofen.

The round chapel in Nuremberg-Altenfurt originates from the second half of the 12th century. Examples of early Roman-Carolingian architecture and statues can be found in Heidenheim, Forchheim and in most of the Franconian cloisters originating from these times. The Cathedral at Eichstätt, which belongs to the Franconian cultural circle, is a monument with many architectural styles.

The first railway stations and railway bridges were created in Nuremberg and in Franconia as people began to use the steam power generated in railway locomotives. The architecture of suitability and rational aesthetic changed the picture of our towns, in many cases still medieval or Biedermeier.

While Munich had been given a Greek-Roman countenance in the 19th century, Franconia remained German, traditional German – in other words Franconian. There is however, no Franconian monotony in the appearance of our towns and cities, no uniform unity of style: the variety finds its ensemble in its unity and that which is new is measured by tradition. One avoids breaking with the past, without letting history rob us of the freedom of new forms and risks. In all architectural styles, from the Romanesque through to the functional rationality of the glass and steel architecture of the present, examples of high perfection and audacity gone wrong can be found in Franconian towns and villages.

The first German railway station was built on the Nuremberg Plärrer in gothic hall style. In the 19th century gothic historism was often indulged in when constructing railway and other official buildings. But at the beginning of the 20th century buildings became quite

Lebensqualität pur
The Pure Quality of Life

Die Altstadt von Dinkelsbühl mit ihren schmucken Fachwerkhäusern ist eng mit dem Begriff der Romantik verknüpft.

The old city of Dinkelsbühl with its decorative half-timbered houses is closely linked with the term of romanticism.

tektur viele gelungene und denkmalpflegerisch geschützte Hausfronten hinterlassen. Das Künstlerhaus am Königstor ist eine polyphone Mischung von barocken Anklängen; dagegen trug der Hauptbahnhof eine Kuppel und noch heute in freier Stilisierung eine Renaissancefassade.

Den Wohnungsbau vor und nach dem Ersten Weltkrieg beherrschte die Gartenstadtidee, in der sozialer Wohnungsbau und Eigentumsbildung gefördert wurden.

Im Nürnberger Stadion wurden die Erkenntnisse der modernen Sportstättenbauten berücksichtigt. Die Ehrenhalle im Luitpoldhain beeindruckt durch ihre klassische Strenge und die römische Proportion der Arkaden.

Die Reichsparteitagsbauten am Dutzendteich haben als politische Architektur der NS-Zeit mit der fränkischen Bauarchitekturgeschichte nichts zu tun. Dem Stile nach handelt es sich um späthellenistische und römische Adaptionen. Die Säulentribüne auf dem Zeppelinfeld ist dem Zeus-Altar von Pergamon nachempfunden; der Kongressbau, in dem heute das Dokumentationszentrum Reichsparteitagsgelände untergebracht ist, hat das römische Colosseum der flavischen Imperatoren zum Vorbild.

Am Nürnberger Plärrer wurde anfangs der fünfziger Jahre das erste Hochhaus in Bayern errichtet. Im Stadtteil Langwasser, wo nach Speers Planung das Märzfeld für das Reichsparteitagsgelände errichtet werden sollte, entstand die Trabantenstadt Langwasser. Auf ähnlich triste Weise hat man in ganz Deutschland und Europa versucht, Wohnungsbau und Städtebau zu verbinden. ☐

modern: Art Nouveau has left many successful and listed house fronts in Nuremberg's architecture. The artists' house on the Königstor is a polyphone mixture of Baroque similarities; in contrast the main railway station carried a cupola and still today a Renaissance facade in free stylisation.

The idea of a garden city predominated the building of houses before and after the First World War when the building of council houses and the creation of ownership was promoted.

In the Nuremberg stadium the knowledge of building modern sports centres was taken into consideration. The Ehrenhalle in Luitpoldhain is impressive in its classic severity and the Roman proportions of the arcades.

As political architecture of the NS period the Reichsparteitag buildings on the Dutzendteich have nothing to do with Franconian architectural history. From the style it would appear to be about late Hellenistic and Roman adaptation. The column tribune on the Zeppelin field are adapted from the Zeus altar of Pergamon; the congress building, which today accommodates the documentation centre Reichsparteitagsgelände, had the Roman Coliseum of the Flavian emperors as model.

At the beginning of the fifties, the first high-rise building in Bavaria was built on the Nuremberg Plärrer. The satellite town of Langwasser was built in the Langwasser district where, according to Speer's planning, the Märzfeld should be used for erecting the Reichsparteitagsgelände. Attempts had been made all over Germany and Europe to combine house building with urban development in an equally dismal manner. ☐

Lebensqualität pur
The Pure Quality of Life

Die Würzburger Residenz zählt zu den bedeutendsten Bauwerken des Barock und wird in einem Atemzug mit Versailles, Paris und Schönbrunn bei Wien genannt.

The Würzburg Residence is one of the most important buildings of the Baroque period and is mentioned in the same breath as Versailles, Paris and Schönbrunn near Vienna.

Vielfalt ist Trumpf – Hotellerie und Gastronomie

Werner Behringer

Klima, Lage und Topographie, gewachsene Traditionen und regionale Besonderheiten der Metropolregion Nürnberg im Herzen Frankens sind die Grundlage für unterschiedliche kulinarische Akzente. Fränkische Produkte genießen dabei vielfach Weltruhm. Spitzenköche, Top-Sommeliers und ausgezeichnete Restaurants und Hotels bringen marktfrische Gerichte aus der Region zu Tisch. Sie bestimmen die gastronomische Landschaft Frankens.

Aktuelle Umfragen zu den Assoziationen von Gästen zu kulinarischen Spezialitäten aus der Metropolregion Nürnberg belegen weiter, dass Essen und Trinken zu den schönsten Erlebnissen einer Frankenreise gehören und nahezu jeder zweite Deutsche Franken mit Frankenwein und Weinlandschaften in Verbindung bringt. Genuss ohne lange Anfahrtswege, verbunden mit einem Kulturprogramm, dafür ist die Metropolregion Nürnberg die richtige Destination, kurzum, sie ist Ausdruck fränkischer Lebensqualität!

Das Land der Metropolregion Nürnberg ist weithin als Weinfranken und Bierfranken bekannt und geschätzt. Unsere weitgehend unberührten Naturlandschaften sind besonders gesegnet mit fruchtbarem Boden, mit glasklarem Quellwasser, mit sonnigen Rebhängen, duftenden Wiesen und dichten Wäldern. Dort reifen erstklassige Zutaten, die unsere Köche, Winzer und Bierbrauer ganz frisch verarbeiten können. Original regional auf den Tisch unserer Gäste: Das knusprig gebratene Schweineschäufele, die auf aromatischem Buchenholzfeuer gegrillte Nürnberger Rostbratwurst (fingerklein und exakt 25 g schwer), die „Königin" der Würste, der zarte Aischgründer Karpfen, der raffiniert gewürzte Junglammrücken, das mit Rosmarin geschmorte Zicklein, die goldgelb gebackenen Fische, die fangfrischen Flusskrebse und vieles mehr. Zubereitet von Köchen mit Tradition und Leidenschaft. Köchen aus der Region, die sich voll mit dieser identifizieren. An jeder Ecke, auf jedem Platz trifft man auf fränkische Würste, und überall werden sie verschie-

Climate, location and topography, mature traditions and regional specialities of the metropolitan region of Nuremberg in the heart of Franconia are the foundation for different culinary accents. At the same time Franconian products enjoy worldwide fame. Top chefs, top sommeliers and excellent restaurants and hotels bring garden-fresh meals from the region to the table. They set the tone of Franconia's gastronomic landscape.

Current surveys on how guests associate culinary specialities from the metropolitan region of Nuremberg prove that eating and drinking belong to the most exciting experiences of a journey through Franconia and almost every second German connects Franconia with Franconian wine and wine landscapes. Enjoyment without needing to go far, combined with a cultural programme, then the metropolitan region of Nuremberg is the correct destination, in short it expresses Franconian quality of life!

The countryside of the metropolitan region of Nuremberg is widely known and appreciated as Weinfranken (wine-Franconia) and Bierfranken (beer-Franconia). Our almost untouched natural landscapes are particularly blessed with fertile earth, with crystal clear well water, with sunny vine slopes, sweet smelling meadows and dense forests. This is where the top-class ingredients mature which our chefs, vintners and brewers can process direct from the field. Originally regional to the plates of our guests: crispy roast blade of pork, Nuremberg sausages grilled on aromatic beech wood fires (as small as a finger and weighing exactly 25 g) the "Queen" of sausages, the tender Aischgründer carp, the cleverly seasoned rack of young lamb, kid braised in rosemary, golden baked fish, freshly-caught river crayfish and much more. Prepared by chefs with tradition and passion. Chefs from the region, who fully identify with it. At every corner, on every market square one can buy Franconian sausages and they are all prepared differently. Franconia is the world's sausage heaven.

Variety is Trump – The Hotel and Catering Trades

Lebensqualität pur
The Pure Quality of Life

Die auf Buchenholz gegrillte Nürnberger Rostbratwurst wird oft im traditionellen Zinnherzen serviert.

The roast sausages grilled over beech wood are often served in traditional tin hearts.

Stilvolle, traditionsreiche Eleganz vereint mit moderner Ausstattung: Im Le Méridien Grand Hotel Nürnberg erwartet den Gast ein einzigartiges Ambiente.
Marmorbäder, Klimaanlage und viele Annehmlichkeiten mehr bieten in den 186, im Jugendstil möblierten Zimmern und Suiten den Komfort zum Wohlfühlen.
Der besondere Charme und Esprit des Art Déco-Stils sowie raffinierte Cocktail-Kreationen und leichte Snacks in der Atelier-Bar laden zum Entspannen und Genießen ein. Spezialitäten der lokalen und internationalen Küche werden in der Brasserie serviert.
Ob Bankett, Meeting oder Konferenz – der außergewöhnliche Tagungsbereich für 20 bis 250 Personen bietet zeitgemäße Technik und professionellen Service. Besonders beeindruckend ist der historische Ballsaal, dekoriert mit Motiven aus Richard-Wagner-Opern.
Das Le Méridien Grand Hotel Nürnberg liegt am Rande der Altstadt. Alle wichtigen Museen, Sehenswürdigkeiten und Einkaufsstraßen sind bequem zu Fuß zu erreichen. Hauptbahnhof und U-Bahn in Richtung Flughafen und Messe sind ebenfalls nur wenige Schritte entfernt.

Stylish, traditional elegance combined with modern appointments: In the Le Méridien Grand Hotel Nürnberg a unique ambience awaits the guest.
The marble baths, air-conditioning in most rooms and the many other conveniences in the 186 rooms and suites, furnished in Art Nouveau style, offer comfort which gives a sense of well being.
The special charm and esprit of the Art Deco style as well as the ingenious cocktail creations and light snacks offered in the Atelier Bar invite one to relax and enjoy. Specialities from the local and international cuisine are served in the Brasserie.
Whether banquets, meetings or conferences – the unusual conference area which can cater for between 20 and 250 people offers up-to-date technology and professional service. Particularly impressive is the historic ballroom decorated with motives from Richard Wagner operas.
The Le Méridien Grand Hotel Nürnberg is situated on the edge of the old city. All the important museums, sights and shops can be easily reached on foot. The main railway station and underground for the airport and trade fair area are also just a few steps away.

Information

Gründungsjahr: 1895

Zimmer:
186 Zimmer und Suiten in gehobener und exklusiver Ausstattung

Angebotsspektrum:
– Business Center
– sieben individuell gestaltete Tagungsräume
– Restaurant Brasserie
– Atelier-Bar
– Sauna
– Fitnesscenter

Year founded: 1895

Rooms:
186 rooms and suites are furnished in a fined and exclusive manner

Services offered:
– business centre
– seven individually designed conference rooms
– Brasserie restaurant
– Atelier bar
– sauna
– fitness centre (gym)

Le Méridien Grand Hotel Nürnberg

Lebensqualität pur
The Pure Quality of Life

Zu einer kulinarischen Entdeckungsreise durch die Region gehört selbstverständlich auch die Haute Cuisine.

Naturally Haute Cuisine is part of a culinary journey of discovery through the region.

denartig zubereitet. Franken ist der Wursthimmel der Welt.

Im Glas ein spritziger, trockener Riesling von den sonnigen Rebhängen am Main oder der Bad Windsheimer Bucht, oder ein sattgoldenes Bier mit feinem Schaum aus der Region mit der größten Brauereidichte der Welt.

Und dann die süße Versuchung: die Lebkuchen mit ihren exotischen Gewürzen aus 1001 Nacht, die Pralinen mit ihrem zartbitteren, schokoladigen Schmelz, die knusprigen Schneeballen mit einem Hauch von feinstem Puderzucker und die sommerfrischen Hefekuchen mit ihrem fruchtigen Belag frisch aus dem Obstgarten. All dies genießt der Gast in einer Region, wo herzliche Gastfreundschaft, gutes Essen und Trinken und eine ruhige Übernachtung Lebensphilosophie sind.

Die kulinarischen Traditionen sind in Franken eher rustikal, geprägt durch eine klösterliche und bäuerliche Welt, in der nahrhafte Verpflegung für hart arbeitende

In the glass a lively dry Riesling from the sunny sloping vineyards on the river Main or the Bad Windsheim bay, or a deep-golden beer with a fine foam from the region with the biggest brewery density in the world.

And then the sweet temptation: gingerbread with its exotic spices from Aladdin's realm, chocolates with plain dark chocolate glaze, crispy snowballs with a breath of the finest icing sugar and summer-fresh yeast cakes with fruity coverings fresh from the orchard. All this can be enjoyed by the guest in a region where hearty hospitality, a good meal and drink and a quiet, comfortable bed are part of their philosophy of life.

The culinary traditions in Franconia are rather rustic, monastic and farming worlds have left their mark in which nourishing food and drink was needed for hard-working people. But in the metropolitan region of Nuremberg today gourmets also get their money's worth. This is not least an expression of the structural changes which have taken place over the last decades. Franconia can offer excellent multi-star restaurants in homely surroundings just as much as it can serve uncomplicated, hearty food.

Since the eighties a trend in Franconia's culinary landscape has become particularly noticeable. The gastronomically highly-qualified younger generation is making small places of pilgrimage for gourmets out of old-established, middle-class country pubs at moderate

Sonnige Rebhänge machen den Fränkischen Wein zu einem ganz besonderen Tropfen.

Sun-filled vineyards make the Franconian wine a very special one.

Menschen gefragt war. Aber in der Metropolregion Nürnberg kommen heute auch Gourmets voll auf ihre Kosten. Dieses ist nicht zuletzt Ausdruck eines Strukturwandels in den letzten Jahrzehnten. Mit hervorragenden Sternerestaurants in heimeliger Umgebung kann Franken genauso aufwarten wie mit bodenständiger, deftiger Kost.

Seit den achtziger Jahren wird ein Trend in der kulinarischen Landschaft Frankens besonders deutlich. Aus alteingesessenen, gutbürgerlichen Landgasthöfen macht die gastronomisch hoch qualifizierte jüngere Generation kleine Gourmettempel zu moderaten Preisen. Neben der „Haute Cuisine" verleugnen sie aber nicht ihre Herkunft und bieten auch heimische Spezialitäten an. Die Gastronomieszene hat sich in den letzten Jahrzehnten radikal verändert: von der Eckkneipe zur Trendgastronomie für das Szenepublikum.

Auch in der Hotellerie kann die Metropolregion alle Sparten anbieten. Vom 5-Sterne-Hotel bis zur Pension ist für jeden Geschmack und Geldbeutel etwas dabei. Designer- und Wellness-Hotels liegen voll im Trend der Zeit und bieten auch den Geschäftsreisenden Entspannung und Erholung. Wenn auch in der Hotellandschaft der Metropolregion Nürnberg der Geschäftsreise- und Städtetourismus überwiegt, so nimmt der private Tourismus im Ferienland Franken erfreulich zu. Beispielgebend sei hier der Playmobil FunPark in Zirndorf genannt, aber auch die vielen kulturellen Sehenswürdigkeiten wie das Weltkulturerbe Limes bei Weißenburg und das Gesamtensemble der Domstadt Bamberg.

Insbesondere in Nürnberg, Fürth und Erlangen sind Ketten- und Großhotels internationaler Herkunft entstanden. Es gibt fast keine Hotelkette, die nicht in der Region ansässig ist. Die herausragende Messestadt Nürnberg steht im harten Konkurrenzkampf mit anderen großen Standorten in Europa. Dadurch entstanden in den letzten 20 Jahren weitere Großhotels mit einer Gesamtkapazität von etwa 13 000 Betten in Nürnberg selbst und 20 000 Betten im unmittelbaren Einzugsbereich.

prices. They are not denying their origins and their menus also offer local specialities as well as "Haute Cuisine" dishes. The gastronomic scene has changed radically in the last decades: from the pub on the corner to trendy gastronomy for scenesters.

The metropolitan region offers visitors all the branches of hotel business. Whether a 5-star hotel or "bed and breakfast", there is something to suit everyone and his budget. Designe and wellness hotels are fully in trend at the moment and even provide relaxation and recuperation for business people. Even if business trips and city tourism predominate in the metropolitan region of Nuremberg's hotel trade, private tourism in the holiday country of Franconia is happily on the increase. One good example is the Playmobil FunPark in Zirndorf but there are also many other cultural sights such as the Limes, a world cultural heritage near Weißenburg and the entire ensemble of the cathedral town of Bamberg.

Chain and mass hotels of international origin have been erected, particularly in Nuremberg, Fürth and Erlangen and in fact there is hardly a hotel chain that is not represented in the region. As one would expect, the popular trade fair city of Nuremberg is in keen competition with other business locations all over Europe. This has resulted in many other major hotels being built over the last 20 years with a total capacity of 13,000 beds in Nuremberg alone and a further 20,000 in its immediate catchment area.

Lebensqualität pur
The Pure Quality of Life

Events und Veranstaltungen mit Format

Hartwig Reimann

Die Metropolregion Nürnberg – eine Region, in der immer was los ist. Für jeden Geschmack hat der Wirtschaftsraum etwas zu bieten und lockt jedes Jahr viele Reisende in das Herz Europas. Es gibt viele Gründe, warum die Metropolregion so stark besucht wird. Einer davon sind die zahlreichen Events und Veranstaltungen, die die Kulturlandschaft dieser Region prägen. Die Bandbreite reicht vom klassischen Theater, über ausgezeichnete Festivals und Großveranstaltungen bis hin zu Spitzen- und Breitensport. Dieses breit gefächerte Angebot bedeutet eine hohe Lebensqualität der weltoffenen Metropole, die ihr bereits in zahlreichen europa- und weltweiten Umfragen bestätigt wurde. Vor allem das harmonierende Nebeneinander von Tradition und Moderne prägen ihr Bild und begründen die Beliebtheit dieser Region.

Zu den renommiertesten Festivals in Nürnberg gehört die Internationale Orgelwoche. Die Nürnberger Musica Sacra ist das größte und älteste Ereignis für geistliche Musik und ein Höhepunkt im europäischen Kulturkalender. Das Bardentreffen gilt auch international als eines der größten Festivals für Weltmusik. Im Rahmen des kostenlosen und multikulturellen Fests treffen sich hier Liedermacher aus aller Welt. Dabei ist das Publikum so bunt wie die Schar der Musiker. Bis zu 200 000 Menschen ziehen alljährlich in die Nürnberger Innenstadt.

Zwei hervorragende Orchester, Tausende von Besuchern, Picknick im Park – das ist das Nürnberger Klassik Open-Air: ein Musikerlebnis der besonderen Art. Die Nürnberger Philharmoniker und die Nürnberger Symphoniker laden jedes Jahr zu Europas größten sommerlichen Konzerten unter freiem Himmel im Luitpoldhain ein.

So richtig glamourös geht es zu, wenn sich die Prominenz jedes Jahr im Herbst zum Nürnberger Opernball ein Stelldichein gibt. In der herrlichen Kulisse der Nürnberger Staatsoper feiern rund 3000 Gäste eine rauschende Ballnacht. International am bekanntesten sind die Wagner-Festspiele in Bayreuth. Für eine Eintrittskarte lässt ein Opernfan alles stehen

The metropolitan region of Nuremberg – a region in which something is always going on. The economic area has something to offer to suit all tastes and attracts many visitors to the heart of Europe each year. There are many reasons why the metropolitan region is so well visited. One of them is the countless number of events so characteristic of this region. They range from classical theatre over extremely well-organised festivals and major events through to top and popular sports. This wide selection signifies a high quality of life in the cosmopolitan metropolis as countless European and global surveys have confirmed. But it is primarily the harmonious juxtaposition of tradition and modern that leaves its mark and provides the foundation for the region's popularity.

The International Organ Week is one of the best known festivals in Nuremberg. The Nuremberg Musica Sacra is the largest and oldest event for religious music and is a highlight in the European culture calendar. The Bardentreffen also counts internationally as one of the largest festivals for world music. Within the framework of the entrance-free and multicultural festival, songmakers from all over the world meet here performing for an audience that is as colourful as the horde of musicians taking part. Up to 200,000 people drift every year into Nuremberg's inner city.

Two outstanding orchestras, thousands of visitors, Picnic in the Park – that is the Nuremberg classic open-air: a musical adventure of the special sort. The Nuremberg Philharmonic and the Nuremberg Symphonic Orchestra extend invitations each year to some of Europe's largest open air summer concerts in the Luitpoldhain.

It is really glamorous when prominent figures get together each year in autumn for the Nuremberg Opera Ball. In the gorgeous surroundings of the Nuremberg State Opera House some 3,000 guests celebrate a sumptuous ball. Best known internationally are the Wagner-Festival productions in Bayreuth and an opera fan will drop everything for an admission ticket: It takes seven years on average – politicians and prominent

Events of Stature

und liegen: Sieben Jahre dauert es im Durchschnitt – Politiker und Prominente ausgenommen – bis man an eine der begehrten Karten kommt.

Christoph Willibald Gluck war vor Wolfgang Amadeus Mozart der wichtigste Opernkomponist der zweiten Hälfte des 18. Jahrhunderts. Im Jahr 2005 widmete das Staatstheater Nürnberg dem Komponisten zum ersten Mal ein eigenes Festival. Um ihn zu würdigen und sein Andenken als Sohn der Region zu pflegen, sollen in Zukunft die „Internationalen Gluck-Festspiele" als Triennale im Dreijahresrhythmus stattfinden.

Rock im Park ist für alle Jungen und Junggebliebenen und natürlich für jeden Rockfan ein Muss.

Europas größtes Klassikkonzert findet alljährlich unter freiem Himmel im Luitpoldhain statt.

Europe's largest classical concert is held every year in the open air in Luitpoldhain.

people excepted – until one can get hold of one of the much sought after tickets.

Christoph Willibald Gluck was the most important composer of operas in the 18th century prior to Wolfgang Amadeus Mozart. In the year 2005 the State Theatre Nuremberg dedicated for the first time his own festival to the composer. In order to acknowledge him and to maintain his memory as a son of the region, the "International Gluck-Festival production" is to take

Vielfalt ist dabei Trumpf, so dass immer Pfingsten ein buntes Treiben rund um das Frankenstadion herrscht.

Aber nicht nur die Metropole Nürnberg, sondern auch alle anderen Städte und Landkreise der Metropolregion warten mit Veranstaltungen der Spitzenklasse auf. So verwandelt sich alle zwei Jahre Ansbach in den internationalen Treffpunkt für Freunde der Musik von Johann Sebastian Bach.

Nachdem Kaspar Hauser 1828 in Nürnberg auftauchte und binnen kürzester Zeit Berühmtheit erlangte, siedelte er 1831 nach Ansbach, wo er zwei Jahre später einem ungeklärten Mord zum Opfer fiel. Seit 1998 stellt sich die Stadt Ansbach alle zwei Jahre mit den Kaspar-Hauser-Festspielen der Aufgabe, durch eine umfangreiche Auswahl früherer und neuer Arbeiten das Einzigartige am Phänomen Kaspar Hauser verständlich zu machen.

Ebenfalls im zweijährigen Turnus trifft sich die jiddische Musik in Fürth auf dem internationalen Klezmer-Festival. In der Goldschlägerstadt Schwabach hat sich die Biennale „Ortung – Kunst im Zeichen des Goldes" auch durch ihre ungewöhnlichen Präsentationsorte rasch internationale Beachtung erworben. Ein wahrer Senkrechtstarter in der Jazz-Szene ist das „New Orleans Music-Festival" in Wendelstein. Die Veranstaltung zieht jährlich über 20 000 Fans an und beeindruckt mit umjubelten Straßenparaden.

Erlangen beherbergt ebenfalls drei kulturelle

Die Goldschlägerstadt Schwabach hat einen festen Platz auf der kulturellen Landkarte der Metropolregion.

The gold beater city of Schwabach has a firm place on the cultural map of the metropolitan region.

place in the future as a tri-annual in a three-year rhythm.

Rock in the Park is a must for all juveniles, those who have remained young at heart and naturally for each and every rock fan. Variety is the trump card so that every Whitsun a colourful hustle and bustle holds sway in and around the Frankenstadion.

Not only the metropolis of Nuremberg organises top-class events but also all other cities and districts in the metropolitan region. Every second year for example, Ansbach changes into an international meeting place for friends of Johann Sebastian Bach's music.

In 1828 Kaspar Hauser appeared in Nuremberg achieving fame within a very short time and in 1831 he settled in Ansbach, where he became the victim of an unsolved murder two years later. Every second year since 1998 the city of Ansbach takes on the task of making clear the uniqueness of the phenomena of Kaspar Hauser by organising the Kaspar-Hauser-Festival programme with a wide range of earlier and later works.

In a similar two-year cycle, the Yiddish Music in Fürth meets at the international Klezmer-Festival. The

Höhepunkte mit internationalem Format. Deutschlands schönstes Literaturfest ist dort zu Hause. Als Spiegel der Literaturszene, Forum für neue Trends und Podium für Neu- und Wiederentdeckungen ist das Poetenfest ein Leckerbissen für Profis und Liebhaber zeitgenössischer Literatur.

Beim Internationalen Figurentheater-Festival werden die Grenzen zwischen Figurentheater, Schauspiel, bildender Kunst und neuen Medien fließend. Das Erlanger Figurentheater-Festival hat sich zu einem der wichtigsten Termine des „anderen Theaters" entwickelt und ist das größte Festival seiner Art. Erlangen ist zudem Austragungsort des Internationalen Comic-Salons. Der Comic-Salon vereint eine große Fachmesse und ein breites Veranstaltungsprogramm. Alle zwei Jahre trifft sich hier, was in der Comic-Szene Rang und Namen hat.

Von Ende Juni bis Ende Juli steht in Bamberg in der alten Hofhaltung neben dem Dom eine große Tribüne. Dann wird der malerisch mittelalterliche Innenhof des historischen Gebäudes zur Kulisse für die Calderón-Festspiele. Das Ensemble des E.T.A.-Hoffmann-Theaters gibt Aufführungen unter freiem Himmel – mit einem ganz besonderen Flair.

Aber nicht nur im Musik- und Kulturbereich hat die Region viel zu bieten. Die Metropolregion ist auch das Zuhause von Spitzensport-Events. Jedes Jahr versammeln sich 100 000 Menschen zum „Speedweekend", um die Elite der Tourenwagen- und Formel-3-Piloten mitten in Nürnberg zu bewundern. Beim Quelle Challenge, Fränkische Schweiz- oder Brombachsee-Marathon können sich die Teilnehmer im Leistungssport messen. Ob im Rother Ultra-Triathlon oder anderen Veranstaltungen: Die Teilnehmer werden von tausenden Zuschauern bejubelt und zu Höchstleistungen angetrieben. Besonders stolz ist die Metropolregion, Austragungsort der Fußball-Weltmeisterschaft 2006 zu sein. Über 45 000 Fans dürfen sich auf fulminante Fußballereignisse im eigens umgebauten Frankenstadion freuen.

All die genannten Events sind aber nur die Spitze des Eisberges. Die Metropolregion Nürnberg bietet noch viel mehr Veranstaltungen und Programme mit Format, die (fast) keine Wünsche mehr offen lassen. Dafür wird sie sowohl von ihren Gästen als auch den Menschen, die dort leben, geschätzt und geliebt.

Rock im Park ist mit Rock am Ring (Eifel) das dienstälteste und größte Festival Deutschlands. Der Ring hat jährlich 70 000 Besucher, Rock im Park hat rund 50 000 Fans.

Lebensqualität pur
The Pure Quality of Life

biennial "Ortung – Kunst im Zeichen des Goldes" has quickly found international acclaim through its unusual presentation locations in the gold-beaters' city of Schwabach. A real whiz kid of the jazz scene is the "New Orleans Music-Festival" in Wendelstein. This event annually draws more than 20,000 fans and its well-cheered street parades leave an indelible impression.

Erlangen also accommodates three cultural highlights with international flair. The most beautiful of Germany's literature festivals is here at home. As a mirror of the literature scene, a forum for new trends and a podium for new and re-discoveries, the poets' festival is a delicacy for professionals and lovers of contemporary literature.

At the international figure theatre festival the boundaries between figure theatre, drama, the fine arts and new media are fluid. The Erlangen Figure Theatre Festival has developed into one of the most important dates on the calendar of the "other sort of theatre" and is the largest festival of its sort. Erlangen is also the venue of the international comic salon. The comic salon combines a major specialised trade fair with a wide programme of events. Every second year everybody who is anybody in the comic scene meets here.

In Bamberg a large tribune is set up in the old Hofhaltung next to the cathedral from the end of June to the end of July. Then the picturesque medieval inner yard of the historical building becomes the backdrop for the Calderón-Festival. The ensemble of the E.T.A.-Hoffmann-theatre gives performances in the open air – with quite a distinct flair.

The region not only has a lot to offer in the music and culture sectors. The metropolitan region is also the home of top sporting events. Each year some 100,000 people gather at the "Speed weekend", to admire the elite of touring car and formula 3 pilots in the middle of Nuremberg. At the Quelle Challenge, Franconian Switzerland or Brombach Lake Marathon participants can compare their performances in competitive sports. Whether in the Ultra-Triathlon in Roth or at other events: Participants are cheered on by thousands of spectators pushing them to give their utmost. The metropolitan region is particularly proud to be the venue of the Football World Championship 2006. More than 45,000 fans will be able to enjoy themselves with brilliant football in their specially renovated Frankenstadion.

All the events mentioned however, are only the tip of the iceberg. The metropolitan region of Nuremberg has many more events and programmes of format on offer, programmes which (almost) leave nothing to be desired. That is why it is so highly regarded and indeed loved by its guests as well as the people who live there.

Rock in the Park is, together with Rock on the Ring (Eifel), Germany's longest serving and largest festival. The Ring has 70,000 visitors each year; the Rock in the Park has some 50,000 fans.

Naturerlebnis für Jung und Alt – der Tiergarten

Dr. Dag Encke

Der Tiergarten Nürnberg ist mit 1,1 Millionen Besuchern pro Jahr eine der wichtigsten Freizeitstätten der Region. Der alte, 1912 gegründete Tiergarten musste den Baumaßnahmen für das Reichsparteitagsgelände weichen, sodass 1939 ein neuer Tiergarten am Schmausenbuck entstand. Die Wahl für den neuen Standort fiel für die Belange des Tiergartens sowohl für die damalige Zeit als auch für die Entwicklung eines modernen Zoos ideal aus. Mit 70 Hektar ist der Tiergarten Nürnberg der zweitgrößte Zoo Deutschlands mit außerordentlich weiträumigen Gehegen in naturnahen Lebensräumen. Die Wege führen auf etwa 15 Kilometern durch die urwüchsige Landschaft des Reichswalds mit seinen roten Sandsteinklippen und durch offene Landschaften aus Wasser und Wiesen. Mit dieser Lage ist der Tiergarten Nürnberg ein in Deutschland einzigartiger Landschaftszoo.

Aus den vorhandenen Landschaften des Tiergartens entwickelte sich ein phantastischer Tierbestand, der sich passgenau in die Lebensräume einfügt mit Vertretern der Wälder, Steppen und des Wassers aus allen Kontinenten: Seekühe, Delphine und Kaimane aus den Küstengebieten und Flussläufen Südamerikas, Schabrackentapire, Panzernashörner und Weißhandgibbons aus den Regenwäldern Südostasiens, Rotrückenducker, Bongos und Gorillas aus den Wäldern Afrikas, Kulane, Kropfgazellen und Przewalskipferde aus den Wüsten Zentralasiens und Tiere eurasischer Hochgebirge vom Steinbock bis zum Mishmi-Takin stellen nur einige Beispiele hoch bedrohter Tierarten dar, für deren Zucht Nürnberg einen weltweiten Namen errang.

Die Delphinhaltung in Nürnberg ist ein Publikumsmagnet, der jährlich rund 400 000 Besucher aus der gesamten Region anlockt. Im Rahmen der Modernisierung des Zoos plant der Tiergarten eine Wasserlandschaft, die den Lebensraum Wasser vom offenen Meer bis in die Flussläufe des Amazonas thematisiert und gestalterisch vermittelt. Diese Anlage für Delphine,

The Nuremberg Zoo with its 1.1 million visitors per year is one of the region's most important leisure locations. The old zoo, founded in 1912, was forced to give way to the construction measures for the Reichsparteitagsgelände, so that in 1939 a new zoo was created at the Schmausenbuck. The choice of new location was ideal as far as the zoo for that period in time and also as far as the development of a modern zoo was concerned. With its 70 hectares the Nuremberg Zoo is the second largest one in Germany with exceptionally spacious enclosures in areas which have been kept as close to nature as possible. The almost 15 kilometres of paths lead round through unspoiled landscape of the Reichswald with its red sandstone cliffs and through open landscapes of water and meadows. With such a location the Nuremberg Zoo is a unique landscape zoo.

A fantastic animal population has been developed in the zoo's existing countryside, one which fits precisely into the habitat available and includes representatives of forests, steppe and water from all the continents of earth: sea cows, dolphins and caymans from the coastal areas and river courses of South America, Malayan tapirs, Indian rhinoceros and white hand gibbons from the rain forests of South East Asia, red-back duiker, bongos and gorillas from the forests of Africa, kulans, goitred gazelles and Przewalski horses from the deserts of Central Asia and animals of the Eurasian High Mountains from ibex to mishmi-takin represent just a few of the highly endangered animal species for whose breeding Nuremberg has achieved worldwide fame.

Keeping dolphins in Nuremberg is a public attraction, annually drawing some 400,000 visitors from the entire region. Within the framework of zoo modernisation, plans have been made for a waterscape to make the habitat of water from the open sea to the river courses of the Amazon a subject for discussion and a method of communicating how they are laid out. This layout for dolphins, sea lions and sea cows will be a

Young and Old Experience Nature – the Zoo

Lebensqualität pur
The Pure Quality of Life

Das Delphinarium mit täglichen Vorführungen ist eine der Attraktionen im Nürnberger Zoo.

The Delphinarium with daily demonstration is one of the attractions in the Nuremberg Zoo.

> **Information**
>
> **Gründungsjahr:** 1912, Neubau 1939
>
> **Fläche:** rund 70 ha
>
> **Besucher:** 1,1 Mio. pro Jahr
>
> **Thematische Schwerpunkte:**
> Lebensraum Wald, Wasser & Wüste
>
> **Bildungsprogramm:**
> Zooschule (über 8000 betreute Schüler pro Jahr), Naturkundehaus, Sonderführungen
>
> **Auswilderungsprojekte:**
> Przewalskipferde, Steinböcke, Bartgeier, Ural-Käuze
>
> **Zuchtprogramme:**
> 38 Tierarten, darunter Seekühe, Schabrackentapire, Panzernashörner, Somali-Wildesel, Große Tümmler

Seelöwen und Seekühe wird zum Meilenstein auf dem Weg vom Zoo zum Naturschutzzentrum, der von den wissenschaftlich geleiteten Zoos weltweit eingeschlagen wird.

Die Arbeit des Tiergartens beruht auf den vier Säulen Erholung, Bildung, Forschung und Naturschutz. Voraussetzung für unaufdringliche Bildungsarbeit ist ein Tiergarten, der – Kindern und Erwachsenen – Erholung in der Natur und Erlebnisse mit der Natur und den Tieren anbietet. Dies wird im Tiergarten auf vielfältige Weise erreicht. Ein Streichelzoo in Kombination mit einem JAKO-O-Großspielplatz, der mit einer Kleinbahn vom Eingang aus zu erreichen ist, ist zentraler Anlaufpunkt für Kinder. Durch direkte Begegnungen mit den Haustieren werden tierschutzrelevante Themen kindgerecht zugänglich gemacht. Vorführungen mit Seelöwen und Delphinen vermitteln Aspekte des Naturschutzes von der Ökologie bis zur Bedrohung von Meeressäugern. Lehrpfade und interaktive Spiele führen junge und alte Besucher auf einfache Weise an komplexe Themen heran.

Eine eigene Zooschule mit zwei Lehrkräften bietet Schulen wertvollen Ergänzungsunterricht zur Biologie und zur Bedeutung der Biodiversität. Ein Naturkundehaus mit Ausstellungen und Vortragsreihen ergänzt das Angebot für viele Zielgruppen.

Der Betrieb des Tiergartens hält außerdem eine eigene landwirtschaftliche Produktion auf 80 Hektar vor und unterhält 200 Hektar Stadtforst.

milestone on the route from being a zoo to a nature conservation centre, as has been chosen by scientifically managed zoos all over the world.

The work of the zoo is based on the four pillars of recuperation, education, research and nature conservation. Preconditions for unobtrusive education is a zoo which offers – children and adults alike – recuperation in natural surroundings and the experiences which nature and animals offer. The zoo has achieved this in many ways. A pet's zoo in combination with a JAKO-O-large playground reached by a small train from the entrance is a central starting point for children. By directly encountering pets, subjects of conservation are made approachable at childhood level. Demonstrations with sea lions and dolphins pass on aspects of conservation from ecology through to threats to other sea mammals. Nature trails and interactive games draw younger and older visitors alike into complex subjects using simple methods.

A zoo class with two teachers provides schools with valuable supplementary lessons on biology and the significance of biodiversity. A house of natural history with exhibitions and series of lectures round off the offers for many target groups.

The management of the zoo also maintains its own agricultural production on 80 hectares and maintains 200 hectares of municipal forest.

> **Information**
>
> **Year founded:** 1912, newly constructed 1939
>
> **Surface area:** about 70 ha
>
> **Visitors:** 1.1 million per year
>
> **Subject focal points:**
> habitat forest,
> water & desert
>
> **Educational programme:**
> zoo class (more than 8,000 schoolchildren per year), house of natural history, special tours
>
> **Projects of releasing into the wilds:**
> Przewalski horses, ibex, bearded vultures, Ural-owls
>
> **Breeding programme:**
> 38 animal species amongst them sea cows, Malayan tapirs, Indian rhinoceros, Somalian wild donkeys, bottlenose dolphins

Dieses Löwenbaby gehört zu den jüngsten Bewohnern des Nürnberger Zoos.

This lion cub is one of the youngest citizens in the Nuremberg Zoo.

Eine neue Anlage für Eisbären, Seelöwen und Pinguine mit Unterwasserfenster wurde 2004 eröffnet.

A new enclosure for the ice bears, sea lions and penguins with underwater windows was opened in 2004.

Attraktive Sportangebote für Amateure und Profis

Dr. Thomas Bach

Das sportliche Leistungspotenzial einer Region steht und fällt mit ihren Sportstätten und -angeboten. Die Metropolregion Nürnberg ist naturgemäß nicht dafür bekannt, dass ihre Vertreter im Riesenslalom oder Abfahrtslauf stets die allerhöchsten Preise abräumen. Kein Wunder, denn die Wintersportverhältnisse sind nicht von alpiner Qualität, wenngleich es selbst in Franken eine stattliche Zahl von kleinen Skiliften und attraktiven Langlaufloipen gibt. Berge kann ein Wirtschaftsraum im wörtlichen Sinne nicht versetzen, aber

The sporting potential of a region stands and falls with its sports organisations and what they have to offer. The metropolitan region of Nuremberg is naturally not well known for its representatives walking off with the best prizes for the giant slalom or downhill events. This is hardly surprising when one considers that winter sporting conditions are not of alpine quality even if there are a respectable number of small ski lifts and attractive cross country courses in Franconia. An economic area cannot, literally speaking, move mountains,

Große Volksläufe gehören zum festen Sportprogramm der Metropolregion: hier der Städtemarathon Erlangen–Herzogenaurach.

Mass races belong to the metropolitan region's fixed sports programme: the city marathon in Erlangen–Herzogenaurach.

es gibt eine ganze Menge Faktoren, an denen man arbeiten kann – und die Metropolregion Nürnberg hat dies in den vergangenen Jahren schon hervorragend getan.

Neben dem 1. FC Nürnberg und seinem Weltmeisterschaftsstadion blickt die Region stolz auf zahlreiche andere Institutionen im Hochleistungssport. Ob Basketball, Eishockey, Fechten, Handball, Kegeln,

but there are very many factors on which one could work – and the metropolitan region of Nuremberg has done just that in the past few years, in an excellent manner.

In addition to the 1. FC Nürnberg and its championship stadium, the region is keeping a proud eye on countless other institutions in top competitive sports. Whether basketball, ice hockey, fencing, handball,

Attractive Sports Arrangements for Amateurs and Professionals

Lebensqualität pur
The Pure Quality of Life

Die „Arena Nürnberger Versicherung" ist Heimstätte der Nürnberg Ice Tigers in der DEL und außerdem Austragungsort von Eishockey-Länderspielen wie hier Deutschland gegen USA.

The "Arena Nürnberger Versicherung" is the home of the Nuremberg Ice Tigers in the DEL and also the venue for international ice hockey matches such as Germany against the USA pictured here.

Der weltgrößte Triathlon in der Langdistanz ist der „Quelle Challenge" in Roth.

The world's largest triathlon in long distance is the "Quelle Challenge" in Roth.

Radsport, Ringen, Schwimmen, Tanzen oder Tennis: In fränkischen Landen wird erstklassiger Sport geboten. So viel, dass man vor lauter Bäumen oft die Blümchen gar nicht sieht. Leider wird nämlich gern vergessen, dass in der Region auch weniger prominente Sportler leben, die in ihrer Disziplin weltweit führend sind. Wer zum Beispiel erinnert sich noch daran, dass bei den Paralympics in Sydney eine Bayreutherin namens Christiane Pape die Goldmedaille im Tischtennis gewonnen hat?

Die Erfolge der Leistungssportler sind nicht, wie man denken könnte, nur für sie selbst von Belang – sie haben zum Teil weitreichende Konsequenzen für die Sportart insgesamt, für ihren Heimatort und letzten Endes sogar für den Freizeitwert einer Region. Wer würde schon Kerpen kennen, wenn Michael Schumacher nicht von dort käme? Apropos Automobilsport: Mit dem Norisring-Rennen strahlt auch diese Disziplin namhaft von Nürnberg aus. So wie wir viele Tennisplätze in Deutschland heute Boris Becker und Steffi Graf verdanken, ist der Leistungssport nur die Spitze des Eisbergs. Aber durch diese Spitze wird man auf den Breitensport aufmerksam. Beide zusammen wiederum sorgen dafür, dass weitere Hochleistungen möglich werden – ein Kreislauf. An den Stellen, wo dieser Kreislauf gut funktioniert, profitieren auch die Freizeitsportler und die regionale Wirtschaft davon.

Aus Tauberbischofsheim weiß ich, welche Bedeutung der Sport für einen Ort haben kann. Der dortige Olympiastützpunkt hat seine Aufgaben inzwischen vom Fechten auf andere Disziplinen ausgeweitet und betreut nun auch Kaderathleten etwa aus den Bereichen Tischtennis, Tennis, Schwimmen oder Radfahren. Um das Fechtzentrum herum sind Angebote wie ein Internat, ein Tagungszentrum, eine physiotherapeutische Einrichtung und eine sportpsychologische Beratung entstanden. Der Bekanntheitsgrad von Tauberbischofsheim hängt ungefähr so vom Fechtsport ab wie der Bekanntheitsgrad Schifferstadts von seinen Ringern. Und die Greuther Fürth setzen immer wieder den Namen der Kleeblattstadt auf die Wahrnehmungs-Agenda. Die geistige Landkarte Deutschlands entsteht – auch im Ausland – zum großen Teil durch Orte sportlicher Höchstleistungen.

Was kann nun eine Region tun, um ihr Sportangebot so attraktiv wie möglich zu machen? Sie muss den Sport strategisch klug fördern! Das gilt sowohl für den Leistungssport als auch für den Breitensport, denn sie bedingen einander. Für den Breiten- und Freizeitsport müssen besonders viele, für den Leistungssport

bowling, cycling, wrestling, swimming, dancing or tennis: First-class sports are available in all the areas of Franconia. In fact there are so many that quite often one can't see the flowers for trees. Unfortunately it is frequently forgotten that a few less prominent sportspeople live in the region who are world leaders in their disciplines. Who, for instance, can remember that in the Paralympics in Sydney a Bayreuther named Christiane Pape won the gold medal in table tennis?

The successes of top sportspeople are not only, as one could think, of significance to themselves – they sometimes also have far-reaching consequences for the type of sport, for their native country and in the end even for the leisure qualities of a region. Who would know where Kerpen was if it weren't for Michael Schumacher? Apropos automobile sport: With the Norisring races even this discipline radiates its identification with Nuremberg. In the same way that it is thanks to Boris Becker and Steffi Graf that we have so many tennis courts in Germany today, top performance sports are only the tip of the iceberg. But these top sports also draw attention to popular sports. Both of them in turn make sure that further top performances become at all possible – they become a spiral. In those areas where the cycle or spiral functions well hobby sportspeople and the regional economy also profit from it.

From Tauberbischofsheim I know the importance which sport can have for a town. The Olympia centre there has in the meantime spread its tasks from fencing to other disciplines and now looks after cadre athletes for instance from the sectors of table tennis, tennis, swimming and cycling. Around the fencing centre services such as a boarding school, a conference centre, a physiotherapy institution and sports psychology counselling have developed. The degree of Tauberbischofsheim's fame depends almost just as much on fencing as Schifferstadt's does on its wrestlers. And the Greuther Fürth always set the name of the clover town on the perception agenda. The mental map of Germany is created – for people from overseas too – to a large extent by places of top sporting performances.

What can a region do to make the sports it can offer as attractive as possible? It must promote sport with clever strategies! This applies to both popular sports and top sports because they depend on each other. For popular and hobby sports particularly many conditions must be created whereas particularly good conditions must be created for top sports. Whoever wants to have the best swimmers of the world must offer them competitive training opportunities – otherwise they will

Lebensqualität pur
The Pure Quality of Life

Klettern an den Haselstaudener Wänden in der Fränkischen Schweiz bei Forchheim

Climbing on the Haselstauden cliffs in Franconian Switzerland near Forchheim

| Ballonfahrer im Abendrot | *Balloon drivers in the sunset* |

besonders gute Bedingungen geschaffen werden. Wer die besten Schwimmer der Welt haben will, der muss ihnen auch konkurrenzfähige Trainingsmöglichkeiten offerieren – sonst hat es sich bald ausgekrault. Auch im Sport gibt es nämlich zunehmend wirtschaftlichen Wettbewerb, wie im Bereich des Triathlons in Roth (früher „Ironman") sehr deutlich wurde. Erfreulicherweise hat Roth hier ja seine Marktführerschaft trotz eines Etikettenwechsels behaupten können.

Mindestens genauso wichtig sind aber auch die Sportstätten für Hobbysportler, aus denen sich schließlich die Profis hervortun. Für sie braucht man nicht die großen Arenen, sondern die vielen brauchbaren Plätze zum Bolzen, Inline-Skaten, Klettern, Rudern, Laufen etc. Die Innenstädte lassen hierfür wenig Raum. Sport braucht aber Platz, um zu funktionieren. Diesen Platz muss sich die Metropolregion immer wieder mit Klugheit und Kreativität erkämpfen, so wie sich auch die Sportler selbst ihre vorderen Plätze erkämpfen müssen. An globalen Gegebenheiten wie den Bergen und dem Schnee lässt sich vielleicht nicht viel machen. An den Sportstätten dagegen hört die Arbeit nie auf. □

"crawl off" somewhere else. There is increasing economic competition in sport too, as became very clear for instance in the sector of the triathlon in Roth (the earlier "iron man"). Happily Roth has been able to maintain its market leadership in spite of the change of label.

For hobby sportspeople, sports centres are just as important; after all, this is where all the professionals originate. They don't need the big arenas, much more they need smaller, practical places to kick a ball around, do inline skating, practice climbing, rowing, running etc. Inner cities have precious little room for it. But sport needs plenty of room to function. The metropolitan region has to fight for this room time and again with cleverness and creativity just as sportspeople themselves have to fight to become first. There is not much that can be done about global facts such as mountains and snow but the work on the sports centres never stops. □

Lebensqualität pur
The Pure Quality of Life

Früh übt sich, wer Erfolg haben will: Segelregatta auf dem Dechsendorfer Weiher

One needs plenty of practice to be successful: a sailing regatta on the Dechsendorfer Weiher

„Tooooooooar in Nürnberg!"

Günther Koch

Teurer und wichtiger als alles andere auf der Welt ist und bleibt für Fußballfans – auch in der Metropolregion – ihr Verein.

Mit dem ehemals „ruhmreichen" und deutschen Rekordmeister 1. FC Nürnberg ging es leider in den letzten 38 Jahren etwa im selben Maße und im selben Tempo, in dem der Fußball aus einer reinen Sportveranstaltung zu einem knallharten, hoch professionellen Wirtschafts-Wettbewerb mutierte, unaufhaltsam abwärts.

Lediglich beim Endspiel um den DFB-Pokal am 1. Mai 1982 in Frankfurt mit einer mehr als unglücklichen 2:4 Niederlage – trotz 2:0 Führung zur Halbzeit – gegen den rasanten Emporkömmling FC Bayern München und mit der kurzen, ebenfalls unglücklich verlaufenden Teilnahme am UEFA-Pokalwettbewerb im Herbst 1988 gegen den AS Rom, mit einem 2:1 Sieg in Rom, flackerte noch mal so etwas Ähnliches wie Hoffnung auf, wenigstens halbwegs Anschluss ans neue knallharte Fußball-Business halten zu können.

Seit der 9. und damit bisher letzten deutschen Meisterschaft im Jahr 1968 (Wabra, Hilpert, Leupold, Popp, Ferschl, L. Müller, Wenauer, Brungs, Cebinac, H. Müller, Schöll, Starek, Strehl, Volkert, Trainer Max Merkel) ist der 1. FCN bislang sechs Mal in die 2. Liga abgestiegen (1969/79/84/94/99 und 2003) und darüber hinaus ein weiteres Mal sogar in die Regionalliga im Jahr 1996. Schlimmer geht's fast nimmer.

Doch wir alle lieben und verfluchen diesen unseren Club, dessen unerreichter Max Morlock 1954 sogar Weltmeister in Bern wurde – genau so wie übrigens Charly Mai aus der Nachbarstadt Fürth. Womit wir bei der SpVgg Greuther Fürth wären, die, trotz ebenfalls immerhin drei Meistertiteln aus der Frühzeit des Fußballs, seit Einführung der Fußball-Bundesliga im Jahr 1963 immer zweitklassig blieb – bisher.

Die Nürnberger lieben ihren Club – trotz aller Misserfolge. Die Fürther ihre Spielvereinigung – trotz aller Rückschläge.

For a football fan there is nothing dearer or more important in the world than his club – and the metropolitan region is no exception.

With the once "glorious" and former German record holder 1. FC Nürnberg the descent over the last 38 years has, unfortunately, been at the same rate and at the same speed in which football has mutated from a mere sporting event into a really hard, highly professional economic competition – unstoppable.

It was only in the final of the DFB cup on 1st Mai 1982 in Frankfurt with a more or less unlucky defeat of 2:4 – in spite of leading 2:0 at half time – against the upstart FC Bayern München and with the short, equally unlucky participation in the UEFA cup competition in autumn 1988 against AS Rome, with a 2:1 victory in Rome, when something similar to hope flared up again that there was at least half a chance of connecting up with the new hard football business.

Since the 9th and, up to now, last German Championship in 1968 (Wabra, Hilpert, Leupold, Popp, Ferschl, L. Müller, Wenauer, Brungs, Cebinac, H. Müller, Schöll, Starek, Strehl, Volkert, trainer Max Merkel) the 1. FCN has been relegated into the 2nd league for the sixth time (1969/79/84/94/99 and 2003), and, making matters worse, one more time in the regional league in 1996. It can hardly get worse.

But don't we all love and curse our club, whose unequalled Max Morlock was even world champion in 1954 in Bern – incidentally just like Charly Mai from the neighbouring city of Fürth. Bringing us to the SpVgg Greuther Fürth, which, in spite of also being champions three times in the early days of football have remained second class since the introduction of the German football league in 1963 –, 'till now that is.

People of Nuremberg love their club – in spite of all its flops. The Fürther love their Spielvereinigung – in spite of all its setbacks.

Are we Franconians backwards or at best unrealistic because of it? No we are not!

"Goooooooal in Nuremberg!"

Lebensqualität pur
The Pure Quality of Life

Confederations Cup 2005: Deutschland gegen Brasilien im Frankenstadion, das seit März 2006 offiziell den Namen easyCredit Stadion trägt.

Confederations Cup 2005: Germany vs. Brazil in the Frankenstadion which received the official name of easyCredit Stadion in March 2006.

Treu und leidensfähig: Fans des „Clubs" haben es in der Vergangenheit nicht immer leicht gehabt.

Faithful and long-suffering: Fans of the "Club" haven't always had it easy in the past.

Sind wir Franken deshalb rückständig oder zumindest realitätsfern? Nein!

Bei uns in Franken ist halt alles etwas gemütlicher, dabei deutlich preisgünstiger, normaler und manchmal sogar schöner als anderswo in Deutschland. Fußballerisch betrachtet, beherrschen wir mittlerweile das Leiden dank unserer Cluberer und unserer Fürther sogar richtig gut. Über seltene und dann völlig unerwartete Siege freuen wir uns natürlich umso mehr – vor allem intensiver und auch länger.

Unser Fußball-Unglück hat zumindest einen Vorteil. Fast immer finden wir Anlass zum Jammern und Schimpfen: erstens über unseren Club und zweitens über die Fürther, die noch kein einziges Mal aufgestiegen sind und gar nicht einmal wissen, wie das ist und ob sie das überhaupt wollen. Natürlich träumen auch wir, für die der Fußball fast das Wichtigste im Leben ist, von besseren Zeiten, und dass die Metropolregion auch fußballerisch wieder vorne mitmischen kann und nicht nur mitleidig belächelt wird.

Ende 2005 passierte dann – in der fußballerisch betrachtet eher „Minipol-Region" – plötzlich und völlig unerwartet höchst Merkwürdiges: Der 1. FC Nürnberg, unser aller Club, hatte plötzlich wieder mal einen richtig guten und tüchtigen Trainer und holte mit ihm in vier Spielen sieben Punkte in der 1. Bundesliga. Die rote Laterne war man los. Zur gleichen Zeit schlich der nicht von allen Nürnbergern geliebte Nachbar, die

In Franconia things are a bit more gemütlich (easy) and at the same time considerably cheaper, more normal and sometimes even more beautiful than in other places in Germany. From a football fan's angle, we have, in the meantime, mastered our suffering thanks to our clubbers and our Fürther, you could even say we have mastered it really well. Naturally, we are even more delighted about the rare and fully unexpected wins – for even longer and more intensively than ever.

Our football misfortune has had at least one advantage. We can almost always find a reason for moaning and groaning: firstly about our club and secondly about the Fürther, who haven't been promoted once and don't know how it is or whether they even want to be promoted. Of course we, those of us for whom football the most important thing in life is, also dream of better times, that the metropolitan region is footballish involved at the top of the table again and not only to be pitifully smiled on.

At the end of 2005 something completely unexpected and highly unusual happened in the rather "football minipolitan Region": The 1. FC Nürnberg, the most important club of all for us, suddenly had a really good and competent trainer once again and managed to get seven points in four games in the 1st German league. The red light kept at the end of the train had been passed on. At the same time, the SpVgg Greuther Fürth, a neighbour not loved by all Nurembergers, crept almost unnoticed to the top of the table of the 2nd German league.

The long suffering fans of the 1. FCN at the bottom of the league didn't understand the sudden, beautiful new world any more. Two victories and a draw within a few weeks! If this carried on we'd have nothing to grumble about. Melancholy abounded. Perhaps we won't be relegated in 2006 after all? "Mensch, Maier" (oh, boy!) was the only thing to be said. If that's the case then all we clubbers will probably suddenly love all those

Lebensqualität pur
The Pure Quality of Life

Jubelnde Club-Spieler: Ein Bild, das die Anhänger des 1. FC Nürnberg in der Zukunft häufig sehen möchten.

Celebrating Club players: A picture that the fans of the 1. FC Nürnberg would like to see more often in the future.

SpVgg Greuther Fürth, beinahe unbemerkt an die Tabellenspitze der 2. Bundesliga.

Die leidgeprüften Fans des Tabellenletzten 1. FCN verstanden die plötzlich neue, schöne Welt nicht mehr. Zwei Siege und ein Unentschieden innerhalb von wenigen Wochen! Wenn das so weitergeht, kann man ja gar nicht mehr schimpfen. Man wurde richtig melancholisch. Vielleicht steigen wir 2006 ja doch nicht ab? „Mensch, Maier" könnte man dann nur sagen. Dann würden wir Cluberer wegen des aus dem Osten stammenden neuen Trainers Hans Meyer vermutlich auf einmal alle „Ossis" lieben, ja vielleicht sogar die fränkischen „Wessis" aus Nürnbergs „Vorstadt" Fürth. Dann dürften aus Clubsicht sogar die wenigstens einmal – aber bitte nur für ein Jahr – aufsteigen. Fürths Trainer Möhlmann würde zum „Wundermann" und die Metropolregion wäre auch fußballerisch nach über 60 Jahren endlich wieder erstklassig. Das wär' echt ein Traum! Allerdings fast nicht auszuhalten.

Im Vergleich dazu wäre sogar der Gewinn der Weltmeisterschaft am 9. Juli in Berlin durch Klinsmanns Buben im Endspiel gegen Brasilien weniger sensationell bzw. fast unwichtig . . .

In diesem Sinne: Ein herzliches fränkisches Willkommen zur FIFA-WM 2006 in Nürnberg, liebe Gäste aus England, Ghana, Kroatien, Mexiko, Iran, Japan, Trinidad/Tobago und USA zu den vier Vorrundenspielen.

Im Achtelfinale werden wir dann geradezu enthusiastisch den Zweiten aus der Gruppe C, also vermutlich Argentinien oder die Niederlande oder aber die Freunde aus Serbien-Montenegro oder gar von der Elfenbeinküste im Frankenstadion begrüßen dürfen sowie auf der anderen Seite den Ersten aus der Gruppe D, also womöglich die großartigen Portugiesen oder Angola bzw. abermals Mexiko oder Iran, die schon am 11. Juni das erste Spiel in Nürnberg bestreiten. „Toooooooaar in Nürnberg!" – für wen auch immer . . .

"Ossis" (Easterners) because of Hans Meyer the new trainer who originated in the East(ern Germany), perhaps we'll even love the Franconian "Wessis" (Westerners) from Nuremberg's "suburb town" of Fürth. If that were the case, even they would be allowed to be promoted, from the club's point of view just the once – and please, only for one year. Fürth's trainer Möhlmann would become "Wonder man" and the metropolitan region would, footballish speaking, become a first class region for the first time in 60 years. That would be unbelievable! Almost unbearable.

In comparison, even winning the world championship on 9th July in Berlin with Klinsmann's lads in the final against Brazil would be less sensational or even almost unimportant . . .

In this respect: A hearty Franconian welcome to the FIFA-WM 2006 in Nuremberg, dear guests from England, Ghana, Croatia, Mexico, Iran, Japan, Trinidad/Tobago, and USA for the four qualifying games.

In the round of the last sixteen we shall be able to enthusiastically welcome the second from group C, probably Argentina or the Netherlands or our friends from Serbia-Montenegro or even from the Ivory Coast in the Frankenstadion as well as from the other side, the first from group D, possibly the splendid Portuguese or Angolans and/or once again Mexico or Iran, who will play their first game in Nuremberg on 11th June. "Gooooooool in Nuremberg!" – for whoever it is . . .

Kulturelle und wirtschaftliche Vielfalt in der Bierregion Bamberg

Rainer Keis

Es ist Sommer und in einem kleinen Kunststoff verarbeitenden Betrieb irgendwo im Landkreis Bamberg unterhalten sich zwei Kollegen. Am Ende dieses Gesprächs sagt der eine: „Lass uns doch heute Abend auf einen Keller gehen und ein schönes kühles Bier trinken."

Als Leser werden Sie sich jetzt sicherlich fragen: Seit wann geht man auf einen Keller, um Bier zu trinken? Dies ist kein Druckfehler, sondern hat etwas mit der Bamberger Biertradition zu tun. Dass man auf einen Keller geht, hängt mit der erhöhten Lage der Bierkeller zusammen, die im Umfeld der Ortschaften an den Sandsteinhängen angelegt wurden. Diese Keller, die Sommer wie Winter eine gleichbleibende Temperatur gewährleisten, dienten seit jeher als Lager für gebrautes Bier. In den Sommermonaten wurden sie zum Bierausschank genutzt.

In der Stadt und im Landkreis Bamberg gibt es noch 82 Privatbrauereien – bei insgesamt 220 000 Einwohnern. Während in Russland auf eine Brauerei 350 000 Einwohner kommen, in den USA – immerhin das Land mit den meisten Brauereien weltweit – 200 000 Einwohner, so kommen im Bamberger Land auf eine Brauerei rund 2600 Einwohner. Damit besitzt der Landkreis Bamberg die höchste Brauereidichte der Welt!

Bier ist eine Art flüssige Weltanschauung. Bier prägt Menschen und Landschaften, und das Bamberger Land ist Bierfranken. Beim Bier ist es wie beim Wein: Jeder Sud schmeckt ein bisschen anders, je nachdem welcher Brauer welchen Hopfen und welches Wasser verwendet. Es sind keine großen Brauereien, und genau darin liegt der Reiz. Oft sind es Kleinstanlagen, die nur für den Bedarf in der eigenen Gastwirtschaft konzipiert sind. Daher liegen die Preise für dieses „Grundnahrungsmittel" so einmalig niedrig. Wo, außer bei uns, bekommen sie „a Seidla" Bier (halber Liter) für rund 1,80 Euro? Ein „Stoff" für Genießer – und solche die es werden wollen.

It is summer and in a small plastic-processing factory somewhere in the district of Bamberg two colleagues are having a chat. At the end of the chat one says to the other: "Let's go up into a cellar tonight and have a nice cool beer."

Reading this, you will no doubt have asked yourself since when does one go up into a cellar to have a beer. This is not a printing error, it has something to do with beer tradition in Bamberg. The fact that you go up into a cellar is connected with the raised level of the beer cellars laid out in the sandstone slopes surrounding the villages and towns of the area. These cellars guarantee a stable temperature summer and winter alike and have always served as storerooms for beer. In the summer months they are also used for serving beer.

In the city and district of Bamberg there are still 82 private breweries – for a total of 220,000 inhabitants. While in Russia there is one brewery for 350,000 inhabitants and in the USA – the country with the most breweries in the world – 200,000 inhabitants, so in the county of Bamberg there are some 2,600 inhabitants for each brewery. Looking at these figures, the district of Bamberg has the highest brewery density in the world!

Beer is a sort of liquid philosophy of life. Beer leaves its influence on people and the countryside and the Bamberg district is beer Franconia. It's the same with beer as it is with wine: Every brew tastes a little bit different depending on which brewer uses which hops with which water. They are not major breweries and therein lies their charm. Often they are very small installations which have only been designed for supplying their own pub or restaurant. This is also the reason why the price of this "basic foodstuff" is so exceptionally low. Where else, except in our area, can you get "a Seidla" beer (half a litre) for about 1.80 Euro? "Stuff" for gourmets – and those who want to become such.

Up in the beer cellar, our two "Kunststoffler" (plastic workers) are comfortably enjoying a cool fresh beer

Cultural and Economic Variety in the Beer Region of Bamberg

Lebensqualität pur
The Pure Quality of Life

Im Sommer gehören die zahlreichen Bierkeller in der Region Bamberg zu den beliebtesten Ausflugszielen.

In the summer the countless beer cellars of the Bamberg region are some of the best-loved destinations.

Unsere „Kunststoffler" genießen auf dem Bierkeller, gemütlich unter einer Schatten spendenden Kastanie sitzend, ein kühles frisches Bier – im traditionellen Steinkrug („Seidla") serviert. Sie sind so in das Gespräch vertieft, dass sie nicht bemerkt haben, wie sich ihr „Seidla" Rauchbier so langsam geleert hat. Das Rauchbier, das stets als charakteristische Biersorte mit Bamberg in Verbindung gebracht wird, erhält sein spezifisches Raucharoma durch die Trocknung des Grünmalzes direkt über dem Buchenholzfeuer. Beim zweiten Bier entscheiden sie sich aber für das wohl meistgetrunkenste Bier im Bamberger Land, das Lager- oder Kellerbier. Dieses ist ein untergäriges, unfiltriertes Bier mit einem niedrigen Kohlensäuregehalt (ungespundet).

Während sie ihr Bier genießen, sinnieren die beiden „Kunststoffler" über die Vorteile und Qualitäten der hiesigen Region. Die drei Naturparks Fränkische Schweiz im Osten, der Steigerwald im Westen und die Hassberge im Norden des Landkreises laden zu den unterschiedlichsten Freizeitaktivitäten ein: Ob Rad fahren, Mountainbiking, Paddeln im Flussparadies Franken, Segelfliegen, Paragliding oder Klettern – für alle Aktiven bietet der Landkreis Bamberg das Richtige.

Doch auch Kunst- und Kulturbegeisterte kommen auf ihre Kosten: Das Collegium Musicum in Pommersfelden, die Frühlingsserenaden in Schloss Seehof, der Ebracher Musiksommer, der Theatersommer Fränkische Schweiz oder das Levi Strauss Museum in Buttenheim (Geburtshaus des gleichnamigen Jeanserfinders) sorgen für ein abwechslungsreiches Programm. Das kulturelle Zentrum bildet das UNESCO-Weltkulturerbe Altstadt Bamberg: Musikliebhaber schätzen die Konzerte der weltberühmten Bamberger Symphoniker – Bayerische Staatsphilharmonie. Theaterfreunde kommen im E.T.A.-Hoffmann-Theater auf ihre Kosten, Kunstbegeisterte im Internationalen Künstlerhaus Villa Concordia.

Doch nicht nur die weichen Standortfaktoren überzeugen, sondern auch das wirtschaftliche Umfeld leistet seinen Beitrag. Der Landkreis Bamberg als Investitionsstandort ist geprägt durch seine ökonomische Vielfalt: ein ausgewogener Branchenmix mit vielen, vor allem kleinen und mittleren Unternehmen – dem Rückgrat der deutschen Wirtschaft. Einen wichtigen Wirtschaftszweig stellt die Kunststoff verarbeitende Industrie dar. Ob Unternehmen, die Zahnpastatuben herstellen oder Dichtprofile für Aluminiumtüren

served in a traditional earthenware mug (a "Seidla") sitting in the shadow of a chestnut tree. They are so involved in their discussion that they haven't noticed that the "Seidla" Rauchbier has slowly emptied. Rauchbier, which has always been connected with Bamberg as a characteristic sort of beer, gets its specific smoky aroma by drying the green malt directly over a beechwood fire. But for the second beer, they decide on the beer most drunk in the Bamberg area, the lager or cellar beer. This is a bottom-fermented unfiltered beer with a low carbonic acid content (unbunged).

While they are enjoying their beer, both "Kunststoffler" ponder on the advantages and qualities of the local region. The three nature parks of Franconian Switzerland in the east, the Steiger Forest in the west and the Hass Mountains in the north of the district invite one to partake in a wide variety of leisure activities: Cycling, mountain biking, paddling in the river paradise of Franconia, gliding, paragliding or climbing – the district of Bamberg has something to offer for everyone.

Fans of art and culture can also thoroughly enjoy themselves: the Collegium Musicum in Pommersfelden, the spring serenades in Schloss Seehof, the Ebrach Music Summer, the Franconian Switzerland Theatre Summer or the Levi Strauss Museum in Buttenheim (birthplace of the jeans inventor of the same name) provide a well-assorted programme. The cultural centre is formed by the UNESCO-world cultural heritage of the old city of Bamberg: Music fans appreciate the concerts of the world-renowned Bamberg Symphony – Bavarian State Philharmonic Orchestra. Theatre fans can enjoy themselves in the E.T.A.-Hoffmann-Theatre, and art enthusiasts in the international artists' house Villa Concordia.

But not only soft factors of business location are convincing arguments, the economic sphere also makes its contribution. The district of Bamberg as a location for investments is meaningful because of its economical variety: a well-balanced mixture of branches with many concerns, primarily small and medium-sized – that form the backbone of the German economy. One important economic branch is the synthetics-processing industry. Whether concerns produce toothpaste tubes or sealing profiles for aluminium doors and windows for automobile manufacturers – they all have their headquarters in the district of Bamberg. It should generally be noted that the automobile supply industry in the Bamberg and Upper Franconian

Lebensqualität pur
The Pure Quality of Life

Schloss Weißenstein in Pommersfelden ist eine der schönsten Barockanlagen Frankens.

Castle Weißenstein in Pommersfelden is one of the most beautiful Baroque installations in Franconia.

und Fenster für die Automobilhersteller – sie alle haben ihren Sitz im Landkreis Bamberg. Generell ist anzumerken, dass die Automobilzulieferindustrie in der Region Bamberg und Oberfranken eine wichtige Rolle spielt. Rund 44 000 Arbeitnehmer in etwa 250 Unternehmen sind im oberfränkischen Automobilzulieferbereich tätig – der überwiegende Anteil entfällt dabei auf den Raum Bamberg.

Die Elektroindustrie ist die beschäftigungsstärkste Branche im Freistaat Bayern. Auch in der Region Bamberg zeichnet sich diese Tendenz ab: Die hier traditionell ansässigen Betriebe sind vor allem auf dem Gebiet der elektronischen Bauelemente und Schalttechnik tätig. Doch auch Unternehmen in den Bereichen Mess-, Regelungs- und Steuerungstechnik, Automatisierungssysteme und Unterhaltungselektronik sind zahlreich vertreten.

Das Bamberger Land bietet eine gelungene Symbiose aus frischen, weltoffenen Ideen, gepaart mit traditionsbewussten Menschen in einer intakten Umwelt und einer vielfältigen Wirtschaftsstruktur.

regions plays a very important role. Some 44,000 employees in approximately 250 concerns are employed in the Upper Franconian automobile supply sector – most of them in the Bamberg area.

The electro industry is the strongest employment branch in the Free State of Bavaria. This tendency can also be seen in the region of Bamberg: The concerns traditionally resident here are primarily active in the sector of electronic components and switch engineering. But concerns in the sectors of measuring, regulating and control technologies, automation systems and entertainment electronics are also well represented.

The Bamberg area offers a successful symbiosis of fresh, cosmopolitan ideas paired with tradition-conscious people in an intact environment and a manifold economic structure.

Metropolregion Nürnberg – Kern und Netz

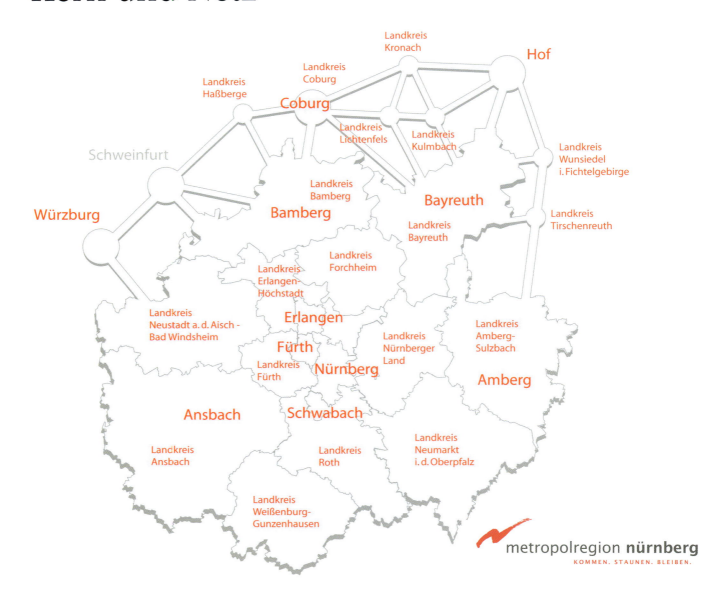

Wichtige Kennzahlen für den Kern der Metropolregion

Bevölkerung:	2,5 Millionen
Unternehmen:	110 000 plus 40 000 weitere Selbstständige
Beschäftigte:	864 000
Bruttoinlandsprodukt:	71 Mrd. Euro
Exportquote:	40 Prozent

Key figures for the core metropolitan region

Population:	*2.5 million*
Companies:	*110,000 plus 40,000 self-employed persons*
Employees:	*864,000*
Gross domestic product:	*71 billion Euro*
Export quota:	*40 percent*

Metropolitan Region of Nuremberg – Core and Net

Strukturdaten der Metropolregion

Metropolregionen sind im Verständnis der Ministerkonferenz für Raumordnung „Motoren der gesellschaftlichen, wirtschaftlichen, sozialen und kulturellen Entwicklung mit guter Erreichbarkeit auf europäischer und internationaler Ebene und weiter Ausstrahlung in das Umland."

Die Metropolregion Nürnberg besteht aus der Kernregion und einer Netzregion. Zur Kernregion gehören die acht Städte Amberg, Ansbach, Bamberg, Bayreuth, Erlangen, Fürth, Nürnberg und Schwabach sowie die zwölf Landkreise Amberg-Sulzbach, Ansbach, Bamberg, Bayreuth, Erlangen-Höchstadt, Forchheim, Fürth, Neumarkt i. d. Oberpfalz, Neustadt a. d. Aisch-Bad Windsheim, Nürnberger Land, Roth und Weißenburg-Gunzenhausen.

Weitere Gebietskörperschaften haben Beitrittsinteresse bekundet.

Handels- und Messezentrum von internationalem Rang
- EU-Prädikat „Gateway to Eastern Europe"
- Internationaler Messe- und Kongressplatz mit 160 000 Quadratmetern Ausstellungsfläche und über 60 Fachmessen und Kongressen
- Hohe Einkaufszentralität mit leichter Erreichbarkeit für 5,2 Millionen Einwohner im Umkreis von 100 Kilometern

Zentrale Lage mit hervorragender Verkehrsanbindung
- Flugverkehr (Internationaler Airport Nürnberg):
  3,8 Millionen Fluggäste pro Jahr;
  Business Traveller Award: bester Flughafen seiner Größenordnung;
  über 80 tägliche Nonstop-Verbindungen zu allen wichtigen europäischen Metropolen in weniger als zwei Stunden Flugzeit
- Europäischer Fernstraßenknotenpunkt im Schnittpunkt der Autobahnen:
  Paris–Prag
  Warschau–Berlin–Rom
  London–Brüssel–Frankfurt–Wien–Budapest
  Stockholm–Hannover–Zürich–Mailand
- Schienennetz: im Schnittpunkt von ICE- und internationalen Fernverkehrsstrecken
- Schifffahrt: Main-Donau-Kanal als Bindeglied einer 3500 Kilometer langen Wasserstraße zwischen Nordsee/Rhein und Donau/Schwarzem Meer;
  Güterverkehrszentrum Hafen Nürnberg:
  Gesamtumschlag über 10 Millionen Tonnen jährlich;
  trimodales Terminal (Verladung Schiff–Bahn–Straße)

Innovations- und Gründerregion
- Gründerregion:
  Spitzenplatz unter den deutschen Metropolen beim Anteil von Gründern und Jungunternehmern an den Erwerbstätigen
- Innovationsregion:
  in der Spitzengruppe der High-Tech-Regionen mit dem höchsten Innovationspotenzial; TOP-FIVE-Position im Patentatlas Deutschland
- Bildung und Wissenschaft:
  15 Hochschulen, davon vier Universitäten und elf Fachhochschulen; über 80 000 Studierende; Franconian International School

Structural data of the metropolitan region

According to the ministerial council for regional planning (which awards the title), Metropolitan Regions are "motors for corporate, economic, social and cultural development, with good accessibility on a European and international level and an additional positive impact on the surrounding area."

The metropolitan region of Nuremberg consists of the core region and a network region. The eight cities of Amberg, Ansbach, Bamberg, Bayreuth, Erlangen, Fürth, Nuremberg and Schwabach belong to the core region, as do the twelve rural districts of Amberg-Sulzbach, Ansbach, Bamberg, Bayreuth, Erlangen-Höchstadt, Forchheim, Fürth, Neumarkt i. d. Oberpfalz, Neustadt a. d. Aisch-Bad Windsheim, Nürnberger Land, Roth and Weißenburg-Gunzenhausen.

Other area bodies have indicated interest in entry.

Centre of commerce and exhibition of international standing
- *EU designation "Gateway to Eastern Europe"*
- *international exhibition and congress venue with 160,000 square metres of exhibition space and more than 60 trade fairs and congresses*
- *good shopping centrality with easy accessibility for 5.2 million inhabitants within a radius of 100 kilometres*

Central position with outstanding transport links:
- *air traffic (Nuremberg International Airport):
  3.8 million travellers per year;
  Business Traveller Award: best airport of its size;
  more than 80 non-stop flights a day to all key European metropolises in under two hours flying time*
- *a hub in the European major road network at the point of intersection of the motorways:
  Paris–Prague
  Warsaw–Berlin–Rome
  London–Brussels–Frankfurt–Vienna–Budapest
  Stockholm–Hanover–Zurich–Milan*
- *rail links: an important point of interchange for ICE and international long-distance routes*
- *shipping: Main-Danube-Canal as a key link in a 3,500 kilometres waterway joining North Sea/Rhine and Danube/Black Sea;
  Nuremberg Harbour and Logistics Centre:
  total turnover of more than 10 million tons a year;
  trimodal terminal (loading ship–rail–road)*

Innovation and business founder region
- *business founder region:
  top ranked amongst the German metropolises in terms of share of business founders and young entrepreneurs amongst working population*
- *innovation region:
  in the top group of high-tech regions with the greatest innovation potential; TOP FIVE position in the German Patent Atlas*
- *education and science:
  15 colleges of higher education, thereof four universities and eleven universities of applied sciences; over 80,000 students; Franconian International School*

Register
Index

VERZEICHNIS DER PR-BILDBEITRÄGE

Die nachstehenden Firmen, Verwaltungen und Verbände haben mit ihren Public-Relations-Beiträgen das Zustandekommen dieses Buches in dankenswerter Weise gefördert.

LIST OF ILLUSTRATED CONTRIBUTIONS

We thank the following companies, administrations and associations which with their public relations contributions have made the production of this book possible.

ADAC Nordbayern e. V., Nürnberg 214, 215
    www.adac.de/nordbayern / mitgliederservice@nby.adac.de

Aicher Recycling GmbH, Max, Nürnberg 186, 187
    www.mar.de / info@mar.de

alpha Gruppe, Nürnberg 96
    www.alpha-gruppe.com / info@alpha-gruppe.com

AVL DiTEST GmbH, Fürth 200
    www.avlditest.com / info.fue@avl.com

Barth & Sohn GmbH & Co. KG, Joh., Nürnberg 30, 31
    www.johbarth.com / info@johbarth.de

Baumüller Holding GmbH & Co. KG, Nürnberg 192, 193
    www.baumueller.de / marketing@baumueller.de

BAUSTOFF UNION GmbH & Co. KG, Nürnberg 59
    www.baustoff-union-franken.de / info@bu-nbg.de

Bayerische Beamtenkrankenkasse Versicherungsdienste
  BEV GmbH, Nürnberg 109
    www.bev.de / info@bev.de

Bayerische Hypo- und Vereinsbank AG, Nürnberg 219
    www.hypovereinsbank.de / info@hvb.de

Register
Index

BEN Buchele Elektromotorenwerke GmbH, Nürnberg 61
    www.benbuchele.de / info@benbuchele.de

BERG Zeitarbeit GmbH, Nürnberg 212, 213
    www.berg-zeitarbeit.de / info@berg-zeitarbeit.de

Berufsförderungswerk Nürnberg gGmbH 217
    www.bfw-nuernberg.de / info@bfw-nuernberg.de

BIOTRONIK GmbH & Co. KG, Erlangen 168, 169
    www.biotronik.com / info@biotronik.com

CeramTec AG Innovative Ceramic Engineering, Lauf a. d. Pegnitz 178
    www.ceramtec.com / info@ceramtec.de

Convoi Deutschland GmbH, Nürnberg 156
    www.convoi.com / info@convoi.com

CSC JÄKLECHEMIE GmbH & Co. KG, Nürnberg 206, 207
    www.csc-jaekle.de / chemikalien@csc-jaekle.de

Diakonie Neuendettelsau 106, 107
    www.diakonieneuendettelsau.de / info@diakonieneuendettelsau.de

DTZ Dialyse Trainings-Zentren gGmbH, Nürnberg 100
    www.dtz-gmbh.de / info@DTZ-GmbH.de

ECKART GmbH & Co. KG, Velden 28
    www.eckart.net / info.eckart@altanachemie.com

ESAB ARCOS, Georg Hartner GmbH, Nürnberg 69
    www.esabarcos.de / EAGH.GmbH@t-online.de

Eschenbach Optik GmbH + Co., Nürnberg 50
    www.eschenbach-optik.de / mail@eschenbach-optik.de

ESS – Erlanger Sicherheits-Service GmbH, Erlangen 176
    www.ess-erlangen.de / info@ess-erlangen.de

E-T-A Elektrotechnische Apparate GmbH, Altdorf 196
    www.e-t-a.com / info@e-t-a.de

Faurecia Exhaust Systems, Fürth 25
    www.faurecia.com / info@stadeln.faurecia.com

FCI Automotive Deutschland GmbH, Nürnberg 20, 21
    www.fciconnect.com / fcinuernberg@fciconnect.com

Ferngas Nordbayern GmbH, Nürnberg 184
    www.ferngas-nordbayern.de / info@ferngas-nordbayern.de

FrankenData Softwareengineering GmbH & Co. KG, Erlangen 166
    www.frankendata.de / fd@frankendata.de

GfK Gruppe, Nürnberg 19
    www.gfk.de / www.gfk.com / public.affairs@gfk.com

Gießerei Heunisch GmbH, Bad Windsheim 27
    www.heunisch-guss.com / info@heunisch-guss.com

GMÖHLING Transportgeräte GmbH, Fürth 32
    www.gmoehling.com / verkauf@gmoehling.com

Gutmann Werke AG, Hermann, Weißenburg 26
    www.gutmann.de / info@gutmann.de

Handwerkskammer für Mittelfranken, Nürnberg 66
    www.hwk-mittelfranken.de / info@hwk-mittelfranken.de

HBW-Gubesch Kunststoff-Engineering GmbH, Emskirchen 181
    www.hbw-gubesch.de / info@hbw-gubesch.de

Hofmann GmbH, I. K., Nürnberg 211
    www.hofmann.info / info@hofmann.info

Hofmann GmbH & Co., Friedrich, Büchenbach 208
    www.hofmann-denkt.de / info@hofmann-denkt.de

HONSEL GMBH & CO. KG, Druckguss Werk Nürnberg 194, 195
    www.honsel.com / h.schwendner@nuernberg.honsel.com

Hüttinger GmbH, Kurt, Schwaig 216
    www.huettinger.de / info@huettinger.de

infowerk ag, Nürnberg 204
    www.infowerk.de / info@infowerk.de

IZB Informatik-Zentrum, Standort Nürnberg 162
    www.izb.de / info@izb.de

Register
Index

K&M Transporte, Nürnberg 76
   www.kumtransporte.com / Klaus.Rotter@kumtransporte.com

Le Méridien Grand Hotel, Nürnberg 246
   www.grand-hotel.de / LeMeridien@grand-hotel.de

LEONI AG, Nürnberg 160, 161
   www.leoni.com / info@leoni.com

LOOS INTERNATIONAL Loos Deutschland GmbH, Gunzenhausen 189
   www.loos.de / vertrieb@loos.de

MAN Nutzfahrzeuge Gruppe, Geschäftseinheit Motoren, Nürnberg 57
   www.man-mn.com/engines / www.man-mn.com

Messebau Wörnlein GmbH, Nürnberg 88
   www.woernlein.de / info@woernlein.de

Müller GmbH & Co. Press- und Spritzgusswerk KG, Joseph, Nürnberg 199
   www.joseph-mueller.de / gl@joseph-mueller.de

MUNKERT • KUGLER + PARTNER Steuerberater • Wirtschaftsprüfer •
Rechtsanwälte GbR, Nürnberg 45
   www.munkert-kugler.de / info@munkert-kugler.de

N-ERGIE Aktiengesellschaft, Nürnberg 185
   www.n-ergie.de / dialog@n-ergie.de

Nestlé Schöller GmbH & Co. KG, Nürnberg 24
   www.schoeller.de / info-sl@schoeller.de

norisbank Aktiengesellschaft, Nürnberg 220
   www.norisbank.de / service@norisbank.de

NORMA Lebensmittelfilialbetrieb GmbH & Co. KG, Nürnberg 52, 53
   www.norma-online.de / info@norma-online.de

Nürnberger Wach- und Schließgesellschaft mbH, Nürnberg 210
   www.nwsgmbh.de / info@nwsgmbh.de

NWL Laser-Technologie GmbH, Ottensoos 198
   www.nwl-laser.de / info@nwl-laser.de

Omnibusverkehr Franken GmbH (OVF), Nürnberg 85
   www.ovf.de / info@ovf.de

Orth GmbH Assekuranzmakler, J. L., Nürnberg 221
   www.jlo.de / orth@jlo.de

OSSBERGER GmbH + Co, Weißenburg 190
   www.ossberger.de / ossberger@ossberger.de

PAUSCH technologies, Hans Pausch GmbH & Co., Erlangen 172
   www.pausch.de / info@pausch.de

Pfrimmer Nutricia GmbH, Erlangen 174
   www.pfrimmer-nutricia.de / information@nutricia.com

PSYMA GROUP AG, Rückersdorf 60
   www.psyma.com / info@psyma.com

Retterspitz GmbH, Schwaig 173
   www.retterspitz.de / info@retterspitz.de

Rödl & Partner GbR, Nürnberg 40, 41
   www.roedl.de / info@roedl.de

Sasse Elektronik GmbH, Schwabach 33
   www.sasse-elektronik.de / info@sasse-elektronik.de

Schaeffler Gruppe, Herzogenaurach 46, 47
   www.ina.com / info@de.ina.com

Schwanhäußer Industrie Holding GmbH & Co. KG, Heroldsberg 23
   www.schwan-stabilo.com / pr@stabilo.com

sebald druck GmbH, u.e., Nürnberg 165
   www.schlottgruppe.de / www.uesebald.de / dialog@uesebald.de

Seminar- und Wellnesshotel Residenz Bad Windsheim 234
   www.rbw-hotel.de / hotel@r-b-w.net

servicelogiQ GmbH, Nürnberg 209
   www.servicelogiq.com / info@servicelogiq.com

Siemens Aktiengesellschaft, Niederlassung Nürnberg 36, 37
   www.siemens.de

SIPOS Aktorik GmbH, Nürnberg 64
   www.sipos.de / www.sipos.com / info@sipos.de

STAEDTLER Mars GmbH & Co. KG, Schreib- und
Zeichengeräte-Fabriken, Nürnberg 42
   www.staedtler.de / info@staedtler.de

SÜD-WEST-PARK Management GmbH, Nürnberg 98
   www.suedwestpark.de / info@suedwestpark.de

Register
Index

SUSPA Holding GmbH, Altdorf 58
   www.suspa.com / infochairline@de.suspa.com

tabacon Tabakwaren GmbH & Co. Holdinggesellschaft KG,
   Nürnberg 54, 55
   www.tabacon.de

TADANO FAUN GmbH, Lauf a. d. Pegnitz 29
   www.tadanofaun.de / info@tadanofaun.de

Telefonbuch Verlag Hans Müller GmbH & Co. KG, Nürnberg 205
   www.muellerverlag.de / info@muellerverlag.de

Telle GmbH, Erwin, Nürnberg 63
   www.telle.de / info@telle.de

uniVersa Versicherungen, Nürnberg 108
   www.universa.de / info@universa.de

UVEX WINTER HOLDING GmbH & Co. KG, Fürth 48, 49
   www.uvex.de / holding@uvex.de

Verkehrsverbund Großraum Nürnberg GmbH (VGN) 84
   www.vgn.de / info@vgn.de

Volksbank Raiffeisenbank Nürnberg eG 218
   www.vr-bank-nuernberg.de / mail@vr-bank-nuernberg.de

WEILBURGER Graphics GmbH, Gerhardshofen 62
   www.weilburger-graphics.de / info@weilburger-graphics.de

WEILER Werkzeugmaschinen GmbH, Emskirchen 68
   www.weiler.de / info@weiler.de

WÖHRL AG, Nürnberg 34
   www.woehrl.de / info@woehrl.de

ZEITLAUF® GmbH antriebstechnik & Co KG, Lauf a. d. Pegnitz 201
   www.zeitlauf.com / info@zeitlauf.com

Ziehm Imaging GmbH, Nürnberg 170, 171
   www.ziehm.com / info@ziehm-eu.com

Bildquellen
Picture Sources

Kurt Fuchs, Presse-Foto-Design, Erlangen: Titel/Innentitel 1, 2 u. 5, S. 13–15, 38, 39, 70, 73, 78/79, 80, 81, 83, 87, 90–93, 95, 103, 111, 113, 115–117, 123, 125–127, 129, 132, 139–141, 142 o., 145, 146, 148, 152, 154, 158, 163, 167, 174 o., 175, 177, 179, 180, 183, 197, 203, 223, 224, 226, 229–231, 233 u., 235, 237, 238, 241, 243, 245, 247, 248, 250, 251, 257, 258, 259 o., 261–263, 266, 267, 269, 271.

Bodo Nussdorfer, Bielefeld: S. 20, 21, 30–34, 40, 54, 55, 57 u., 59–61, 63, 64 u., 68 u. re., 69, 76, 84, 85, 98, 100, 107, 108 o., 109, 162, 168–171, 173, 176, 178, 181, 186, 187, 189, 192, 193, 198 o., 199, 209, 210, 214 o., 216, 217 u., 219.

Archiv (Werkaufnahmen): S. 10, 19, 23 Mitte und u., 24–26, 28 u., 29, 36, 37, 42, 45 o., 46, 47, 48 o., 50, 52, 53, 57 o., 64 o., 66, 68 o. und u. li., 88, 108 u., 151, 153, 160, 161, 165, 174 u., 184, 185, 194, 195, 198 u., 200, 211, 214 Mitte und u., 215, 218, 221, 272.

Heinz Ackermann, Erlangen: S. 172; Martin Barth, Nürnberg: S. 205 u.; Bavaria Luftbild, München: S. 28 o.; Bayreuther Festspiele GmbH, Bayreuth: S. 137; Dr. Manfred Becker, Gerhardshofen: S. 62; Ingo Bertz, Bad Windsheim: S. 234; Christine Dierenbach, Nürnberg: S. 16, 265; dpa Picture-Alliance GmbH, Frankfurt (Main): S. 135 o.; Fachhochschule Ansbach: S. 71; Feddersenarchitekten: S.106 o.; Flughafen Nürnberg GmbH, Nürnberg: Titel/Innentitel 4, S. 75, 77; Georg-Simon-Ohm-Fachhochschule Nürnberg: S. 119, 121; Germanisches Nationalmuseum Nürnberg: S. 131, 133; Gräflich Pappenheim'sche Verwaltung, Pappenheim: S. 225; Christian Habermeier, Scheinfeld: S. 27; Handwerkskammer für Mittelfranken, Nürnberg: S. 67; Sabine Haymann, Staatstheater Nürnberg: S. 149; A. Heinrich, Carboneras (Spanien): S. 156 u.; Thomas Hierl, Nürnberg: S. 217 o.; Torsten Hönig, Nürnberg: S. 212; Manfred Hoersch, Eckental: S. 23 o.; Manfred Jarisch, München: S. 41; Mark Kemming, Schnaittach: S. 201; Jörg Koch/ddp, Berlin: Titel/Innentitel 3, S. 135 u.; Sabine Kothes: S. 106 u.; Roland Kretschmer, Altdorf: S. 196; Ioni Laibarös, Nürnberg: S. 96 u.; Herbert Liedel, Nürnberg: S. 205 o.; Josef Mang, Segelfliegerverein Weißenburg: S. 190; MEV Verlag GmbH, Augsburg: S. 105; Sammy Minkoff, Eching: S. 48 u.; Stephan Minx: S. 220 u.; Stefanos Notopoulos, München: S. 45 u.; Nürnberg Messe GmbH, Nürnberg: S. 89; Nürnberger Nachrichten, Nürnberg: S. 252/253; Ludwig Olah, Nürnberg: S. 213; Petzoldt Fotografie, Nürnberg: S. 49; T. Preusche, Edinburgh (Schottland): S. 156 o.; Frank Schmidt, Fürth: S. 246; Jürgen Seidel, Nürnberg: S. 204 u.; Staab Architekten, Berlin: S. 96 o.; Stadt Bayreuth: S. 233 o.; Stadt Schwabach: S. 142 u.; Werner Stubenvoll, Nürnberg: S. 204 o.; TEAM Challenge, Roth: S. 259 u.; Tiergarten Nürnberg: S. 255; Thomas Tjiang: S. 220 o.; Stefan Tomaszewski, Erlangen: S. 166; Tourist-Information Roth: S. 227; Tschapka Fotografie, Roth: S. 208; W. M. Photofabrik GmbH, Nürnberg: S. 206, 207; werk:b, Altdorf: S. 58.